# STONE
# AGE
# ECONOMICS

# STONE
# AGE
# ECONOMICS

## BY
## MARSHALL
## SAHLINS

ALDINE PUBLISHING COMPANY
Chicago

# The Author

*Marshall Sahlins* is Professor of Anthropology at the
University of Chicago. He received his Ph.D. from
Columbia University in 1954 and has taught there, at the
University of Michigan, and at the University of
Paris–Nanterre. Professor Sahlins was a fellow at the
Center for Advanced Study in Behavioral Sciences in 1963-64,
and in 1967-68 held a Guggenheim Fellowship. His many
contributions to the literature include *Social Stratification
in Polynesia, Moala, Tribesmen,* and numerous articles in
professional journals.

First published 1972 by
Aldine · Atherton, Inc.

First paperback edition 1974

Second printing, 1976

Address all inquiries to
Aldine Publishing Company
529 South Wabash Avenue
Chicago, Illinois 60605

ISBN 0-202-01098-8 (cloth)
      0-202-01099-6 (paper)
Library of Congress Catalog Number 75-169506

Printed in the United States of America

FOR JULIA, PETER, AND ELAINE

# Acknowledgments

I thank especially two institutions, and the excellent staff associated with them, for the aid and facilities provided during critical periods of my research and writing. In 1963-64 I held a fellowship at the Center for Advanced Study in the Behavioral Sciences (Palo Alto), in 1967-69 an office and the run of the Laboratoire d'Anthropologie Sociale du Collège de France (Paris). Although I had no official position in the Laboratoire, M. Claude Lévi-Strauss, the director, received me with a courtesy and generosity I should have difficulty reciprocating, were he ever in turn to visit my village.

A John Simon Guggenheim fellowship during my first year in Paris (1967-68) and a Social Science Research Council Faculty Research Fellowship (1958-61) also contributed important support during the gestation period of these essays.

That period has been so long and so full of beneficial intellectual encounters that it would be impossible to list all the colleagues and students who have, in one way or another, influenced the course of the work. Out of long years of friendship and discussion, however, I make three exceptions: Remo Guidieri, Elman Service, and Eric Wolf. Their ideas and criticisms, always accompanied by encouragement, have been of inestimable value to me and to my work.

Several of the essays have been published in whole, in part, or in translation during the past several years. "The Original Affluent Society" appeared in abbreviated form as "La première société d'abondance" in *Les Temps Modernes* (No. 268, Oct. 1968, 641–80). The first part of Chapter 4 was originally published as "The Spirit of the Gift" in *Echanges et communications* (Jean Pouillon and P. Maranda, eds., The Hague: Mouton, 1969). The second part of Chapter 4 appeared as "Philosophie politique de *l'Essai sur le don,*" in *L'Homme* (Vol. 8[4], 1968, 5–17). "On the Sociology of Primitive Exchange" was published first in *The Relevance of Models for Social Anthropology* (M. Banton, ed., London: Tavistock [ASA Monographs, 1], 1965). I thank the publishers of all of the above for permission to reproduce these articles.

"The Diplomacy of Primitive Trade," initially published in *Essays in Economic Anthropology* (June Helm, ed., Seattle: American Ethnological Society, 1965), has been entirely revised for the present book.

# Contents

# Introduction

I have written the several essays of this volume at various times over the past ten years. Some were written especially for the present publication. All were conceived and are here assembled in the hope of an anthropological economics, which is to say, in opposition to business-like interpretations of primitive economies and societies. Inevitably the book inscribes itself in the current anthropological controversy between "formalist" and "substantivist" practices of economic theory.

Endemic to the science of Economics for over a century, the formalist-substantivist debate seems nevertheless lacking in history, for nothing much seems to have changed since Karl Marx defined the fundamental issues in contraposition to Adam Smith (cf. Althusser et al., 1966, Vol. 2). Still, the latest incarnation in the form of anthropology has shifted the emphasis of discussion. If the problem in the beginning was the "naive anthropology" of Economics, today it is the "naive economics" of Anthropology. "Formalism versus substantivism" amounts to the following theoretical option: between the ready-made models of orthodox Economics, especially the "microeconomics," taken as universally valid and applicable *grosso modo* to the primitive societies; and the necessity—supposing this formalist position unfounded—of developing a new analysis more appropriate to the historical societies in question and to the intellectual history of Anthropology. Broadly speaking, it is a choice between the perspective of Business, for the formalist method must consider the primi-

tive economies as underdeveloped versions of our own, and a cultural-
ist study that as a matter of principle does honor to different societies
for what they are.

No solution is in sight, no ground for the happy academic conclusion that "the answer lies somewhere in between." This book is substantivist. It thus takes on a familiar structure, as provided by
traditional substantive categories. The first essays concern production: "The Original Affluent Society" and "The Domestic Mode
of Production." (The latter has been divided for convenience into two
sections, Chapters 2 and 3, but these make up one continuous argument.) The chapters following turn to distribution and exchange:
"The Spirit of the Gift," "On the Sociology of Primitive Exchange,"
"Exchange Value and the Diplomacy of Primitive Trade." But as the
exposition is at the same time an opposition, this sequence harbors
also a more concealed strategy of debate. The lead chapter accepts
battle on formalist terms. "The Original Affluent Society" does not
challenge the common understanding of "economy" as a relation
between means and ends; it only denies that hunters find any great
disparity between the two. The following essays, however, would
definitively abandon this entrepreneurial and individualist conception
of the economic object. "Economy" becomes a category of culture
rather than behavior, in a class with politics or religion rather than
rationality or prudence: not the need-serving activities of individuals,
but the material life process of society. Then, the final chapter returns
to economic orthodoxy, but to its problems, not to its *problématique*.
The attempt in the end is to bring the anthropological perspective to
bear on the traditional work of microeconomics, the explanation of
exchange value.

In all this, the aim of the book remains modest: merely to perpetuate
the possibility of an anthropological economics by a few concrete
examples. In a recent issue of *Current Anthropology,* a spokesman of
the opposed position announced with no apparent regret the untimely
demise of substantive economics:

> The wordage squandered in this debate does not add up to its intellectual
> weight. From the beginning the substantivists (as exemplified in the justly
> famous works of Polanyi and others) were heroically muddled and in error.
> It is a tribute to the maturity of economic anthropology that we have been

able to find in what the error consisted in the short space of six years. The paper . . . written by Cook (1966) when he was a graduate student neatly disposes of the controversy. . . . Social science being the sort of enterprise [!] it is, however, it is virtually impossible to down a poor, useless, or obfuscating hypothesis, and I expect the next generation of creators of high-level confusion will resurrect, in one guise or another, the substantive view of the economy (Nash, 1967, p. 250).

How then to describe the present work, which is neither the second coming nor otherwise bears the slightest trace of immortality? One can only hope there has been some mistake. Perhaps, as with Mark Twain in a similar case, the reports of the death of substantivism have been grossly exaggerated.

In any event, I refrain from the attempt at mouth-to-mouth resuscitation in the form of methodological discussion. The recent literature of "economic anthropology" is already overinflated with talk at this level. And while many of the arguments seem models of good sense, the total effect has been to confirm everyone in his original prejudice. ("He who's convinced against his will/Is of the same opinion still.") Reason has proven a poor arbiter. Meanwhile the audience to the debate is rapidly declining, out of boredom, prompting even some of the main participants to now declare themselves ready to go to work. That too is the spirit of this book. Officially, as a participant in a discipline that considers itself a science, I would rest the case on the essays themselves, and on the belief they explain matters better than the competing theoretical mode. Such is the traditional and the healthy procedure: let all the flowers bloom, and we shall see which bear real fruit.

But the official position is not, I confess, my deepest conviction. It seems to me that this tissue of metaphors on the natural sciences dressed up as "social science," this anthropology, has shown as little capacity for agreement on the empirical adequacy of a theory as on its logical sufficiency. For unlike mathematics where "truth and the interest of men oppose not each other," as Hobbes said long ago, in social science nothing is indisputable because social science "compareth men and meddleth with their right and profit," so that "as often as reason is against a man, a man is against reason." The decisive differences between formalism and substantivism, as far as their acceptance is at issue, if not so far as their truth, are ideological. Embodying the wisdom of native bourgeois categories, formal

economics flourishes as ideology at home and ethnocentrism abroad.
As against substantivism, it draws great strength from its profound
compatibility with bourgeois society—which is not to deny, either,
that the conflict with substantivism can become a confrontation of
(two) ideologies.

When the early physicists and astronomers, working in the shadow
of established ecclesiastic dogmas, commended themselves to God
and Sovereign, they knew what they were doing. The present work
plays on the same contradiction: not in the illusion that the dogmas
will prove flexible, but the gods just. The political-ideological differences between formal and anthropological thought may well be ignored in the writing, but that does not render them much less
consequent to the outcome. We are told substantivism is dead. Politically, at least for a certain part of the world, it may be so; that flower
was nipped in the bud. It is also conceivable that bourgeois economics
is doomed, scheduled by history to share the fate of the society that
nurtured it. In either event, it is not for current anthropology to
decide. We are at least enough of a science to know that is the
prerogative of society, and of the academic sons of heaven who hold
its mandate. In the meantime, we cultivate our gardens, waiting to see
if the gods will shower rain or, like those of certain New Guinea tribes,
just urinate upon us.

# 1

# The Original Affluent Society

If economics is the dismal science, the study of hunting and gathering economies must be its most advanced branch. Almost universally committed to the proposition that life was hard in the paleolithic, our textbooks compete to convey a sense of impending doom, leaving one to wonder not only how hunters managed to live, but whether, after all, this was living? The specter of starvation stalks the stalker through these pages. His technical incompetence is said to enjoin continuous work just to survive, affording him neither respite nor surplus, hence not even the "leisure" to "build culture." Even so, for all his efforts, the hunter pulls the lowest grades in thermodynamics—less energy/capita/year than any other mode of production. And in treatises on economic development he is condemned to play the role of bad example: the so-called "subsistence economy."

The traditional wisdom is always refractory. One is forced to oppose it polemically, to phrase the necessary revisions dialectically: in fact, this was, when you come to examine it, the original affluent society. Paradoxical, that phrasing leads to another useful and unexpected conclusion. By the common understanding, an affluent society is one in which all the people's material wants are easily satisfied. To assert that the hunters are affluent is to deny then that the human condition is an ordained tragedy, with man the prisoner at hard labor of a perpetual disparity between his unlimited wants and his insufficient means.

For there are two possible courses to affluence. Wants may be

1

"easily satisfied" either by producing much or desiring little. The familiar conception, the Galbraithean way, makes assumptions peculiarly appropriate to market economies: that man's wants are great, not to say infinite, whereas his means are limited, although improvable: thus, the gap between means and ends can be narrowed by industrial productivity, at least to the point that "urgent goods" become plentiful. But there is also a Zen road to affluence, departing from premises somewhat different from our own: that human material wants are finite and few, and technical means unchanging but on the whole adequate. Adopting the Zen strategy, a people can enjoy an unparalleled material plenty—with a low standard of living.

That, I think, describes the hunters. And it helps explain some of their more curious economic behavior: their "prodigality" for example—the inclination to consume at once all stocks on hand, as if they had it made. Free from market obsessions of scarcity, hunters' economic propensities may be more consistently predicated on abundance than our own. Destutt de Tracy, "fish-blooded bourgeois doctrinaire" though he might have been, at least compelled Marx's agreement on the observation that "in poor nations the people are comfortable," whereas in rich nations "they are generally poor."

This is not to deny that a preagricultural economy operates under serious constraints, but only to insist, on the evidence from modern hunters and gatherers, that a successful accomodation is usually made. After taking up the evidence, I shall return in the end to the real difficulties of hunting-gathering economy, none of which are correctly specified in current formulas of paleolithic poverty.

### Sources of the Misconception

"Mere subsistence economy" "limited leisure save in exceptional circumstances," "incessant quest for food," "meagre and relatively unreliable" natural resources, "absence of an economic surplus," "maximum energy from a maximum number of people"—so runs the fair average anthropological opinion of hunting and gathering.

> The aboriginal Australians are a classic example of a people whose economic resources are of the scantiest. In many places their habitat is even more severe than that of the Bushmen, although this is perhaps not quite true in the northern portion. . . . A tabulation of the foodstuffs which the

aborigines of northwest central Queensland extract from the country they inhabit is instructive. . . . The variety in this list is impressive, but we must not be deceived into thinking that variety indicates plenty, for the available quantities of each element in it are so slight that only the most intense application makes survival possible (Herskovits, 1958, p 68–69).

Or again, in reference to South American hunters:

The nomadic hunters and gatherers barely met minimum subsistence needs and often fell far short of them. Their population of 1 person to 10 or 20 square miles reflects this. Constantly on the move in search of food, they clearly lacked the leisure hours for nonsubsistence activities of any significance, and they could transport little of what they might manufacture in spare moments. To them, adequacy of production meant physical survival, and they rarely had surplus of either products or time (Steward and Faron, 1959, p. 60; cf. Clark, 1953, p. 27 f; Haury, 1962, p. 113; Hoebel, 1958, p. 188; Redfield, 1953, p. 5; White, 1959).

But the traditional dismal view of the hunters' fix is also preanthropological and extra-anthropological, at once historical and referable to the larger economic context in which anthropology operates. It goes back to the time Adam Smith was writing, and probably to a time before anyone was writing.[1] Probably it was one of the first distinctly neolithic prejudices, an ideological appreciation of the hunter's capacity to exploit the earth's resources most congenial to the historic task of depriving him of the same. We must have inherited it with the seed of Jacob, which "spread abroad to the west, and to the east, and to the north," to the disadvantage of Esau who was the elder son and cunning hunter, but in a famous scene deprived of his birthright.

Current low opinions of the hunting-gathering economy need not be laid to neolithic ethnocentrism, however. Bourgeois ethnocentrism will do as well. The existing business economy, at every turn an ideological trap from which anthropological economics must escape, will promote the same dim conclusions about the hunting life.

Is it so paradoxical to contend that hunters have affluent economies, their absolute poverty notwithstanding? Modern capitalist societies, however richly endowed, dedicate themselves to the proposition of scarcity. Inadequacy of economic means is the first principle of the world's wealthiest peoples. The apparent material status of the economy seems to be no clue to its accomplishments; something has to be

1. At least to the time Lucretius was writing (Harris, 1968, pp. 26–27).

said for the mode of economic organization (cf. Polanyi, 1947, 1957, 1959; Dalton, 1961).

The market-industrial system institutes scarcity, in a manner completely unparalleled and to a degree nowhere else approximated. Where production and distribution are arranged through the behavior of prices, and all livelihoods depend on getting and spending, insufficiency of material means becomes the explicit, calculable starting point of all economic activity.[2] The entrepreneur is confronted with alternative investments of a finite capital, the worker (hopefully) with alternative choices of remunerative employ, and the consumer. . . . Consumption is a double tragedy: what begins in inadequacy will end in deprivation. Bringing together an international division of labor, the market makes available a dazzling array of products: all these Good Things within a man's reach—but never all within his grasp. Worse, in this game of consumer free choice, every acquisition is simultaneously a deprivation, for every purchase of something is a foregoing of something else, in general only marginally less desirable, and in some particulars more desirable, that could have been had instead. (The point is that if you buy one automobile, say a Plymouth, you cannot also have the Ford—and I judge from current television commercials that the deprivations entailed would be more than just material.)[3]

That sentence of "life at hard labor" was passed uniquely upon us. Scarcity is the judgment decreed by our economy—so also the axiom of our Economics: the application of scarce means against alternative ends to derive the most satisfaction possible under the circumstances. And it is precisely from this anxious vantage that we look back upon hunters. But if modern man, with all his technological advantages, still hasn't got the wherewithal, what chance has this naked savage with his puny bow and arrow? Having equipped the hunter with bourgeois impulses and paleolithic tools, we judge his situation hopeless in advance.[4]

2. On the historically particular requisites of such calculation, see Codere, 1968, [especially pp. 574-575.]

3. For the complementary institutionalization of "scarcity" in the conditions of capitalist production, see Gorz, 1967, pp. 37–38.

4. It deserves mention that contemporary European-Marxist theory is often in accord with bourgeois economics on the poverty of the primitive. Cf. Boukharine, 1967; Mandel, 1962, vol. 1; and the economic history manual used at Lumumba University

Yet scarcity is not an intrinsic property of technical means. It is a relation between means and ends. We should entertain the empirical possibility that hunters are in business for their health, a finite objective, and that bow and arrow are adequate to that end.[5]

But still other ideas, these endemic in anthropological theory and ethnographic practice, have conspired to preclude any such understanding.

The anthropological disposition to exaggerate the economic inefficiency of hunters appears notably by way of invidious comparison with neolithic economies. Hunters, as Lowie put it blankly, "must work much harder in order to live than tillers and breeders" (1946, p. 13). On this point evolutionary anthropology in particular found it congenial, even necessary theoretically, to adopt the usual tone of reproach. Ethnologists and archaeologists had become neolithic revolutionaries, and in their enthusiasm for the Revolution spared nothing denouncing the Old (Stone Age) Regime. Including some very old scandal. It was not the first time philosophers would relegate the earliest stage of humanity rather to nature than to culture. ("A man who spends his whole life following animals just to kill them to eat, or moving from one berry patch to another, is really living just like an animal himself"[Braidwood, 1957, p. 122].) The hunters thus downgraded, anthropology was free to extol the Neolithic Great Leap Forward: a main technological advance that brought about a "general availability of leisure through release from purely food-getting pursuits" (Braidwood, 1952, p. 5; cf. Boas, 1940, p. 285).

In an influential essay on "Energy and the Evolution of Culture," Leslie White explained that the neolithic generated a "great advance in cultural development . . . as a consequence of the great increase in the amount of energy harnessed and controlled per capita per year by means of the agricultural and pastoral arts" (1949, p. 372). White further heightened the evolutionary contrast by specifying *human effort* as the principal energy source of paleolithic culture, as opposed to the *domesticated plant and animal resources* of neolithic culture.

---

(listed in bibliography as "Anonymous, n.d.").

5. Elman Service for a very long time almost alone among ethnologists stood out against the traditional view of the penury of hunters. The present paper owes great inspiration to his remarks on the leisure of the Arunta (1963, p. 9), as well as to personal conversations with him.

This determination of the energy sources at once permitted a precise low estimate of hunters' thermodynamic potential—that developed by the human body: "average power resources" of one-twentieth horse-power per capita (1949, p. 369)—even as, by eliminating human effort from the cultural enterprise of the neolithic, it appeared that people had been liberated by some labor-saving device (domesticated plants and animals). But White's problematic is obviously misconceived. The principal mechanical energy available to both paleolithic and neolithic culture is that supplied by human beings, as transformed in both cases from plant and animal sources, so that, with negligible exceptions (the occasional direct use of nonhuman power), the amount of energy harnessed per *capita* per year is the same in paleo-lithic and neolithic economies—and fairly constant in human history until the advent of the industrial revolution[6].

Another specifically anthropological source of paleolithic discon-tent develops in the field itself, from the context of European observa-tion of existing hunters and gatherers, such as the native Australians, the Bushmen, the Ona or the Yahgan. This ethnographic context tends to distort our understanding of the hunting-gathering economy in two ways.

First, it provides singular opportunities for naïveté. The remote and exotic environments that have become the cultural theater of modern hunters have an effect on Europeans most unfavorable to the latter's assessment of the former's plight. Marginal as the Australian or Kala-hari desert is to agriculture, or to everyday European experience, it is a source of wonder to the untutored observer "how anybody could live in a place like this." The inference that the natives manage only to eke out a bare existence is apt to be reinforced by their marvelously varied diets (cf. Herskovits, 1958, quoted above). Ordinarily including

6. The evident fault of White's evolutionary law is the use of "per capita" measures. Neolithic societies in the main harness a *greater total amount of energy* than preagricul-tural communities, because of the greater number of energy-delivering humans sus-tained by domestication. This overall rise in the social product, however, is not necessarily effected by an increased productivity of labor—which in White's view also accompanied the neolithic revolution. Ethnological data now in hand, (see text *infra*) raise the possibility that simple agricultural regimes are not more efficient thermody-namically than hunting and gathering—that is, in energy yield per unit of human labor. In the same vein, some archaeology in recent years has tended to privilege stability of settlement over productivity of labor in explanation of the neolithic advance (cf. Braid-wood and Wiley, 1962).

objects deemed repulsive and inedible by Europeans, the local cuisine lends itself to the supposition that the people are starving to death. Such a conclusion, of course, is more likely met in earlier than in later accounts, and in the journals of explorers or missionaries than in the monographs of anthropologists; but precisely because the explorers' reports are older and closer to the aboriginal condition, one reserves for them a certain respect.

Such respect obviously has to be accorded with discretion. Greater attention should be paid a man such as Sir George Grey (1841), whose expeditions in the 1830s included some of the poorer districts of western Australia, but whose unusually close attention to the local people obliged him to debunk his colleagues' communications on just this point of economic desperation. It is a mistake very commonly made, Grey wrote, to suppose that the native Australians "have small means of subsistence, or are at times greatly pressed for want of food." Many and "almost ludicrous" are the errors travellers have fallen into in this regard: "They lament in their journals that the unfortunate Aborigines should be reduced by famine to the miserable necessity of subsisting on certain sorts of food, which they have found near their huts; whereas, in many instances, the articles thus quoted by them are those which the natives most prize, and are really neither deficient in flavour nor nutritious qualities." To render palpable "the ignorance that has prevailed with regard to the habits and customs of this people when in their wild state," Grey provides one remarkable example, a citation from his fellow explorer, Captain Sturt, who, upon encountering a group of Aboriginals engaged in gathering large quantities of mimosa gum, deduced that the " 'unfortunate creatures were reduced to the last extremity, and, being unable to procure any other nourishment, had been obliged to collect this mucilaginous.' " But, Sir George observes, the gum in question is a favorite article of food in the area, and when in season it affords the opportunity for large numbers of people to assemble and camp together, which otherwise they are unable to do. He concludes:

> Generally speaking, the natives live well; in some districts there may be at particular seasons of the year a deficiency of food, but if such is the case, these tracts are, at those times, deserted. It is, *however, utterly impossible for a traveller or even for a strange native to judge whether a district affords an abundance of food, or the contrary* . . . But

in his own district a native is very differently situated; he knows exactly what it produces, the proper time at which the several articles are in season, and the readiest means of procuring them. According to these circumstances he regulates his visits to different portions of his hunting ground; *and I can only say that I have always found the greatest abundance in their huts* (Grey, 1841, vol. 2, pp. 259-262, emphasis mine; cf. Eyre, 1845, vol. 2, p. 244f).[7]

In making this happy assessment, Sir George took special care to exclude the *lumpen-proletariat* aboriginals living in and about European towns (cf. Eyre,1845, vol.2, pp. 250, 254-255). The exception is instructive. It evokes a second source of ethnographic misconceptions: the anthropology of hunters is largely an anachronistic study of ex-savages—an inquest into the corpse of one society, Grey once said, presided over by members of another.

The surviving food collectors, as a class, are displaced persons. They represent the paleolithic disenfranchised, occupying marginal haunts untypical of the mode of production: sanctuaries of an era, places so beyond the range of main centers of cultural advance as to be allowed some respite from the planetary march of cultural evolution, because they were characteristically poor beyond the interest and competence of more advanced economies. Leave aside the favorably situated food collecters, such as Northwest Coast Indians, about whose (comparative) well-being there is no dispute. The remaining hunters, barred from the better parts of the earth, first by agriculture, later by industrial economies, enjoy ecological opportunities something less than the later-paleolithic average.[8] Moreover, the disruption accomplished in the past two centuries of European imperialism has been especially severe, to the extent that many of the ethnographic notices that constitute the anthropologist's stock in trade are adulterated culture goods. Even explorer and missionary accounts, apart from their ethnocentric misconstructions, may be speaking of afflicted economies (cf. Service, 1962). The hunters of eastern Canada of whom we read in the *Jesuit Relations* were committed to the fur trade in the

7. For a similar comment, referring to missionary misinterpretation of curing by blood consumption in eastern Australia, see Hodgkinson, 1845, p. 227.

8. Conditions of primitive hunting peoples must not be judged, as Carl Sauer notes, " 'from their modern survivors, now restricted to the most meagre regions of the earth, such as the interior of Australia, the American Great Basin, and the Arctic tundra and taiga. The areas of early occupation were abounding in food' " (cited in Clark and Haswell, 1964, p. 23).

early seventeenth century. The environments of others were selectively stripped by Europeans before reliable report could be made of indigenous production: the Eskimo we know no longer hunt whales, the Bushmen have been deprived of game, the Shoshoni's piñon has been timbered and his hunting grounds grazed out by cattle.[9] If such peoples are now described as poverty-stricken, their resources "meagre and unreliable," is this an indication of the aboriginal condition—or of the colonial duress?

The enormous implications (and problems) for evolutionary interpretation raised by this global retreat have only recently begun to evoke notice (Lee and Devore, 1968). The point of present importance is this: rather than a fair test of hunters' productive capacities, their current circumstances pose something of a supreme test. All the more extraordinary, then, the following reports of their performance.

### *"A Kind of Material Plenty"*

Considering the poverty in which hunters and gatherers live in theory, it comes as a surprise that Bushmen who live in the Kalahari enjoy "a kind of material plenty," at least in the realm of everyday useful things, apart from food and water:

> As the /Kung come into more contact with Europeans—and this is already happening—they will feel sharply the lack of our things and will need and want more. It makes them feel inferior to be without clothes when they stand among strangers who are clothed. But in their own life and with their own artifacts *they were comparatively free from material pressures.* Except for food and water (important exceptions!) of which the Nyae Nyae /Kung have a sufficiency—but barely so, judging from the fact that all are thin though not emaciated—they all had what they needed or could make what they needed, for every man can and does make the things that men make and every woman the things that women make. . . . *They lived in a kind of material plenty* because they adapted the tools of their living to materials which lay in abundance around them and which were free for anyone to take (wood, reeds, bone for weapons and implements, fibers for cordage, grass for shelters), or to materials which were at least sufficient for the needs of the population. . . . The /Kung could always use more ostrich egg

---

9. Through the prison of acculturation one glimpses what hunting and gathering might have been like in a decent environment from Alexander Henry's account of his bountiful sojourn as a Chippewa in northern Michigan: see Quimby, 1962.

shells for beads to wear or trade with, but, as it is, enough are found for
every woman to have a dozen or more shells for water containers—all she
can carry—and a goodly number of bead ornaments. In their nomadic
hunting-gathering life, travelling from one source of food to another
through the seasons, always going back and forth between food and water,
they carry their young children and their belongings. With plenty of most
materials at hand to replace artifacts as required, the /Kung have not
developed means of permanent storage and have not needed or wanted to
encumber themselves with surpluses or duplicates. They do not even want
to carry one of everything. They borrow what they do not own. With this
ease, they have not hoarded, and the accumulation of objects has not
become associated with status (Marshall, 1961, pp. 243–44, emphasis
mine).

Analysis of hunter-gatherer production is usefully divided into two
spheres, as Mrs. Marshall has done. Food and water are certainly
"important exceptions," best reserved for separate and extended treatment. For the rest, the nonsubsistence sector, what is here said of the
Bushmen applies in general and in detail to hunters from the Kalahari
to Labrador—or to Tièrra del Fuego, where Gusinde reports of the
Yahgan that their disinclination to own more than one copy of utensils frequently needed is "an indication of self-confidence." "Our
Fuegians," he writes, "procure and make their implements with little
effort" (1961, p. 213).[10]

In the nonsubsistence sphere, the people's wants are generally easily
satisfied. Such "material plenty" depends partly upon the ease of
production, and that upon the simplicity of technology and democracy of property. Products are homespun: of stone, bone, wood, skin—
materials such as "lay in abundance around them." As a rule, neither
extraction of the raw material nor its working up take strenuous
effort. Access to natural resources is typically direct—"free for
anyone to take"—even as possession of the necessary tools is general
and knowledge of the required skills common. The division of labor
is likewise simple, predominantly a division of labor by sex. Add in
the liberal customs of sharing, for which hunters are properly famous,

10. Turnbull similarly notes of Congo Pygmies: "The materials for the making of
shelter, clothing, and all other necessary items of material culture are all at hand at
a moment's notice." And he has no reservations either about subsistence: "Throughout
the year, without fail, there is an abundant supply of game and vegetable foods" (1965,
p. 18).

and all the people can usually participate in the going prosperity, such as it is.

But, of course, "such as it is": this "prosperity" depends as well upon an objectively low standard of living. It is critical that the customary quota of consumables (as well as the number of consumers) be culturally set at a modest point. A few people are pleased to consider a few easily-made things their good fortune: some meagre pieces of clothing and rather fugitive housing in most climates;[11] plus a few ornaments, spare flints and sundry other items such as the "pieces of quartz, which native doctors have extracted from their patients" (Grey, 1841, vol. 2, p. 266); and, finally, the skin bags in which the faithful wife carries all this, "the wealth of the Australian savage" (p. 266).

For most hunters, such affluence without abundance in the nonsubsistence sphere need not be long debated. A more interesting question is why they are content with so few possessions—for it is with them a policy, a "matter of principle" as Gusinde says (1961, p. 2), and not a misfortune.

Want not, lack not. But are hunters so undemanding of material goods because they are themselves enslaved by a food quest "demanding maximum energy from a maximum number of people," so that no time or effort remains for the provision of other comforts? Some ethnographers testify to the contrary that the food quest is so successful that half the time the people seem not to know what to do with themselves. On the other hand, *movement* is a condition of this success, more movement in some cases than others, but always enough to rapidly depreciate the satisfactions of property. Of the hunter it is truly said that his wealth is a burden. In his condition of life, goods can become "grievously oppressive," as Gusinde observes, and the more so the longer they are carried around. Certain food collectors do have canoes and a few have dog sleds, but most must carry themselves all the comforts they possess, and so only possess what they can comfortably carry themselves. Or perhaps only what the women can carry: the men are often left free to react to the sudden opportunity of the chase or the sudden necessity of defense. As Owen Lattimore

11. Certain food collectors not lately known for their architectural achievements seem to have built more substantial dwellings before being put on the run by Europeans. See Smythe, 1871, vol. 1, pp. 125-128.

wrote in a not too different context, "the pure nomad is the poor nomad." Mobility and property are in contradiction.

That wealth quickly becomes more of an encumbrance than a good thing is apparent even to the outsider. Laurens van der Post was caught in the contradiction as he prepared to make farewells to his wild Bushmen friends:

> This matter of presents gave us many an anxious moment. We were humiliated by the realization of how little there was we could give to the Bushmen. Almost everything seemed likely to make life more difficult for them by adding to the litter and weight of their daily round. They themselves had practically no possessions: a loin strap, a skin blanket and a leather satchel. There was nothing that they could not assemble in one minute, wrap up in their blankets and carry on their shoulders for a journey of a thousand miles. They had no sense of possession (1958, p. 276).

A necessity so obvious to the casual visitor must be second nature to the people concerned. This modesty of material requirements is institutionalized: it becomes a positive cultural fact, expressed in a variety of economic arrangements. Lloyd Warner reports of the Murngin, for example, that portability is a decisive value in the local scheme of things. Small goods are in general better than big goods. In the final analysis "the relative ease of transportation of the article" will prevail, so far as determining its disposition, over its relative scarcity or labor cost. For the "ultimate value," Warner writes, "is freedom of movement." And to this "desire to be free from the burdens and responsibilities of objects which would interfere with the society's itinerant existence," Warner attributes the Murngin's "undeveloped sense of property," and their "lack of interest in developing their technological equipment" (1964, pp. 136-137).

Here then is another economic "peculiarity"—I will not say it is general, and perhaps it is explained as well by faulty toilet training as by a trained disinterest in material accumulation: some hunters, at least, display a notable tendency to be sloppy about their possessions. They have the kind of nonchalance that would be appropriate to a people who have mastered the problems of production, even as it is maddening to a European:

> They do not know how to take care of their belongings. No one dreams of putting them in order, folding them, drying or cleaning them, hanging

them up, or putting them in a neat pile. If they are looking for some particular thing, they rummage carelessly through the hodgepodge of trifles in the little baskets. Larger objects that are piled up in a heap in the hut are dragged hither and yon with no regard for the damage that might be done them. The European observer has the impression that these [Yahgan] Indians place no value whatever on their utensils and that they have completely forgotten the effort it took to make them.[12] Actually, no one clings to his few goods and chattels which, as it is, are often and easily lost, but just as easily replaced. . . . The Indian does not even exercise care when he could conveniently do so. A European is likely to shake his head at the boundless indifference of these people who drag brand-new objects, precious clothing, fresh provisions, and valuable items through thick mud, or abandon them to their swift destruction by children and dogs. . . . Expensive things that are given them are treasured for a few hours, out of curiousity; after that they thoughtlessly let everything deteriorate in the mud and wet. The less they own, the more comfortable they can travel, and what is ruined they occasionally replace. Hence, they are completely indifferent to any material possessions (Gusinde, 1961, pp. 86–87).

The hunter, one is tempted to say, is "uneconomic man." At least as concerns nonsubsistence goods, he is the reverse of that standard caricature immortalized in any *General Principles of Economics,* page one. His wants are scarce and his means (in relation) plentiful. Consequently he is "comparatively free of material pressures," has "no sense of possession," shows "an undeveloped sense of property," is "completely indifferent to any material pressures," manifests a "lack of interest" in developing his technological equipment.

In this relation of hunters to worldly goods there is a neat and important point. From the internal perspective of the economy, it seems wrong to say that wants are "restricted," desires "restrained," or even that the notion of wealth is "limited." Such phrasings imply in advance an Economic Man and a struggle of the hunter against his own worse nature, which is finally then subdued by a cultural vow of poverty. The words imply the renunciation of an acquisitiveness that in reality was never developed, a suppression of desires that were never broached. Economic Man is a bourgeois construction—as Marcel Mauss said, "not behind us, but before, like the moral man." It is not that hunters and gatherers have curbed their materialistic "im-

12. But recall Gusinde's comment: "Our Fuegians procure and make their implements with little effort" (1961, p. 213).

pulses"; they simply never made an institution of them. "Moreover, if it is a great blessing to be free from a great evil, our [Montagnais] Savages are happy; for the two tyrants who provide hell and torture for many of our Europeans, do not reign in their great forests,—I mean ambition and avarice . . . as they are contented with a mere living, not one of them gives himself to the Devil to acquire wealth" (LeJeune, 1897, p. 231).

We are inclined to think of hunters and gatherers as *poor* because they don't have anything; perhaps better to think of them for that reason as *free*. "Their extremely limited material possessions relieve them of all cares with regard to daily necessities and permit them to enjoy life" (Gusinde, 1961, p. 1).

## Subsistence

When Herskovits was writing his *Economic Anthropology* (1958), it was common anthropological practice to take the Bushmen or the native Australians as "a classic illustration of a people whose economic resources are of the scantiest," so precariously situated that "only the most intense application makes survival possible." Today the "classic" understanding can be fairly reversed—on evidence largely from these two groups. A good case can be made that hunters and gatherers work less than we do; and, rather than a continuous travail, the food quest is intermittent, leisure abundant, and there is a greater amount of sleep in the daytime per capita per year than in any other condition of society.

Some of the substantiating evidence for Australia appears in early sources, but we are fortunate especially to have now the quantitative materials collected by the 1948 American-Australian Scientific Expedition to Arnhem Land. Published in 1960, these startling data must provoke some review of the Australian reportage going back for over a century, and perhaps revision of an even longer period of anthropological thought. The key research was a temporal study of hunting and gathering by McCarthy and McArthur (1960), coupled to McArthur's analysis of the nutritional outcome.

Figures 1.1 and 1.2 summarize the principal production studies. These were short-run observations taken during nonceremonial peri-

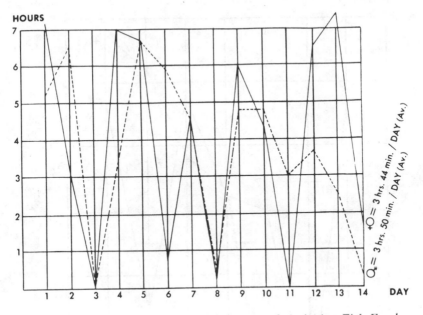

*Figure 1.1.* *Hours per Day in Food-Connected Activities: Fish Creek Group (McCarthy and McArthur, 1960)*

ods. The record for Fish Creek (14 days) is longer as well as more detailed than that for Hemple Bay (seven days). Only adults' work has been reported, so far as I can tell. The diagrams incorporate information on hunting, plant collecting, preparing foods, and repairing weapons, as tabulated by the ethnographers. The people in both camps were free-ranging native Australians, living outside mission or other settlements during the period of study, although such was not necessarily their permanent or even their ordinary circumstance.[13]

13. Fish Creek was an inland camp in western Arnhem Land consisting of six adult males and three adult females. Hemple Bay was a coastal occupation on Groote Eylandt; there were four adult males, four adult females, and five juveniles and infants in the camp. Fish Creek was investigated at the end of the dry season, when the supply of vegetable foods was low; kangaroo hunting was rewarding, although the animals became increasingly wary under steady stalking. At Hemple Bay, vegetable foods were plentiful; the fishing was variable but on the whole good by comparison with other

(continued on p. 17)

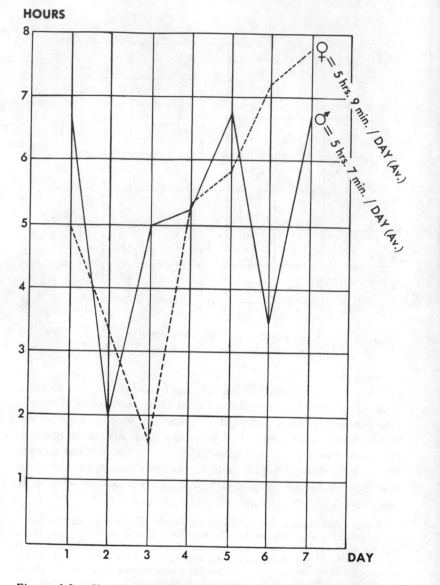

Figure 1.2. Hours per Day in Food-Connected Activities: Hemple Bay Group (McCarthy and McArthur, 1960)

One must have serious reservations about drawing general or historical inferences from the Arnhem Land data alone. Not only was the context less than pristine and the time of study too brief, but certain elements of the modern situation may have raised productivity above aboriginal levels: metal tools, for example, or the reduction of local pressure on food resources by depopulation. And our uncertainty seems rather doubled than neutralized by other current circumstances that, conversely, would lower economic efficiency: these semi-independent hunters, for instance, are probably not as skilled as their ancestors. For the moment, let us consider the Arnhem Land conclusions as experimental, potentially credible in the measure they are supported by other ethnographic or historic accounts.

The most obvious, immediate conclusion is that the people do not work hard. The average length of time per person per day put into the appropriation and preparation of food was four or five hours. Moreover, they do not work continuously. The subsistence quest was highly intermittent. It would stop for the time being when the people had procured enough for the time being, which left them plenty of time to spare. Clearly in subsistence as in other sectors of production, we have to do with an economy of specific, limited objectives. By hunting and gathering these objectives are apt to be irregularly accomplished, so the work pattern becomes correspondingly erratic.

In the event, a third characteristic of hunting and gathering unimagined by the received wisdom: rather than straining to the limits of available labor and disposable resources, these Australians seem to *underuse* their objective economic possibilities.

> The quantity of food gathered in one day by any of these groups could in every instance have been increased. Although the search for food was, for the women, a job that went on day after day without relief [but see our Figures 1.1 and 1.2], they rested quite frequently, and did not spend all the hours of daylight searching for and preparing food. The nature of the men's

---

coastal camps visited by the expedition. The resource base at Hemple Bay was richer than at Fish Creek. The greater time put into food-getting at Hemple Bay may reflect, then, the support of five children. On the other hand, the Fish Creek group did maintain a virtually full-time specialist, and part of the difference in hours worked may represent a normal coastal-inland variation. In inland hunting, good things often come in large packages; hence, one day's work may yield two day's sustenance. A fishing-gathering regime perhaps produces smaller if steadier returns, enjoining somewhat longer and more regular efforts.

food-gathering was more sporadic, and if they had a good catch one day they frequently rested the next. . . . Perhaps unconsciously they weigh the benefit of greater supplies of food against the effort involved in collecting it, perhaps they judge what they consider to be enough, and when that is collected they stop (McArthur, 1960, p. 92).

It follows, fourthly, that the economy was not physically demanding. The investigators' daily journal indicates that the people pace themselves; only once is a hunter described as "utterly exhausted" (McCarthy and McArthur, 1960, pp. 150f). Neither did the Arnhem Landers themselves consider the task of subsistence onerous. "They certainly did not approach it as an unpleasant job to be got over as soon as possible, nor as a necessary evil to be postponed as long as possible" (McArthur, 1960, p. 92).[14] In this connection, and also in relation to their underuse of economic resources, it is noteworthy that the Arnhem Land hunters seem not to have been content with a "bare existence." Like other Australians (cf. Worsley, 1961, p. 173), they become dissatisfied with an unvarying diet; some of their time appears to have gone into the provision of diversity over and above mere sufficiency (McCarthy and McArthur, 1960, p. 192).

In any case, the dietary intake of the Arnhem Land hunters was adequate—according to the standards of the National Research Council of America. Mean daily consumption per capita at Hemple Bay was 2,160 calories (only a four-day period of observation), and at Fish Creek 2,130 calories (11 days). Table 1.1 indicates the main daily consumption of various nutrients, calculated by McArthur in percentages of the NRCA recommended dietary allowances.

*Table 1.1. Mean daily consumption as percentage*
*of recommended allowances*
*(from McArthur, 1960)*

|  | Calories | Protein | Iron | Calcium | Ascorbic Acid |
|---|---|---|---|---|---|
| Hemple Bay | 116 | 444 | 80 | 128 | 394 |
| Fish Creek | 104 | 544 | 33 | 355 | 47 |

14  At least some Australians, the Yir-Yiront, make no linguistic differentiation between work and play (Sharp, 1958, p. 6).

Finally, what does the Arnhem Land study say about the famous question of leisure? It seems that hunting and gathering can afford extraordinary relief from economic cares. The Fish Creek group maintained a virtually full-time craftsman, a man 35 or 40 years old, whose true specialty however seems to have been loafing:

> He did not go out hunting at all with the men, but one day he netted fish most vigorously. He occasionally went into the bush to get wild bees' nests. *Wilira* was an expert craftsman who repaired the spears and spear-throwers, made smoking-pipes and drone-tubes, and hafted a stone axe (on request) in a skillful manner; apart from these occupations he spent most of his time talking, eating and sleeping (McCarthy and McArthur, 1960, p. 148).

Wilira was not altogether exceptional. Much of the time spared by the Arnhem Land hunters was literally spare time, consumed in rest and sleep (see Tables 1.2 and 1.3). The main alternative to work, changing off with it in a complementary way, was sleep:

> Apart from the time (mostly between definitive activities and during cooking periods) spent in general social intercourse, chatting, gossiping and so on, some hours of the daylight were also spent resting and sleeping. On the average, if the men were in camp, they usually slept after lunch from an

*Table 1.2. Daytime rest and sleep,*
*Fish Creek group*
*(data from McCarthy and McArthur, 1960)*

| Day | ♂ Average | ♀ Average |
|---|---|---|
| 1 | 2'15" | 2'45" |
| 2 | 1'30" | 1'0" |
| 3 | Most of the day | |
| 4 | Intermittent | |
| 5 | Intermittent and most of late afternoon | |
| 6 | Most of the day | |
| 7 | Several hours | |
| 8 | 2'0" | 2'0" |
| 9 | 50" | 50" |
| 10 | Afternoon | |
| 11 | Afternoon | |
| 12 | Intermittent, afternoon | |
| 13 | — | — |
| 14 | 3'15" | 3'15" |

Table 1.3. Daytime rest and sleep, Hemple Bay group
(data from McCarthy and McArthur, 1960)

| Day | ♂ Average | ♀ Average |
|-----|-----------|-----------|
| 1 | — | 45″ |
| 2 | Most of the day | 2′45″ |
| 3 | 1′0″ | — |
| 4 | Intermittent | Intermittent |
| 5 | — | 1′30″ |
| 6 | Intermittent | Intermittent |
| 7 | Intermittent | Intermittent |

hour to an hour and a half, or sometimes even more. Also after returning from fishing or hunting they usually had a sleep, either immediately they arrived or whilst game was being cooked. At Hemple Bay the men slept if they returned early in the day but not if they reached camp after 4.00 p.m. When in camp all day they slept at odd times and always after lunch. The women, when out collecting in the forest, appeared to rest more frequently than the men. If in camp all day, they also slept at odd times, sometimes for long periods (McCarthy and McArthur, 1960, p. 193).

The failure of Arnhem Landers to "build culture" is not strictly from want of time. It is from idle hands.

So much for the plight of hunters and gatherers in Arnhem Land. As for the Bushmen, economically likened to Australian hunters by Herskovits, two excellent recent reports by Richard Lee show their condition to be indeed the same (Lee, 1968; 1969). Lee's research merits a special hearing not only because it concerns Bushmen, but specifically the Dobe section of /Kung Bushmen, adjacent to the Nyae Nyae about whose subsistence—in a context otherwise of "material plenty"—Mrs. Marshall expressed important reservations. The Dobe occupy an area of Botswana where /Kung Bushmen have been living for at least a hundred years, but have only just begun to suffer dislocation pressures. (Metal, however, has been available to the Dobe since

1880–90). An intensive study was made of the subsistence production of a dry season camp with a population (41 people) near the mean of such settlements. The observations extended over four weeks during July and August 1964, a period of transition from more to less favorable seasons of the year, hence fairly representative, it seems, of average subsistence difficulties.

Despite a low annual rainfall (6 to 10 inches), Lee found in the Dobe area a "surprising abundance of vegetation." Food resources were "both varied and abundant," particularly the energy-rich mangetti nut—"so abundant that millions of the nuts rotted on the ground each year for want of picking" ( all references in Lee, 1969, p. 59).[15] His reports on time spent in food-getting are remarkably close to the Arnhem Land observations. Table 1.4 summarizes Lee's data.

The Bushman figures imply that one man's labor in hunting and gathering will support four or five people. Taken at face value, Bushman food collecting is more efficient than French farming in the period up to World War II, when more than 20 percent of the population were engaged in feeding the rest. Confessedly, the comparison is misleading, but not as misleading as it is astonishing. In the total population of free-ranging Bushmen contacted by Lee, 61.3 percent (152 of 248) were effective food producers; the remainder were too young or too old to contribute importantly. In the particular camp under scrutiny, 65 percent were "effectives." Thus the ratio of food producers to the general population is actually 3 : 5 or 2 : 3. *But,* these 65 percent of the people "worked 36 percent of the time, and 35 percent of the people did not work at all"! (Lee, 1969, p. 67).

*good point*

For each adult worker, this comes to about two and one-half days labor per week. ("In other words, each productive individual supported herself or himself and dependents and still had 3-1/2 to 5-1/2 days available for other activities.") A "day's work" was about six hours; hence the Dobe work week is approximately 15 hours, or an average of 2 hours 9 minutes per day. Even lower than the Arnhem Land norms, this figure however excludes cooking and the preparation of implements. All things considered, Bushmen subsistence labors are probably very close to those of native Australians.

15. This appreciation of local resources is all the more remarkable considering that Lee's ethnographic work was done in the second and third years of "one of the most severe droughts in South Africa's history" (1968, p. 39; 1969, p. 73 n.).

*Table 1.4. Summary of Dobe Bushmen work diary (from Lee, 1969)*

| Week | Mean Group Size* | Man-Days of Consumption† | Man-Days of Work | Days of Work/ Week/Adult | Index of Subsistence Effort‡ |
|---|---|---|---|---|---|
| 1 (July 6-12) | 25.6 (23-29) | 179 | 37 | 2.3 | .21 |
| 2 (July 13-19) | 28.3 (23-37) | 198 | 22 | 1.2 | .11 |
| 3 (July 20-26) | 34.3 (29-40) | 240 | 42 | 1.9 | .18 |
| 4 (July 27-Aug. 2) | 35.6 (32-40) | 249 | 77 | 3.2 | .31 |
| 4-week totals | 30.9 | 866 | 178 | 2.2 | .21 |
| Adjusted totals§ | 31.8 | 668 | 156 | 2.5 | .23 |

*Group size shown in average and range. There is considerable short-term population fluctuation in Bushmen camps.

†Includes both children and adults, to give a combined total of days of provisioning required/week.

‡This index was constructed by Lee to illustrate the relation between consumption and the work required to produce it: $S = W/C$, where $W$ = number of man-days of work, and $C$ = man days of consumption. Inverted, the formula would tell how many people could be supported by a day's work in subsistence.

§Week 2 was excluded from the final calculations because the investigator contributed some food to the camp on two days.

Also like the Australians, the time Bushmen do not work in subsistence they pass in leisure or leisurely activity. One detects again that characteristic paleolithic rhythm of a day or two on, a day or two off—the latter passed desultorily in camp. Although food collecting is the primary productive activity, Lee writes, "the majority of the people's time (four to five days per week) is spent in other pursuits, such as resting in camp or visiting other camps" (1969, p. 74):

> A woman gathers on one day enough food to feed her family for three days, and spends the rest of her time resting in camp, doing embroidery, visiting other camps, or entertaining visitors from other camps. For each day at home, kitchen routines, such as cooking, nut cracking, collecting firewood, and fetching water, occupy one to three hours of her time. This rhythm of steady work and steady leisure is maintained throughout the year. The hunters tend to work more frequently than the women, but their schedule is uneven. It is not unusual for a man to hunt avidly for a week and then do no hunting at all for two or three weeks. Since hunting is an unpredictable business and subject to magical control, hunters sometimes experience a run of bad luck and stop hunting for a month or longer. During these periods, visiting, entertaining, and especially dancing are the primary activities of men (1968, p. 37).

The daily per-capita subsistence yield for the Dobe Bushmen was 2,140 calories. However, taking into account body weight, normal activities, and the age-sex composition of the Dobe population, Lee estimates the people require only 1,975 calories per capita. Some of the surplus food probably went to the dogs, who ate what the people left over. "The conclusion can be drawn that the Bushmen do not lead a substandard existence on the edge of starvation as has been commonly supposed" (1969, p. 73).

Taken in isolation, the Arnhem Land and Bushmen reports mount a disconcerting if not decisive attack on the entrenched theoretical position. Artificial in construction, the former study in particular is reasonably considered equivocal. But the testimony of the Arnhem Land expedition is echoed at many points by observations made elsewhere in Australia, as well as elsewhere in the hunting-gathering world. Much of the Australian evidence goes back to the nineteenth century, some of it to quite acute observers careful to make exception of the aboriginal come into relation with Europeans, for "his food supply is restricted, and . . . he is in many cases warned off from the waterholes which are the centers of his best hunting grounds" (Spencer and Gillen, 1899, p. 50).

The case is altogether clear for the well-watered areas of southeastern Australia. There the Aboriginals were favored with a supply of fish so abundant and easily procured that one squatter on the Victorian scene of the 1840s had to wonder "how that sage people managed to pass their time before my party came and taught them to smoke" (Curr, 1965, p. 109). Smoking at least solved the economic problem— nothing to do: "That accomplishment fairly acquired . . . matters went on flowingly, their leisure hours being divided between putting the pipe to its legitimate purpose and begging my tobacco." Somewhat more seriously, the old squatter did attempt an estimate of the amount of time spent in hunting and gathering by the people of the then Port Phillip's District. The women were away from the camp on gathering expeditions about six hours a day, "half of that time being loitered away in the shade or by the fire"; the men left for the hunt shortly after the women quit camp and returned around the same time (p. 118). Curr found the food thus acquired of "indifferent quality" although "readily procured," the six hours a day "abundantly sufficing" for that purpose; indeed the country "could have supported twice the number of Blacks we found in it" (p. 120). Very similar comments were made by another old-timer, Clement Hodgkinson, writing of an analogous environment in northeastern New South Wales. A few minutes fishing would provide enough to feed "the whole tribe" (Hodgkinson, 1845, p. 223; cf. Hiatt, 1965, pp. 103-104). "Indeed, throughout all the country along the eastern coast, the blacks have never suffered so much from scarcity of food as many commiserating writers have supposed" (Hodgkinson, 1845, p. 227).

But the people who occupied these more fertile sections of Australia, notably in the southeast, have not been incorporated in today's stereotype of an Aborigine. They were wiped out early.[16] The European's relation to such "Blackfellows" was one of conflict over the continent's riches; little time or inclination was spared from the

16. As were the Tasmanians, of whom Bonwick wrote: "The Aborigines were never in want of food; though Mrs. Somerville has ventured to say of them in her 'Physical Geography' that they were 'truly miserable in a country where the means of existence were so scanty.' Dr. Jeannent, once Protector, writes: 'They must have been superabundantly supplied, and have required little exertion or industry to support themselves.' "(Bonwick, 1870, p. 14).

process of destruction for the luxury of contemplation. In the event, ethnographic consciousness would only inherit the slim pickings: mainly interior groups, mainly desert people, mainly the Arunta. Not that the Arunta are all that bad off—ordinarily, "his life is by no means a miserable or a very hard one" (Spencer and Gillen, 1899, p. 7).[17] But the Central tribes should not be considered, in point of numbers or ecological adaptation, typical of native Australians (cf. Meggitt, 1964). The following tableau of the indigenous economy provided by John Edward Eyre, who had traversed the south coast and penetrated the Flinders range as well as sojourned in the richer Murray district, has the right to be acknowledged at least as representative:

> Throughout the greater portion of New Holland, where there do not happen to be European settlers, and invariably when fresh water can be permanently procured upon the surface, the native experiences no difficulty whatever in procuring food in abundance all the year round. It is true that the character of his diet varies with the changing seasons, and the formation of the country he inhabits; but it rarely happens that any season of the year, or any description of country does not yield him both animal and vegetable food. . . . Of these [chief] articles [of food], many are not only procurable in abundance, but in such vast quantities at the proper seasons, as to afford for a considerable length of time an ample means of subsistence to many hundreds of natives congregated at one place. . . . On many parts of the coast, and in the larger inland rivers, fish are obtained of a very fine description, and in great abundance. At Lake Victoria . . . I have seen six hundred natives encamped together, all of whom were living at the time upon fish procured from the lake, with the addition, perhaps, of the leaves of the mesembryanthemum. When I went amongst them I never perceived any scarcity in their camps. . . . At Moorunde, when the Murray annually inundates the flats, fresh-water cray-fish make their way to the surface of the ground . . . in such vast numbers that I have seen four hundred natives live upon them for weeks together, whilst the numbers spoiled or thrown away would have sustained four hundred more. . . . An unlimited supply of fish is also procurable at the Murray about the beginning of December. . . . The number [of fish] procured . . . in a few hours is incredible. . . . Another very favourite article of food, and equally abundant at a particular season of the year, in the eastern portion of the continent, is a species of

17. This by way of contrast to other tribes deeper in the Central Australian Desert, and specifically under "ordinary circumstances," not the times of long-continued drought when "he has to suffer privation" (Spencer and Gillen, 1899, p. 7).

moth which the natives procure from the cavities and hollows of the mountains in certain localities. . . . The tops, leaves, and stalks of a kind of cress, gathered at the proper season of the year . . . furnish a favourite, and inexhaustible supply of food for an unlimited number of natives. . . . There are many other articles of food among the natives, equally abundant and valuable as those I have enumerated (Eyre, 1845, vol. 2, pp. 250-254).

Both Eyre and Sir George Grey, whose sanguine view of the indigenous economy we have already noted ("I have always found the greatest abundance in their huts") left specific assessments, in hours per day, of the Australians' subsistence labors. (This in Grey's case would include inhabitants of quite undesirable parts of western Australia.) The testimony of these gentlemen and explorers accords very closely with the Arnhem Land averages obtained by McCarthy and McArthur. "In all ordinary seasons," wrote Grey, (that is, when the people are not confined to their huts by bad weather) "they can obtain, *in two or three hours* a sufficient supply of food for the day, but their usual custom is to roam indolently from spot to spot, lazily collecting it as they wander along" (1841, vol. 2, p. 263; emphasis mine). Similarly, Eyre states: "In almost every part of the continent which I have visited, where the presence of Europeans, or their stock, has not limited, or destroyed their original means of subsistence, I have found that the natives could usually, *in three or four hours,* procure as much food as would last for the day, and that without fatigue or labour" (1845, pp. 254-255; emphasis mine).

The same discontinuity of subsistence of labor reported by McArthur and McCarthy, the pattern of alternating search and sleep, is repeated, furthermore, in early and late observations from all over the continent (Eyre, 1845, vol. 2, pp. 253-254; Bulmer, in Smyth, 1878, vol. 1, p. 142; Mathew, 1910, p. 84; Spencer and Gillen, 1899, p. 32; Hiatt, 1965, pp. 103-104). Basedow took it as the general custom of the Aboriginal: "When his affairs are working harmoniously, game secured, and water available, the aboriginal makes his life as easy as possible; and he might to the outsider even appear lazy" (1925, p. 116).[18]

Meanwhile, back in Africa the Hadza have been long enjoying a

18. Basedow goes on to excuse the people's idleness on the grounds of overeating, then to excuse the overeating on the grounds of the periods of hunger natives suffer, which he further explains by the droughts Australia is heir to, the effects of which have been exacerbated by the white man's exploitation of the country.

Assiduous

comparable ease, with a burden of subsistence occupations no more strenuous in hours per day than the Bushmen or the Australian Aboriginals (Woodburn, 1968). Living in an area of "exceptional abundance" of animals and regular supplies of vegetables (the vicinity of Lake Eyasi), Hadza men seem much more concerned with games of chance than with chances of game. During the long dry season especially, they pass the greater part of days on end in gambling, perhaps only to lose the metal-tipped arrows they need for big game hunting at other times. In any case, many men are "quite unprepared or unable to hunt big game even when they possess the necessary arrows." Only a small minority, Woodburn writes, are active hunters of large animals, and if women are generally more assiduous at their vegetable collecting, still it is at a leisurely pace and without prolonged labor (cf. p. 51; Woodburn, 1966). Despite this nonchalance, and an only limited economic cooperation, Hadza "nonetheless obtain sufficient food without undue effort." Woodburn offers this "very rough approximation" of subsistence-labor requirements: "Over the year as a whole probably an average of less than two hours a day is spent obtaining food" (Woodburn, 1968, p. 54).

Interesting that the Hadza, tutored by life and not by anthropology, reject the neolithic revolution in order to *keep* their leisure. Although surrounded by cultivators, they have until recently refused to take up agriculture themselves, "mainly on the grounds that this would involve too much hard work."[19] In this they are like the Bushmen, who respond to the neolithic question with another: "Why should we plant, when there are so many mongomongo nuts in the world?" (Lee, 1968, p. 33). Woodburn moreover did form the impression, although as yet unsubstantiated, that Hadza actually expend less energy, and probably less time, in obtaining subsistence than do neighboring cultivators of East Africa (1968, p. 54).[20] To change continents but not contents, the fitful economic

19. This phrase appears in a paper by Woodburn distributed to the Wenner-Gren symposium on "Man the Hunter," although it is only elliptically repeated in the published account (1968, p. 55). I hope I do not commit an indiscretion or an inaccuracy citing it here.

20. "Agriculture is in fact the first example of servile labor in the history of man. According to biblical tradition, the first criminal, Cain, is a farmer" (Lafargue, 1911[1883], p. 11 n.).

It is notable too that the agricultural neighbours of both Bushmen and Hadza are quick to resort to the more dependable hunting-gathering life come drought and threat

commitment of the South American hunter, too, could seem to the European outsider an incurable "natural disposition":

> . . . the Yamana are not capable of continuous, daily hard labor, much to the chagrin of European farmers and employers for whom they often work. Their work is more a matter of fits and starts, and in these occasional efforts they can develop considerable energy for a certain time. After that, however, they show a desire for an incalculably long rest period during which they lie about doing nothing, without showing great fatigue. . . . It is obvious that repeated irregularities of this kind make the European employer despair, but the Indian cannot help it. It is his natural disposition (Gusinde, 1961, p. 27).[21]

The hunter's attitude towards farming introduces us, lastly, to a few particulars of the way they relate to the food quest. Once again we venture here into the internal realm of the economy, a realm sometimes subjective and always difficult to understand; where, moreover, hunters seem deliberately inclined to overtax our comprehension by customs so odd as to invite the extreme interpretation that either these people are fools or they really have nothing to worry about. The former would be a true logical deduction from the hunter's nonchalance, on the premise that his economic condition is truly exigent. On the other hand, if a livelihood is usually easily procured, if one can usually expect to succeed, then the people's seeming imprudence can no longer appear as such. Speaking to unique developments of the market economy, to its institutionalization of scarcity, Karl Polanyi said that our "animal dependence upon food has been bared and the naked fear of starvation permitted to run loose. Our humiliating enslavement to the material, which all human culture is designed to mitigate, was deliberately made more rigorous" (1947, p. 115). But

---

of famine (Woodburn, 1958, p. 54; Lee, 1968, pp. 39–40).

21. This common distaste for prolonged labor manifested by recently primitive peoples under European employ, a distaste not restricted to ex-hunters, might have alerted anthropology to the fact that the traditional economy had known only modest objectives, so within reach as to allow an extraordinary disengagement, considerable "relief from the mere problem of getting a living."

The hunting economy may also be commonly underrated for its presumed inability to support specialist production. Cf. Sharp, 1934–35, p. 37; Radcliffe-Brown, 1948, p. 43; Spencer, 1959, pp. 155, 196, 251; Lothrup, 1928, p. 71; Steward, 1938, p. 44. If there is not specialization, at any rate it is clearly for lack of a "market," not for lack of time.

our problems are not theirs, the hunters and gatherers. Rather, a pristine affluence colors their economic arrangements, a trust in the abundance of nature's resources rather than despair at the inadequacy of human means. My point is that otherwise curious heathen devices become understandable by the people's confidence, a confidence which is the reasonable human attribute of a generally successful economy.[22]

Consider the hunter's chronic movements from camp to camp. This nomadism, often taken by us as a sign of a certain harassment, is undertaken by them with a certain abandon. The Aboriginals of Victoria, Smyth recounts, are as a rule "lazy travellers. *They have no motive to induce them to hasten their movements*. It is generally late in the morning before they start on their journey, and there are many interruptions by the way" (1878, vol. 1, p. 125; emphasis mine). The good *Pere* Biard in his *Relation* of 1616, after a glowing description of the foods available in their season to the Micmac ("Never had Solomon his mansion better regulated and provided with food ") goes on in the same tone:

> In order to thoroughly enjoy this, their lot, our foresters start off to their different places with as much pleasure as if they were going on a stroll or an excursion; they do this easily through the skillful use and great convenience of canoes . . . so rapidly sculled that, without any effort, in good weather you can make thirty or forty leagues a day; nevertheless we scarcely see these Savages posting along at this rate, for their days are all nothing but pastime. They are never in a hurry. Quite different from us, who can never do anything without hurry and worry . . . (Biard, 1897, pp. 84–85).

22. At the same time that the bourgeois ideology of scarcity was let loose, with the inevitable effect of downgrading an earlier culture, it searched and found in nature the ideal model to follow if man (or at least the workingman) was ever to better his unhappy lot: the ant, the industrious ant. In this the ideology may have been as mistaken as in its view of hunters. The following appeared in the *Ann Arbor News,* January 27, 1971, under the head, "Two Scientists Claim Ants a little Lazy": Palm Springs, Calif. (AP)—"Ants aren't all they are reported [reputed?] to be," say Drs. George and Jeanette Wheeler.

The husband-wife researchers have devoted years to studying the creatures, heroes of fables on industriousness.

"Whenever we view an anthill we get the impression of a tremendous amount of activity, but that is merely because there are so many ants and they all look alike," the Wheelers concluded.

"The individual ants spend a great deal of time just loafing. And, worse than that, the worker ants, who are all females, spend a lot of time primping."

Certainly, hunters quit camp because food resources have given out in the vicinity. But to see in this nomadism merely a flight from starvation only perceives the half of it; one ignores the possibility that the people's expectations of greener pastures elsewhere are not usually disappointed. Consequently their wanderings, rather than anxious, take on all the qualities of a picnic outing on the Thames.

A more serious issue is presented by the frequent and exasperated observation of a certain "lack of foresight" among hunters and gatherers. Oriented forever in the present, without "the slightest thought of, or care for, what the morrow may bring" (Spencer and Gillen, 1899, p. 53), the hunter seems unwilling to husband supplies, incapable of a planned response to the doom surely awaiting him. He adopts instead a studied unconcern, which expresses itself in two complementary economic inclinations.

The first, prodigality: the propensity to eat right through all the food in the camp, even during objectively difficult times, "as if," LeJeune said of the Montagnais, "the game they were to hunt was shut up in a stable." Basedow wrote of native Australians, their motto "might be interpreted in words to the effect that while there is plenty for today never care about tomorrow. On this account an Aboriginal is inclined to make one feast of his supplies, in preference to a modest meal now and another by and by" (1925, p. 116). LeJeune even saw his Montagnais carry such extravagance to the edge of disaster:

> In the famine through which we passed, if my host took two, three, or four Beavers, immediately, whether it was day or night, they had a feast for all neighboring Savages. And if those people had captured something, they had one also at the same time; so that, on emerging from one feast, you went to another, and sometimes even to a third and a fourth. I told them that they did not manage well, and that it would be better to reserve these feasts for future days, and in doing this they would not be so pressed with hunger. They laughed at me. "Tomorrow" (they said) "we shall make another feast with what we shall capture." Yes, but more often they capture only cold and wind (LeJeune, 1887, pp. 281-283).

Sympathetic writers have tried to rationalize the apparent impracticality. Perhaps the people have been carried beyond reason by hunger: they are apt to gorge themselves on a kill because they have gone so long without meat—and for all they know they are likely to soon do so again. Or perhaps in making one feast of his supplies a man is

Superfluous

responding to binding social obligations, to important imperatives of sharing. LeJeune's experience would confirm either view, but it also suggests a third. Or rather, the Montagnais have their own explanation. They are not worried by what the morrow may bring because as far as they are concerned it will bring more of the same: "another feast." Whatever the value of other interpretations, such self-confidence must be brought to bear on the supposed prodigality of hunters. More, it must have some objective basis, for if hunters and gatherers really favored gluttony over economic good sense, they would never have lived to become the prophets of this new religion.

A second and complementary inclination is merely prodigality's negative side: the failure to put by food surpluses, to develop food storage. For many hunters and gatherers, it appears, food storage cannot be proved technically impossible, nor is it certain that the people are unaware of the possibility (cf. Woodburn, 1968, p. 53). One must investigate instead what in the situation precludes the attempt. Gusinde asked this question, and for the Yahgan found the answer in the selfsame justifiable optimism. Storage would be "superfluous,"

> because throughout the entire year and with almost limitless generosity the sea puts all kinds of animals at the disposal of the man who hunts and the woman who gathers. Storm or accident will deprive a family of these things for no more than a few days. Generally no one need reckon with the danger of hunger, and everyone almost anywhere finds an abundance of what he needs. Why then should anyone worry about food for the future! . . . Basically our Fuegians know that they need not fear for the future, hence they do not pile up supplies. Year in and year out they can look forward to the next day, free of care. . . . (Gusinde, 1961, pp. 336, 339).

Gusinde's explanation is probably good as far as it goes, but probably incomplete. A more complex and subtle economic calculus seems in play—realized however by a social arithmetic exceedingly simple. The advantages of food storage should be considered against the diminishing returns to collection within the compass of a confined locale. An uncontrollable tendency to lower the local carrying capacity is for hunters *au fond des choses*: a basic condition of their production and main cause of their movement. The potential drawback of storage is exactly that it engages the contradiction between wealth and mobility. It would anchor the camp to an area soon depleted of natural food supplies. Thus immobilized by their accumulated stocks, the people may suffer by comparison with a little hunting and gathering elsewhere, where nature has, so to speak, done considerable storage of her own—of foods possibly more desirable in diversity as well as amount than men can put by. But this fine calculation—in any event probably symbolically impossible (cf. Codere,1968)—would be worked out in a much simpler binary opposition, set in social terms such as "love" and "hate." For as Richard Lee observes (1969, p. 75), the technically neutral activity of food accumulation or storage is morally something else again, "hoarding." The efficient hunter who would accumulate supplies succeeds at the cost of his own esteem, or else he gives them away at the cost of his (superfluous) effort. As it works out, an attempt to stock up food may only reduce the overall output of a hunting band, for the have-nots will content themselves with staying in camp and living off the wherewithal amassed by the more prudent. Food storage, then, may be technically feasible, yet economically undesirable, and socially unachievable.

If food storage remains limited among hunters, their economic confidence, born of the ordinary times when all the people's wants are easily satisfied, becomes a permanent condition, carrying them laughing through periods that would try even a Jesuit's soul and worry him so that—as the Indians warn—he could become sick:

> I saw them, in their hardships and in their labors, suffer with cheerfulness. . . . I found myself, with them, threatened with great suffering; they said to me, "We shall be sometimes two days, sometimes three, without eating, for lack of food; take courage, *Chihiné,* let thy soul be strong to endure suffering and hardship; keep thyself from being sad, otherwise thou wilt be sick; see how we do not cease to laugh, although we have little to eat" (LeJeune, 1897, p. 283; cf. Needham, 1954, p. 230).

## Rethinking Hunters and Gatherers

> Constantly under pressure of want, and yet, by travelling, easily able to supply their wants, their lives lack neither excitement or pleasure (Smyth, 1878, vol. 1, p. 123).

Clearly, the hunting-gathering economy has to be revaluated, both as to its true accomplishments and its true limitations. The procedural fault of the received wisdom was to read from the material circumstances to the economic structure, deducing the absolute difficulty of such a life from its absolute poverty. But always the cultural design improvises dialectics on its relationship to nature. Without escaping the ecological constraints, culture would negate them, so that at once the system shows the impress of natural conditions and the originality of a social response—in their poverty, abundance.

What are the real handicaps of the hunting-gathering *praxis?* Not "low productivity of labor," if existing examples mean anything. But the economy is seriously afflicted by the *imminence of diminishing returns*. Beginning in subsistence and spreading from there to every sector, an initial success seems only to develop the probability that further efforts will yield smaller benefits. This describes the typical curve of food-getting within a particular locale. A modest number of people usually sooner than later reduce the food resources within convenient range of camp. Thereafter, they may stay on only by absorbing an increase in real costs or a decline in real returns: rise in costs if the people choose to search farther and farther afield, decline in returns if they are satisfied to live on the shorter supplies or inferior foods in easier reach. The solution, of course, is to go somewhere else. Thus the first and decisive contingency of hunting-gathering: it requires movement to maintain production on advantageous terms.

But this movement, more or less frequent in different circumstances, more or less distant, merely transposes to other spheres of production the same diminishing returns of which it is born. The manufacture of tools, clothing, utensils, or ornaments, however easily done, becomes senseless when these begin to be more of a burden than a comfort. Utility falls quickly at the margin of portability. The construction of substantial houses likewise becomes absurd if they must soon be abandoned. Hence the hunter's very ascetic conceptions of material welfare: an interest only in minimal equipment, if that; a valuation of smaller things over bigger; a disinterest in acquiring two or more of most goods; and the like. Ecological pressure assumes a rare form of concreteness when it has to be shouldered. If the gross product is trimmed down in comparison with other economies, it is not the hunter's productivity that is at fault, but his mobility.

Almost the same thing can be said of the demographic constraints of hunting-gathering. The same policy of *débarassment* is in play on the level of people, describable in similar terms and ascribable to similar causes. The terms are, cold-bloodedly: diminishing returns at the margin of portability, minimum necessary equipment, elimination of duplicates, and so forth—that is to say, infanticide, senilicide, sexual continence for the duration of the nursing period, etc., practices for which many food-collecting peoples are well known. The presumption that such devices are due to an inability to support more people is probably true—if "support" is understood in the sense of carrying them rather than feeding them. The people eliminated, as hunters sometimes sadly tell, are precisely those who cannot effectively transport themselves, who would hinder the movement of family and camp. Hunters may be obliged to handle people and goods in parallel ways, the draconic population policy an expression of the same ecology as the ascetic economy. More, these tactics of demographic restraint again form part of a larger policy for counteracting diminishing returns in subsistence. A local group becomes vulnerable to diminishing returns—so to a greater velocity of movement, or else to fission—in proportion to its size (other things equal). Insofar as the people would keep the advantage in local production, and maintain a certain physical and social stability, their Malthusian practices are just cruelly consistent. Modern hunters and gatherers, working their notably inferior environments, pass most of the year in very small groups widely spaced out. But rather than the sign of underproduction, the wages of poverty, this demographic pattern is better understood as the cost of living well.

Hunting and gathering has all the strengths of its weaknesses. Periodic movement and restraint in wealth and population are at once imperatives of the economic practice and creative adaptations, the kinds of necessities of which virtues are made. Precisely in such a framework, affluence becomes possible. Mobility and moderation put hunters' ends within range of their technical means. An undeveloped mode of production is thus rendered highly effective. The hunter's life is not as difficult as it looks from the outside. In some ways the economy reflects dire ecology, but it is also a complete inversion.

Reports on hunters and gatherers of the ethnological present—specifically on those in marginal environments—suggest a mean of three to five hours per adult worker per day in food production. Hunters keep banker's hours, notably less than modern industrial workers (unionized), who would surely settle for a 21–35 hour week. An interesting comparison is also posed by recent studies of labor costs among agriculturalists of neolithic type. For example, the average adult Hanunoo, man or woman, spends 1,200 hours per year in swidden cultivation (Conklin, 1957, p. 151); which is to say, a mean of three hours twenty minutes per day. Yet this figure does not include food gathering, animal raising, cooking and other direct subsistence efforts of these Philippine tribesmen. Comparable data are beginning to appear in reports on other primitive agriculturalists from many parts of the world. The conclusion is put conservatively when put negatively: hunters and gatherers need not work longer getting food than do primitive cultivators. Extrapolating from ethnography to prehistory, one may say as much for the neolithic as John Stuart Mill said of all labor-saving devices, that never was one invented that saved anyone a minute's labor. The neolithic saw no particular improvement over the paleolithic in the amount of time required per capita for the production of subsistence; probably, with the advent of agriculture, people had to work harder.

There is nothing either to the convention that hunters and gatherers can enjoy little leisure from tasks of sheer survival. By this, the evolutionary inadequacies of the paleolithic are customarily explained, while for the provision of leisure the neolithic is roundly congratulated. But the traditional formulas might be truer if reversed: the amount of work (per capita) increases with the evolution of culture, and the amount of leisure decreases. Hunters' subsistence labors are characteristically intermittent, a day on and a day off, and modern hunters at least tend to employ their time off in such activities as daytime sleep. In the tropical habitats occupied by many of these existing hunters, plant collecting is more reliable than hunting itself. Therefore, the women, who do the collecting, work rather more regularly than the men, and provide the greater part of the food supply. Man's work is often done. On the other hand, it is likely to be highly erratic, unpredictably required; if men lack leisure, it is then in the Enlightenment sense rather than the literal. When Condorcet attributed the hunter's unprogressive condition to want of "the leisure in which he can indulge in thought and enrich his understanding with new combinations of ideas," he also recognized that the economy was a "necessary cycle of extreme activity and total idleness." Apparently what the hunter needed was the *assured* leisure of an aristocratic *philosophe*.

Hunters and gatherers maintain a sanguine view of their economic state despite the hardships they sometimes know. It may be that they sometimes know hardships because of the sanguine views they maintain of their economic state. Perhaps their confidence only encourages prodigality to the extent the camp falls casualty to the first untoward circumstance. In alleging this is an affluent economy, therefore, I do not deny that certain hunters have moments of difficulty. Some do find it "almost inconceivable" for a man to die of hunger, or even to fail to satisfy his hunger for more than a day or two (Woodburn, 1968, p. 52). But others, especially certain very peripheral hunters spread out in small groups across an environment of extremes, are exposed periodically to the kind of inclemency that interdicts travel or access to game. They suffer—although perhaps only fractionally, the shortage affecting particular immobilized families rather than the society as a whole (cf. Gusinde, 1961, pp. 306-307).

Still, granting this vulnerability, and allowing the most poorly situated modern hunters into comparison, it would be difficult to prove that privation is distinctly characteristic of the hunter-gatherers. Food shortage is not the indicative property of this mode of production as opposed to others; it does not mark off hunters and gatherers as a class or a general evolutionary stage. Lowie asks:

> But what of the herders on a simple plane whose maintenance is periodically jeopardized by plagues—who, like some Lapp bands of the nineteenth century were obliged to fall back on fishing? What of the primitive peasants who clear and till without compensation of the soil, exhaust one plot and pass on to the next, and are threatened with famine at every drought? Are they any more in control of misfortune caused by natural conditions than the hunter-gatherer? (1938, p. 286)

Above all, what about the world today? One-third to one-half of humanity are said to go to bed hungry every night. In the Old Stone Age the fraction must have been much smaller. *This* is the era of hunger unprecedented. Now, in the time of the greatest technical power, is starvation an institution. Reverse another venerable formula: the amount of hunger increases relatively and absolutely with the evolution of culture.

This paradox is my whole point. Hunters and gatherers have by force of circumstances an objectively low standard of living. But taken as their *objective,* and given their adequate means of production, all the people's material wants usually can be easily satisfied. The evolution of economy has known, then, two contradictory movements: enriching but at the same time impoverishing, appropriating in relation to nature but expropriating in relation to man. The progressive aspect is, of course, technological. It has been celebrated in many ways: as an increase in the amount of need-serving goods and services, an increase in the amount of energy harnessed to the service of culture, an increase in productivity, an increase in division of labor, and increased freedom from environmental control. Taken in a certain sense, the last is especially useful for understanding the earliest stages of technical advance. Agriculture not only raised society above the distribution of natural food resources, it allowed neolithic communities to maintain high degrees of social order where the requirements of human existence were absent from the natural order. Enough food could be harvested in some seasons to sustain the people while no food would grow at all; the consequent stability of social life was critical for its material enlargement. Culture went on then from triumph to triumph, in a kind of progressive contravention of the biological law of the minimum, until it proved it could support human life in outer space—where even gravity and oxygen were naturally lacking.

Other men were dying of hunger in the market places of Asia. It has been an evolution of structures as well as technologies, and in that respect like the mythical road where for every step the traveller advances his destination recedes by two. The structures have been political as well as economic, of power as well as property. They developed first within societies, increasingly now between societies. No doubt these structures have been functional, necessary organizations of the technical development, but within the communities they have thus helped to enrich they would discriminate in the distribution of wealth and differentiate in the style of life. The world's most primitive people have few possessions, *but they are not poor.* Poverty is not a certain small amount of goods, nor is it just a relation between means and ends; above all it is a relation between people. Poverty is a social status. As such it is the invention of civilization. It has grown with civilization, at once as an invidious distinction between classes and more importantly as a tributary relation—that can render agrarian peasants more susceptible to natural catastrophes than any winter camp of Alaskan Eskimo.

All the preceding discussion takes the liberty of reading modern hunters historically, as an evolutionary base line. This liberty should not be lightly granted. Are marginal hunters such as the Bushmen of the Kalahari any more representative of the paleolithic condition than the Indians of California or the Northwest Coast? Perhaps not. Perhaps also Bushmen of the Kalahari are not even representative of marginal hunters. The great majority of surviving hunter-gatherers lead a life curiously decapitated and extremely lazy by comparison with the other few. The other few are very different. The Murngin, for example: "The first impression that any stranger must receive in a fully functioning group in Eastern Arnhem Land is of industry. . .

And he must be impressed with the fact that with the exception of very young children . . . there is no idleness" (Thomson, 1949a, pp. 33-34). There is nothing to indicate that the problems of livelihood are more difficult for these people than for other hunters (cf. Thomson, 1949b). The incentives of their unusual industry lie elsewhere: in "an elaborate and exacting ceremonial life," specifically in an elaborate ceremonial exchange cycle that bestows prestige on craftsmanship and trade (Thomson, 1949a, pp. 26, 28, 34 f, 87 passim). Most other hunters have no such concerns. Their existence is comparatively colorless, fixed singularly on eating with gusto and digesting at leisure. The cultural orientation is not Dionysian or Apollonian,but"gastric," as Julian Steward said of the Shoshoni. Then again it may be Dionysian, that is, Bacchanalian: "Eating among the Savages is like drinking among the drunkards of Europe. Those dry and ever-thirsty souls would willingly end their lives in a tub of malmsey, and the Savages in a pot full of meat; those over there talk only of drinking, and these here only of eating" (LeJeune, 1897, p. 249).

It is as if the superstructures of these societies had been eroded, leaving only the bare subsistence rock, and since production itself is readily accomplished, the people have plenty of time to perch there and talk about it. I must raise the possibility that the ethnography of hunters and gatherers is largely a record of incomplete cultures. Fragile cycles of ritual and exchange may have disappeared without trace, lost in the earliest stages of colonialism, when the intergroup relations they mediated were attacked and confounded. If so, the "original" affluent society will have to be rethought again for its originality, and the evolutionary schemes once more revised. Still this much history can always be rescued from existing hunters: the "economic problem" is easily solvable by paleolithic techniques. But then, it was not until culture neared the height of its material achievements that it erected a shrine to the Unattainable: *Infinite Needs*.

# 2

# The Domestic Mode of
# Production: The Structure of
# Underproduction

This chapter is constructed on an observation in apparent contradiction to the pristine "affluence" I have just taken so much trouble to defend: the primitive economies are underproductive. The main run of them, agricultural as well as preagricultural, seem not to realize their own economic capacities. Labor power is underused, technological means are not fully engaged, natural resources are left untapped.

This is not the simple point that the output of primitive societies is low: it is the complex problem that production is low relative to existing possibilities. So understood, "underproduction" is not necessarily inconsistent with a pristine "affluence." All the people's material wants might still be easily satisfied even though the economy is running below capacity. Indeed, the former is rather a condition of the latter: given the modest ideas of "satisfaction" locally prevailing, labor and resources need not be exploited to the full.

In any event, there are indications of underproduction from many parts of the primitive world, and the first task of the essay is to give some sense of the evidence. Beyond any initial attempt at explanation, the discovery of this tendency—more precisely of several related tendencies of the primitive economic performance—seems of greater importance. I raise the possibility that underproduction is in the nature of the economies at issue; that is, economies organized by domestic groups and kinship relations.

41

*Dimensions of Underproduction*

UNDERUSE OF RESOURCES

The major evidence for underexploitation of productive resources comes from agricultural societies, especially those practicing slash-and-burn cultivation. Probably this is a function of research procedures rather than a dubious special privilege of the subsistence type. Similar observations have been made of hunting and of herding economies, but anecdotally for the most part, and without benefit of a practicable measure. Slash-and-burn agriculture, on the other hand, uniquely lends itself to quantified assessments of economic capacity. And in almost all the cases so far investigated, still not numerous but from many different parts of the globe, especially where the people have not been confined to "native reserves," the actual production is substantially less than the possible.

Slash-and-burn, an agriculture of neolithic origin, is widely practiced today in tropical forests. It is a technique for opening up and bringing under cultivation a patch of forest land. The standing growth is first cleared by axe or machete and, after a period of drying out, the accumulated debris is burned off—thus the inelegant name, slash-and-burn. A cleared plot is cultivated for one or two seasons, rarely more, then abandoned for years, usually with a view toward restoration of fertility through reversion to forest. The area may then be opened again for another cycle of cultivation and fallow. Typically the period of fallow is several times the period of use; hence, the community of cultivators, if it is to remain stable, must always hold in reserve several times the area it has under production at any given moment. Measures of productive capacity must take this requirement into consideration; also the period of garden use, the period of fallow, the amount of land required per capita for subsistence, the amount of arable land within range of the community, and the like. So long as these measures are careful to respect the normal and customary practices of the people concerned, the final estimate of capacity will not be utopian—that is, what might be done with a free choice of techniques—but only what could be done by the agricultural regime as it stands.

Nevertheless, there are inescapable uncertainties. Any "productive capacity" so estimated is partial and derivative: partial, because the investigation is restricted in advance to the cultivation of food, other dimensions of production left aside; derivative, because "capacity" takes the form of a *population* maximum. What research yields is the optimum number of people that can be supported by the existing means of production. "Capacity" appears as a determinate population size or density, a critical mass that cannot be surpassed without some change in 'agricultural practice or conception of livelihood. Beyond that point is a dangerous ground of speculation which daring ecologists, identifying the optimum population as the "critical carrying capacity" or "critical population density," all the same do not hesitate to enter. "Critical carrying capacity" is the theoretical limit to which the population could be taken without degrading the land and compromising the agricultural future. But it is characteristically difficult to project from the existing "optimum" to the persisting "critical"; such questions of long-term adaptation are not decided by the short-term data. We have to be content with a more limited, if possibly defective, understanding: what the agricultural system as constituted can do.

W. Allan (1949, 1965) was the first to devise and apply a general index of population capacity for slash-and-burn agriculture. Several versions and variants of Allan's formula[1] have since appeared, notably those of Conklin (1959), Carneiro (1960), and a complicated refinement fashioned by Brown and Brookfield for the New Guinea Highlands (1963). These formulas have been applied to specific ethnographic sites and, with less precision, to broad cultural provinces dominated by slash-and-burn production. Outside of reservations, in traditional agricultural systems, the results, although highly variable, are highly consistent in one respect: the existing population is generally inferior to the calculable maximum, often remarkably so.[2]

Table 2.1 summarizes a certain number of ethnographic studies of

1. Following the slight rephrasing by Brown and Brookfield (1963), Allan's formula is: "carrying capacity" = 100 CL/P where *P* is the percentage of arable available to the community, *L* is the mean acreage per capita under cultivation and *C* a factor of the number of garden units needed for a full cycle, calculated as fallow period + cultivation period/fallow period. The result of 100 CL/P is the amount of land required to support one person in perpetuity. This is then converted into a density per square mile or square kilometer.

2. This conclusion is framed for the population, globally considered, practicing a determinate form of agriculture; it does not preclude that localized subgroups (families,

Table 2.1. Relation of actual to potential population, swidden cultivators

| Group | Location | Population (size or density) | | Actual as Percentage of Potential | Source |
|---|---|---|---|---|---|
| | | Actual | Potential Maximum | | |
| Naregu Chimbu | New Guinea | 288/m² | 453/m² | 64 | Brown and Brookfield 1963 |
| Tsembaga * (Maring) | New Guinea | 204 (local pop) | 313-373 | 55-65 | Rappaport 1967 |
| Yagaw Hanaoo | Philippines | 30/km² (arable) | 48/km² (arable) | 63 | Conklin 1957 |
| Lamet† | Laos | 2.9/km² | 11.7-14.4/km² | 20-25 | Izikowitz 1951 |
| Iban | Borneo | 23/m² (Sut Valley) 14/m² (Baleh) | 35-46m² | 50-66 (s) 30-40 | Freeman 1955 |

| Group | Location | Population (size or density) | | Actual as Percentage of Potential | Source |
| | | Actual | Potential Maximum | | |
| --- | --- | --- | --- | --- | --- |
| Kuikuru | Brazil | 145 (village) | 2041 | 7 | Carneiro 1960 |
| Ndembu (Kanongesha Chiefdom) | N. Rhodesia | 3.17/m² | 17-38/m² | 8-19 | Turner 1957 |
| W. Lala‡ | N. Rhodesia | < 3/m² | 4/m² | < 75 | Allan 1965: 114 |
| Swaka‡ | N. Rhodesia | < 4/m² | 10+/m² | < 40 | Allan 1965: 122-123 |
| Dogomba‡ | Ghana | 25-50/m² | 50-60/m² | 42-100 | Allan 1965: 240 |

*Mean population capacity, between maximum and minimum pig-herd, here tabulated.

†The Lamet figures are calculated from Izikowitz's rough estimates, with the further assumption that only five percent of the countryside is arable. The results are probably far from accurate. However, we have the ethnographer's assurance that Lamet villages have considerably more land at their disposal than they need (use) (1951, p. 43).

‡Allan presents data on several African populations, confined to reserves or otherwise subjected to disturbances of colonialism, that are over the capacity of the traditional system. These are excluded here. The Serenji Lala, however, may be an exception. (Most of Allan's estimates seem more approximate than the other studies tabulated above.)

45

population capacity from several world areas of shifting agriculture. Two of these studies, those of the Chimbu and Kuikuru, merit special comment.

The Chimbu example is indeed theoretically privileged, not only for the unusually sophisticated techniques developed by the investigators, but because these techniques were tested on a system of peak density in one of the most densely occupied areas of the primitive world. The Naregu section of Chimbu studied by Brown and Brookfield certainly upholds the New Guinea Highlands' reputation: a mean density of 288 people/square mile. Yet this density is only 64 percent of the prevailing agricultural capacity. (The result of 64 percent is an average for 12 clan and subclan territories of Naregu; the range was from 22 to 97 percent of capacity; Table 2.2 gives the breakdown by territory.) Brown and Brookfield also made wider but less precise estimates for the 26 tribal and subtribal sections of Chimbu as a whole, yielding conclusions of the same order: mean population at 60 percent of capacity.[3]

The Kuikuru, on the other hand, illustrate another kind of extreme: the scale of the disparity that may exist between potential and reality. The Kuikuru village of 145 persons is only seven percent of the calculable maximum population (Carneiro, 1960). Given the Kuikurus' agricultural practices, their present population of 145 is supported from the cultivation of 947.25 acres. In fact, the community has a base of 13,350 acres (arable), sufficient for 2,041 persons.

Although studies such as these remain few, the results they present do not appear to be exceptional nor limited to the instances in question. On the contrary, reputable and sober authorities have been tempted to generalize to the same effect about wide geographical areas with which they are familiar. Carneiro, for example (projecting from Kuikuru but in a way that presumes them unusually well off), consid-

---

lineages, villages), under the given rules of recruitment and land tenure, will not experience "population pressure." Such of course is a structural problem, not posed by technology or resources *per se*.

3. Four of the 26 groups were above capacity. All four, however, fall into the two lowest of four categories of data-reliability developed by Brown and Brookfield. Only Naregu received the highest classification of reliability. Groups in the second highest had the following indexes of actual to potential population: 0.8 (two cases), 0.6, 0.5, 0.4, and 0.3.

Table 2.2.   *Actual and maximum population capacities*
*of Naregu Chimbu Groups\**
*(from Brown and Brookfield, 1963, pp. 117, 119)*

| Group | Total Population | | Population Density per Square Mile | | Proportion of Actual to Maximum Density |
|---|---|---|---|---|---|
| | Actual | Maximum | Actual | Maximum | |
| Kingun-Sumbai | 279 | 561 | 300 | 603 | 0.49 |
| Bindegu | 262 | 289 | 524 | 578 | 0.91 |
| Togl-Konda | 250 | 304 | 373 | 454 | 0.82 |
| Kamaniambugo | 205 | 211 | 427 | 439 | 0.97 |
| Mondu-Ninga | 148 | 191 | 361 | 466 | 0.77 |
| Sunggwakani | 211 | 320 | 271 | 410 | 0.66 |
| Domkani | 130 | 223 | 220 | 378 | 0.58 |
| Buruk-Maima, Damagu | 345 | 433 | 371 | 466 | 0.80 |
| Komu-Konda | 111 | 140 | 347 | 438 | 0.79 |
| Bau-Aundugu | 346 | 618 | 262 | 468 | 0.56 |
| Yonggomakani | 73 | 183 | 166 | 416 | 0.40 |
| Wugukani | 83 | 370 | 77 | 343 | 0.22 |
| | $\Sigma$ 2443 | $\Sigma$ 3843 | $\bar{X} = 288$ | $\bar{X} = 453$ | $\bar{X} = 0.64$ |

\*The capacities reported by Brown and Brookfield include a small allowance (.03 acres/capita) for a cash crop, coffee, as well as an allowance for a tree crop, pandanus (0.02 acres/capita). The food-crop requirement of 0.25 acres/capita also includes an amount for pig food and some food sold. The allowance for pigs, however, is not adjusted to maximum herd size.

ers that traditional agriculture in the South American Tropical Forest Zone was capable of sustaining village populations on the order of 450 people; whereas the modal community throughout this extensive area was only 51–150 (1960). The Congo forest of Africa, according to Allan, was likewise underpopulated over wide stretches—"well below the apparent carrying capacity of the land for the traditional systems of land use" (1965, p. 223). Again in West Africa, particularly Ghana before the cocoa boom, Allan reports that "population densities in the central forest zone were far below the critical levels" (p. 228; cf. pp. 229, 230, 240). J. E. Spencer frames a similar opinion of shifting cultivation in Southeast Asia. Impressed by the unusually high densities of upland New Guinea, Spencer is inclined to believe "most shifting-cultivator societies are operating at less than maximum potential so far as their agricultural system is concerned" (1966, p. 16). His interpretation is of interest:

> Light areal density patterns of population are naturally associated with many groups following shifting cultivation because of their intrinsic social system. . . . This cultural tradition cannot be interpreted in terms of the carrying capacity of the land, so that the social phenomenon, rather than the literal carrying capacity of the land itself, has assumed the dynamic role of controlling population density (Spencer, 1966, pp. 15-16).

Let us underline the point, at the same time reserving it for fuller discussion later. Spencer says that the social-cultural organization is not designed after the technical limits of production, to maximize output, but rather impedes development of the productive means. If this position runs counter to a certain ecological thinking, it is nevertheless repeated by several ethnographers of underproduction. For the Ndembu, in Turner's view (1957), it is the contradictions of customary modes of residence and descent, coupled to an absence of political centralization, that set off village fission and population dispersal at a level inferior to the agricultural capacity. Izikowitz (1951), speaking of Lamet, and Carneiro of Amazonian Indians (1968) alike hold the weakness of the community polity responsible for an undue centrifugal segmentation. Quite generally among the tribal cultivators, the intensity of land use seems a specification of the social-political organization.

To return to the technical facts and their distribution: slash-and-burn agriculture is a major form of production among extant primitive societies, perhaps the dominant form.[4] Inquiries in a number of communities, from several different world areas, confirm that (outside native reserves) the agricultural system is running below its technical capacity. More broadly, extensive areas of Africa, Southeast Asia, and South American occupied by swidden cultivators are authoritatively judged under-exploited. May we be permitted to con-

4. According to a recent FAO report, some 14 million square miles, occupied by 200 million people, are still exploited by slash-and-burn (cited in Conklin, 1961, p. 27). Of course, not all of this is primitive domain.

clude that the dominant form of primitive production is underproduction?[5]

Much less can be said about the performance of other common production types. There are suggestions that hunting-gathering may be no more intensive than slash-and-burn agriculture. But the interpretation of resource underuse among hunters presents special difficulties, even apart from the lack of a practicable measure. It is usually not possible to determine whether an apparent underproduction of the moment nonetheless represents a long-term adaptation to recurrent shortages, bad years when it would be possible to support only a fraction of the present population. All the more pertinent, then, the following remark of Richard Lee on /Kung Bushman subsistence, as the period of field observation included the third year of a prolonged drought such as rarely visits even the Kalahari Desert:

> It is impossible to define "abundance" of resources absolutely. However, one index of *relative* abundance is whether or not a population exhausts all the food available from a given area. By this criterion, the habitat of the Dobe-area Bushmen is abundant in naturally occuring foods. By far the

5. The consistent discrepancy between population density and agricultural capacity, even where the former attains 200–plus people/square mile, raises more than one passionate theoretical question. What are we to make of the popular inclination to invoke demographic pressure on resources in explanation of diverse economic and political developments ranging from the intensification of production to the elaboration of patrilineal structure or the formation of the state? First of all, it is not evident that archaic economies know a tendency to reach, let alone exceed, the population capacity of their means of production. On the other hand, it is evident that current mechanistic explanations from demographic cause—or, conversely, the inference of "population pressure" from an observed economic or political "effect"—are often oversimplified. In any given cultural formation, "pressure on land" is not in the first instance a function of technology and resources, but rather of the producers *access* to *sufficient* means of livelihood. The latter clearly is a specification of the cultural system—relations of production and property, rules of land tenure, relations between local groups, and so forth. Except in the theoretically improbable case in which the customary rules of access and labor are consistent with optimum exploitation of land, a society may experience "population pressure" of various kinds and degrees at global densities below its technical capacity of production. Thus the threshold of demographic pressure is not an absolute determination of the means of production but is relative to the society at issue. Moreover, how this pressure is organizationally experienced, the level of the social order to which it is communicated, *as well as the character of the response,* also depend on the institutions in place. (This point is well made by Kelly's study of the problem in the New Guinea Highlands, 1968.) Hence both the definition of population pressure and its social effects pass by way of the existing structure. Consequently, any explanation of historical events or developments, such as warfare or the origin of the state, that ignores this structure is theoretically suspect.

most important food is the Mongomongo (mangetti) nut. . . . Although tens
of thousands of pounds of these nuts are harvested and eaten each year,
thousands more rot on the ground each year for want of picking (Lee, 1968,
p. 33; see also pp. 33–35).

Woodburn's comments on Hadza hunting carry the same implication:

> I have already mentioned the exceptional abundance of game animals in
> this area. Although Hadza, in common probably with all other human
> societies, do not eat all the types of animals available to them—they re-
> ject civet, monitor lizard, snake, terrapin among others—they do eat an
> unusually wide range of animals.. . . In spite of the large number of spe-
> cies which they are both able to hunt and regard as edible, the Hadza do
> not kill very many animals and it is probable that even in the radically
> reduced area they occupied in 1960 more animals could have been killed
> of every species without endangering the survival of any species in ques-
> tion (Woodburn, 1968, p. 52).

In a work primarily devoted to subsistence agriculture, Clark and
Haswell (1964, p. 31) make a daring argument about preagricultural
resource use that at least invites contemplation. Basing their calculations on certain data for East Africa summarized by Pirie (1962),[6] and
positing certain conservative assumptions about animal reproduction
rates in the wild, Clark and Haswell estimate that the annual natural
yield of meat is forty times greater than necessary to support a hunting
population living at one person/20 square kilometers (1/7.7 square
miles) and exclusively on animal foods—that is to say, the animal
reproduction fully utilized would support five persons per square
mile. This without diminishing the natural supply. Whether hunters
need such a margin of safety is another, unanswered question, although Clark and Haswell rather think they do.

A further implication of Pirie's East African figures is that the wild
animal yield per area of natural grazing land is higher than the output
of pastoral nomadism in adjacent regions (cf. Worthington, 1961).
Again, Clark and Haswell generalize to an interesting judgment of
pastoralist land use:

6. These Pirie had himself culled from the Arusha symposium on *Conservation of
Nature and Natural Resources in Modern African States* (1961). This publication was
not available to me on writing. Pirie's article, moreover, raises some question about the
control of predators (p. 411), the significance of which is unclear but which may have
bearing on the figures for wild animal yields.

We should remind ourselves that the primitive pastoral communities, found where the land is not forested . . . live at a density of about 2 persons/sq. km. Though not so wasteful of the land and its resources as are the primitive hunting peoples, they nevertheless fall far short of fully exploiting the potential mean output of land, which Price estimates at 50 kg. liveweight gain/ha./year (5 tons liveweight gain/sq. km.). Even if we half this figure, as some would do, it seems clear that primitive pastoral peoples ' . . . are unable to exploit the full growth of grass in favourable seasons of the year (1964 ).

Without technical means of accumulating fodder, as the authors recognize, pastoralists are of course restricted to the livestock they can support in poorer rather than favorable seasons. Still, Clark and Haswell's conclusion finds some support from Allan. As a rough conjecture, Allan supposes that East African pastoralists know a "critical population density" on the order of seven persons per square mile. But from a series of actual cases, "It would seem that population densities of surviving pastoral peoples are usually well below this figure, even in the more favourable of the regions they still occupy" (Allan, 1965, p. 309). [7]

We seem perilously close to that characteristic failing of interdisciplinary study—an enterprise which often seems to merit definition as the process by which the unknowns of one's own subject matter are multiplied by the uncertainties of some other science. But enough said at least to raise doubt about the efficiency of resource exploitation in the primitive economies.

UNDERUSE OF LABOR-POWER

That the labor forces of primitive communities are also underused is easier to document, thanks to a greater ethnographic attention. (Besides, this dimension of primitive underproduction conforms closely to European prejudices, so that many others besides anthropologists have noticed it, although the more appropriate deduction from the cultural differences might have been that Europeans are overworked.) It is only necessary to keep in mind that the manner by which labor-power is withheld from production is not everywhere the

7. Allan, on the other hand, finds among pastoralists some urge to accumulate cattle that may outstrip pasturage capacities, and at least two peoples, Masai and Mukogodo, with an apparent "excess of livestock in relation to the economic requirements of simple pastoralism" (1965, p. 311).

same. The institutional modalities vary considerably: from marked cultural abbreviations of the individual working-life span to immoderate standards of relaxation—or, what is probably a better understanding of the latter, very moderate standards of "sufficient work."

One of the main conclusions of Mary Douglas's brilliant comparison of Lele and Bushong economies is that in some societies people work for a much greater part of their lifetime than in others. "Everything the Lele have or do," Douglas wrote, "the Bushong have more and can do better. They produce more, live better as well as populating their region more densely than the Lele" (1962, p. 211). They produce more largely because they work more, as demonstrated along one dimension by the remarkable diagram Douglas presents of male working life span in the two societies (Figure 2.1 ).Beginning before age 20 and finishing after 60, a Bushong man is productively occupied almost twice as long as a Lele, the latter retiring comparatively early from a career that began well after physical maturity. Without intending to repeat Douglas's detailed analysis, some of the reasons might be noted briefly for their pertinence to the present discussion. One is the Lele practice of polygyny, which as a privilege of the elders entails for younger men a considerable postponement of marriage, hence of adult responsibilities.[8] Moving into the political

*Figure 2.1.   Male Working-Span: Lele and*
*Bushong*
*(after Douglas, 1962, p. 231)*

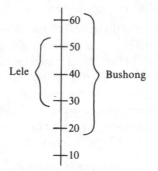

8. This is not at all unique to Lele. Polygyny in a society of more or less balanced sex ratio usually means late first marriages for most men. While an only casual interest

domain, Douglas's more general explanations of the Lele-Bushong contrast strike a note already familiar. But Douglas carries the analysis to new dimensions. It is not only differences in political scale or morphology that make one or another system more effective economically, but the different relations they entail between the powers that be and the process of production.[9]

Scant use of young adult labor, however, is not characteristic of the Lele alone. It is not even the exclusive privilege of agricultural societies. Hunting and gathering do not demand of !Kung Bushmen that famous "maximum effort of a maximum number of people." They manage quite well without the full cooperation of younger men, who are fairly idle sometimes to the age of 25:

> Another significant feature of the composition of the [!Kung Bushmen] work force is the late assumption of adult responsibility by the adolescents. Young people are not expected to provide food regularly until they are married. Girls typically marry between the ages of 15 and 20, and boys about five years later, so that it is not unusual to find healthy, active teenagers visiting from camp to camp while their older relatives provide food for them (Lee, 1968, p. 36).

This contrast between the indolence of youth and industry of elders may appear also in a developed political setting, as in centralized African chiefdoms such as Bemba. Now the Bemba are not markedly polygynous. Audrey Richards proposes yet another explanation, one that calls to anthropological mind still other examples:

> In pre-European days there was a complete change of ambition between . . . youth and age. The young boy, under the system of matrilocal marriage [entailing bride-service in the wife's family], had no individual responsibility for gardening. He was expected to cut trees [for making gardens], but his main way of advance in life was to attach himself to a chief or to a man of rank and not to make large gardens or to collect material goods. He often went on border raids or foraging expeditions. He did not expect to work in earnest until middle age, when his children were "crying from hunger" and he had settled down. Nowadays we saw in concrete cases the immense difference between the regularity of work done by the old and young.[10]

---

in production is not also necessary, it is at least consistent and often encountered.

9. Again I merely raise the point here, reserving it for fuller discussion later (Chapter 3).

10. The concrete case described in greatest detail concerns the village of Kasaka, for

This is partly due to the new insubordination of the boys, but partly also to a perpetuation of an old tradition. In our society youths and adolescents have, roughly speaking, the same economic ambitions throughout youth and early manhood. . . . Among the Bemba this was not so, any more than it was among such warrior peoples as the Masai of East Africa with their regular age-sets.[11] Each individual was expected to be first a fighter and later a cultivator and the father of a family (Richards, 1961, p. 402).

In sum, for a variety of cultural reasons, the life time working span may be seriously curtailed. Indeed, economic obligations can be totally unbalanced in relation to physical capacity, the younger and stronger adults largely disengaged from production, leaving the burden of society's work to the older and weaker.

An unbalance to the same effect may obtain in the division of labor by sex. Half the available labor power may be providing a disproportionately small fraction of the society's output. Differences of this kind are common enough, at least in the subsistence sector, to have long lent credence to crude materialist explanations of the customary descent rule, matrilineal or patrilineal, by the specific economic weight of female versus male labor.

I have myself had ethnographic occasion to observe a marked unbalance in the sexual division of labor. Excluded from agriculture, the women of the Fijian island of Moala show much slighter interest than do their men in main productive activities. True that the women, especially younger women, maintain the homes, cook, fish periodically, and are charged with certain crafts. Yet the ease they enjoy by comparison with their sisters elsewhere in Fiji, where women do cultivate, is enough to credit the local saying that "in this land, women rest." One Moalan friend confided that all they really did was

---

which Richards recorded a general calendar of activities covering mainly September 1933, and work diaries of 38 adults over 23 days (Richards, 1961, pp. 162-64 and Table E). Only the old men worked regularly, "those reckoned by the Government as too feeble to pay tax." Richards observes: "Five old men worked 14 days out of 20; seven young men worked seven days out of 20 . . . it is obvious that any community in which the young and active males work exactly half as much as the old must suffer as regards its food production" (p. 164 n). The records refer to a season of less-than-average agricultural intensity, but not the famous Bemba hunger period.

11. "The herding of livestock does not absorb the energies of the entire [Masai] population, and the young men from the ages of about sixteen to thirty live apart from their families and clans as warriors" (Forde, 1963 [1934], p. 29 f).

sit around all day and break wind. (This was a slander; gossip was the more consuming occupation.) The reverse emphasis, on female labor, is probably more widespread in primitive communities (exception made for pastoralists, where the women often—but sometimes many of the men too—are not concerned with the daily husbandry).[12]

One example we have already noted is worth repeating, as it again concerns hunters, who less than anyone might be thought able to afford the extravagance of one whole idle sex out of the two usually available. Yet such are the Hadza that the men pass six months a year (the dry season) in gambling—effectively inhibiting those who have lost their metal-tipped arrows from hunting big game the rest of the year (Woodburn, 1968, p. 54).

It is impossible from these few instances to infer an extent, let alone attribute a universality, to the differential economic engagement by sex and age. Again I would merely raise a problem, which is also to cast a doubt on a common presupposition. The problem concerns the composition of the labor force. This composition is clearly a cultural and not simply a natural (physical) specification. Clearly too, the cultural and natural specifications need not correspond. By custom the individual working career is variously abbreviated or alleviated, and whole classes of the able-bodied, perhaps the most able-bodied, are exempted from economic concern. In the event, the disposable working force is something less than the available labor-power, and the remainder of the latter is otherwise spent or dissipated. That this diversion of manpower is sometimes necessary is not contested. It may well be functional, even inevitable, to the society and economy as organized. But that is the problem: we have to do with the organized withdrawal of important social energies from the economic process. Nor is it the only problem. Another is how much the others, the effective producers, actually do work.

While no anthropologist today would concede the truth of the imperialist ideology that the natives are congenitally lazy, and many would testify rather that the people are capable of sustained labor,

---

12. Cf. Clark, 1938, p. 9; Rivers, 1906, pp. 566–67. As for middle-eastern Arabs, however, "The male Arab is quite content to pass the day smoking, chatting and drinking coffee. Herding the camels is his only office. All the work of erecting tents, looking after sheep and goats and bringing water, he leaves to his women" (Awad, 1962, p. 335).

probably most would also observe that the motivation to do so is not constant, so that work is in fact irregular over the longer or shorter term. The work process is sensitive to interference of various kinds, vulnerable to suspension in favor of other activities as serious as ritual, as frivolous as repose. The customary working day is often short; if it is protracted, frequently it is interrupted; if it is both long and unremitting, usually this is only seasonal. Within the community, moreover, some people work much more than others. By the norms of the society, let alone of the *stakhonovite*, considerable labor-power remains underemployed. As Maurice Godelier writes, labor is not a scarce resource in most primitiv‿ societies (1969, p. 32).[13]

In the subsistence sector, a man's normal working day (in season) may be as short as four hours, as among the Bemba (Richards, 1961, pp. 398-399), the Hawaiians (Stewart, 1828, p. 111) or the Kuikuru (Carneiro, 1968, p. 134), or peɪhaps it is six hours, as for /Kung Bushmen (Lee, 1968, p. 37) or Kapauku (Pospisil, 1963, pp. 144-145). Then again, it may last from early to late:

> But let us follow a (Tikopian) working party as they leave home on a fine morning, bound for the cultivations. They are going to dig turmeric, for it is August, the season for the preparation of this highly valued sacred dye. The group sets off from the village of Matautu, straggles along the beach to Rofaea and then turning inland begins to ascend the path running up to the crest of the hills. The turmeric plant ... grows on the mountain-side and to reach the orchard ... involves a steep climb of several hundred feet ... The party consists of Pa Nukunefu and his wife, their young daughter, and three older girls, these latter having been coopted from the households of friends and neighbors ... Soon after these people arrive they are joined by Vaitere, a youth whose family owns the neighbouring orchard ... The work is of very simple nature ... Pa Nukunefu and the women share the work fairly among them, he doing most of the clearing of vegetation and the digging, they some of the digging and replanting, and nearly all the cleaning and sorting ... the tempo of the work is an easy one. From time to time members of the party drop out for a rest, and to chew betel. To this end, Vaitere, who takes no very active part in the work itself, climbs a nearby tree to collect some leaves of *pita*, the betel plant. . . . About mid-morning the customary refresh-

13. Among Tiv, " 'Labor' is the factor of production in greatest supply" (Bohannan and Bohannan, 1968, p. 76).

ment is provided in the shape of green coconuts, for which Vaitere is again sent to climb . . . . The whole atmosphere is one of labour diversified by recreation at will . . . . Vaitere, as the morning draws on, busies himself with the construction of a cap out of banana leaf, his own invention, and of no practical use . . . . So between work and leisure the time passes, until as the sun declines perceptibly from the zenith the task of the party is done, and bearing their baskets of turmeric roots they go off down the mountain-side to their homes (Firth, 1936, pp. 92-93.).

On the other hand, the daily labors of Kapauku seem more sustained. Their workday begins about 7:30 a.m. and proceeds fairly steadily until a late morning break for lunch. The men return to the village in the early afternoon, but the women continue on until four or five o'clock. Yet the Kapauku "have a conception of balance in life": if they work strenuously one day, they rest the next.

> Since the Kapauku have a conception of balance in life, only every other day is supposed to be a working day. Such a day is followed by a day of rest in order to "regain the lost power and health." This monotonous fluctuation of leisure and work is made more appealing to the Kapauku by inserting into their schedule periods of more prolonged holidays (spent in dancing, visiting, fishing, or hunting . . .). Consequently, we usually find only some of the people departing for their gardens in the morning, the others are taking their "day off." However, many individuals do not rigidly conform to this ideal. The more conscientious cultivators often work intensively for several days in order to complete clearing a plot, making a fence, or digging a ditch. After such a task is accomplished, they relax for a period of several days, thus compensating for their "missed" days of rest (Pospisil, 1963, p. 145).

Following this course of moderation in all things, Kapauku over the long run allow an unextraordinary amount of time to agriculture. From records that he kept through an eight-month period (Kapauku cultivation is not seasonal) and on the assumption of a potential eight-hour day, Pospisil estimates that Kapauku men spend approximately one-fourth their "working time" in gardening, the women about one-fifth. More precisely, men average 2h18m/day in agricultural tasks, the women 1h42m. Pospisil writes: "These relatively small portions of total working time seem to cast serious doubt on the claim, so often made, that native cultivation methods are wasteful, time consuming and economically inadequate"(1963, p. 164). For the rest, aside from relaxation and "prolonged holidays," Kapauku men are more concerned with politicking and exchange than with other areas of production (crafts, hunting, house building).[14]

In their studied habit of one day on, one day off, Kapauku are perhaps unusual for the regularity of their economic tempo,[15] but not for its intermittency. A similar pattern was documented in Chapter One for hunters: Australians, Bushmen, and other peoples—their labors chronically punctuated by days of slack, not to mention sleep. And notoriously among many agriculturalists of seasonal regime the same cadence recurs, although on a different time scale. Agricultural off-seasons are given over as much to relaxation and diversion, to rest, ceremony and visiting, as they are to other works. Taken over the extended term, therefore, all these modes of livelihood reveal themselves unintensive: they make only fractional demands on the available labor-power.

Fractional use of labor-power is detectable also in the individual work-diaries sometimes collected by ethnographers. Although these diaries typically account for only a very few people as well as a very brief time, they are usually extensive enough to show important domestic differences in economic effort. At least one of the six or seven people concerned turns out to be the village indolent (cf. Provinse, 1937; Titiev, 1944, p. 196). The diaries thus manage to convey a suggestion of unequal productive commitment, that is to say, a relative underemployment of some even within the unspectacular conscientiousness of all. A certain flavor of this pattern, if not an accurate measure, is provided in Table 2.3, a reproduction of F. Nadel's journal for three Nupe farm families (1942, pp. 222-224).[16] The two weeks of observation fall into different periods of the annual cycle. The second week is a time of peak intensity.

14. Here is another society, however, in which labor obligation seems unevenly divided by sex, and also by age-class. For in addition to gardening, Kapauku women do a substantial amount of fishing, pig tending, and housework, even as their men are sometimes away three and four months in trading or war expeditions, and the unmarried men in particular maintain all the while a steady indifference to cultivation (Pospisil, 1963, p. 189).

15. Although Tiv also "prefer to work very hard and at a terrific pace and then do almost nothing for a day or two" (Bohannan and Bohannan, 1968, p. 72).

16. Of course, even as there remains a question whether such a slight record can be representative of the Nupe economic condition, it is also questionable whether Nupe are truly representative of a primitive economy.

Table 2.3. *Journal of three Nupe farm families*
*(after Nadel 1942, pp. 222-224)*

| *N.* | *M.* | *K.* |
|---|---|---|
| *Labor Group: Father and Three Sons* | *Labor Group: Father and One Son* | *Labor Group: One Man* |

**31.5.1936**

| | | |
|---|---|---|
| Goes out to farm about 8 A.M. Eats midday meal on the farm, and returns about 4 P.M. | Goes out to farm together with *N.*, whose farm is close to his own. Also returns with him. | Is away from Kutigi; went to a neighboring village for the funeral of his sister. |

**1.6.1936**

| | | |
|---|---|---|
| As previous day. | As previous day. | Returns in the evening. |

**2.6.1936**

| | | |
|---|---|---|
| Stays at home, together with sons. | Stays at home, and visits *N.* in the evening. | Goes out to farm about 10 A.M., and returns at 4 P.M. |

**3.6.1936**

| | | |
|---|---|---|
| Stays at home. Sons go out to farm in the morning, but are back at 2 P.M. in time to attend the market, which is held today. | Stays at home, works on garden plots round the house. Son goes out to farm. | Stays at home; says he is tired from the journey. |

**4.6.1936**

| | | |
|---|---|---|
| Goes out to farm at 8 A.M., returns for midday meal; sons stay longer. | Goes out to farm at 8 A.M.., returns after midday meal. | Goes out to farm at 8 A.M., returns after midday meal. |

**5.6.1936 (Friday)**

| | | |
|---|---|---|
| Stays at home, together with sons. Attends mosque in the afternoon. | Stays at home. Visits *N.* in the evening. | Stays at home. His brother, who lives in a hamlet, comes on a visit. |

*Table 2.3. (Continued)*

| N. | M. | K. |
|---|---|---|
| Labor Group: Father and Three Sons | Labor Group: Father and One Son | Labor Group: One Man |

**6.6.1936**

| | | |
|---|---|---|
| Stays at home, says he is tired. Works on garden plots, but will go to farm tomorrow. Sons go out to farm. | Goes out to farm at 8 A.M. , returns for midday meal. | Goes out to farm at 8 A.M. , returns for midday meal. |

**22.6.1936**

| | | |
|---|---|---|
| Goes out to farm at 8 A.M. , returns at 4 P.M. One son goes to Sakpe to attend wedding of a friend. | Goes out to farm at 7 A.M., returns after 4 P.M.. | Goes out to farm at 8 A.M. , returns after 4 P.M.. |

**23.6.1936**

| | | |
|---|---|---|
| Goes out to farm at 8 A.M. , returns for midday meal. He hurt his hand and cannot work properly. His sons stay on; one son still in Sakpe. | Goes out to farm at 8 A.M. , returns for midday meal. | Goes out to farm at 8 A.M. , returns after 4 P.M.. |

**24.6.1936**

| | | |
|---|---|---|
| Goes out to farm at 8 A.M., but returns early as his hand hurts. Son who went to Sakpe returns in the evening. | Goes out to farm at 7 A.M. , returns after 4 P.M.. | Stays at home as he is tired and has stomach trouble. |

**25.6.1936**

| | | |
|---|---|---|
| Stays at home, his hand not yet well. Sons go out to farm. | Goes out to farm at 7 A.M. , returns after 4 P.M.. | Goes out to farm at 7 A.M. , returns after 5 P.M.. |

Table 2.3. (Concluded)

| N. | M. | K. |
|---|---|---|
| Labor Group: Father and Three Sons | Labor Group: Father and One Son | Labor Group: One Man |
| **26.6.1936 (Friday)** | | |
| Stays at home. | Stays at home. | Goes out to farm at 8 A.M., returns after 4 P.M. |
| **27.6.1936** | | |
| Goes out to farm at 8 A.M., returns at 5 P.M. | Goes out to farm at 8 A.M., returns after 4 P.M. | Goes out to farm at 7 A.M., returns for midday meal. |
| **28.6.1936** | | |
| Stays at home because tax clerk of chief had summoned all elders. Sons go out to farm. | Stays at home for same reason as N. Son goes out to farm. | Goes out to farm at 7 A.M., but returns early to meet the tax clerk. |

Audrey Richard's diaries for two Bemba villages lend themselves to quantitative assessment. The first and longer, from Kasaka village, is presented in Table 2.4: it covers the activities of 38 adults over 23 days (September 13–October 5, 1934). This was a season of reduced agricultural labor, although not the Bemba hungry period. Men engaged in little or no work for approximately 45 percent of the time. Only half their days could be classed as productive or working days, of an average duration of 4.72 hours of labor (but see below, where the figure of 2.75 hours for a working day was apparently calculated on a base of all available days). Women's time was more equally divided between working days (30.3 percent), days of part-time work (35.1 percent) and days of little or no work (31.7 percent). For both men and women, this unstrenuous program would be modified during the busier agricultural season.[17] Table 2.5, representing the work of 33 adults of Kampamba village over

17. Theoretically November to March, but see Richards, 1962, p. 390.

*Table 2.4. Distribution of activities: Kasaka Village, Bemba
(after Richards, 1962, Appendix E)\**

|  | Men (n = 19) | Women (n = 19) |
|---|---|---|
| 1. Days mainly working† | garden work, hunting, fishing, crafts, house-building, work for Europeans . . . 220 (50%) | gardening, fishing, work for chiefs, work for Europeans, etc . . . 132 (30.3%) |
| Mean duration of full working day | 4.72 hrs/day | 4.42 hrs/day |
| 2. Days of part-time work‡ | "in village," "away," "at home" . . . 22 (5%) | "in village," "no garden work," "away" . . . 153 (35.19%) |
| 3. Days mainly not working | "leisure," visits to relatives,§ beer-drinks . . . 196 (44.5%) | "leisure," visits to relatives, beer-drinks . . . 138 (31.7%) |
| 4. Illness | carrying sick . . . 2 (0.5%) | confinement . . . 13 (3%) |

\*N = 38; days tabulated = 23.

†The categories 1-4 and classification of data under these rubrics are my own.

‡Richards specifies that even when remaining in the village, women do much domestic work; therefore, she rarely uses the category "leisure" to describe their days, preferring instead "no garden work." "Leisure" on the other hand means "a day spent in sitting, talking, drinking, or doing handicrafts." I have thus put "no garden work" (as well as "in village," "at home" and, for want of further information, "away") in a category of "part-time work," while "leisure" is classed in the category "days mainly not working." "Leisure" includes Christian Sundays.

§ Richards indicates that "walks" in her table mean "visits to relatives" unless otherwise specified; I include such "walks" here.

seven to ten days of January 1934, attests to the periodic intensification of productive tempo.[18]

If these tables for the Bemba could be extended over a full year, they would probably yield results similar to those obtained by Guillard (1958) for the Toupouri of North Cameroon, shown in Table 2.6.[19]

And if such systems as the Bemba and Toupouri were plotted graphically over the year, they would probably resemble the diagrams de Schlippe accumulated for the Azande—one of these is presented in Figure 2.2.

But work schedules such as these, with their generous reservations of time to fete and repose, should not be interpreted from the anxious vantage of European compulsions.[20] The periodic deflection from "work" to "ritual" by peoples such as the Tikopians or Fijians, must

18. Richards's comments on the duration of the working day provide additional pertinent information: "Bemba rise at 5 a.m. in the hot weather, but come reluctantly from their huts at 8 or even later in the cold season, and their working day is fixed accordingly . . . the Bemba in his unspecialized society does different tasks daily and a different amount of work each day. The diary of men's and women's activities . . . shows that in Kampamba the men were employed on five quite separate occupations . . . in the course of ten days, and at Kasaka . . . various ritual observances, visits from friends or Europeans, interrupted the daily routine constantly. Domestic needs tie the women to certain daily tasks . . . but even then their garden work varies greatly from day to day. The working hours also change in what seems to us a most erratic manner. In fact I do not think the people ever conceive of such periods as the month, week, or day in relation to regular work at all. . . . The whole bodily rhythm of the Bemba differs completely from that of a peasant in Western Europe, let alone an industrial worker. For instance at Kasaka, in a slack season, the old men worked 14 days out of 20 and the young men seven; while at Kampamba in the busier season, the men of all ages worked on an average of 8 out of 9 working days [Sunday not included]. The average working day in the first instance was 2-3/4 hours for men and 2 hours gardening plus 4 hours domestic work for the women, but the figures varied from 0 to 6 hours a day. In the second case the average was 4 hours for the men and 6 for the women, and the figures showed the same daily variation" (1962, pp. 393-394).

19. Cf. the analogous report from the Cameroons cited by Clark and Haswell (1964, p. 117).

20. "A strange delusion possesses the working classes of the nations where capitalist civilization holds its sway. This delusion drags in its train the individual and social woes which for two centuries have tortured sad humanity. This delusion is the love of work, the furious passion for work, pushed even to the exhaustion of the vital force of the individual and his progeny. Instead of opposing this mental aberration, the priests, the economists and the moralists have cast a sacred halo over work" (Lafargue, 1909, p. 9).

Table 2.5. *Distribution of activities: Kampana Village, Bemba (after Richards, 1962, Appendix E)\**

|  | ♂ *(n = 16, 10 days)* | ♀ *(n = 17, 7 days)* |
|---|---|---|
| 1. Days mainly working | 114 (70.8%) | 66 (62.9%) |
| 2. Days of part-time work | 9 (5.6%) | 21 (20%) |
| 3. Days mainly not working | 29 (18%) | 17 (16.2%) |
| 4. Illness | 9 (5.6%) | 1 (1%) |

\*For explanation of the categories adopted, see Table 2.4.

be made without prejudice, for their linguistic categories know no such distinction, but conceive both activities sufficiently serious as to merit a common term (so the "Work of the Gods"). And what are we to construe of those Australian Aborigines—the Yir Yiront—who do not discriminate between "work" and "play"? (Sharp, 1958, p. 6)

Table 2.6. *Distribution of activities over year, Toupouri (after Guillard 1958)\**

|  | Men (n = 11) | | | Women (n = 18) | | |
|---|---|---|---|---|---|---|
|  | Average Man-Days per Year | | | Average Man-Days per Year | | |
|  | Number | Percent | Range | Number | Percent | Range |
| Agriculture | 105.5 | 28.7 | 66.5-155.5 | 82.1 | 22.5 | 42-116.5 |
| Other work | 87.5 | 23.5 | 47-149 | 106.6 | 29.0 | 83-134.5 |
| Rest and non-productive† | 161.5 | 44.4 | 103.5-239 | 164.4 | 45.2 | 151-192 |
| Illness | 9.5 | 2.6 | 0-30 | 3.0 |  | 0-40 |

\*N = 29 working persons.

†Category includes marketing and visits (often indistinguishable), feasts and rituals, and repose. It is not absolutely clear that for men the time in hunting and fishing was excluded here. Women's days in the village were calculated by Guillard as one-half "other work," one-half rest.

Perhaps equally arbitrary are many cultural definitions of inclement weather, serving as pretext, it seems, for suspending production under conditions somewhere short of the human capacity for discomfort. Yet it would be insufficient simply to suppose that production is thus subject to arbitrary interference: to interruption by other obligations, themselves "noneconomic" but not by that character unworthy of people's respect. These other claims—of ceremony, diversion, sociability and repose—are only the complement or, if you will, the superstructural counterpart of a dynamic proper to the economy. They are not simply imposed upon the economy from without, for there is within, in the way production is organized, an intrinsic discontinuity. The economy has its own cutoff principal: it is an economy of concrete and limited objectives.

Consider the Siuai of Bougainville. Douglas Oliver describes in terms by now familiar how garden work submits to diverse cultural obstructions, leaving the real output clearly below the possible:

> There is, of course no *physical* reason why this labor output could not be increased. There is no serious land-shortage, and a labor "stretch-out" could be and often is undertaken. Siuai women work hard at their gardens but not nearly so hard as some Papuan women; it is conceivable that they could work much longer and harder without doing themselves physical injury. That is to say, it is conceivable by *other* standards of work. Cultural rather than physical factors influence Siuai standards of "maximum working hours." Garden work is taboo for long periods following upon death of a kinsman or friend. Nursing mothers may spend but a few hours daily away from their babies, who, because of ritual restrictions, often may not be carried into the gardens. And aside from these ritual restrictions upon continuous garden work, there are less spectacular limitations. It is conventional to cease working during even light showers; it is customary to start for the garden only after the sun is well up, and to leave for home in mid-afternoon. Now and then a married couple will remain in their garden site all night sleeping in a lean-to, but only the most ambitious and enterprising care to discomfort themselves thus (Oliver, 1949 [3], p. 16).

But in another connection Oliver explains more fundamentally why Siuai working standards are so modest—because, except for politically ambitious people, they are *sufficient:*

> As a matter of fact, natives took pride in their ability to estimate their immediate personal consumption needs, and to produce just enough taro

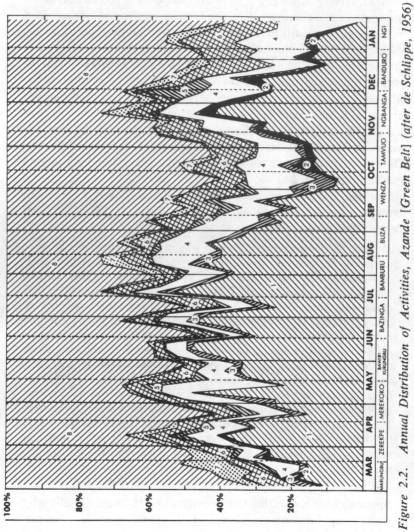

Figure 2.2. *Annual Distribution of Activities, Azande [Green Belt] (after de Schlippe, 1956)*

1. Agricultural work.

2. Gathering of wild produce, including honey, chillies, mushrooms, caterpillars, berries, roots, salt grass, and divers others.

3. Hunting and fishing.

4. Processing at home of agricultural produce and of produce of gathering, including beer brewing oil and salt making, and so on. These four items taken together could be called food production at or near home.

5. Marketing, including cotton markets, as well as weekly food markets, either selling or buying, and absences for the purpose of acquiring tools, clothes, and other goods in shops or elsewhere.

6. Other occupations at home, mainly housebuilding and craftsmanship, but also repairing, putting things in order, and such like.

7. Work outside home, including hunting and fishing expeditions, work for chief or district, salaried work for Government or E.P.B., and work for neighbors in beer parties.

8. No work for various reasons—including chiefs' courts, ceremonies and rituals, sickness at home, in hospital or at the witchdoctor's, childbirth, rest, and leisure.

The graph does not represent man-days given to various tasks but the number of days (or percentage of days) the type of activity occurred.

to satisfy them. I write "personal consumption needs" advisedly, because there is very little commercial or ritual exchange of taro. Nevertheless, personal consumption needs vary considerably: there is a lot of difference between the amount of taro consumed by an ordinary man with his one or two pigs, and an ambitious social-climber with his ten or twenty. The latter has to cultivate more and more land in order to feed his increasing number of pigs and to provide vegetable food for distribution among guests at his feasts (Oliver, 1949 [4], p. 89).

Production has its own constraints. If these are sometimes manifest as the deployment of labor to other ends, it should not be thus obscured to the analysis. Sometimes it is not even disguised to observation: as of certain hunters, for example, who once again become the revealatory case because they seem to need no excuse to stop working once they have enough to eat.[21] All this can be phrased another way: from the point of view of the existing mode of production, a considerable proportion of the available labor-power is *excess*. And the system, having thus defined sufficiency, does not realize the surplus of which it is perfectly capable:

> There is no doubt at all that the Kuikuru could produce a surplus of food over the full productive cycle. At the present time a man spends only about 3-1/2 hours a day on subsistence—2 hours on horticulture, and 1-1/2 hours on fishing. Of the remaining 10 or 12 waking hours of the day the Kuikuru men spend a great deal of it dancing, wrestling, in some form of informal recreation, and in loafing. A good deal more of this time could easily be devoted to gardening. Even an extra half hour a day spent on agriculture would enable a man to produce a substantial surplus of manioc. However, as conditions stand now there is no reason for the Kuikuru to produce such a surplus, nor is there any indication that they will (Carneiro, 1968, p. 134).

In brief, it is an economy of production for use, for the livelihood

---

21. See the reference to McCarthy and MacArthur's study of Australian hunting in Chapter 1. "The quantity of food gathered in any one day by any of these groups could in every instance be increased. . . ." Woodburn writes to the same effect of the Hadza: "When a man goes off into the bush with his bow and arrows, his main interest is usually to satisfy his hunger. Once he has satisfied his hunger by eating berries or by shooting and catching some small animal, he is unlikely to make much effort to shoot a large animal. . . . Men most often return from the bush empty-handed but with their hunger satisfied" (1968, p. 53; cf. p. 51). Women, meanwhile, are doing essentially the same.

of the producers. Having come to this conclusion, our discussion links up with established theory in economic history. It also makes connection with understandings long established in anthropological economics. Firth had effectively made this point in 1929, when commenting on the discontinuity of Maori labor in comparison with European tempos and incentives (1959a, p. 192 f). In the 1940's Gluckman wrote as much about the Bantu in general and the Lozi in particular (1943, p. 36; cf. Leacock, 1954, p. 7).

There will be much more to say theoretically about domestic production for use. For now I rest on the descriptive comment that in primitive communities an important fraction of existing labor resources may be rendered excessive by the mode of production.

HOUSEHOLD FAILURE

A third dimension of primitive underproduction, the final one here considered, is perhaps the most dramatic; at least it is the most serious for the people concerned. A fair percentage of domestic groups persistently fail to produce their own livelihood, although organized to do so. They occupy the lower end of a very large range of variation in household production, variation in appearance uncontrolled, but consistently observed in primitive societies of different circumstance, tradition and location. Once more the evidence is not definitive. But coupled to the logic of the case, it seems enough to encourage the following theoretical suggestion: that this variation, notably including a substantial degree of domestic economic failure, is a constituted condition of primitive economy.[22]

I was myself first struck by the magnitude of household production differences while working in Fiji, collecting estimates of food cultivation from the household heads in a number of Moalan villages. These were mainly estimates, so I cite the results merely as an example of the anecdotal comment to be found often in the monographic literature:

Differences in production within any given village are even more critical

22. Again this is no necessary contradiction to the "original affluent society" of Chapter 1, which was defined on the collective level and in terms of consumption, not production. The deficiencies here indicated in domestic production do not at all preclude amelioration by interhousehold distribution. On the contrary, they make intelligible the intensity of such distribution.

than output differences between villages. At least no Moalan village seems to be starving, whereas it is apparent that some men do not produce enough food for family needs. At the same time no village [with one possible exception] appears to have much surfeit, whereas some families are producing considerably more food than they can consume . . . familial differences in production of such . . . magnitude occur in every village and with respect to virtually every staple, secondary, and minor crop (Sahlins, 1962a, p. 59).

C. Daryll Forde's investigation of yam staple cultivation among 97 families in the Yakö village of Umor, shown in Figure 2.3, is more precise, and certainly more graphic. Forde remarks that, although a representative Yakö family of husband, one or two wives and three or four children will have one and one-half acres of yams under cultivation each year, 10 of the 97 he sampled were cultivating less than half an acre and 40 percent between a half and one acre. The same kind of deficit occurs in the output curve: mean production per house was 2,400–2,500 yams (medium-sized units), but the mode was only 1,900; a large proportion of families fell toward the lower end

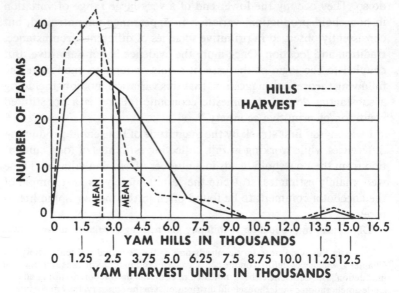

*Figure 2.3.  Yam Production, Umor Village, Yakö (after Forde, 1964)*

of the scale. And some of those at the lower end were below the customary subsistence requirement:

> It would be . . . incorrect to assume that there are no substantial variations from household to household in yam consumption. Although there is probably no gross insufficiency of supply of this staple food, there are at opposite ends of the scale households which, through inefficiency, sickness or other misfortune secure much less than they need by local standards, and others in which the *fufu* bowl is always heaped full (Forde, 1946, p. 59; cf. p. 64).

The situation depicted in Derek Freeman's classic study of rice production among the Iban is yet more serious (Freeman, 1955). But this example, covering the 25 families of Rumah Nyala village, carries two important reservations. First, the Iban maintain a considerable trade in their rice staple with mercantile centers of Sarawak—although in fact Iban families do not always produce enough for subsistence, let alone a surplus for export.[23] Secondly, the period of observation, 1949–50, was an exceptionally bad year. By Freeman's estimate—approximate, as he cautions—only eight of the 25 households were able to harvest a normal consumption quota (including rice for seed, animal feed, ritual expenses and beer). Table 2.7 summarizes yields in relation to consumption requirements for 1949–50. In ordinary years this distribution would probably be inverted, to show a normal rate of household failure on the order of 20 to 30 percent.

> At first sight, the fact that only about one third of *bilek* families managed to secure their normal requirements seems surprising, but it must be remembered that the 1949–50 season was an exceptionally bad one. . . . Nonetheless, it seems probable that even in normal years it is not uncommon for a minor percentage of households to fall below the ordinary level of subsistence as we have defined it. In the absence of reliable data we can do no more than make an informed guess. From my discussions with Iban informants, I would expect that in normal years from 70% to 80% of *bilek* families would attain their ordinary requirements, and that in favourable

---

23. By contrast, in a parallel study of six household outputs among the Lamet of Laos, Izikowitz (1951) found considerable variation, but all on the surplus-over-subsistence side. (The Lamet apparently depend more on rice sales than the Iban, and have apparently done so for a longer time.) Cf. also Geddes, 1954, on the Land Dayak.

*Table 2.7.  Rice yields in relation to normal consumption
requirements, 25 families of Rumah Nyala (1949-50)
(after Freeman, 1955, p. 104)*

| Rice Yield as a Percentage of Normal Requirements | Number of Households | Percentage of Households in Total Community |
|:---:|:---:|:---:|
| over 100% | 8 | 32 |
| 76-100% | 6 | 24 |
| 51-75% | 6 | 24 |
| 26-50% | 4 | 16 |
| under 25% | 1 | 4 |

seasons virtually all would be successful. . . . There are probably few, if any, Iban families which have not, at some time or another, found themselves in straitened circumstances with insufficient *padi* for their barest needs (Freeman, 1955, p. 104).

Another enthnographic example, to some degree making up by its precision for its modesty of scale, is Thayer Scudder's study (1962) of cereal cultivation among the 25 families of Mazulu village, Gwembe Tonga (Northern Rhodesia). The region is plagued by famine, but the yield of Mazulu farms is not of present moment; the first question is whether the several households had *planted* sufficient acreage to assure their subsistence. Scudder adduces a figure of one acre/capita as normally sufficient.[24] But as indicated in Table 2.8, presenting the results of Scudder's field study, four of the Mazulu households come seriously short of this level, and altogether 10 of the 20 fail to reach

24. However, it may be that the figure of one acre/head was determined in part from the actual tendency of gardens to cluster around that ratio—coupled with evidence from a neighboring region that such an amount should suffice. The norm of one acre/capita, moreover, does not make allowance for differential food requirements of men, women, and children, important when assessing the economic success of particular households. In a later section discussing household labor intensity (Chapter 3), such adjustments are made in the Mazulu data.

Table 2.8.  *Household variations in output/capita,*
*Mazulu village, Valley Tonga, 1956-57*
*(after Scudder, 1962, pp. 258-261)\**

| House | Acreage Cultivated/ Capita | Relation to Estimated Subsistence Norm/Capita |
|-------|----------------------------|-----------------------------------------------|
| A | 1.52 | +.52 |
| B | 0.86 | −.14 |
| C | 1.20 | +.20 |
| D | 1.13 | +.13 |
| E | 0.98 | −.02 |
| F | 1.01 | +.01 |
| G | 1.01 | +.01 |
| H | 0.98 | −.02 |
| I | 0.87 | −.13 |
| J | 0.59 | −.41 |
| K | 0.56 | −.44 |
| L | 0.78 | −.22 |
| M | 1.05 | +.05 |
| N | 0.91 | −.09 |
| O | 1.71 | +.71 |
| P | 0.96 | −.04 |
| Q | 1.21 | +.21 |
| R | 1.05 | +.05 |
| S | 2.06 | +1.06 |
| T | 0.69 | −.31 |

\*For further discussion of Mazulu production in relation to subsistence, including attempt at a more detailed analysis, see Chapter 4.

it. The domestic differences seem distributed as a normal curve around the point of per capita subsistence.

Enough said? Nothing is more tiresome than an anthropology "among-the" book: among the Arunta this, among the Kariera that. Nor is anything scientifically proven by the endless multiplication of examples—except that anthropology can be boring. But the last proposition does not need an elaborate demonstration, and neither does the one under discussion. For certain forms of production, notably hunting and fishing, the likelihood of differential success is known to common sense and experience. Besides and more generally, insofar as production is organized by domestic groups, it is established on a fragile and vulnerable base. The familial labor force is normally small and often sorely beset. In any "large enough community" the several households will show a considerable range in size and composition, range that may well leave some susceptible to disastrous mischance. For some must be unfavorably composed in the ratio of effective workers to dependent non-producers (mostly children and the aged). Of course others are in this respect more fortunately balanced, even overbalanced, on the side of capable producers. Yet any given family is subject to this kind of variation over time and the domestic growth cycle, just as at any given time certain families must find themselves facing economic difficulties. Thus a third apparent dimension of primitive underproduction: an interesting percentage of households chronically fail to provide their own customary livelihood.

## Elements of the Domestic Mode of Production

The foregoing constitutes a first empirical experience of widespread and profound tendencies of underproduction in the primitive economies. The succeeding is a first attempt to explain these tendencies theoretically by reference to a widespread and profound structure of the economies in question, the domestic mode of production. Necessarily the analysis will be as generalized as the phenomena are broadly distributed and variably expressed, a procedure which demands as an initial task certain methodological apologies.

APOLOGIES FOR GENERALITY

In a confrontation with a particular ethnographic case of underproduction, no abstract explanation can be as satisfactory as an accounting of the specific forces in play: the existing social and political relations, rights of property, ritual impediments to the deployment of labor, and the like.[25] But insofar as the several forms of underproduction noted earlier are generally discovered in the primitive economies, no particular analysis of them will satisfy either. For then they belong

25. Of the Lele, for example, nothing said here will be as satisfactory as Mary Douglas's excellent analysis (1960).

to the nature of the economies at issue, and in that capacity must be interpreted from equally general conditions of economic organization. Such is the analysis attempted here.

Yet the general only exists in particular forms. So the well-known methodological reservation of a well known social anthropologist remains pertinent: what is the use, he asked, of putting into comparison a society you have not first thoroughly understood? To this a colleague of mine once replied, as we walked along a dim academic corridor: "How can you understand a society you have not first compared?" This unhappy conjuncture of truths seems to leave anthropology in the position of a railroad engineer in the state of Connecticut, where (I am told) there is a law on the books to the effect that two trains moving in opposite directions along parallel tracks must, when they meet, come to a complete stop, and neither one may start up again until the other has passed out of sight. Undaunted anthropologists adopt cunning devices to break the impasse; for example, generalization by means of the "ideal type." The "ideal type" is a logical construct founded at once on pretended knowledge and pretended ignorance of the real diversity in the world—with the mysterious power of rendering intelligible any particular case. The solution has a dignity equal to the problem. Perhaps then it will excuse this chapter, which is written in the genre.

But how to justify certain other tactics even less respectable? From time to time the discussion will take clear leave of "reality," ignoring the apparent facts for what it is pleased to consider "the permanent fact." Penetrating beyond kinship, ritual, chieftainship—in sum, the main institutions of primitive society—it claims to see in the household system the first principles of economic performance. Yet the domestic economy cannot be "seen" in isolation, uncompromised by the greater institutions to which it is always subordinated. And even more reprehensible than this analytic arrogance, although in a way its inevitable result, the argument will be discovered on occasion in a scandalous flirtation with the state of nature—not exactly the latest anthropological approach. Philosophers who have examined the foundations of society, Rousseau said, have all felt the need to return to the state of nature, but none of them ever got there. The master thereupon proceeded to repeat the failure, but so magnificently this time as to leave the conviction that is really was useful to speak of things "that no longer exist, that perhaps never existed, that probably shall never exist, and yet of which it is necessary to have correct ideas in order to better judge our present condition."

But then, even to speak of *"the* economy" of a primitive society is an exercise in unreality. Structurally, "the economy" does not exist. Rather than a distinct and specialized organization, "economy" is something that generalized social groups and relations, notably kinship groups and relations, *do.* Economy is rather a function of the society than a structure, for the armature of the economic process is provided by groups classically conceived "noneconomic." In particular, production is instituted by domestic groups, these ordinarily ordered as families of one kind or another. The household is to the tribal economy as the manor to the medieval economy or the corporation to modern capitalism: each is the dominant production-institution of its time. Each represents, moreover, a determinate mode of production, with an appropriate technology and division of labor, a characteristic economic objective or finality, specific forms of property, definite social and exchange relations between producing units— and contradictions all its own.[26] In brief, to explain the observed disposition toward underproduction in the primitive economies, I would reconstruct the "independent domestic economy" of Karl Bücher and earlier writers—but relocated now somewhat *chez* Marx, and redecorated in a more fashionable ethnography.

For the domestic groups of primitive society have not yet suffered demotion to a mere consumption status, their labor power detached from the familial circle and, employed in an external realm, made subject to an alien organization and purpose. The household is as such charged with production, with the deployment and use of labor-

26. "Mode of production" is here differently employed than by Terray (following Althusser and Balibar) in his important work *Le Marxisme devant les sociétés primitives* (1969). Apart from the obvious difference in attention to superstructural "instances," the main contrast concerns the theoretical importance accorded various forms of cooperation, that is, as constituting corporate structures in control of productive forces over and against the domestic units. Such an importance is here refused, and from this divergence follow many of the others. Nevertheless, in spite of these significant differences, it will be obvious that the present perspective joins with Terray's on many points, and also with that of Meillassoux (1960; 1964), which was the basis for Terray's work.

power, with the determination of the economic objective. Its own inner relations, as between husband and wife, parent and child, are the principal relations of production in society. The built-in etiquette of kinship statuses, the dominance and subordination of domestic life, the reciprocity and cooperation, here make the "economic" a modality of the intimate. How labor is to be expended, the terms and products of its activity, are in the main domestic decisions. And these decisions are taken primarily with a view toward domestic contentment. Production is geared to the family's customary requirements. Production is for the benefit of the producers.

I hasten to add two reservations, which are also two final apologies for generality.

First, the convenient identification of "domestic group" with "family" that I allow myself is too loose and imprecise. The domestic group in the primitive societies is usually a family system, but this is not always so, and where it is, the term "family" must cover a variety of specific forms. Households of a community are sometimes morphologically heterogenous: apart from families, they include other kinds of domestic units composed, for example, of persons of a given age-class. Again, although it is also comparatively rare, families may be completely submerged in domestic groups the dimensions and structure of a lineage. Where the household is a family system, still the forms vary from nuclear to extended, and within the latter category from polygynous through matrilocal, patrilocal, and a variety of other types. Finally, the domestic group is internally integrated in different manners and degrees, as may be judged by the patterns of daily cohabitation, commensality and cooperation. Although the essential qualities of production to be discussed—dominance of the sexual division of labor, segmentary production for use, autonomous access to productive means, centrifugal relations beween producing units—appear to hold across these formal variations, the proposition of a domestic mode of production is surely a highly ideal type. And if one is nevertheless permitted to speak of a domestic mode of production, it is always and only in summary of many different modes of domestic production.

Secondly, I do not suggest that the household everywhere is an exclusive work group, and production merely a domestic activity.

Local techniques demand more or less cooperation, so production may be organized in diverse social forms, and sometimes at levels higher than the household. Members of one family may regularly collaborate on an individual basis with kith and kin from other houses; certain projects are collectively undertaken by constituted groups such as lineages or village communities. But the issue is not the social composition of work. Larger working parties are in the main just so many ways the domestic mode of production realizes itself. Often the collective organization of work merely disguises by its massiveness its essential social simplicity. A series of persons or small groups act side by side on parallel and duplicate tasks, or they labor together for the benefit of each participant in turn. The collective effort thus momentarily compresses the segmentary structure of production without changing it permanently or fundamentally. Most decisive, cooperation does not institute a *sui generis* production-structure with its own finality, different from and greater than the livelihood of the several domestic groups and dominant in the production process of the society. Cooperation remains for the most part a technical fact, without independent social realization on the level of economic control. It does not compromise the autonomy of the household or its economic purpose, the domestic management of labor-power or the prevalence of domestic objectives across the social activities of work.

These apologies offered, I pass to the description of the principal aspects of the domestic mode of production (DMP), with a view fixed to the implications of this mode for the character of the economic performance.

DIVISION OF LABOR

By its composition, the household makes up a kind of *petite* economy. In response to the technical scale and diversity of production, it is even expandable to a degree: the combination of nuclear elements in some form of extended family seems to make its debut as the social organization of an economic complexity. But more important than its size, familial control of production rests on another aspect of its composition. The family contains within itself the division of labor dominant in the society as a whole. A family—it is from the beginning and at the minimum a man and wife, an adult male and an adult female. Hence, from its inception a family combines the two essential social elements of production. Division of labor by sex is not the only economic specialization known to primitive societies. But it is the *dominant* form, transcending all other specialization in this sense: that the normal activities of any adult man, taken in conjunction with the normal activities of an adult woman, practically exhaust the customary works of society. Therefore marriage, among other things, establishes a generalized economic group constituted to produce the local conception of livelihood.

THE PRIMITIVE RELATION BETWEEN MAN AND TOOL

Here is a second correlation, equally elementary: between the domestic mode, atomized and small scale, and a technology of similar dimensions. The basic apparatus can usually be handled by household groups; much of it can be wielded autonomously by individuals. Other technological limitations are likewise consistent with the supremacy of the domestic economy: implements are homespun, thus—as most skills—simple enough to be widely available; productive processes are unitary rather than decomposed by an elaborate division of labor, so that the same interested party can carry through the whole procedure from the extraction of the raw material to the fabrication of the finished good.

But a technology is not comprehended by its physical properties alone. In use, tools are brought into specific relationships with their users. On the largest view, this relationship and not the tool itself is the determinate historic quality of a technology. No purely physical difference between the traps of certain spiders and those of certain (human) hunters, or between the bee's hive and the Bantu's, is historically as meaningful as the difference in the instrument-user relation. The tools themselves are not different in principle, or even in efficiency. Anthropologists are only satisfied by the extratechnological observation that in invention and use the human instrument expresses "conscious ingenuity" (symboling), the insect's tool, inherited physiology ("instinct")—"what distinguishes the worst architect from the best of bees is this, that the architect raises his structure in imagination before he erects it in reality" (Marx, 1967a, vol. 1, p. 178). Tools, even good tools, are prehuman. The great evolutionary divide is in the relationship: tool-organism.

The human capacities once achieved, ingenuity in turn loses its differentiating power. The world's most primitive peoples—judged as such on the plane of overall cultural complexity—create unparalled technical masterpieces. Dismantled and shipped to New York or London, Bushman traps lie now gathering dust in the basements of a hundred museums, powerless even to instruct because no one can figure out how to put them back together again. On a very broad view of cultural evolution, technical developments have accumulated not so much in ingenuity as along a different axis of the man-tool relationship. It is a question of the distribution of energy, skill, and intelligence between the two. In the primitive relation of man to tool, the balance of these is in favor of man; with the inception of a "machine age" the balance swings definitively in favor of the tool.[27]

The primitive relation between man and tool is a condition of the domestic mode of production. Typically, the instrument is an artificial extension of the person, not simply designed for individual use, but as an attachment that increases the body's mechanical advantage (for example, a bow-drill or a spear thrower), or performs final operations (for example, cutting, digging) for which the body is not naturally well equipped. The tool thus delivers human energy and skill more than energy and skill of its own. But the latest technology would invert this relationship between man and tool. It becomes debatable which is the tool:

> The share of the operative workman in the machine industry is (typically) that of an attendant, an assistant, whose duty it is to keep pace with the machine process and to help out with workmanlike manipulation at points where the machine process engaged is incomplete. His work supplements the machine process, rather than makes use of it. On the contrary

27. Of course a great deal of knowledge is required for the development and maintenance of modern machinery; the above sentence confines itself to the relation of man and tool in the process of production.

the machine process makes use of the workman (Veblen, 1914, pp. 306–7)[28].

The theoretical value placed by modern evolutionary anthropology on technology as such is historically contingent. Man is now dependent on machines, and the evolutionary future of culture seems to hinge on the progress of this hardware. At the same time, prehistory is by and large a record of instruments—as a well-known archaeologist is reputed to have said, "the people, they're dead." These banal truths I think help explain the analytical privilege often conceded to primitive technology, perhaps as mistaken however as it is entrenched for its exaggeration of the importance of tool over skill, and correlatively for its perception of the progress of man from ape to ancient empire as a series of petty industrial revolutions initiated by the development of new tools or new energy sources. For the greater part of human history, labor has been more significant than tools, the intelligent efforts of the producer more decisive than his simple equipment. The entire history of labor until very recently has been a history of skilled labor. Only an industrial system could survive on the proportion of unskilled workers as now exists; in a similar case, the paleolithic perishes. And the principal primitive "revolutions," notably the neolithic domestication of food resources, were pure triumphs of human technique: new ways of relating to the existing energy sources (plants

28. Marx's appreciation of the machine revolution, earlier of course than Veblen's, is very close to the latter in wording: "Along with the tool, the skill of the workman in handling it passes over to the machine. . . . In handicrafts and manufacture, the workman makes use of a tool, in the factory, the machine makes use of him. There the movements of the instrument of labour proceed from him, here it is the movements of the machine that he must follow. In [prefactory] manufacture the workmen are parts of a living mechanism. In the factory we have a lifeless mechanism independent of the workman, who becomes its mere living appendage. . . . Every kind of capitalist production, in so far as it is not only a labour-process, but also a process of creating surplus-value, has this in common, that it is not the workman that employs the instruments of labour, but the instruments of labour that employ the workman" (1967a, vol 1., pp. 420–23). For Marx, it should be noted, the critical turning point in the man-tool relation was not the substitution of nonhuman power, but the attachment of tools to a transmission and motor-mechanism; the last might still be human but the workman had effectively been alienated from the instruments of labor, the skill of handling them now passing over to the machine. This is the indicative criterion of the machine and the real beginning of the industrial revolution.

and animals) rather than new tools or new sources (see Chapter 1). The hardware of subsistence production may very well decline in the passage from the paleolithic to the neolithic—even as the output goes up. What is the Melanesian's digging stick to the sealing gear of an Alaskan Eskimo? Up to the time of the true industrial revolution, the product of human labor probably increased much more in return to the worker's skill than to the perfection of his tools.

A discussion of the importance of human techniques is not as tangential as it might seem to this analysis of the DMP. It helps underwrite a major theoretical suggestion: that in the archaic societies, social-political pressure must often present itself the most feasible strategy of economic development. People are the most malleable as well as the most important side of the primitive man-tool relationship. Take into consideration, besides, the ethnographic testimony of underexploitation: that resources are often not fully turned to account, but between the actual production and the possibility there remains considerable room for maneuver. The great challenge lies in the intensification of labor: getting people to work more, or more people to work. That is to say, the society's economic destiny is played out in its relations of production, especially the political pressures that can be mounted on the household economy.

But an intensification of labor will have to take a dialectical course, because many properties of the DMP make it refractory at once to the exercise of political power and the enlargement of production. Of first importance is the contentment of the household economy with its own self-appointed objective: livelihood. The DMP is intrinsically an anti-surplus system.

PRODUCTION FOR LIVELIHOOD

The classic distinction between "production for use" (that is, for the producers) and "production for exchange" was, from the beginning of an economic anthropology, at least in the Anglo-Saxon countries, interred in the graveyard of prehistoric concepts. True that Thurnwald had adopted these concepts to set off the primitive from modern monetary economies (1932). And nothing could prevent their reincarnation in various ethnographic contexts (see "Underuse of Labor Power" above). But when Malinowski (1921) defined the "Tribal

Economy" in opposition (partly) to Bücher's "Independent Domestic Economy" (1911), the notion of production for use was effectively put aside before its theoretical usefulness had been exhausted.

Perhaps the problem was that "production for use" or "independent domestic economy" could be interpreted two different ways, one of which proved indefensible—so the other was generally ignored. These phrases suggest a condition of domestic autarky, untrue for the producing units of any real society. The households of primitive communities are not usually self-sufficient, producing all they need and needing all they produce. Certainly there is exchange. Even aside from the presents given and received under inescapable social obligations, the people may work for a frankly utilitarian trade, thus indirectly getting what they need.

Still, it is "what they need": the exchange, and the production for it, are oriented to livelihood, not to profits. This is a second rendering of the classic distinction, and the more fundamental; more fundamental than a certain exchange is the *producer's relation to the productive process.* It is not merely "production for use" but production for *use value,* even through the acts of exchange, and as opposed to the quest for exchange value. On this reading, the DMP does find a place in the received categories of economic history. Even with exchange, the domestic mode is cousin to Marx's "simple circulation of commodities," thus to the celebrated formula C → M → C′: the manufacture of commodities (C) for sale in the market in order to obtain wherewithal (M, money) for the purchase of other, specific commodities (C′). "Simple circulation" is of course more pertinent to peasant than to primitive economies. But like peasants, primitive peoples remain constant in their pursuit of use values, related always to exchange with an interest in consumption, so to production with an interest in provisioning. And in this respect the historical opposite of *both* is the bourgeois entrepreneur with an interest in exchange value.

The capitalist process has a different starting point and another calculus. The "general formula for capital" is the transformation of a given money sum into more of the same by way of the commodity: M → C → M′, the engagement of labor-power and physical means for the fabrication of a good whose sale realizes the highest possible return on an original capital. Livelihood and gain, "production for

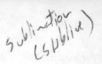

use" and "production for exchange" pose thus contrasting finalities of production—and, accordingly, contrasting intensities of production.

For one is an economic system of determinate and finite objectives while the other holds out the indefinite goal of "as much as possible." It is a difference of quality as well as quantity: in the first place of quality. Production for livelihood envisions not only a moderate quota of good things, but these of a *specific useful character* responding to the producers' customary requirements. Yet where the domestic economy seeks merely to reproduce itself, production for exchange (value) would constantly exceed itself: in the accumulation of a generalized "wealth." It is not the production of goods in particular but of an abstract "wealth." And "the sky's the limit." By definition, $M' \leqslant M$ is a failure of the practice $M \to C \to M'$; by competition, $M' \to \infty$ is the formula of success. How sublime, Marx wrote, seems the ancient conception that made man the objective of production, in comparison with a modern world where production is the objective of man—and wealth the objective of production (1967b, vol. 1, p. 450).

To consider but one implication—of which we have already had ethnographic testimony: work in a system of production for use has unique possibilities of defining a term. Production is under no compulsion to proceed to the physical or gainful capacity, but inclined rather to break off for the time being when livelihood is assured for the time being. Production for use is discontinuous and irregular, and on the whole sparing of labor-power. Whereas, in production organized by and for exchange value:

> Le but de travail n'est plus, dès lors, tel produit spécifique ayant des rapports particuliers avec tel ou tel besoin de l'individu, c'est l'argent, richesse ayant une forme universelle, si bien que le zèle au travail de l'individu ne connaît plus de limites: indifférent à ses propres particularités, le travail revêt toutes les formes qui servent ce but. Le zèle se fait inventif et crée des objets nouveaux pour le besoin sociale. . . . (Marx, 1967b, vol. 1, p. 165).

It is regrettable that Economic Anthropology chose largely to ignore this distinction between production for use and production for exchange. Recognition of the difference in productivity between them had served the study of economic history honorably and well. In a famous case Henri Pirenne thus explained the decline of agriculture in early medieval Europe, when the economy was left without outlets by the Arab seizure of the Mediterranean and lapsed at once from commercial exchange to local self-sufficiency and from higher to lower productivity:

> ... the regression of agricultural methods is obvious. It was useless to make the soil yield more than was required to satisfy the needs of the cultivator, for since the surplus could not be exported it would neither improve the condition of the tiller of the soil nor increase the rental value of the land. The farmer was therefore satisfied with a minimum of care and effort, and agronomic science was allowed to fall into oblivion, until the possiblity of selling the crops should once more encourage the owners of the soil to adopt improved and more lucrative methods. But then the land would begin to be regarded as a value, and not as a means of subsistence (Pirenne, 1955, p. 99).

And now the classic opposition reappears as the "dual economy" of "underdeveloped" countries. Boeke, author of the principle, describes the contrast in performance this way:

> Another respect in which an Eastern differs from a Western society is the fact that *needs are very limited.* This is connected with the limited development of exchange, with the fact that most people have to provide for themselves, that families have to be content with what they are able to produce themselves, so that needs necessarily have to remain modest in quantity and quality. Another consequence of this is that the economic motive does not work continuously. Therefore ... economic activity is also intermittent. Western economy tends in a diametrically opposite direction ... (Boeke, 1953, p. 39).

But as witnesses to the colonial confrontation of the two economies, anthropologists have had the opportunity to experience the historic difference as an ethnographic event. In obdurate patterns of indigenous labor and "irrational" responses to prices, they have seen production for use—in crises, therefore in essence. For the traditional economy of finite objectives insists on asserting itself even as it is broken and harnessed to the market. Perhaps that helps explain how the rational West could live for a very long time with two contradictory prejudices about the "natives" capacity for work. On the one hand, a vulgar anthropology was contending the people had to labor constantly just to survive, given their technical incapacities; on the other hand, it was only too evident that "the natives are congenitally lazy." If the first was a colonialist rationale, the second testifies to a certain deficiency of the ideology: for some reason it proved necessary to beat the people into shouldering the white man's burden. Recruited as plantation hands, they frequently showed themselves unwilling to work steadily. Induced to raise a cash crop, they would not react "appropriately" to market changes: as they were interested mainly in acquiring specific items of consumption, they produced that much less when crop prices rose, and that much more when prices fell off. And the introduction of new tools or plants that increased the productivity of indigenous labor might only then shorten the period of necessary work, the gains absorbed rather by an expansion of rest than of output (cf. Sharp, 1952; Sahlins, 1962a). All these and similar responses express an enduring quality of traditional domestic production, that it is production of use values, definite in its aim, so discontinuous in its activity.

In brief, by this characteristic of DMP—that it is a production of use values—we return to underproduction, the empirical observation of which was the beginning of inquiry. The domestic system entertains limited economic goals, qualitatively defined in the terms of a way of living rather than quantitatively as an abstract wealth. Work is accordingly unintensive: intermittent and susceptible to all manner of interruption by cultural alternatives and impediments ranging from heavy ritual to light rainfall. Economics is only a part-time activity of the primitive societies, or else it is an activity of only part of the society.

Otherwise said, the DMP harbors an antisurplus principle. Geared to the production of livelihood, it is endowed with the tendency to come to a halt at that point. Hence if "surplus" is defined as output above the producers' requirements, the household system is not organized for it. Nothing within the structure of production for use pushes it to transcend itself. The entire society is constructed on an obstinate economic base, therefore on a contradiction, because unless the domestic economy is forced beyond itself the entire society does not survive. Economically, primitive society is founded on an antisociety.

CHAYANOV'S RULE

There is a more exact way of appreciating this unintensive use of productive forces. I offer a mixed series of theoretical and statistical reflections mounting to the conclusion that the domestic system sets norms of livelihood limited not only absolutely but in relation to the society's potential; that indeed, in the community of domestic producing groups, the greater the relative working capacity of the household the less its members work. The last is a capital discovery of A. V. Chayanov, here acknowledged by calling it "Chayanov's rule."

A preliminary understanding is that the three elements of the DMP so far identified—small labor force differentiated essentially by sex, simple technology, and finite production objectives—are systematically interrelated. Not only is each in reciprocal bond with the others, but each by its own modesty of scale is adapted to the nature of the others. Let any one of these elements show an unusual inclination to develop, it meets from the others the increasing resistance of an incompatibility. The normal systematic resolution of this tension is restoration of the status quo ("negative feedback"). Only in the event of an historic conjuncture of additional and external contradictions ("overdetermination") would the crisis pass over into destruction and transformation. Specifically, the norm of domestic livelihood tends to be inert. It cannot move above a certain level without testing the capacities of the domestic labor force, either directly or through the technological change required for a higher output. The standard of livelihood does not substantially increase without putting into question the existing family organization. And it has an ultimate ceiling set by the possibility of any household order to provide adequate forces and relations of production. So long, therefore, as the domestic mode prevails, the customary idea of livelihood will be suitably restrained.

Moreover, if the internal contradictions set off by rising standards thus define an absolute limit, the external contradictions will determine an equilibrium which is low relative to the society's economic capacities.

Because, whatever the nature of social relations between households, from the anarchy of nature to the amity of kinship, the customary norm of welfare has to be fixed at a level attainable by the larger number of them, leaving underexploited the powers of the most efficient minority. Potentially, the several households of a community differ greatly in per capita output, if only because they are at different stages of the familial development cycle, so must vary in their ratio of effective producers to dependent children and elders. But suppose the conventions of domestic well-being were adapted to the households of greatest working capacity. Society is then faced with one of two intolerable conditions, depending on the proximity of existing interhousehold relations to the poles of anarchy and solidarity. No relations prevailing, (or hostile relations) the success of only a few and the inevitable failure of the many is an economic invitation to violence. Or, given an extensive kinship, distribution by the happy few in favor of the many poor merely creates a general and permanent discrepancy between the convention of domestic welfare and the reality.

Taking together then these abstract and preliminary reasonings: on pain of engaging internal and external contradictions, revolution and war, or at least continuous sedition, the customary economic targets of the DMP have to be held within certain limits, these inferior to the overall capacity of the society, and wasteful particularly of the labor-power of more effective households.

"In the family farm," writes A. V. Chayanov, "rates of labor intensity are considerably lower than if labor were fully utilized. In all areas investigated, farm families possess considerable stocks of unused time" (1966, pp. 75-76). This observation, summing up extensive research on Russian agriculture of the immediate prerevolutionary period, allows us to continue the argument in an entirely different register without missing an essential beat. True that Chayanov and his co-workers developed their theory of precapitalist domestic economy in the special context of simple commodity circulation.[29] Yet, para-

---

29. Long unknown in the Anglo-Saxon world, Chayanov's work (1966) assembles a large array of statistical information and intellectual ponderation of passionate interest to the student of precapitalist economies. (This praise is not to be tempered by the obvious disagreement between the theoretical perspective of the present work and the marginalist reading Chayanov gives in the end to his more substantial reflections.)

doxically, a fragmented peasant economy may more clearly than any primitive community present on the empirical level certain profound tendencies of the DMP. In the primitive case these tendencies are concealed and transfigured by general social relations of solidarity and authority. But the peasant domestic economy, articulated rather to the market by exchange than to other households by corporate kinship, without pretence manifests to inspection the deep structure of the DMP. It manifests in particular an underuse of labor-power, as many of Chayanov's tables testify. Table 2.9 is typical.

Chayanov moved beyond the mere observation of a general underuse of manpower. He investigated in detail the variation in intensity by household. Bringing to bear a study of his own among 25 Volokolamsk farm families, he was able to show, first, that these differences are quite remarkable: a threefold range of variation from 78.8 working days/worker/year in the least industrious household to 216.0 working days per worker in the most industrious.[30] Then, most revealing, Chayanov plotted the differences in intensity/household against variations in domestic composition figured in terms of number of consumers. A ratio of household size to effective manpower (dependency ratio), the last is essentially an index of household economic strength in relation to its appointed tasks of livelihood. The relative working capacity of the domestic group can be understood to increase as the index descends towards unity. Chayanov demonstrates (Table 2.10) that the intensity of labor in the domestic group *decreases* accordingly.

Chayanov's demonstration might seem a superfluous refinement of the obvious, particularly if the domestic economy of finite objectives is taken for granted. All it says statistically is what one would then expect logically; namely, the smaller the relative proportion of workers the more they must work to assure a given state of domestic well-being, and the greater the proportion the less they work. Phrased more generally, however, and in a way that says nothing about the finality of the DMP except by the invitation to comparison with other economies, Chayanov's rule suddenly seems magnified several theo-

30. Chayanov supplies the complete table for 25 families (1966, p. 77). The average number of working days/worker/year was 131.8; the median, 125.8.

Table 2.9. Distribution of peasant labor by sector in three areas of czarist Russia* (after Chayanov, 1966, p. 74)†

|  | Percentage of Working Time in: | | | | | |
| District | Agriculture | Crafts and Trades | Total "Productive Labor" | Housework | Unused Time | Festivals‡ |
| --- | --- | --- | --- | --- | --- | --- |
| Vologda Uezd (Vologda Guberniya) | 24.7 | 18.1 | 42.8 | 4.4 | 33.8 | 19.8 |
| Volokolamsk Uezd (Moscow Guberniya) | 28.6 | 8.2 | 36.8 | 43.2 | | 20.0 |
| Starobel'sk Uezd (Khar'kov Guberniya) | 23.6 | 4.4 | 28.0 | 3.0 | 42.0 | 27.0 |

*n not given.

†It is regrettable that many of Chayanov's statistical tables, fashioned in the main from reports of Czarist agricultural inspectors, lack the kinds of precision that modern study must consider indispensable, notably with regard to the character of the sample, operational defintions of categories employed, and the like.

‡The figures of this column evoke Lafargue's critique of the bourgeois revolution: "Under the Old Regime, the laws of the Church guaranteed the laborer ninety rest days, fifty-two Sundays and thirty-eight holidays, during which he was strictly forbidden to work. This was the great crime of Catholicism, the principal cause of the irreligion of the industrial and commercial bourgeoisie: under the revolution, when once it was in the saddle, it abolished all holidays and replaced the week of seven days by that of ten, in order that the people might no longer have more than one rest day out of ten. It emancipated the laborers from the yoke of the Church in order better to subjugate them under the yoke of work" (1909, p. 32 n).

Table 2.10. *Intensity of work in relation to household*
*composition: 25 Volokolamsk families*
*(after Chayanov, 1966, p. 78)\**

| Index of consumers/worker | 1.01-1.20 | 1.21-1.40 | 1.41-1.60 | 1.61+ |
|---|---|---|---|---|
| Working-days/worker/ year (household average) | 98.8 | 102.3 | 157.2 | 161.3 |

\*The same relation between intensity of production and effectiveness of the domestic group is shown in another table, covering several peasant regions and using output/worker measured in rubles rather than intensity measured in workdays (p. 78). I excerpt part of that table:

| Consumer/Worker Ratio | Output (Rubles) per Worker | | |
|---|---|---|---|
| | Starobel'sk Uezd | Vologda Uezd | Vel'sk Uezd |
| 1.00-1.15 | 68.1 | 63.9 | 59.2 |
| 1.16-1.30 | 99.0 | 106.95 | 61.2 |
| 1.31-1.45 | 118.3 | 122.64 | 76.1 |
| 1.46-1.60 | 128.9 | 91.7 | 79.5 |
| 1.61+ | 156.4 | 117.9 | 95.5 |

retical powers: *Intensity of labor in a system of domestic production for use varies inversely with the relative working capacity of the producing unit.*

Productive intensity is inversely related to productive capacity. The rule of Chayanov felicitously summarizes and supports several propositions we had made along the way. It confirms the deduction that the norm of livelihood does not adapt to maximum household efficiency but settles rather at a level within reach of the majority, so wasting a certain potential among the most effective. At the same time, this means that no compulsion to surplus output is built into the DMP. But then, the plight of the least effective domestic groups, especially the substantial percentage that do not meet their own requirements, seems all the more serious. For the households of greater working capacity are not automatically extending themselves on behalf of the poorer. Nothing in the organization of production itself provides systematic compensation for its own systematic defects.

## PROPERTY

On the contrary, rather than producing for others, a certain autonomy in the realm of property strengthens each household's devotion to its own interests.

We need not be so fascinated with "title" to property as with entitlement, nor with abstract claims of "ownership" so much as real privileges of use and disposition. A stockholder in A.T.&T. believed himself endowed by his five shares to chop down a telephone pole placed noxiously in front of his picture window. Anthropologists have likewise learned by experience to separate various rights of property—income, use, control—inasmuch as these may be divided among different holders in the same thing. Also we have proved tolerant enough to recognize separate rights that are not exclusive by nature but differ mainly in the power of one holder to override decisions of the other: ranked overrights, as between a chief and his followers; or segmentary overrights, as between a corporate lineage and its constituent households. The path of anthropological progress is now strewn with terminological corpses, the ghosts of most of which are better avoided. The issue of present concern is the privileged position of domestic groups, whatever the coexisting tenures.

For these coexisting tenures are typically superposed to the family rather than interposed between the family and its means of production. In the event, the higher "owners" in the primitive societies—chiefs, lineages, clans—stand in a relation of the second degree to production, as mediated by the entrenched domestic groups. Chiefly ownership—"of the land, the sea and the people," as the Fijians say—is a particularly revealing case. It is an "ownership" more inclusive than exclusive, and more political than economic: a derived claim on the product and productive means in virtue of an inscribed superiority over the producers. In this it differs from a bourgeois ownership that confers control over the producers by a claim upon productive means. Whatever the resemblances in ideology of "ownership," the two systems of property work differently, the one (chieftainship) a right to things realized through a hold on persons, the other (bourgeois) a hold on persons realized through a right to things:[31]

| chiefly "ownership" | bourgeois ownership |
|---|---|
| ↓ | ↓ |
| producers | means of production and product |
| ↓ | ↓ |
| means of production and product | producers |

The household in the tribal societies is usually *not* the exclusive owner of its resources: farmlands, pastures, hunting or fishing territories. But across the ownership of greater groups or higher authorities, even by means of such ownership, the household retains the primary relation to productive resources. Where these resources are undivided, the domestic group has unimpeded access; where the land is allotted, it has claim to an appropriate share. The family enjoys the *usufruct,* it is said, the use-right, but all the privileges entailed are not obvious from the term. The producers determine on a day-to-day basis *how* the land shall be used. And to them falls the priority of appropriation and disposition of the product; no claim of any supervening group or authority legitimately goes so far as to deprive the household of its livelihood. All this is undeniable and irreducible: the right of the family as a member of the proprietary group or community to directly and independently exploit for its own support a due share of the social resources.

As an *economic* rule, there is no class of landless paupers in primitive society. If expropriation occurs it is accidental to the mode of production itself, a cruel fortune of war for instance, and not a systematic condition of the economic organization. Primitive peoples have invented many ways to elevate a man above his fellows. But the

31. "In the first place the wealth of the old tribal and village communities was in no sense a domination over men. And secondly, even in societies moving in class antagonisms, insofar as wealth includes domination over men, it is mainly and almost exclusively a domination over men *by virtue of,* and *through the intermediary of,* the domination over things" (Engels, 1966, p. 205).

producers' hold on their own economic means rules out the most compelling history has known: exclusive control of such means by some few, rendering dependent the many others. The political game has to be played on levels above production, with tokens such as food and other finished goods; then, usually the best move, as well as the most coveted right of property, is to give the stuff away.

POOLING

The domestic segregation constructed into production and property is completed by an inner-directed circulation of the household product. An inevitable consequence of production at once specialized by sex and oriented to collective use, this centripetal movement of goods differentiates the household economy from the world even as it reiterates the group's internal solidarity. The effect is magnified where distribution takes the form of eating together, in a daily ritual of commensality that consecrates the group as a group. Usually the household is a consumption unit in this way. But at the least, householding demands some *pooling* of goods and services, placing at the disposition of its members what is indispensable to them. On one hand, then, the distribution transcends the reciprocity of functions, as between man and woman, upon which the household is established. Pooling abolishes the differentiation of the parts in favor of the coherence of the whole; it is the constituting activity of a group. On the other hand, the household is thereby distinguished forever from others of its kind. With these other houses, a given group might eventually entertain reciprocal relations. But reciprocity is always a "between" relation: however solidary, it can only perpetuate the separate economic identities of those who so exchange.

Lewis Henry Morgan called the program of the domestic economy "communism in living." The name seems apposite, for householding is the highest form of economic sociability: "from each according to his abilities and to each according to his needs"—from the adults that with which they are charged by the division of labor; to them, but also to the elders, the children, the incapacitated. regardless of their contributions, that which they require. The sociological precipitate is a group with an interest and destiny apart from those outside and a prior claim on the sentiments and resources of those within. Pooling closes the domestic circle; the circumference becomes a line of social and economic demarcation. Sociologists call it a "primary group"; people call it "home."

ANARCHY AND DISPERSION

Considered in its own terms, as a structure of production, the DMP is a species of anarchy.

The domestic mode anticipates no social or material relations between households except that they are alike. It offers society only a constituted disorganization, a mechanical solidarity set across the grain of a segmentary decomposition. The social economy is fragmented into a thousand petty existences, each organized to proceed independently of the others and each dedicated to the homebred principle of looking out for itself. The division of labor? Beyond the household it ceases to have organic force. Instead of unifying society by sacrificing the autonomy of its producing groups, the division of labor here, as it is principally a division of labor by sex, sacrifices the unity of society to the autonomy of its producing groups. Nor is any higher cause entertained by the household's access to productive resources, or again by the economic priorities codified in domestic pooling. Viewed politically, the DMP is a kind of natural state. Nothing within this infrastructure of production obliges the several household groups to enter into compact and cede each one some part of its autonomy. As the domestic economy is in effect the tribal economy in miniature, so politically it underwrites the condition of primitive society—society without a Sovereign. In principle each house retains, as well as its own interests, all the powers that are wanted to satisfy them. Divided thus into so many units of self-concern, functionally uncoordinated, production by the domestic mode has all the organization of the so many potatoes in a certain famous sack of potatoes.

That is in essence the primitive structure of production. But of course not in appearance. In appearance, primitive society is a poor likeness of primordial incoherence. Everywhere the petty anarchy of domestic production is counterposed by larger forces and greater organization, institutions of social-economic order that join one house to another and submit all to a general interest. Still, these grand forces of integration are not given in the dominant and immediate relations of production. On the contrary, precisely as they are negations of domestic anarchy, they owe part of their meaning and existence to the disorder they would suppress. And if in the end anarchy is banished from the surface of things, it is not definitively exiled. It continues, a persistent disarray lurking in the background, so long as the household remains in charge of production.

Here, then, I appeal the apparent facts to the permanent fact. "In the background" is a discontinuity of power and interest, lending itself moreover to a dispersion of people. In the background is a state of nature.

Interesting that almost all the philosophers who have felt the need to go back there—granted not one of them ever made it—saw in that condition a specific distribution of population. Almost all sensed some centrifugal tendency. Hobbes sent back ethnographic report that the life of man was solitary, poor, nasty, brutish and short. Underline (for once) the "solitary." It was a life apart. And the same notion of original isolation appears ever and again, from Herodutus to K. Bücher, in the schemes of those who dared speculate on man in nature. Rousseau took several positions, the most pertinent to our purpose in the *Essai sur l'origine des langues*.[32] In the earliest times the only society was the family, the only laws, of nature, and the only mediator between men, force—in other words, something like the domestic mode of production. And this "barbaric" epoch was, for Rousseau, the golden age,

> not because men were united, but because they were separated. Each one, it is said, considered himself master of everything; that could be: but no one knew of nor coveted more than he had in hand; his needs, far from bringing him nearer his fellows, drove him away. Men, if you will, attacked

32. The scheme of the *Discourse on the Origin of Inequality among Men* is more complicated. True that men in the first period were isolated, but for lack of sociable qualities. By the time Rousseau brought in the potential conflict that in the analyses of others (such as Hobbes) was functionally linked to dispersion, something like society already existed and the earth was fully occupied. However, it is clear that Rousseau had the same understanding of the relation between private force and dispersion, because he felt compelled to explain in footnote why at this later time people were not centrifugally scattered, that is, because the earth had already been filled (1964, vol. 3, pp. 221-222).

each other upon meeting, but they rarely met. Everywhere reigned the state
of war, and all the earth was at peace (translation mine).

Maximum dispersion is the settlement pattern of the state of nature.
To understand what conceivable significance this can promise the
present analysis—that is, supposing the reader has not already abandoned the effort to its apparent folly—it is necessary to ask why the
political philosophers thus rendered natural man far-flung and for the
most part alone. The obvious answer is that the sages posited nature
by a simple opposition to culture, stripped then of everything artificial, which is nothing less than society. The residue could only be man
in isolation—or perhaps man in the family, that concord of natural
lust, as Hobbes called it—even if the man in question was really the
rugged individual become now so common in society that he claimed
to be only natural. ("L'état de nature, c'est le bourgeois sans société.")
But beyond the obvious, this conception of a scattered distribution
was also a logical and functionalist deduction, a reflection upon the
necessary deployment of men supposing the natural rather than the
political state were in effect. Where the right to proceed by force is
held generally rather than monopolized politically, there discretion is
the better part of valor and space the surest principle of security.
Minimizing conflict over resources, goods, and women, dispersal is
the best protector of persons and possessions. In other words, this division of force that the philosophers imagined forced them also to
imagine a humanity divided, putting the greatest distance between
one another just as a kind of functional precaution.

I am at the most abstract, the most hypothetical, in brief, the
wildest point of speculation: that the deeper structure of the economy,
the domestic mode of production, is like the state of nature, and the
characteristic movement of the latter is also its own. Left to its own
devices, the DMP is inclined toward a maximum dispersion of home-
steads, because maximum dispersion is the absence of interdependence and a common authority, and these are by and large the way
production is organized. If within the domestic circle the decisive
motions are centripetal, between households they are centrifugal,
spinning off into the thinnest probable distribution—an effect pro-

ceeding in reality to the extent it is not checked by greater institutions of order and equilibrium.

This is so extreme that I must cite some possibility of its ethnographic relevance, even at the cost of recapitulating known facts and anticipating later arguments. Carneiro, as we had seen earlier, took some care to show that villages of the Amazon Tropical Forest are typically inferior to the 1,000 or even 2,000 inhabitants they might sustain on existing agricultural practices. He rejects, therefore, the usual explanation of small village size, to wit, that it is due to shifting cultivation:

> I would like to argue that a factor of greater importance has been the ease and frequency of village fissioning for reasons not related to subsistence [that is, to techniques of subsistence]. . . . The facility with which this phenomenon occurs suggests that villages may seldom get a chance to increase in population to the point at which they begin to press hard on the carrying capacity of the land. The centrifugal forces that cause villages to break apart seem to reach a critical point well before this happens. What the forces are that lead to village fission falls outside the present discussion. Suffice it to say that many things may give rise to factional disputes within a society, and that the larger the community the more frequent these disputes are likely to be. By the time a village in the Tropical Forest attains a population of 500 or 600 the stresses and strains within it are probably such that an open schism, leading to the hiving off of a dissident faction, may easily occur. If internal political controls were strong, a large community might succeed in remaining intact despite factionalism. But chieftainship was notoriously weak among most Amazonian villages, so that the political mechanisms for holding a growing community together in the face of increasingly strong divisive forces were all but lacking (Carneiro, 1968, p. 136).

My point is that primitive society is founded on an economic disconformity, a segmentary fragility that lends itself to and reverberates particular local causes of dispute, and in the absence of "mechanisms for holding a growing community together" realizes and resolves the crisis by fission. We have noticed that the domestic mode of production is discontinuous in time; here we see it is also discontinuous in space. And as the former discontinuity accounts for a certain underuse of labor, the latter implies a persistent underexploitation of resources. Our very roundabout and theoretical tour of the domestic mode of production thus comes back to its empirical point of departure. Constituted on an uncertain household base, which is in any case restrained in material objectives, stinted in its use of labor power and cloistered in relation to other groups, the domestic mode of production is not organized to give a brilliant performance.

# 3

# The Domestic Mode of Production: Intensification of Production

Clearly the domestic mode of production can only be "a disarray lurking in the background," always present and never happening. It never really happens that the household by itself manages the economy, for by itself the domestic stranglehold on production could only arrange for the expiration of society. Almost every family living solely by its own means sooner or later discovers it has not the means to live. And while the household is thus periodically failing to provision itself, it makes no provision (surplus) either for a public economy: for the support of social institutions beyond the family or of collective activities such as warfare, ceremony, or the construction of large technical apparatus—perhaps just as urgent for survival as the daily food supply. Besides, the inherent underproduction and underpopulation posed by the DMP can easily condemn the community to the role of victim in the political arena. The economic defects of the domestic system are overcome, or else the society is overcome.

The total empirical process of production is organized then as a hierarchy of contradictions. At base, and internal to the domestic system, is a primitive opposition between "the relations" and "the forces": domestic control becomes an impediment to development of the productive means. But this contradiction is reduced by imposing upon it another: between the household economy and the society at large, the domestic system and the greater institutions in which it is inscribed. Kinship, chieftainship, even the ritual order, whatever else they may be, appear in the primitive societies as economic forces. The grand strategy of economic intensification enlists social structures beyond the family and cultural superstructures beyond the productive practice. In the event, the final material product of this hierarchy of contradictions, if still below the technological capacity, is above the domestic propensity.[1]

The foregoing announces the overall theoretical line of our inquiry, the perspectives opened up by analysis of the DMP. At the same time, it suggests the course of further discussion: the play of kinship and politics on production. But to avoid a sustained discourse on generalities, to give some promise of applicability and verification, it is necessary first to attempt some measure of the impact of concrete social systems upon domestic production.

## On a Method for Investigating the Social Inflection of Domestic Production

Given a system of household production for use, theory says that the intensity of labor per worker will increase in direct relation to the domestic ratio of consumers to workers (Chayanov's rule).[2] The greater the relative number of consumers, the more each producer (on average) will have to work to provide an acceptable per capita output for the household as a whole. Fact, however, has already suggested certain violations of the rule, if only because domestic groups with relatively few workers are especially liable to falter. In these households, labor intensity falls below the theoretical expectation. Yet more important—because it accounts for some of the domestic default, or at least for its acceptability—the real and overall social structure of the community does not for its own part envision a Chayanov slope of intensity, if only because kin and political relations between house-

1. The determination of the main organization of production at an infrastructural level of kinship is one way of facing the dilemma presented by primitive societies to Marxist analyses, namely, between the decisive role accorded by theory to the economic base and the fact that the dominant economic relations are in quality superstructural, e.g., kinship relations (see Godelier, 1966; Terray, 1969). The scheme of the preceding paragraphs might be read as a transposition of the infrastructure-superstructure distinction from different types of institutional order (economy, kinship) to different orders of kinship (household versus lineage, clan). In truth, however, the present *problématique* was not directly framed to meet this dilemma.

2. The same can be phrased also as an inverse relation between intensity and the proportion for workers, a formulation used earlier and to which we return presently

holds, and the interest in others' welfare these relations entail, must impel production above the norm in certain houses in a position to do so. That is to say, a social system has a specific structure and inflection of household labor intensity, deviating in a characteristic way and extent from the Chayanov line of normal intensity.

I offer two extended illustrations, from two quite different societies, to suggest that the Chayanov deviation can be depicted graphically and calculated numerically. In principle, with a few statistical data not difficult to collect in the field, it should be possible to construct an intensity profile for the community of households, a profile that indicates notably the amount and distribution of surplus labor. In other words, by the variation in domestic production, it should be possible to determine the economic coefficient of a given social system.

The first example returns to Thayer Scudder's study of cereal production in the Valley Tonga village of Mazulu. This study was considered earlier in connection with domestic differences in subsistence production (Chapter 2). Table 3.1 presents the Mazulu materials in fuller form and in a different arrangement now including the number of consumers and gardeners by household and the domestic indices of labor composition (consumers/gardeners) and labor intensity (acres/gardener). The Mazulu data offer no direct measure of labor intensity, such as the actual hours people work; intensity has to be understood indirectly by the surface cultivated per worker. Immediately an error of some unknown degree is introduced, since the effort expended/acre is probably not the same for all gardeners. Moreover, in the attempt to account for the fractional dietary requirements and labor contributions of different sex and age classes, some estimates had to be made, as a detailed census is not available and the population breakdown in Scudder's production tables (1962, Appendix B) is not entirely specific. Insofar as possible, I apply the following rough and apparently reasonable formula for assessing consumption requirements: taking the adult male as standard (1.00), preadolescent children are computed as 0.50 consumers and adult women as 0.80 consumers.[3] (This is why the consumer column yields a figure less

---

3. All persons indicated in Scudder's table as "unmarried people for whom the wife

(continued on p. 106)

Table 3.1. *Household variations in intensity of labor: Mazulu Village, Valley Tonga, 1956-57 (after Scudder, 1962, pp. 258-261)*

| Household | Number of Members | Number of Consumers | Number of Gardeners | Total Acreage Cultivated | Ratio of Consumers/ Gardener | Acres Cultivated/ Gardener |
|-----------|-------------------|---------------------|---------------------|--------------------------|------------------------------|----------------------------|
| O | 1 | 1.0 | 1.0 | 1.71 | 1.00 | 1.71 |
| Q | 5 | 4.3 | 4.0 | 6.06 | 1.08 | 1.52 |
| B | 3 | 2.3 | 2.0 | 2.58 | 1.15 | 1.29 |
| S | 3 | 2.3 | 2.0 | 6.18 | 1.15 | 3.09 |
| A | 8 | 6.6 | 5.5 | 12.17 | 1.20 | 2.21 |
| D* | 2 | 1.3 | 1.0 | 2.26 | 1.30 | 2.26 |
| C | 6 | 4.1 | 3.0 | 7.21 | 1.37 | 2.40 |
| M | 6 | 4.1 | 3.0 | 6.30 | 1.37 | 2.10 |
| H | 6 | 4.3 | 3.0 | 5.87 | 1.43 | 1.96 |
| R | 7 | 5.1 | 3.5 | 7.33 | 1.46 | 2.09 |
| G | 10 | 7.6 | 5.0 | 10.11 | 1.52 | 2.02 |
| K† | 14 | 9.4 | 6.0 | 7.88 | 1.57 | 1.31 |

| Household | Number of Members | Number of Consumers | Number of Gardeners | Total Acreage Cultivated | Ratio of Consumers/ Gardener | Acres Cultivated/ Gardener |
|---|---|---|---|---|---|---|
| I | 5 | 3.3 | 2.0 | 4.33 | 1.65 | 2.17 |
| N | 5 | 3.3 | 2.0 | 4.55 | 1.65 | 2.28 |
| P | 5 | 3.3 | 2.0 | 4.81 | 1.65 | 2.41 |
| E | 8 | 5.8 | 3.5 | 7.80 | 1.66 | 2.23 |
| F | 9 | 5.6 | 3.0 | 9.11 | 1.87 | 3.04 |
| T | 9 | 6.1 | 3.0 | 6.19 | 2.03 | 2.06 |
| L* | 7 | 4.1 | 2.0 | 5.46 | 2.05 | 2.73 |
| J | 4 | 2.3 | 1.0 | 2.36 | 2.30 | 2.36 |

*In families D and L, the head of the house was absent in European employ during the entire period. He is not calculated in the household's figures, although the money he brings back to the village will presumably contribute to the family's subsistence.

†The head of the house, K, worked part time in European employ. He also cultivated and figures in the computations for his household.

than the total household size, and usually not a whole number.) Finally, adjustments had to be made for calculation of the domestic labor force. A few very small plots appearing in Scudder's table were evidently the work of quite young persons; probably these were training plots in the charge of younger adolescents. Gardeners listed by Scudder as cultivating less than 0.50 acres and belonging to the youngest generation of the family are thus counted as 0.50 workers.

Manifestly, I must insist on the illustrative character of the Mazulu example. In addition to the several errors potentially introduced by one's own manipulations, the very small numbers involved—there are only 20 households in the community—cannot inspire a grand statistical confidence. But as the aim is merely to suggest a feasibility and not to prove a point, these several deficiencies, while surely regrettable, do not seem fatal.[4]

What then do the Mazulu materials illustrate? For one, that Chayanov's rule holds—in a general way. That the rule holds in general, although not in detail, is evident by inspection of the final columns of Table 3.1. The acreage cultivated/gardener mounts in rough relation to the domestic index of consumers/gardener. A procedure like Chayanov's own would show the same, with a little more exactness. Following Chayanov's methods, Table 3.2 groups the variation in acreage/worker by regular intervals of the consumer/worker index:

---

must cook", and who were not further tabulated as gardeners, were counted as preadolescent children. Probably some dependent elders have thus slipped in as 0.50 consumers.

    4. Besides incertainties in the data, there are external complications, some of which are indicated in footnotes to Table 3.1. One, however, must be considered in greater detail. There is a modest amount of cash cropping in Mazulu, mainly of tobacco, with the proceeds invested principally in animal stock. The effects upon the domestic production of cereals are not altogether clear, but the figures on hand probably have not been seriously deformed by crop sales. The total volume of produce sale is quite limited; of subsistence crops in particular, insignificant. At the time of study, Scudder writes, "most valley Tonga were essentially subsistence cultivators who rarely sell a guinea's worth of produce per annum" (1962, p. 89). Nor did cash cropping appear an alternative to subsistence gardening, that is, as a means of food purchase, so capable of direct interference in cereal cultivation. Finally, in such cases of simple commodity production, it must be considered whether trade actually removes the exchangeable food surplus from internal community circulation. It happens that those Tongan farmers who convert produce into animal stock are precisely the ones most subject to imperious requests from relatives at times of food shortage—for animals constitute a reserve that may be again sold for grain (pp. 89 f, 179-180; Colson, 1960, p. 38 f).

*Table 3.2.  Household variations in acreage/gardener: Mazulu\**

| Consumers/Worker | 1.00-1.24 | 1.25-1.49 | 1.50-1.74 | 1.75-1.99 | 2.00+ |
|---|---|---|---|---|---|
| Average household acreage/gardener | 1.96 | 2.16 | 2.07 | 3.04 | 3.28 |
| (Number of cases) | (5) | (5) | (6) | (1) | (3) |

*One further complication of the Mazulu data: in richer households able to provide beer for outside workers, some of the labor expended does not come immediately from the domestic group in question. On one hand, then, the figures for acreage cultivated/worker do not do justice to the actual force of the Chayanov principle–richer houses are working less than indicated, poorer more. On the other hand, some portion of the beer so provided may represent the congealed labor of the supplying household, so that over the longer run the slope of intensity/worker is closer again to the data reported. Clearly subtle corrections are necessary, or else direct estimates of hours worked per gardener–both beyond the prerogatives given by the present data.

The results are fairly comparable to those Chayanov and his co-workers found for peasant Russia. Yet the Mazulu table also betrays the rule. Clearly the relation between labor intensity and the household ratio of workers is neither consistent nor proportionate over the entire range. Individual houses deviate more or less radically, but not altogether randomly, from the general trend. And the trend itself does not develop evenly: it takes on an irregular curvature, a specific pattern of rise and fall.

All this trend and variation can be plotted on a single graph. The scatter of points in Figure 3.1 represents the distribution of household differences in labor intensity. Each house is fixed relative to the horizontal *(X)* axis by its ratio of consumers/gardener, and along the vertical *(Y)* axis by the acreage cultivated/gardener (cf. Table 3.1). A midpoint to this variation, a kind of average household, can be determined at $X = 1.52$ (c/w), $Y = 2.16$ (a/w).The overall average tendency of household differences in intensity is then calculable by deviations from this mean, that is, as a linear regression computed according to standard formula.[5] The result for Mazulu, the real inten-

5. $6xy = \Sigma (xy)/ \Sigma (x^2)$, where $x =$ the deviation of each unit from the $x$ mean (c/w mean), $y$ the deviation from the $y$ (a/w) mean. Given the limited and scattered

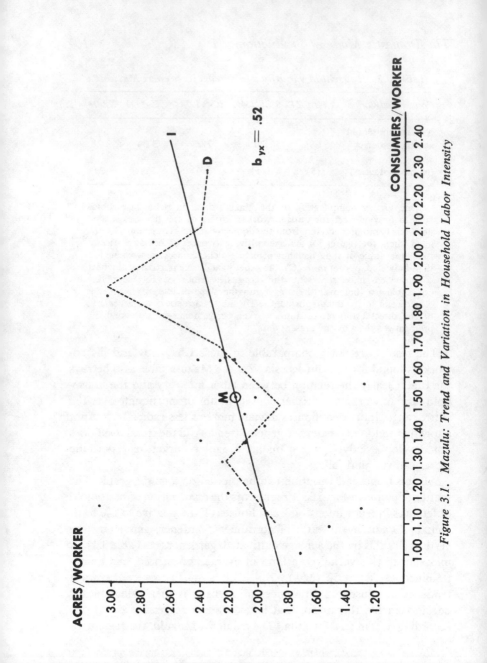

Figure 3.1. *Mazulu: Trend and Variation in Household Labor Intensity*

sity slope of the community, amounts to an increase of 0.52 acres/worker *(Y)* for each additional 1.00 in the ratio of consumers to workers *(X)*. But artificially so. The broken line *(D)* of Figure 3.1 seeks out the truer course of variation, the important propensity to depart from a linear relation between intensity and composition. This line, the *real intensity curve,* is constructed after the mean intensities (columnar means) of 0.20 intervals in the consumers/worker ratio. Note that the curve would have taken a somewhat different path if plotted from the values of Table 3.2. But with so few cases at hand, 20 households, it is difficult to say which version is more valid. Statistical intuition might hold that with more instances the Mazulu curve would be sigmoidal (an ⌒ curve), or perhaps concave upward to the right in exponential fashion. Both of these patterns, and others besides, occur in Chayanov's own tables. What seems more important, however, and consistent with accomplished understandings, is that the variation in labor intensity increases toward both extremes of the c/w range, disturbing or even reversing the more regular incline of the medial section. For at the extremes of household composition, Chayanov's rule becomes vulnerable to contradiction. On one side are households weak in manpower and subject to one or another crippling malchance. (Household J in the Mazulu series, represented by the point furthest right, is an instance in question: a woman widowed at the beginning of the cultivation period and left to support three preadolescent children.) On the other side, the decline of the intensity curve to the left is arrested at some moment because certain domestic groups well endowed in workers are functioning beyond their own necessity. From that point of view (that is, of their own customary requirements), they are working at surplus intensities.

But the surplus output is not exactly indicated by the foregoing procedure. For this it is necessary to construct a *slope of normal intensity,* drawn as much from theory as from reality: a slope describing the variation in labor that would be required to supply each household the customary livelihood, supposing each were left to pro-

---

distribution of household differences, it should be stressed that the regression in the Mazulu case (and in subsequent cases treated) has little predictive or inductive value. It has been adopted here simply as a description of the main drift in the variations.

vision itself. It is necessary, in other words, to project the domestic mode of production as if unimpeded by the larger structures of society. The performance to which the DMP as such is disposed, this line of normal intensity might also then be deemed the true Chayanov slope, for it represents the most rigorous statement of the Chayanov rule. Insofar as it is predicated on production to a definite and customary goal, Chayanov's rule does not admit just any proportionate relation between intensity and relative working capacity. In principle it stipulates strictly the slope of this relation: the domestic intensity of labor must increase by a factor of the customary consumption requirement for every increase of 1.00 in the domestic ratio of consumers to workers. Only in that event will the same (normal) output per capita be achieved by each household, regardless of its particular composition. This, then, is the intensity function that conforms to the theory of domestic production—as the deviation from it in actual practice conforms to the character of the larger society.

How do we determine the true Chayanov slope for Mazulu? According to Scudder, 1.00 acres under cultivation per capita should yield an acceptable subsistence. But "per capita" here applies indiscriminately to men, women and children. As by our earlier computation the village population of 123 reduces to 86.20 full consumers (adult male standard), each consumer of account will demand 1.43 acres for a normal subsistence. The true Chayanov slope is therefore a straight line departing from the origin of both dimensions and rising 1.43 acres/gardener for every increase of 1.00 in the domestic ratio of consumers to workers.

Before proceeding to measure real deviations from this slope, some decision has to be taken between alternative formulations of the Chayanov rule, as this has a practical bearing on the representation of normal intensity. Most of the preceding discussion has been content to refer to intensity rising with the relative number of consumers. Yet the law of Chayanov is just as well expressed as an inverse relation between domestic intensity and the relative number of producers; that is, the fewer the producers to consumers, the more each will have to work. Logically, the two propositions are symmetrical. But sociologically, perhaps not. The first seems to better express the operative constraints, the burdens imposed upon able-bodied producers by the dependents they must feed. Probably that is why Chayanov in effect preferred the direct formulation, and I shall continue to do so.[6]

In Figure 3.2, then, the Chayanov line *(C)* rises upward to the right, intensity increasing with the relative number of consumers by the calculated factor of 1.43 a/w per 1.00 c/w. The line threads its way through a scatter of points. Once more these stand for the *de facto* household differences in labor intensity. But in juxtaposition to the true Chayanov slope, their meaning is transformed: They tell now of the modification imparted to domestic production by the greater organization of society.This modification is summarized also by the deviation of the real intensity slope *(I)* from the Chayanov, insofar as the former— 0.52 a/w for each 1.00 c/w from the means of intensity and composition—represents a reduction of household production differences to their main drift. The positioning of these lines, their manner of intersection within the range of known domestic variations, makes a profile specific to that community of the societal transformation of domestic production (Figure 3.2).

The Mazulu profile can be sharpened and certain of its configurations measured. The empirical production slope *(I)* passes upward to the left of the Chayanov intensity *(C)*, to an important extent because certain households, among them many with favorable manpower resources, are cultivating above their own requirements. They are working at surplus intensities, not simply for their own use, because they are included in a social system of production, not simply a domestic system. They contribute to the larger system *surplus domestic labor.*

Eight of the 20 Mazulu producing groups are so engaged in extraordinary efforts, as shown in Table 3.3. Their own average manpower structure is 1.36 consumers/worker, and their mean intensity 2.40 acres/gardener. Let us mark this point of mean surplus labor, point *S,* on the Mazulu profile (Figure 3.2). Its coordinates express the Mazulu strategy of economic intensification. The vertical distance of *S* over the slope of normal intensity (segment *ES* ) constitutes the mean impulse to surplus labor among productive houses: 0.46 acres/worker or 23.60 percent (as normal intensity at 1.36 c/w is 1.94 a/w). There are 20.50 effective producers in these houses, or 35.60 of the

6. For a diagrammatic indication of Chayanov's rule formulated as an inverse relation, see the interesting analysis of the covariation between domestic labor force and preferred intensities of labor among Indian farm families presented in' Clark and Haswell, 1964, p. 116.

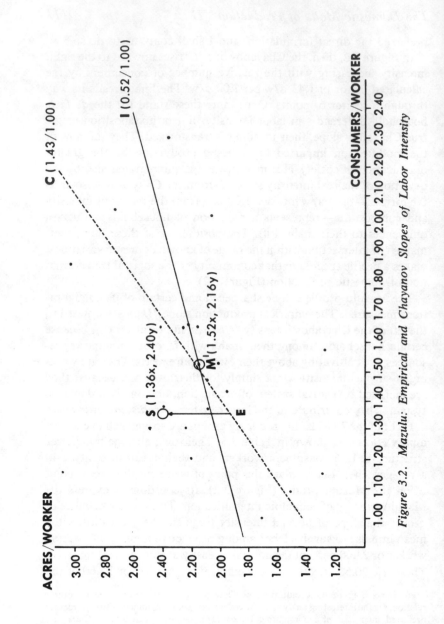

Figure 3.2. Mazulu: Empirical and Chayanov Slopes of Labor Intensity

Table 3.3.  Normal and empirical variations in
domestic labor intensity: Mazulu

| House | Consumers/ Gardener (X) | Acres/ Gardener (Y) | Chayanov Intensity Acres/Gardener (Cy) | Deviation from True Chayanov Slope (Y-Cy) |
|---|---|---|---|---|
| O | 1.00 | 1.71 | 1.43 | +.28 |
| Q | 1.08 | 1.52 | 1.54 | -.02 |
| B | 1.15 | 1.29 | 1.65 | -.36 |
| S | 1.15 | 3.09 | 1.65 | +1.44 |
| A | 1.20 | 2.21 | 1.72 | +.49 |
| D | 1.30 | 2.26 | 1.86 | +.40 |
| C | 1.37 | 2.40 | 1.96 | +.44 |
| M | 1.37 | 2.10 | 1.96 | +.14 |
| H | 1.43 | 1.96 | 2.04 | -.08 |
| R | 1.46 | 2.09 | 2.09 | 0 |
| G | 1.52 | 2.02 | 2.17 | -.15 |
| K | 1.57 | 1.31 | 2.25 | -.94 |
| I | 1.65 | 2.17 | 2.36 | -.19 |
| N | 1.65 | 2.28 | 2.35 | -.08 |
| P | 1.65 | 2.41 | 2.36 | +.05 |
| E | 1.66 | 2.23 | 2.37 | -.14 |
| F | 1.87 | 3.04 | 2.67 | +.37 |
| T | 2.03 | 2.06 | 2.90 | -.84 |
| L | 2.05 | 2.73 | 2.93 | -.20 |
| J | 2.30 | 2.36 | 3.29 | -.93 |

village labor force. Thus 40 percent of the domestic producing groups, comprising 35.60 percent of the working force, are functioning at a mean of 23.60 percent above the normal intensity of labor. So for the *Y*-value of *S.*

The *X* coordinate of the surplus impulse *(S)* will by its relation to mean household composition *(M)* provide an indication of how the intensification tendency is distributed in the community (Figure 3.2). The further *S* falls to the left of the mean composition *(X* = 1.52 c/w), the more surplus labor is a function of higher proportions of workers in the domestic group. A position of *S* nearer the mean, however, indicates a more general participation in surplus labor: further still to the right, *S* would imply an unusual economic activity in households of lesser labor capacity. For Mazulu, the mean surplus impulse *(S)* is clearly left of the village mean. Six of the eight houses functioning at surplus intensities are below average in their ratios of consumers/worker. For all eight, the mean composition is lower than the community average by 0.16 c/w or 10.50 percent.

Finally it is possible from the materials on hand (Tables 3.1 and 3.3) to compute the contribution of surplus (domestic) labor to the total village product. This is done by first calculating the sum of surplus acreage in the several houses producing above normal intensity (number of workers multiplied by the rate of surplus labor for the eight relevant cases). The output thus attributable to surplus labor is 9.21 acres. The total cultivations of Mazulu amount to 120.24 acres. Hence, 7.67 percent of the total village output is the product of surplus labor.

It has to be emphasized that "surplus labor" applies strictly to the domestic groups, and that it is "surplus" in relation to their normal consumption quota. Mazulu village as a whole does not show a surplus expenditure of labor. It is testimony rather to the character and relative ineffectiveness of the existing social strategy that the total acreage cultivated falls slightly below village requirements. (Thus at the point of mean household composition [1.52 c/w], the empirical inflection of production [$I$] passes under the true Chayanov slope [$C$].) A nonproductive class could not live on the output of the Mazulu villagers—at least not without substantial contradiction and potential conflict.

The mathematical reason for village underproduction is obvious. If some domestic groups are functioning above normal intensity, others are working below, to the extent that village output is on balance slightly negative. But this distribution is not accidental. On the contrary, the entire production profile *should be understood as an integrated social system* in its projection of normal domestic intensity as well as its empirical labor slope, in its dimension of domestic underproduction as well as domestic surplus. The subintensive output of some houses is not independent of the surplus labor of others. True that (as far as our information goes) household economic failures seem attributable to circumstances external to the organization of production: illness, death, European influence. Yet it would be misleading to contemplate these failures in isolation from the successes, as if certain families simply proved unable to make it for reasons entirely their own. Some may not have made it precisely because it was clear in advance they could depend on others. And even the underproduction due to unforeseen circumstances is acceptable to society, these vulnerable households tolerable, by virtue of a surplus intensity elsewhere, which in a sense had anticipated in its own dynamic a certain social incidence of domestic tragedy. In an intensity profile such as Figure 3.3, we have to deal with an interrelated distribution of household economic variations—that is, with a social system of domestic production.

The Kapauku of western New Guinea have another system, very different in its pattern, much more pronounced in its strategy of intensification. But then, Kapauku is another *political* system, capable of harnessing domestic economic efforts to the accumulation of exchangeable products, pigs and sweet potatoes primarily, whose sale and distribution are main tactics of an open competition for status (Pospisil, 1963).

Sweet potato cultivation is the key sector of production. The Kapauku to a very large extent, and their pigs to a lesser extent, live by sweet potato. It accounts for over 90 percent of the agricultural land use and seven-eighths of the agricultural labor. Yet the domestic differences in sweet potato production are extraordinary: a tenfold range of variation in output/household as recorded by Pospisil for the 16 houses of Botukebo village over an eight-month period (Table 3.4).

Again for Kapauku we know the intensity of labor only by its product. The intensity column of Table 3.4 is presented as kilograms of sweet potato produced per worker—probably introducing an error analogous to the corresponding Mazulu figures, insofar as different workers expend unequal efforts per unit weight of output. I have taken the liberty, moreover, of revising the ethnographer's household consumer counts, bringing them closer in line with other Melanesian societies by assessing adult women at 0.80 of the adult male requirement, rather than the 0.60 Pospisil had computed from a brief dietary study. (For the other members of the household, children were figured at 0.50 consumers, adolescents at 1.00 and elders of both sexes at 0.80.) Adolescents were calculated at 0.50 workers, following the ethnographer's usage.

Domestic differences in labor intensity compose a very distinctive pattern. No clear Chayanov trend is evident on inspection of Table 3.4. But the apparent irregularity polarizes, or, rather, resolves itself

Table 3.4. Household variation in sweet potato cultivation: Botukebo village, Kapauku (New Guinea), 1955 (after Pospisil, 1963)

| Household (Ethnographer's Code) | Number of Members | Adjusted No. of Consumers* Pospisil | Adjusted No. of Consumers* Revised | Number of Workers | Kilograms/ Household | Ratio of Consumers/Worker (Revised) | Intensity (Kilograms/ Worker) |
|---|---|---|---|---|---|---|---|
| IV | 13 | 8.5 | 9.5 | 8.0 | 16,000 | 1.19 | 2,000 |
| VII | 16 | 10.2 | 11.6 | 9.5 | 20,462 | 1.22 | 2,154 |
| XIV | 9 | 7.3 | 7.9 | 6.5 | 7,654 | 1.22 | 1,177 |
| XV | 7 | 4.8 | 5.6 | 4.5 | 2,124 | 1.25 | 472 |
| VI | 16 | 10.1 | 11.3 | 9.0 | 6,920 | 1.26 | 769 |
| XIII | 12 | 8.9 | 9.5 | 7.5 | 2,069 | 1.27 | 276 |
| VIII | 6 | 5.1 | 5.1 | 4.0 | 2,607 | 1.28 | 652 |
| I | 17 | 12.2 | 13.8 | 10.5 | 9,976 | 1.31 | 950 |
| XVI | 5 | 3.2 | 4.0 | 3.0 | 1,557 | 1.33 | 519 |
| III | 7 | 4.8 | 5.4 | 4.0 | 8,000 | 1.35 | 2,000 |
| V | 9 | 6.4 | 7.4 | 5.5 | 9,482 | 1.35 | 1,724 |
| II | 18 | 12.4 | 14.6 | 10.5 | 20,049 | 1.39 | 1,909 |
| XII | 15 | 9.5 | 10.7 | 7.5 | 7,267 | 1.44 | 969 |
| IX | 12 | 8.9 | 9.5 | 6.5 | 5,878 | 1.46 | 904 |
| X | 5 | 3.6 | 3.8 | 2.5 | 4,224 | 1.52 | 1,690 |
| XI | 14 | 8.7 | 9.1 | 4.5 | 8 898 | 2.02 | 1,978 |

*See text for discussion of "revised" consumer estimates.

†Calculated at adults (♀ and ♂) = 1.00 worker, adolescents and elders of both sexes at 0.50 worker.

into two regularities once the household variations are plotted in graph (Figure 3.3). Everything appears as if the Kapauku village were divided into two populations, each adhering singularly to its own economic inclination in one case, something of a Chayanov trend, intensity increasing with the relative number of consumers, yet in the other "population" just the reverse. And not only are houses of the latter series industrious in proportion to their working capacity, the group as a whole stands at a distinctly higher level than the households of the first series. But then the Kapauku have a big-man system of the Classic Melanesian type (see below, "The Economic Intensity of the Social Order"), a political organization that typically polarizes people's relations to the productive process: grouping on one side the big-men or would-be big-men and their followers, whose production they are able to galvanize, and on the other side those content to praise and live off the ambition of others.[7] The idea seems worth a prediction: that this bifurcate, "fish-tail" distribution of domestic labor intensity will be found generally in the Melanesian big-man systems.

Although not evident to inspection, a light Chayanov trend does actually inhere in the scatter of household intensity variations. It has to be picked up mathematically (again as a linear regression of deviations from the means). On balance, the slope of domestic labor intensity moves upward to the right at the rate of 1,007 kilograms of sweet potato/gardener for each increase (from the mean) of 1.00 in the consumers/gardener ratio. Considered by their respective standard deviations, however, this Kapauku inflection is flatter than the Mazulu empirical slope. In z-units, $b_{yx} = 0.62$ for Mazulu, 0.28 for Botukebo.) Yet more interesting, the Kapauku real inflection stands in an entirely different relation to its slope of normal intensity (Figure 3.4).

I have plotted the slope of normal intensity (the true Chayanov cline) from Pospisil's brief dietary study covering 20 people over six days. The average adult male ration was 2.89 kilograms of sweet potatoes/day—693.60 kilograms, then, for an eight-month period matching the duration of the production study. An inflection of 694 kilograms/worker for each 1.00 in c/w passes substantially under-

7. Subject to the caveat, actually realized in the Botukebo case, where the big-man's production is not extraordinary, that a leader who has successfully piled up credits and followers may eventually slacken his own particular efforts.

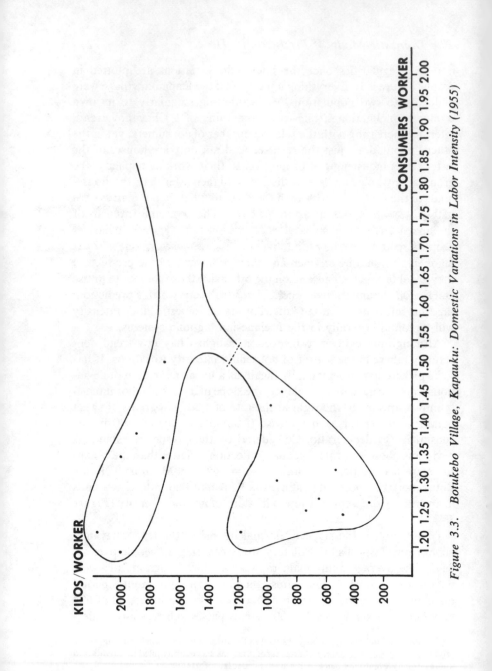

Figure 3.3. *Botukebo Village, Kapauku: Domestic Variations in Labor Intensity (1955)*

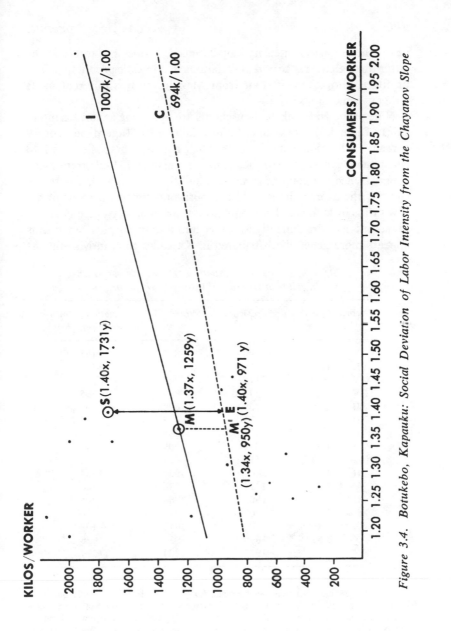

Figure 3.4. Botukebo, Kapauku: Social Deviation of Labor Intensity from the Chayanov Slope

neath the empirical intensity slope, indeed, it does not intersect the latter through the range of real variations in domestic production. The profile is altogether different from Mazulu, and as different in its indicative measures.[8]

Nine of the 16 Botukebo households are operating at surplus intensities (Table 3.5). These nine houses include 61.50 gardeners, or 59 percent of the total working force. Their average composition is 1.40 consumers/gardener, their mean labor intensity, 1,731 kilograms/gardener. Hence the point of mean surplus labor, $S$, falls slightly to the right of the average household composition—by two percent of the c/w ratio. In fact, six of the nine houses are below average composition, but not dramatically so. The impulse to surplus labor thus appears more generally distributed in Kapauku than in Mazulu. At

*Table 3.5. Botukebo, Kapauku: Domestic variation in relation to normal intensity of labor*

| House | C/W | Kilos s.p./Worker | Normal Y | Deviation from Normal Intensity |
|-------|------|-------------------|----------|----------------------------------|
| IV    | 1.19 | 2000 | 825  | +1175 |
| VII   | 1.22 | 2154 | 846  | +1308 |
| XIV   | 1.22 | 1177 | 846  | +331  |
| XV    | 1.25 | 472  | 867  | −395  |
| VI    | 1.26 | 769  | 874  | −105  |
| XIII  | 1.27 | 276  | 881  | −605  |
| VIII  | 1.28 | 652  | 888  | −236  |
| I     | 1.31 | 950  | 909  | +41   |
| XVI   | 1.33 | 519  | 922  | −403  |
| III   | 1.35 | 2000 | 936  | +1064 |
| V     | 1.35 | 1724 | 936  | +788  |
| II    | 1.39 | 1909 | 964  | +945  |
| XII   | 1.44 | 969  | 999  | −30   |
| IX    | 1.46 | 904  | 1013 | −109  |
| X     | 1.52 | 1690 | 1054 | +636  |
| XI    | 2.02 | 1978 | 1401 | +577  |

8. A theoretical argument can be made for inclusion in the domestic quotas of consumption, hence in the slope of normal intensity, an extra amount of sweet potato equivalent to the feed that would be needed to supply a normal per capita pork ration. Apart, however, from arguments also possible to the contrary, the published data do not readily lend themselves to this calculation.

the same time, the strength of this impulse is definitely superior. As expressed by the $Y$ coordinate of $S$, the mean tendency of surplus intensity, at 1,731 kilograms/worker, is 971 kilograms above the normal tendency (segment $SE$). In other words, 69 percent of the Kapauku domestic units, comprising 59 percent of the labor force, are working at an average of 82 percent above normal intensity.

The collective surplus labor of these Kapauku units accounts for 47,109 kilograms of sweet potato. Botukebo total village output is 133,172 kilograms. Thus, 35.37 percent of the social product is the contribution of surplus domestic labor. Taken in comparison with Mazulu (7.67 percent), this figure makes us aware of something heretofore left out of account: the customary household structure is also part of the society's intensification strategy. Botukebo's advantage over Mazulu does not consist solely in a higher rate or more general distribution of surplus labor. Botukebo houses have on average more than twice as many workers, so multiply by that difference their superiority in rate of intensity.

Finally, as the Kapauku intensity profile shows, the effect of surplus labor is to displace real domestic output upward by a sizable amount over the normal. At mean household composition, the empirical inflection of intensity is 309 kilograms/worker (29 percent) higher than the Chayanov slope (segment $M$–$M'$ of Figure 3.4). In terms of the people's own consumption requirements (pigs excluded), Botukebo village as a whole has a surplus output.[9]

Table 3.6 summarizes the differences in production intensity between Mazulu and Botukebo. These differences are the measure of two different social organizations of domestic production.

But clearly the task of research is not finished by the drawing of an intensity profile; it is only thus posed. Before us stretches a work of difficulty and complexity matched only by its promise of an anthropological economics, and consisting not merely in the accumulation of production profiles, but of their interpretation in social terms. For Mazulu and Botukebo this interpretation would dwell on political differences—on the contrast between the big-man system of the Kapauku and traditional political institutions described by the ethno-

9. Pigs included, village production still surpassed the collective subsistence norm (Pospisil, 1963, p. 394f).

Table 3.6. Indices of domestic production: Mazulu and Botukebo

| | Domestic Surplus Impulse* (Intensification Strategy) | | | |
| | Percentage of Households at Surplus Intensity | Percentage of Total Labor Force at Surplus Intensity | Average Production of Surplus in Relation to Normal Intensity | Average Domestic Deviation from Chayanov Norm | Percentage of Total Output Due to Surplus Domestic Labor |
|---|---|---|---|---|---|
| Mazulu | 40 | 35.6 | 123.6 | +2.2% | 7.67 |
| Botukebo | 69 | 59.4 | 182.0 | +32.9% | 35.37 |

*Concerns households working at surplus intensity.

grapher of Tonga as "embryonic," "largely egalitarian" and generally disengaged from the domestic economy (Colson, 1960, pp. 161f). It remains to specify such relations between political form and economic intensification; and also, the less dramatic economic impact of the kinship system, almost imperceptible for its prosaic, everyday character but perhaps not less powerful in the determination of everyday production.

### Kinship and Economic Intensity

The kinship relations prevailing between households must affect their economic behavior. Descent groups and marital alliances of different structure, even interpersonal kin networks of different pattern, should differentially encourage surplus domestic labor. And with varying success, too, kinship relations counter the centrifugal movement of the DMP, to determine a more or less intensive exploitation of local resources. Here then is an idea in some ways banal, in others outrageous, but nevertheless indicative of the kind of problem worth further research: all else being equal, Hawaiian kinship is a more intensive economic system than Eskimo kinship. Because, simply, the Hawaiian system has a greater degree of classification in the Morganian sense: a more extensive identification of collateral with lineal relatives.

Where Eskimo kinship categorically isolates the immediate family, placing others in a social space definitely outside, Hawaiian extends familial relations indefinitely along collateral lines. The Hawaiian household economy risks an analogous integration in the community of households. Everything depends on the strength and spread of solidarity in the kinship system. Hawaiian kinship is in these respects superior to Eskimo. Specifying in this way a wider cooperation, the Hawaiian system should develop more social pressure on households of greater labor resources, especially those of the highest c/w ratios. All other things equal, then, Hawaiian kinship will generate a greater surplus tendency than Eskimo. It will be able also to sustain a higher norm of domestic welfare for the community as a whole. Finally, the same argument implies a greater variation in domestic per capita output for Hawaiian, and a smaller overall variation in intensity per worker.

Besides, the Hawaiian system probably exploits a given territory at a higher level, closer to the technical capacity. For kinship is opposed to the underproduction of the DMP in another way, not just to the centripetal domestic concern for livelihood but to the centrifugal tendency of household dispersion, hence not only to the domestic underuse of labor but to the collective underuse of territory. Against the constituted dispersion of the DMP the system of kinship erects a peace of greater or less effect; so, a corresponding concentration of households and exploitation of resources. The Fijians, who as we have seen conceive a nonrelative as a stranger, hence as a potential enemy and victim, understand by their term "to be acquainted" *(veikilai)* also the meaning "to be related" *(veiweikani)*; and they have no more common word for "peace" than "to live as kinsmen" *(tiko vakavei-weikani)*. Here is one of several primitive versions of that contract lacking in the DMP, a *modus vivendi* where the means of force and production remain segmentary and unalienated. But again different kinship systems, varying in their powers of attraction, must permit varying degrees of spatial concentration. They overcome the fragmentation of domestic production in different measure, and to that extent determine capacities of territorial occupation and exploitation.

Still, the kinship solidarities of primitive societies cannot be undifferentiated, given the inherent cleavages of the domestic mode of production. Even Hawaiian kinship is only formally a universal familiarity; in practice it continually knows invidious distinctions of social distance. The household is never entirely submerged in the larger community, nor are domestic ties ever free from conflict with wider kin relationships. This is a permanent contradiction of primitive society and economy. But it is not an apparent contradiction. Normally it is obscured, repressed by sentiments of sociability that extend to the far reaches of kinship, mystified by an uncritical ideology of reciprocity, above all dissimulated by a continuity of social principles from the family to the larger community, a harmony of organization that makes the lineage seem the household writ large and the chief father to his people. The discovery of the contradiction in the normal course of primitive society therefore takes an act of ethnographic will. Only occasionally comes a crisis, a *crise révélatrice* , to lay bare the structural opposition beyond any possibility of mistaking it. In the absence of that rare chance—or of close observation of the nuances of "reciprocity" (see Chapter 5)—one has recourse at first to certain ethnographic curiosities, proverbs for example, whose elliptical sagesse may put a construction of paradoxes on what seems otherwise a broad sociability.

Thus the same Bemba who define a relative as someone to whom you give food also define a witch as someone "who comes and sits in your house and says, 'I expect you are going to cook soon. What a fine lot of meat you have today,' or 'I expect the beer will be ready this afternoon,' or some such remark" (Richards, 1939, p. 202). Richards reports the artful dodges often employed by Bemba housewives to avoid obligations to share: the concealment of beer upon the appearance of an elderly visiting relative, then met with an, "Alas, Sir, we poor wretches. We have nothing to eat" *(ibid.).*[10]

For the Maori, the conflict between the household and larger interests was current byword: a "squarely-faced opposition," Firth wrote in an early article on the Maori proverbs, a "direct contradiction between sayings which inculcate hospitality and the reverse, liberality and its opposite" (1926, p. 252). On one hand, hospitality "was one of the highest virtues of the native . . . inculcated into all and gained the greatest approval. On the practice of it depended to a large extent reputation and prestige" (p. 247). But Firth was also quick to note a whole set of popular dicta to the contrary. Here were proverbs that privileged an enlightened self-interest over concern for others, the retention of food over its distribution. "Raw food is still possessed," went the adage, "cooked it goes to another"—advising that food be eaten underdone on pain of being obliged to share it out. Or again, "Broil your rat [a favorite Maori dish] with its fur on, lest you be disturbed by someone." One provero recognizes in the noble act of sharing a large residue of discontent:

10. In the same vein, among Ituri Pygmies: "When the hunt returns to camp there is immediate excitement as those who stayed behind crowd around for tales of all that happened, and maybe for a few tidbits of raw meat. In the confusion, men and women alike but particularly women, may be seen furtively concealing some of their spoils under the leaves of their roofs, or in empty pots nearby. For although there will have been some sharing on the scene, there is always more back in the camp, and family loyalty is not that subject to band loyalty that there is no cheating" (Turnbull, 1965, p. 120; cf. Marshall, 1961, p. 231).

> *Haere ana a Manawa yeka*               Glad heart went away,
> *Noho ana a Manawa kuwa*                Bitter mind remained.

Another says this of the irksome cadging of relatives:

> *He huanga ki Matiti*                   A relative in winter,
> *He tama ki Tokerau*                    A son in autumn.

—the man who during the winter planting season is only a distant relative suddenly becomes a son at the autumn harvest.

These contradictions of the Maori proverbial wisdom translate a real conflict of society—"two diametrically opposed principals of conduct working side by side. . . . " Firth, however, did not pause to analyze them as such in their capacity as social facts. He adopted instead that kind of "naive anthropology"[11] conventional to Economic Science: it was at base an opposition between human nature and culture, between the "impulse of the individual to seek his own advantage" and "the expressed morality of the social group." Perhaps Lèvi-Strauss would say the model is after all the Maori's own, for proverb does hold that raw is to cooked as possession is to sharing—that is, nature is to culture as the refusal to share is to reciprocity. In any event, Firth's later detailed analysis of Maori economy (1959a) makes it clear why the opposition of principle was drawn specifically along the line distant relative/son. It was a conflict between extended kinship and the homebred self-interest of the *whanau,* the household, "the basic unit of the Maori economy":

> The *whanau* held group-ownership of certain types of property, and also as a body exercised rights to land and its products. Tasks requiring a small body of workers and co-operation of a not very complex order were performed by the *whanau,* and the apportionment of food was largely managed on this basis. Each family group was a cohesive, self-contained unit, managing its own affairs, both social and economic, except as these affected village or tribal policy. Members of a *whanau,* on the whole, ate, and dwelt together in a distinct group (Firth, 1959a, p. 139)[12]

11. The phrase is L. Althusser's. See his discussion of "L'objet du Capital" (Althusser, Rancière, et al.; 1966, Vol. 2).

12. Firth's interpretation of the social conflict of interest as an opposition between the individual and the society unfortunately lends itself to the grand mystification now prevailing in comparative economics, for the elaboration of which anthropologists join with economists to prove that savages are often moved by a crass self-concern, even as businessmen are pursuing higher ends: hence people everywhere act on mixed "economic" and "noneconomic" motives, and, the classic economizing behavior being

The position of the household in these primitive societies is one of constant dilemma and continuous manoeuvre, temporizing always between domestic welfare and broader obligations toward kinsmen in the hope of satisfying the latter without menacing the former. Apart from the paradoxes of the proverbial wisdom, this tug of war does receive one general expression: in the nuances of traditional "reciprocity." For despite the connotation of equivalence, ordinary reciprocal exchanges are often unbalanced; that is, on the strictly material plane. Repayments are only more or less equal to the initial gifts, and they are only more or less direct in time. The variation is correlated notably with kinship distance. Balance is the material relation of distant kinship; closer to home, exchange becomes more disinterested; there is tolerance of delays or even of complete failure to reciprocate. To observe that kinship plays out in social force as it moves out in social distance is not a sufficient explanation or even a very logical one considering the wide extension of familial categories. More pertinent is the segmentary separation of economic interests. What gives this dissipation of kinship solidarity function and definition, makes meaningful such distinctions as "distant relative"/"son," is the economic determination of home as the place where charity begins. The first premise of "kinship distance" is the DMP. Thus, all the discussion of Chapter 5 on the tactical play of reciprocity can be taken as a case in present point.

Despite the constituted contradiction between the household and the larger kindred, instances of structural breakdown that reveal the conflict are few in the primitive societies. All the more valuable, then,

---

everywhere the same in principle, it is universally valid in analysis. On one hand, if the "native" engages in reciprocal exchange to no net material increment, still he may be looking toward a tangible utility, inasmuch as the gift given now when it can be afforded may be returned later on when it is most needed. On the other hand, the bourgeoisie have been known to contribute to charity and otherwise derive spiritual benefits from material profits. The objective returns to a given deployment of resources, whether to maximum material gain or some other use, are thus confused with the economic subject's own final relation to the process. Both are called "utilities" or "ends." The *de facto* returns in this way confounded with the subjective satisfactions, and the motivations of the subject with the nature of his activity, one is permitted to ignore the real differences in the way goods are handled in favor of apparent resemblances in the satisfactions gained. The attempt of the "formalist school" to detach the principle of individual maximization from its bourgeois context and spread it around the world is fatally marked by this confusion. Cf. Burling, 1962; Cook, 1966; Robbins, 1935; Sahlins, 1969.

Firth's succeeding work on Tikopia, especially the restudy (with Spillius) of 1953-54, when he chanced upon this people celebrated for their hospitality during a trial of famine (Firth, 1959b). Nature had dealt Tikopia a double blow: hurricanes struck in January 1952 and March 1953, doing great damage to houses, trees and standing crops. Food shortages followed, in severity varying from district to district and time to time; generally, the worst occurred between September and November 1953, a period the ethnographers describe as "famine."Still, the people on the whole survived, as did the social system. Yet the first was not entirely due to the second. Kinship beyond the household held on in the formal code, but the code was being systematically honored in the breach, so that even as Tikopian society managed a kind of moral continuity it showed itself founded on a basic discontinuity. It was a revealatory crisis. Firth and Spillius speak of "atomization," of the fragmentation of larger kin groups and "closer integration" of the household. "What the famine did," Firth wrote, "was to *reveal* the solidarity of the elementary family" (1959b, p. 84; emphasis mine).

Economic decomposition set in on several fronts, in property and distribution most notably. Even in planning for recovery after the first hurricane, it was (apart from the chiefs) every household for itself: "the use of resources was nearly in every case intended to safeguard family interests. . . . The range of calculation rarely went beyond this" (p. 64). Attempts were made to abrogate traditional kinship privileges of access to family garden areas (p. 70). Land held in common by close kinsmen became a cause of proprietary contention, sometimes pitting brother against brother, sometimes resulting in a definitive division and precise bounding of fraternal claims (Firth, 1959b; Spillius, 1957, p. 13).

The movement in the sphere of food distribution was more complicated. Exchange showed a predictable pulsation between an expansion of sociability and generosity under trial, and a reversion to domestic isolation as the trial turned into disaster.[13] At those times

13. This pulsation is discussed further in Chapter 5. It is controlled on one hand by the rule that generosity tends to be more widely extended when differences in wealth appear within the community, and on the other, by the ability of the social system, given its constituted solidarities, to support this exceptional generosity, an ability that decreases as the general hardship increases

and in the places food shortage was less severe, the household economy would even efface itself: closely related families suspended their
separate existences to pool supplies in a collective oven. But as the
crisis deepened, an opposed tendency set in, made up of two complementary trends: decrease in sharing and increase of theft.[14] Firth estimated that theft reached a level fivefold higher than its incidence
during his first visit twenty-five years earlier, and where formerly it
was restricted mainly to "semi-luxuries" now it was largely theft of
staples—nor were ritual crops immune, or members of chiefly houses
guiltless. "Nearly everyone was stealing and nearly everyone was
robbed" (Spillius, 1957, p. 12). Meanwhile, after the initial wave of
sociability, the frequency and social range of sharing progressively
declined. Instead of food, visitors got only apologies, perhaps disingenuous. Supplies were hidden from kinsmen, even locked up in boxes
and someone left in the house to guard them. Firth describes such
un-Tikopian behavior as this:

> In some cases the kinsman would suspect there was food in his host's
> house; he would sit and chat and wait, hoping that the host would give way
> and use it. But nearly always the host would hold out until the guest had
> gone before unlocking the box and taking out the food (Firth, 1959b, p.
> 83).

Not that there was a war of every family against every family. The
Tikopians remained polite. As Firth wrote, manners continued if
morals degenerated. But the crisis did test certain structural toleranc-
es. It exposed the weakness of that celebrated *"We, the Tikopia"* by
the strength of the private household. The household proved a fortress
of self-interest which in the crisis cut itself apart, raised its social
drawbridges—when it was not engaged in sallies against the gardens
of kith and kin.

The DMP has to be counteracted and transcended. This not simply
for technical reasons of cooperation, but because the domestic economy is as unreliable as it is apparently functional, a private nuisance
and a public menace. The greater kinship system is one important way
it is counteracted. But the continuing hold of the domestic economy
then leaves its mark on the whole society: a contradiction between the

14. In the terms adopted in Chapter 5, pooling and generalized reciprocity were now
declining in the social sphere, as negative reciprocity extended its range.

infrastructure and the superstructure of kinship that is never entirely suppressed but continues in subtle ways to influence the everyday disposition of goods, and under stress may surface to put the whole economy in a state of segmentary collapse.

## The Economic Intensity of the Political Order

Two words are used for feasts [among the Sa'a], *ngäuhe* and *houlaa:* the meaning of the first is "eating," of the second "fame" (Ivens, 1927, p. 60).

"Without feasts" [a Wogeo man] said, "we would not collect all our chestnuts nor plant so many trees. We would perhaps have enough to eat, but we would never have any really big meals" (Hogbin, 1938-39, p. 324).

In the course of primitive social evolution, main control over the domestic economy seems to pass from the formal solidarity of the kinship structure to its political aspect. As the structure is politicized, especially as it is centralized in ruling chiefs, the household economy is mobilized in a larger social cause. This impulse transmitted by polity to production is often attested ethnographically. For although the primitive headman or chief may be himself driven by personal ambition, he incarnates the collective finalities; he personifies a public economic principle in opposition to the private ends and petty self-concerns of the household economy. Tribal powers that be and would-be powers encroach upon the domestic system to undermine its autonomy, curb its anarchy, and unleash its productivity. "The pace of life in a given Manus village" Margaret Mead observed, "the amount of goods in circulation, and therefore the actual amount of goods in existence depend on the number of leaders in that village. It varies with their enterprise, intelligence, and aggressiveness, and the number of their kin whose cooperation they can enlist" (1937a, pp. 216-217).

Conversely, but to the same rule, Mary Douglas introduces her major monograph on the Lele of Kasai as a study in the failure of authority. And she notes immediately the economic consequence: "Those who have had anything to do with the Lele must have noticed the absence of anyone who could give orders with a reasonable hope of being obeyed. . . . The lack of authority goes a long way to explain their poverty" (1963, p. 1). This negative effect we have seen before, especially in relation to underuse of subsistence resources. As Carneiro perceived it for the Kuikuru, and Izikowitz advances a similar appreciation of Lamet, the issue is between a chronic tendency to divide and disperse the community, and, on the other side, the development of political controls which would check this fission and effect an economic dynamic more appropriate to the society's technical capacity.

I discuss this aspect of the primitive political economy only briefly and schematically.

Everything depends on the political negation of the centrifugal tendency to which the DMP is naturally inclined. Otherwise said (and other factors being equal), the approximation to productive capacity accomplished by any given society is a vector of two contending political principles: on one hand, the centrifugal dispersion inscribed in the DMP—already a kind of reflexive mechanism of peace; on the other hand, the accord that can be installed by prevailing institutions of hierarchy and alliance, whose success is measurable rather by the concentration of population. Of course, more than just the tribal authorities are at issue, and more than their intervention against the primitive reflex of fission. The regional intensity of occupation depends too on relations between communities, relations possibly carried on as much by marriages and lineages as by constituted authorities. My concern here is merely to indicate the *problématique:* each political organization harbors a coefficient of population density, thus in conjunction with the ecological givens, a determinate intensity of land use.

The second aspect of the general problem, the effect of polity upon household labor, I discuss in greater detail. This in part because more ethnographic detail is available. It is even possible to isolate certain formal qualities of leadership structure that imply different degrees of domestic productivity, so hold out the hope of analysis in terms of a social intensity profile. Before these flights of typology, however, we should first consider the structural and ideological means by which power in the primitive societies is realized in production.

The impact of the political system upon domestic production is not

unlike the impact of the kinship system. But then, the organization
of authority is not differentiated from the kinship order, and its economic effect is best understood as a radicalization of the kinship
function. Even many of the greatest African chiefs, and all those of
Polynesia, were not disengaged from the kinship nexus, and it is this
which renders comprehensible the economics of their political acts—
as well as the politics of their economics. Thus I specifically exclude
from this discussion true kings and states, to speak only of societies
where kinship is king and the "king" only a superior kinsman. At the
most we have to deal with "chiefs" properly so-called, and chieftainship is a political differentiation of a kinship order—as kingship is
usually a kinship differentiation of a political order (State). Moreover,
what is true of the most advanced form, chieftainship, is *à plus forte
raison* true of all other kinds of tribal leaders: they hold positions in
and of a network of kinship. And as it is structurally, so ideologically
and in practice the economic role of the headman is only a differentiation of kinship morality. Leadership is here a higher form of kinship,
hence a higher form of reciprocity and liberality. This repeats itself
in ethnographic descriptions from all over the primitive world, even
to the dilemmas posed by chiefly obligations of generosity:

> The [Nambikwara] chief must not merely do well: he must try, and his
> group will expect him to try, to do better than the others. How does the
> chief fulfill these obligations? The first and main instrument of his power
> is his generosity. Generosity is among most primitive peoples, and above
> all in America, an essential attribute of power. It has a role to play even
> in those rudimentary cultures where the notion of property consists merely
> in a handful of rudely fashioned objects. Although the chief does not seem
> to be in a privileged position, from the material point of view, he must have
> under his control surplus quantities of food, tools, weapons, and ornaments
> which, however trifling in themselves, are nonetheless considerable in
> relation to the prevailing poverty. When an individual, a family, or the
> band as a whole, wishes or needs something, it is to the chief that an appeal
> must be made. Generosity is, therefore, the first attribute to be expected
> of a new chief. It is a note which will be struck almost continuously; and
> from the nature, discordant or otherwise, of the sound which results the
> chief can judge of his standing with the band. His "subjects" make the most
> of all this. . . . The chiefs were my best informers; and as I knew the
> difficulties of their position I liked to reward them liberally. Rarely, howev-
> er, did any of my presents remain in their hands for more than a day or

two. And when I moved on, after sharing for several weeks the life of any particular band, its members rejoiced in the acquisition of axes, knives, pearls, and so forth from my stores. The chief, by contrast, was generally as poor, in material terms, as he had been when I arrived. His share, which was very much larger than the average allowance, had all been extorted from him (Lévi-Strauss, 1961, p. 304).

The same refrain appears in the complaint of the Tahitian priest-chief, Ha'amanimani, to the Duff missionaries:

"You give me," says he, "much parow [talk] and much prayers to the Eatora [God], but very few axes, knives, scissars, or cloth." The case is, that whatever he receives he immediately distributes among his friends and dependents; so that for all the numerous presents he had received, he had nothing now to shew, except a glazed hat, a pair of breeches, and an old black coat, which he had fringed with red feathers. And this prodigal behaviour he excuses by saying that, were he not to do so, he should never be a king *(sic)*, nor even remain a chief of any consequence (Duff Missionaries, 1799, pp. 224-225).

This benevolent interest of the headman in the process of distribution, and the political energy he accumulates therefrom, are generated by the field of kinship in which he moves. In one respect it is a matter of prestige. Insofar as the society is socially committed to kin relationships, morally it is commited to generosity; whoever, therefore, is liberal automatically merits the general esteem. Generous, the chief is a paragon among kinsmen. But more profoundly, his generosity is a kind of constraint. "Gifts make slaves," the Eskimo say, "as whips make dogs." Common in any society, this constraint gains in force where the norms of kinship are dominant. Because kinship is a social relation of *reciprocity,* of *mutual* aid; hence, generosity is a manifest imposition of debt, putting the recipient in a circumspect and responsive relation to the donor during all that period the gift is unrequited. The economic relation of giver-receiver is the political relation of leader-follower.[15] This is the working principle. More exactly, it is the operative ideology.

"Ideology" that is revealed as such from the beginning by its con-

15. We shall see shortly that the principle is organized in various ways. But in some instances the entire scheme of rank is left to the free play of generosity, as in Busama, where: "The relation of debtors to creditors forms the basis of the system of leadership" (Hogbin, 1951, p. 122).

tradiction with the larger ideal in which it is fixed, that is, with reciprocity. Always the rank relation, faithful to the qualities of a society it would not abolish, is compensatory. It is conceived in terms of balance, a "mutual helpfulness," a "continual reciprocity."[16] But in strictly material terms the relation cannot be both "reciprocal" and "generous," the exchange at once equivalent and more so. "Ideology," then, because "chiefly liberality" must ignore the contrary flow of goods from people to chief—perhaps by categorizing this as the chief's due—on pain of canceling out the generosity; or else, or in addition, the relation conceals a material unbalance—perhaps rationalized by other kinds of compensation—on pain of negating the reciprocity. We shall find that material unbalances in fact exist; depending on the system, they are borne by one or the other side, headman or people. Yet the conjunction of a norm of reciprocity with a reality of exploitation would not distinguish the primitive political economy from any other: everywhere in the world the indigenous category for exploitation is "reciprocity."[17]

Considered at a more abstract level, the ideological ambiguity of the chiefly office, at once generous and reciprocal, expresses perfectly the contradiction of a primitive nobility: between power and kinship, inequality in a society of amicability. The only reconciliation, of course, is an inequality that is generally beneficial, the only justification of power its disinterestedness; which is to say, economically, a distribution of goods from the chiefs to the people that deepens at the same time it offsets the latter's dependence—and leaves no interpretation of the distribution from people to chiefs but as a moment in a cycle of reciprocity. The ideological ambiguity is functional. On the one hand, the ethic of chiefly generosity blesses the inequality;

---

16. "Mutual helpfulness" (Mead, 1934, p. 335), "continual reciprocity between chief and people" (Firth, 1959a, p. 133), "mutually dependent" (Ivens, 1927, p. 255). For other examples see Richards, 1939. pp. 147–150, 214; Oliver, 1955, p. 342; Drucker, 1937, p. 245. See also Chapter 5. In speaking of "reciprocity" I refer here to the ideological economic relation between headmen and the underlying population, not necessarily to the concrete form. The latter may be technically, "redistribution." Even so, redistribution is conceived and sanctioned as a reciprocal relation, and is in form but a centralization of reciprocities.

17. One reason (or rationale) why Western social science, with its disposition to accept or even privilege the native models, has so much difficulty with "exploitation." Or is it that, having trouble with "exploitation," it is disposed to privilege the native model?

on the other, the ideal of reciprocity denies that it makes any difference.[18]

However it is realized, one thing the ideology of headmanship does not admit: the economic introversion of the DMP. The "liberality" of the chief must stimulate production beyond the usual aims of domestic livelihood, if only in the chief's own household; reciprocity between the ranks will do the same on a more or less general scale. The political economy cannot survive on that restrained use of resources which for the domestic economy is a satisfactory existence.

We return thus to the original point: the political life is a stimulus to production. But it is so to varying degrees. The following paragraphs trace some of the variations in political form that seem to connote differing domestic productivities, beginning with the Melanesian big-man orders.

Open systems of status competition, such as prevail in Melanesia, develop economic impact in the first place from the ambition of aspiring big-men. Intensification appears in their own work and the labors of their own household. The New Guinea Busama clubhouse leader, as Hogbin reports,

> has to work harder than anyone else to keep up his stocks of food. The aspirant for honours cannot rest on his laurels but must go on holding large feasts and piling up credits. It is acknowledged that he has to toil early and late—"His hands are never free from earth, and his forehead continually drips with sweat" (Hogbin, 1951, p. 131).[19]

---

18. If again this ideology seems more widespread than primitive society, perhaps in that respect it can be taken in confirmation of Marx's dictum that what is not visible in modern economy is often seen *en clair* in primitive economy—to which Althusser adds that what is seen *en clair* in primitive economy is that *"l' économique n'est pas directment visible en clair"* (Althusser et al., 1966a, Vol 2, p. 154).

19. Cf. Hogbin, 1939, p. 35; Oliver, 1949, p. 89; 1955, p. 446, for similar passages, or more generally, Sahlins, 1963. One could easily collect the same observations from outside Melanesia. For example: "A man who can afford to acquire all these expensive things which are connected with the cult of the ancestors, and sacrifice so much at these rites, must be a particularly clever person, and thus his reputation and his prestige grow with every feast. In this connection social prestige plays an excessive part, and I should even like to assume that the feast of the ancestors and all connected with it is the driving force in the entire economic and social life of the Lamet. *It forces the more aspiring and ambitious to produce more than what is required for the necessities of life* . . . This striving for prestige plays a particularly important part in the economic life of the Lamet, *and urges them to a surplus production*" (Izikowitz, 1951, pp. 332, 341, emphasis mine).

To this end of accumulation and generosity, the Melanesian leader typically attempts to enlarge his domestic working force, perhaps by polygyny: "'Another woman go garden, another woman go take firewood, another woman go catch fish, another woman cook him— husband he sing out plenty people come kaikai [eat]'" (Landtman, 1927, p. 168). Clearly the Chayanov slope begins to suffer a political deviation; against the rule, certain of the most effective groups are working the most. But the big-man would quickly surpass the narrow base of autoexploitation. Deploying his resources carefully, the emerging leader uses wealth to place others in his debt. Moving beyond his household, he constructs a following whose production may be harnassed to his ambition. The process of intensification in production is thus coupled to reciprocity in exchange. So the Lakalai big-man, with a view toward sponsoring memorial festivals and participating successfully in external trade,

> must not only show personal industry but also be able to call on the industry of others. He must have a following. If he is blessed with many junior kinsmen whose labor he actually commands, he is under less pressure to build up a following. If he is not so blessed, he must acquire his following by assuming responsibility for the welfare of remoter kinsmen. By displaying all of the necessary attributes of a responsible leader, by dutifully sponsoring festivals on behalf of his children, by being ready with wealth to meet his obligations to his in-laws, by buying magic and dances for his children, by assuming whatever burdens he can feasibly carry, he makes himself attractive to older and younger kinsmen alike. . . . His younger kinsmen court his support by volunteering to help him in his undertakings, by cheerfully obeying his calls to work, and by catering to his wishes. They tend increasingly to entrust their wealth to him as trustee in preference to some senior relative (Chowning and Goodenough, 1965– 66, p. 457).

Drawing then from a local group of followers economically engaged to his cause, the big-man opens the final and socially most expansive phase of his ambition. He sponsors or contributes heavily to great public feasts and distributions that reach outside his own circle to establish his dignity, "build his name" Melanesians say, in society at large. For

> the purpose in owning pigs and pig-wealth is not to store them nor to put them on recurrent display: it is to use them. The aggregate effect is a vast

circulating flow of pigs, plumes and shells. The motive force of the flow is the reputation men can gain from ostentatious participation in it. . . . The Kuma "big men" or "men of strength" . . . who command much wealth, are entrepreneurs in the sense they control the flow of valuables between clans by making fresh presentations on their own account and choosing whether or not to contribute to others. Their profit in these transactions is incremental reputation. . . . The aim is not simply to be wealthy, nor even to act as only the wealthy can act: it is to be *known* to be wealthy (Reay, 1959, p. 96).

The big-man's personal career has a general political significance. The big-man and his consuming ambition are means whereby a segmentary society, "acephalous" and fragmented into small autonomous communities, overcomes these cleavages, at least provisionally, to fashion larger fields of relation and higher levels of cooperation. Through concern for his own reputation, the Melanesian big-man becomes a point of articulation in a tribal structure.

It should not be supposed that the big-man of Melanesian type is a necessary condition of the segmentary societies. Chiefs of the Northwest Coast Indian villages achieve the same sort of articulation, and if in their potlatches it is by external feasting similar to the prestige quest of many Melanesian leaders, the chief has an entirely different relation to the internal economy. A Northwest Coast chieftain is a lineage head, and in this capacity is necessarily accorded a certain right to group resources. He is not obliged to establish a personal claim by the dynamic of an autoexploitation put at the others' disposal. Of even greater contrast, a segmentary society may dispense with all but minimal ties between its constituent parts; or else, as in the celebrated case of the Nuer segmentary lineage system, the relations between local groups are fixed mainly and automatically by descent, without recourse to a differentiation among men.

The Nuer pose an alternative to the segmentary politics of personal power and renown: the anonymous and silent government of structure. In classic segmentary lineage systems, headmen have to be content with a local importance at best, and perhaps proven by attributes other than their generosity. The interesting deduction is that the segmentary lineage system has a lower coefficient of intensity than the Melanesian polity.

The Melanesian system can be put to another speculative purpose.

Beyond the contrast it suggests between tribes with and without rulers, in its successive phases of generous autoexploitation and an accumulation funded by reciprocity, the career of the Melanesian big-man makes a transition between two forms of economic authority that elsewhere appear separately and appear to have an unequal economic potential. Autoexploitation is a kind of original and underdeveloped economics of respect. It is often encountered in the autonomous local groups of tribal societies—the Nambikwara "chief" is an example of the genre—and most commonly in the camps of hunters and gatherers:

> No Bushman wants prominence, but Toma went further than most in avoiding prominence; he had almost no possessions and gave away everything that came into his hands. He was diplomatic, for in exchange for his self-imposed impoverty he won the respect and following of all the people there (Thomas, 1959, p. 183).

Authority of this kind has obvious limitations, both economic and political—and the modesty of each sets limits to the other. Only the domestic labor immediately under the control of the headman is politically engaged. While his own household labor pool is expandable to a degree, as by polygyny, neither through structure nor gratitude does the headman gain significant command over the output of other domestic groups. The surplus of one house put to the benefit of others, this *politique* is closest to the ideal of noble liberality—and the weakest economics of leadership. Its principal force is attraction rather than compulsion, and the field of this force is principally restricted to people in direct personal contact with the leader. For under the simple and often capricious technical circumstances, with the labor of so few provisioning it, the headman's "fund of power" (as Malinowski called it) is meagre and rapidly exhausted. Furthermore, it is necessarily diluted in political efficacy, the influence to be had by its distribution, as this distribution is stretched out in social space. The greatest dividends of influence, then, are accrued in the local cohort, and in the form of the respect due a self-effacing generosity. But no one is thereby rendered dependent, and this respect will have to compete with all the other kinds of deference that can be accorded in face-to-face relations. Hence the economic is not necessarily the dominant basis of authority in the simpler societies: by comparison with generational status, or with personal attributes and capacities from the mystical to the oratorical, it may be politically negligible.

At the other extreme is chieftainship properly so-called, as it developed, for example, in high islands of Polynesia, among nomads of interior Asia, and many central and southern African peoples. The contrast of economic and political form seems complete: from autoexploitation—by the sweat of the leader's brow—to tribute, accompanied sometimes by the idea that even to shoulder a burden is beneath the chiefly dignity: for that matter, dignity may require that *he* be carried; from a respect personally accorded to a command structurally bestowed; and from a liberality something less than reciprocal to a reciprocity less than liberal. The difference is institutional. It lies in the formation of hierarchical relations within and between local groups, a regional political frame maintained by a system of chiefs, major and minor, holding sway over segments of greater and lesser order and subordinate all to the one paramount. The integration of parochial groups tenuously broached by Melanesian big-men, if unimaginable to prestigious hunters, is achieved in these pyramidal societies. They are still primitive. The political armature is provided by kinship groups. But these groups make positions of official authority a condition of their organization. Now men do not personally construct their power over others; they come *to* power. Power resides in the office, in an organized acquiesence to chiefly privileges and organized means of upholding them. Included is a specific control over the goods and the services of the underlying population. The people owe in advance their labor and their products. And with these funds of power, the chief indulges in grandiose gestures of generosity ranging from personal aid to massive support of collective ceremonial or economic enterprise. The flow of goods between chiefs and people then becomes cyclical and continual:

> The prestige of a [Maori] chief was bound up with his free use of wealth, particularly food. This in turn tended to secure for him a larger revenue from which to display his hospitality, since his followers and relatives brought him choice gifts. . . . Apart from lavish entertainment of strangers and visitors, the chief also disbursed wealth freely as presents among his followers. By this means their allegiance was secured and he repaid them for the gifts and personal services rendered to him. . . . There was thus a continual reciprocity between chief and people. . . . It was by his accumula-

tion and possession of wealth, and his subsequent lavish distribution of it, that such a man was able to give the spur to . . . important tribal enterprises. He was a kind of channel through which wealth flowed, concentrating it only to pour it out freely again (Firth, 1959a, p. 133).

In advanced forms of chieftainship, of which the Maori is not particularly an illustration, this redistribution is not without material benefit to the chief. If an historical metaphor be permitted: what begins with the would-be headman putting his production to others' benefit, ends, to some degree, with others putting their production to the chief's benefit.

Eventually the ideals of reciprocity and chiefly liberality serve as mystification of the people's dependence. Liberal, the chief only returns to the community what he has received from the community. Reciprocal then? Perhaps he did not return all of that. The cycle has all the reciprocity of the Christmas present the small child gives his father, bought with the money his father had given him. Still this familial exchange is effective socially, and so is chiefly redistribution. Besides, when the timing and diversity of the goods redistributed are taken into consideration, the people may appreciate concrete benefits otherwise unobtainable. In any case, the material residue that sometimes falls to the chief is not the main sense of the institution. The sense is the power residing with the chief from the wealth he has let fall to the people. And in a larger vantage, by thus supporting communal welfare and organizing communal activities, the chief creates a collective good beyond the conception and capacity of the society's domestic groups taken separately. He institutes a public economy greater than the sum of its household parts.

This collective good is also won at the expense of the household parts. Too frequently and mechanically anthropologists attribute the appearance of chieftainship to the production of surplus (for example, Sahlins, 1958). In the historic process, however, the relation has been at least mutual, and in the functioning of primitive society it is rather the other way around. Leadership continually generates domestic surplus. The development of rank and chieftainship becomes, *pari passu*, development of the productive forces.

In brief testimony, the remarkable ability of certain political orders distinguished by advanced ideas of chieftainship to augment and diversify production. Again I use Polynesian examples, partly for the reason that in earlier work I had argued the exceptional productivity of this polity by comparison with the Melanesian (Sahlins, 1963); partly also because a few of the Polynesian societies, Hawaii particularly, take the primitive contradiction between the domestic and public economies to an ultimate crisis—revealatory it seems not only of this disconformity but of the economic and political limits of kinship society.

Comparison with Melanesia would not only compliment the Polynesian achievement in overall production, but for the occupation and improvement of once-marginal areas effected under the aegis of ruling chiefs. To this process the chronic struggles between neighboring chiefdoms often supplied decisive force. Competition probably accounts for a remarkable tendency to invert by culture the ecology of nature: many of the poorer regions of Polynesian high islands were the more intensively exploited. The contrast in this respect between the southeast peninsula of Tahiti and the fertile northwest moved one of Captain Cook's officers, Anderson, to reflect positively Toynbeean: "It shows," he said, "that even the defects of nature . . . have their use in promoting man to industry and art" (cited in Lewthwaite, 1964, p. 33). The Tahitian group is even better known for the integration of offshore atolls in mainland chiefdoms. Here was a political combination of economies so different as to constitute in Melanesia, and even other parts of Polynesia, the basis of entirely different cultural systems. Tetiaroa is the most celebrated example: "the Palm Beach of the South Seas," a complex of thirteen "spit-of-land" coral islets 26 miles north of Tahiti, occupied for marine and coconut production by men of the Pau district chief and as a watering place of the Tahitian nobility. By forbidding all cultivation except coconut and taro on Tetiaroa, the Pau chief forced a continuous exchange with Tahiti. In a punitive action against the chief, Cook once seized 25 canoes en route from Tetiaroa with a cargo of cured fish. "Even in stormy weather, the missionaries [of the Duff] counted 100 canoes on the beach [of Tetiaroa], for there the aristocracy went to feast and fatten, and their flotillas returned 'rich as a fleet of galleons' " (Lewthwaite, 1966, p. 49).

Then again, one might consider the impressive development of taro cultivation in the Hawaiian Islands, notable for its extent, diversity and intensity: the 250-350 different varieties, often recognized for suitability in different microenvironments; the large irrigation networks (as in the Waipio Valley, island of Hawaii, site of a single complex three miles by three-fourths to one mile); irrigation remarkable for the complexity of ditching and protective works (a canal in Waimea, Kauai runs 400 feet around a cliff and up to 20 feet above level, while in the Kalalau Valley a sloping sea wall built of great boulders shelters a broad stretch of shoreward flats); irrigation remarkable again for the utilization of tiny pockets of soil interspersed through rocky lava, and for the terracing of narrow gorges deep into the mountains, "where the least available space has been won." Nor is this to catalogue the manifold ecological specialization of agricultural techniques, the several types of forest as well as wet taro cultivation, and in the swamps a form of chinampa, the "muddyback method." [20]

The relationship between Polynesian chieftainship and the intensification of production can be given historic depth. In Hawaii, at least, the political transformation of marginal areas knows legendary depth: a chief who used his authority to squeeze water out of rocks. On the western side of the Keanae valley, Maui, is a peninsula that stands a mile out to sea and a much longer distance beyond ecological reason: fundamentally barren and rocky, without natural soil, but covered nevertheless with famous acres of taro. Tradition lays the miracle to an old chief, his name now forgotten,

> ... who was constantly at war with the people of Wailua and determined that he must have more good land under cultivation, more food, and more people. So he set all his people to work (they were then living within the valley and going down to the peninsula only for fishing), carrying soil in baskets from the valley down to the lava point. The soil and the banks enclosing the patches were thus, in the course of many years, all transplanted and packed into place. Thus did the watered flats of Keanae originate (Handy, 1940, p. 110).

Perhaps the Hawaiian tradition is not truly historical. Still it is the

20. See Handy, 1940 for these and other details of Hawaiian irrigation. W. Bennett reported of Kauai: "The impressive feature of the agricultural terracing is its tremendous extent. In the valleys in which little disturbance has gone on, particularly the Napali section, the maximum of tillable soil was utilized. On the sides of the valleys the terraces run almost to the base of the great cliffs, where the nature of the talus slopes is not too rocky. Though all these terraces were not irrigated, a great proportion of them were, and the ingenuity of the engineering is remarkable" (1931, p. 21).

true history of Polynesia: a kind of paradigm of which the entire archaeological sequence of the Marquesas as presented by Suggs, for example, is only another version. All Marquesan prehistory recounts the same dialogue between intervalley competition, the exercise of chiefly power, and the occupation and development of marginal areas of the islands (Suggs, 1961).

Is there evidence in Hawaii or Tahiti of political crises comparable to the episode Firth and Spillius described for Tikopia? Do we discover, that is to say, analogous *crises révélatrices,* here exposing the vertical contradiction between the household economy and the chieftainship, as the Tikopian exposed the horizontal contradiction between household and kindred? But then, the Tikopian famine is not irrelevant either to the first question, for the same hurricanes of 1953 and 1954 that shook the kinship structure also almost brought down the chiefs. As the supply of food diminished, economic relations between chiefs and people deteriorated. Customary dues to the clan leaders were neglected; while, to the contrary, stealing from chiefly gardens "became almost barefaced." Said Pa Ngarumea: "When the land is firm people pay respect to the things of the chief, but when there is a famine people go and make sport of them" (Firth, 1959b, p. 92). Moreover, reciprocity in goods is only the concrete mode of the Tikopian political dialogue; its breakdown meant the whole system of political communication was in question. The Tikopian polity had begun to unhinge. An uncommon rift appeared between chiefs and the underlying population. Somber traditions were resurrected— "myths," Spillius considers them—telling how certain chiefs of old, when pressure on the local food supply became unsupportable, drove the commoners en masse off the island. To the present chiefs the idea seemed fantastic, but one private meeting of notables unwittingly provoked a mass mobilization of the people of the Faea district, forewarned by a spirit medium and forearmed to resist a chiefly conspiracy to expel them (Firth, 1959b, p. 93; Spillius, 1957, pp. 16–17). Still the antagonism remained incomplete, the commoners in an undeveloped stage of political consciousness and the chiefs in command throughout. Battle was not given. Indeed, it was never even conceived by Tikopians in the classic form of a popular uprising against the powers that be. On the contrary, it was the chiefs who constituted the danger to the commoners. And to the last, everyone continued to concede the chiefs' traditional privilege of survival, whoever else might have to die—and however much food was being stolen from them. The Tikopian political crisis was thus aborted.[21]

Let us then consider Hawaii, where one can follow conflicts of the same general type to the conclusion of a successful rebellion. Conflicts "of the same general type" in the sense they brought forth the opposition between the chieftainship and domestic interests, but the differences are also important. In Tikopia the political stress was externally induced. It did not unfold from the normal working of Tikopian society, which normally does work, but in the wake of a natural catastrophe. And it could have happened any structural time, at any phase in the development of the system. The political upset in Tikopia was exogenic, abnormal and historically indeterminate. But the rebellions with which Hawaiian traditional history fascinated itself, Hawaiian history had made. They were produced in the normal course of Hawaiian society, and more than endogenic, they were recurrent. These troubles, besides, seem incapable of realization at just any historic stage. They mark rather the maturity of the Polynesian system, the working through of its contradictions to the point of denouement. They reveal the structural limits.

The paramount chiefs of old Hawaii reigned each and independently over a single island, a section of one of the larger islands, sometimes over districts of neighboring islands. The variation is already part of the problem: the tendency, on which traditions discourse at length, for chiefly domains to enlarge and contract, extended once by conquest only to be partitioned again by rebellion. And this cycle was geared to a second, such that the rotation of one would set off the other. Ruling chiefs showed a propensity to "eat the power of the government too much"; that is, to oppress the people economically, which the chiefs found themselves forced to do when the political domain was enlarged, despite their obligations as kinsmen and chiefs to consider the people's welfare, which they nevertheless found difficult to do even when the polity was reduced.

For the administration of merely an ordinary domain would bite deeply into the labor and goods of the common people. The popula-

---

21. Perhaps in part because of the intervention of the colonial power—and the ethnographers who at times acted in quasi-governmental capacity (Spillius, 1957).

tion was dispersed over a wide area; the means of transportation and communication were rudimentary. The chieftainship besides enjoyed no monopoly of force. It had to meet its diverse problems of rule organizationally then, by a certain administrative formation: a bloated political establishment that sought to cope with a proliferation of tasks by a multiplication of personnel, at the same time economizing its scarce real force by an awesome display of conspicuous consumption as intimidating to the people as it was glorifying to the chiefs. But the material weight of this chiefly retinue and the sumptuary airs it affected fell, of course, on the ordinary people. It fell especially on those nearest the paramount, within a range that made transport worthwhile and the threat of sanctions effective. Conscious, it seems, of the logistic burdens they were obliged to impose, the Hawaiian chiefs conceived several means to relieve the pressure, notably including a career of conquest with a view toward enlarging the tributary base. In the successful event, however, with the realm now stretched over distant and lately subdued hinterlands, the bureaucratic costs of rule apparently rose higher than the increases in revenue, so that the victorious chief merely succeeded in adding enemies abroad to a worse unrest at home. The cycles of centralization and exaction are now at their zenith.

At this point, Hawaiian traditions will hint of intrigue and conspiracy mounted against the ruling chief by local followers, perhaps in collusion with distant subjects.[22] The rebellion is launched always by

22. Here is one example of this geopolitics of rebellion: Kalaniopu'u, supreme chief of the large island of Hawaii—the same who was paternal uncle and predecessor of Kamehameha I—held court for a time in the Kona district of the southwest. But, tradition relates, "scarcity of food, after a while, obliged *Kalaniopu'u* to remove his court to the Kohala district [in the northwest], where his headquarters were fixed at Kapaau" (Fornander, 1878–85, Vol. 2, p. 200). What had apparently rendered food scarce in Kona was now repeated in Kohala: "Here the same extravagant, *laissez-faire,* eat and be merry policy continued that had been commenced at Kona, and much grumbling and discontent began to manifest itself among the resident chiefs and cultivators of the land, the 'Makaainana' " *(ibid).* The local grumbling was echoed by a distant rumbling from the outlying district of Puna, across to the island to the southeast. The two factions apparently combine, and the tale then takes on its customary Olympian form, a story of battle joined between great chiefs. The principal rebels were Imakakaloa of Puna and one Nu'uanu, a chief of Ka'u who had once lived in Puna but were now in attendance at Kalaniopu'u's court. These two, as Fornander writes, were "the heads and rallying points" of the unrest. From distant Puna, Imakakaloa "openly resisted the orders of Kalaniopu'u and his ex-

(continued on p. 146)

important chiefs, who of course had their own reasons for challenging the paramount, but had their power to do so as personifications of a more general discontent. The revolt takes form as a court assassination, an armed struggle, or both. And then, as one ethnological bard said, the Hawaiians sat cross-legged upon the ground and told sad stories of the death of kings:

> Many kings have been put to death by the people because of their oppression of the *makaainana* [the commoners]. The following kings lost their lives on account of their cruel exactions on the commoners: Koihala was put to death in Kau, for which reason the district of Kau was called the Wier. Koka-i-ka-lani was an *alii* [chief] who was violently put to death in Kau . . . Enu-nui-kai-malino was an *alii* who was secretly put out of the way by the fishermen in Keahuolu in Kona . . . King Hakau was put to death by the hand of Umi at Waipio valley in Hamakua, Hawaii.[23] Lono-i-ka-makahiki was a king who was banished by the people of Kona. . . . It was for this reason that some of the ancient kings had a wholesome fear of the people (Malo, 1951, p. 195).

It is important that the death of tyrants was taken in charge by men of authority and chiefs themselves. The rebellion was not then a revolution; the chieftainship if overthrown was replaced by a chieftainship. Delivering itself of oppressive rulers, the system did not consequently rid itself of basic contradictions, transcend and transform itself, but continued instead to cycle within the confines of existing institutions. In the object of replacing a bad (exacting) chief by a good (generous) one, the rebellion would have a fair chance of success. In its aftermath, the enlarged political domain would probably fragment, as recalcitrant outdistricts regained their independence. The chieftainship thus decentralized, its economic weight was reduced. Power and oppression returned to the nadir—for the time being.

The epic quality of Hawaiian traditions conceals a more mundane causality. Manifestly, the political cycle had an economic base. The

---

travagant demands for all kinds of property." Nu'uanu, at the side of the paramount, "was strongly suspected of favoring the growing discontent" *(ibid.)* This time, however, the gods were with Kalaniopu'u. Nu'uanu died of a shark bite, and after a series of battles, Imakakaloa was trapped, captured, and duly sacrificed.

23. Hakau is described by another collector of tradition as "rapacious and extortionate beyond endurance of either chiefs or people" (Fornander, 1878–85, vol. 2, p. 76).

great struggles between powerful chiefs and their respective districts were transposed forms of the more essential struggle over domestic labor: whether it was to be more modestly employed in household livelihood or more intensively deployed to political organization. That the chiefs had the right to levy the domestic economy was not contested. The problem was, on one hand, the customary limit to this right, as established by the existing structure, and on the other hand, the regular abuse of it set off by a structural exigency. Hawaiian chieftainship had distanced itself from the people, yet it had never definitively severed the kinship relation. This primitive bond between ruler and ruled remained in force, and with it the usual ethics of reciprocity and chiefly generosity.[24] Malo says of the great storehouses maintained by ruling chiefs that they were "means of keeping the people contented, so they would not desert the king"—this in a passage otherwise remarkable for its political cynicism: "as the rat will not desert the pantry . . . where he thinks food is, so the people will not desert the king while they think there is food in his storehouse" (Malo, 1951, p. 195).

In other words, the chiefly toll on the household economy had a moral limit consistent with the kinship configuration of the society. Up to a point it was the chief's due, but beyond that, highhandedness. The organization set an acceptable proportion between the allocation of labor to the chiefly and domestic sectors. It set a fitting proportion also between retention of the people's goods by the chief and redistribution to the people. It could tolerate only a certain unbalance in these matters. Besides, some propriety ought to be observed. Exaction by force is no customary gift, nor is pillage the chief's due. The chiefs had their own lands, set aside for their support, and received many gifts regularly from the people. When a ruling chief's men seized the people's pigs and plundered their farms, the *"makaainana* were not pleased with this conduct on the part of the king"—it was "tyranny," "abuse of authority" (Malo, 1951, p. 196). Chiefs were too much inclined to work the *makaainana:* "It was a life of weariness . . . they were compelled at frequent intervals to go here and there to do this and that work for the lord of the land" (p. 64). But then let the leader beware: "The people made war on bad kings in old times." Thus did

24. On genealogical idiom see Malo, 1951, p. 52.

the system define and maintain a ceiling on the intensification of domestic production by political means and for public purposes.

Malo, Kamakau and the other custodians of Hawaiian tradition refer habitually to the paramount chiefs as "kings". But the trouble was precisely that they were not kings. They had not broken structurally with the people at large, so they might dishonor the kinship morality only on pain of a mass disaffection. And without a monopoly of force, the probability was that the general discontent would come down on their particular heads. In a comparative perspective, the great disadvantage of the Hawaiian organization was its primitiveness: it was not a state. Its further advance could only have been secured by an evolution in that direction. If Hawaiian society discovered limits to its ability to augment production and polity, this threshold which it had reached but could not cross was the boundary of primitive society itself.

# 4

# The Spirit of the Gift

Marcel Mauss's famous *Essay on the Gift* becomes his own gift to the ages. Apparently completely lucid, with no secrets even for the novice, it remains a source of an unending ponderation for the anthropologist *du métier,* compelled as if by the *hau* of the thing to come back to it again and again, perhaps to discover some new and unsuspected value, perhaps to enter into a dialogue which seems to impute some meaning of the reader's but in fact only renders the due of the original. This chapter is an idiosyncratic venture of the latter kind, unjustified moreover by any special study of the Maori or of the philosophers (Hobbes and Rousseau especially) invoked along the way. Yet in thinking the particular thesis of the Maori *hau* and the general theme of social contract reiterated throughout the *Essay,* one appreciates in another light certain fundamental qualities of primitive economy and polity, mention of which may forgive the following overextended commentary.

## *"Explication de Texte"*

The master concept of the *Essai sur le don* is the indigenous Maori idea *hau,* introduced by Mauss as "the spirit of things and in particular of the forest and the game it contains . . ." (1966, p. 158).[1] The

1. An English translation of *L'Essai sur le don* has been prepared by Ian Cunnison, and published as *The Gift* (London: Cohen and West, 1954).

149

Maori before any other archaic society, and the idea of *hau* above all similar notions, responded to the central question of the *Essay*, the only one Mauss proposed to examine "à fond": *"What is the principle of right and interest which, in societies of primitive or archaic type, requires that the gift received must be repaid? What force is there in the thing given which compels the recipient to make a return?"* (p. 148).

The *hau* is that force. Not only is it the spirit of the *foyer*, but of the donor of the gift; so that even as it seeks to return to its origin unless replaced, it gives the donor a mystic and dangerous hold over the recipient.

Logically, the *hau* explains only why gifts are repaid. It does not of itself address the other imperatives into which Mauss decomposed the process of reciprocity: the obligation to give in the first place, and the obligation to receive. Yet by comparison with the obligation to reciprocate, these aspects Mauss treated only summarily, and even then in ways not always detached from the *hau:* "This rigorous combination of symmetrical and opposed rights and duties ceases to appear contradictory if one realizes that it consists above all of a melange of spiritual bonds between things which are in some degree souls, and individuals and groups which interact in some degree as things" (p. 163).

Meanwhile, the Maori *hau* is raised to the status of a general explanation: the prototypical principle of reciprocity in Melanesia, Polynesia, and the American northwest coast, the binding quality of the Roman *traditio*, the key to gifts of cattle in Hindu India—"What you are, I am; become on this day of your essence, in giving you I give myself" (p. 248).

Everything depends then on the "texte capitale" collected by Elsdon Best (1909) from the Maori sage, Tamati Ranapiri of the Ngati-Raukawa tribe. The great role played by the *hau* in the *Essay on the Gift*—and the repute it has enjoyed since in anthropological economics—stems almost entirely from this passage. Here Ranapiri explained the *hau* of *taonga*, that is, goods of the higher spheres of exchange, valuables. I append Best's translation of the Maori text (which he also published in the original), as well as Mauss's rendering in French.

Best, 1909, p. 439                Mauss, 1966, pp. 158–159

I will now speak of the *hau*, and the ceremony of *whangai hau*. That *hau* is not the *hau* (wind) that blows— not at all. I will carefully explain to you. Suppose that you possess a certain article, and you give that article to me, without price. We make no bargain over it. Now, I give that article to a third person, who, after some time has elapsed, decides to make some return for it, and so he makes me a present of some article. Now, that article that he gives me is the *hau* of the article I first received from you and then gave to him. The goods that I received for that item I must hand over to you. It would not be right for me to keep such goods for myself, whether they be desirable items or otherwise. I must hand them over to you, because they are a *hau* of the article you gave me. Were I to keep such an equivalent for myself, then some serious evil would befall me, even death. Such is the *hau*, the *hau* of personal property, or the forest *hau*. Enough on these points.

Je vais vous parler du *hau*. . . . Le *hau* n'est pas le vent qui souffle. Pas du tout. Supposez que vous possédez un article déterminé *(taonga)* et que vous me donnez cet article; vous me le donnez sans prix fixe. Nous ne faisons pas de marché à ce propos. Or, je donne cet article à une troisième personne qui, après qu'un certain temps s'est écoulé, décide de rendre quelque chose en paiement *(utu)*, il me fait présent de quelque chose *(taonga)*. Or, ce *taonga* qu'il me donne est l'esprit *(hau)* du *taonga* que j'ai recu de vous et que je lui ai donnés à lui. Les *taonga* que j'ai recus pour ces *taonga* (venus de vous) il faut que je vous les rende. Il ne serait pas juste *(tika)* de ma part de garder ces *taonga* pour moi, qu'ils soient désirables *(rawe)*, ou désagreables *(kino)*. Je dois vous les donner car ils sont un *hau* du *taonga* que vous m'avez donné. Si je conservais ce deuxième *taonga* pour moi, il pourrait m'en venir du mal, sérieusement, même la mort. Tel est le *hau*, le *hau* de la propriété personnelle, le *hau* des *taonga*, le *hau* de la forêt. *Kati ena*. (Assez sur ce sujet.)

Mauss complained about Best's abbreviation of a certain portion of the original Maori. To make sure that we would miss nothing of this critical document, and in the hope further meanings might be gleaned from it, I asked Professor Bruce Biggs, distinguished student of the Maori, to prepare a new interlinear translation, leaving the term *"hau,"* however, in the original. To this request he responded most kindly and promptly with the following version, undertaken without consulting Best's translation:[2]

> *Na, mo te hau o te ngaaherehere. Taua mea te hau, ehara i te mea*
> Now, concerning the *hau* of the forest. This *hau* is not the *hau*
>
> *ko te hau e pupuhi nei. Kaaore. Maaku e aata whaka maarama ki a koe.*
> that blows (the wind). No. I will explain it carefully to you.
>
> *Na, he taonga toou ka hoomai e koe mooku. Kaaore aa taaua whakaritenga*
> Now, you have something valuable which you give to me. We have no
>
> *uto mo too taonga. Na, ka hoatu hoki e ahau mo teetehi atu tangata, aa,*
> agreement about payment. Now, I give it to someone else, and,
>
> *ka roa peaa te waa, aa, ka mahara taua tangata kei a ia raa taug taonga*
> a long time passes, and that man thinks he has the valuable,
>
> *kia hoomai he utu ki a au, aa, ka hoomai e ia. Na, ko taua taonga*
> he should give some repayment to me, and so he does so. Now, that
>
> *i hoomai nei ki a au, ko te hau teenaa o te taonga i hoomai ra ki a au*
> valuable which was given to me, that is the *hau* of the valuable which was
>
> *i mua. Ko taua taonga me hoatu e ahau ki a koe. E kore*
> given to me before. I must give it to you. It would not
>
> *rawa e tika kia kaiponutia e ahau mooku; ahakoa taonga pai rawa, taonga*
> be correct for me to keep it for myself, whether it be something very good,
>
> *kino raanei, me tae rawa taua taonga i a au ki a koe. No te mea he hau*
> or bad, that valuable must be given to you from me. Because that valuable
>
> *no te taonga teenaa taonga na. Ki te mea kai kaiponutia e ahau taua taonga*
> is a *hau* of the other valuable. If I should hang onto that valuable
>
> *mooku, ka mate ahau. Koina te hau, hau taonga*
> for myself, I will become *mate*. So that is the *hau*—*hau* of valuables,
>
> *hau ngaaherehere. Kaata eenaa.*
> *hau* of the forest. So much for that.

Concerning the text as Best recorded it, Mauss commented that—despite marks of that "esprit théologique et juridique encore imprécis" characteristic of Maori—"it offers but one obscurity: the intervention of a third person." But even this difficulty he forthwith clarified with a light gloss:

---

2. Hereinafter, I will use the Biggs version except where the argument about Mauss's interpretation requires that one cite only the documents available to him. I take this opportunity to thank Professor Biggs for his generous help.

But in order to rightly understand this Maori jurist, it suffices to say: *"Taonga* and all strictly personal property have a *hau,* a spiritual power. You give me a *taonga,* I give it to a third party, the latter gives me another in return, because he is forced to do so by the *hau* of my present; and I am obliged to give you this thing, for I must give back to you what is in reality the product of the *hau* of your *taonga* (1966, p. 159).

Embodying the person of its giver and the *hau* of its forest, the gift itself, on Mauss's reading, obliges repayment. The receiver is beholden by the spirit of the donor; the *hau* of a *taonga* seeks always to return to its homeland, inexorably, even after being transferred hand to hand through a series of transactions. Upon repaying, the original recipient assumes power in turn over the first donor; hence, "la circulation obligatoire des richesses, tributs et dons" in Samoa and New Zealand. In sum:

> . . . it is clear that in Maori custom, the bond of law, bond by way of things, is a bond of souls, because the thing itself has a soul, is soul. From this it follows that to present something to someone is to present something of oneself. . . . It is clear that in this system of ideas it is necessary to return unto another what is in reality part of his nature and substance; for, to accept something from someone is to accept something of his spiritual essence, of his soul; the retention of this thing would be dangerous and mortal, not simply because it would be illicit, but also because this thing which comes from a person, not only morally but physically and spiritually—this essence, this food, these goods, movable or immovable, these women or these offspring, these rites or these communions—give a magical and religious hold over you. Finally, this thing given is not inert. Animate, often personified, it seeks to return to what Hertz called its *"foyer d'origine"* or to produce for the clan and the earth from which it came some equivalent to take its place (*op. cit.,* p. 161).

## The Commentaries of Lévi-Strauss, Firth and Johansen

Mauss's interpretation of the *hau* has been attacked by three scholars of authority, two of them experts on the Maori and one an expert on Mauss. Their critiques are surely learned, but none I think arrives at the true meaning of the Ranapiri text or of the *hau.*

Lévi-Strauss debates principles. He does not presume to criticize Mauss on Maori ethnography. He does, however, question the reliance on an indigenous rationalization: "Are we not faced here with one of those instances (not altogether rare) in which the ethnologist allows himself to be mystified by the native?" (Lévi-Strauss, 1966, p. 38.) The *hau* is not the reason for exchange, only what one people happen to believe is the reason, the way they represent to themselves an unconscious necessity whose reason lies elsewhere. And behind Mauss's fixation on the *hau,* Lévi-Strauss perceived a general conceptual error that regretably arrested his illustrious predecessor short of the full structuralist comprehension of exchange that the *Essay on the Gift* had itself so brilliantly prefigured: "like Moses leading his people to a promised land of which he would never contemplate the splendor" (p. 37). For Mauss had been the first in the history of ethnology to go beyond the empirical to a deeper reality, to abandon the sensible and discrete for the system of relations; in a unique manner he had perceived the operation of reciprocity across its diverse and multiple modalities. But, alas, Mauss could not completely escape from positivism. He continued to understand exchange in the way it is presented to experience—fragmented, that is to say, into the separate acts of giving, receiving, and repaying. Considering it thus in pieces, instead of as a unified and integral principle, he could do nothing better than to try to glue it back again with this "mystic cement," the *hau.*

Firth likewise has his own views on reciprocity, and in making them he scores Mauss repeatedly on points of Maori ethnography (1959a, pp. 418-421). Mauss, according to Firth, simply misunderstood the *hau,* which is a difficult and amorphous concept, but in any event a more passive spiritual principle than Mauss believed. The Ranapiri text in fact gives no evidence that the *hau* passionately strives to return to its source. Nor did the Maori generally rely on the *hau* acting by itself to punish economic delinquency. Normally in the event of a failure to reciprocate, and invariably for theft, the established procedure of retribution or restitution was witchcraft *(makutu):* witchcraft initiated by the person who had been bilked, usually involving the services of a "priest" *(tohunga),* if operating through the vehicle of the goods detained.[3] Furthermore, adds Firth, Mauss con-

---

3. It seems from Firth's account that the same procedure was used both against thieves and ingrates. I appeal here to Maori authorities for clarification. From my own very limited and entirely textual experience, it seems that the goods of a victimized party were used particularly in sorcery against thieves. Here, where the culprit usually is not known, some portion of the goods remaining—or something from the place they were kept—is the vehicle for identifying or punishing the thief (for example, Best, 1924,

fused types of *hau* that in the Maori view are quite distinct—the *hau* of persons, that of lands and forests, and that of *taonga*—and on the strength of this confusion he formulated a serious error. Mauss simply had no warrant to gloss the *hau* of the *taonga* as the *hau* of the person who gives it. The whole idea that the exchange of gifts is an exchange of persons is *sequitur* to a basic misinterpretation. Ranapiri had merely said that the good given by the third person to the second was the *hau* of the *thing* received by the second from the first.[4] The *hau* of persons was not at issue. In supposing it was, Mauss put his own intellectual refinements on Maori mysticism.[5] In other words, and Lévi-Strauss notwithstanding, it was not a native rationalization after all; it was a kind of French one. But as the Maori proverb says, "the troubles of other lands are their own" (Best, 1922, p. 30).

Firth for his part prefers secular to spiritual explanations of reciprocity. He would emphasize certain other sanctions of repayment, sanctions noted by Mauss in the course of the *Essay:*

> The fear of punishment sent through the *hau* of goods is indeed a supernatural sanction, and a valuable one, for enforcing repayment of a gift. But to attribute the scrupulousness in settling one's obligations to a belief in an active, detached fragment of personality of the donor, charged with nostalgia and vengeful impulses, is an entirely different matter. It is an abstraction which receives no support from native evidence. The main emphasis of the fulfillment of obligation lies, as the work of Mauss himself has suggested, in the social sanctions—the desire to continue useful economic relations, the maintenance of prestige and power—which do not require any hypothesis of recondite beliefs to explain (1959a, p. 421).[6]

---

vol. 1, p. 311). But sorcery against a known person is typically practiced by means of something associated with *him;* thus, in a case of failure to repay, the goods of the deceiver would be more likely to serve as vehicle than the gift of the owner. For further interest and confusion, such a vehicle associated with the victim of witchcraft is known to the Maori as *hau.* One of the entries under *"hau"* in W. Williams's dictionary is: "something connected with a person on whom it is intended to practice enchantment; such as a portion of his hair, a drop of his spittle, or anything which has touched his person, etc., which when taken to the *tohunga* [ritual expert] might serve as a connecting link between his incantations and their object" (Williams, 1892).

4. The intervention of a third party thus offers no obscurity to Firth. The exchange between second and third parties was necessary to introduce a second good that could stand for the first, or for the *hau* of the first (cf. Firth, 1959a, p. 420 n.).

5. "When Mauss sees in the gift exchange an interchange of personalities, 'a bond of souls,' he is following, not native belief, but his own intellectualized interpretation of it" (Firth, 1959a, p. 420).

6. In his latest word on the subject, Firth continues to deny the ethnographic validity of Mauss's views on the Maori *hau,* adding also that no such spiritual belief

The latest to apply for entrance to the Maori "house of learning," J. Prytz Johansen (1954), makes certain clear advances over his predecessors in the reading of the Ranapiri text. He at least is the first to doubt that the old Maori had anything particularly spiritual in mind when he spoke of the *hau* of a gift. Unfortunately, Johansen's discussion is even more labyrinthal than Tamati Ranapiri's, and once having reached the point he seems to let go, searches a mythical rather than a logical explanation of the famous exchange *à trois,* and ends finally on a note of scholarly despair.

After rendering due tribute and support to Firth's critique of Mauss, Johansen observes that the word *hau* has a very wide semantic field. Probably several homonyms are involved. For the series of meanings usually understood as "life principle" or something of the sort, Johansen prefers as a general definition, "a part of life (for example, an object) which is used ritually in order to influence the whole," the thing serving as *hau* varying according to the ritual context. He then makes a point that hitherto had escaped everyone's notice—including, I think, Best's. Tamati Ranapiri's discourse on gifts was by way of introduction to and explanation of a certain ceremony, a sacrificial repayment to the forest for the game birds taken by Maori fowlers.[7] Thus the informant's purpose in this expositing passage was merely to establish the principle of reciprocity, and *"hau"* there merely signified "countergift"—"the Maori in question undoubtedly thought that *hau* means countergift, simply what is otherwise called *utu"* (Johansen, 1954, p. 118).

We shall see momentarily that the notion of "equivalent return" *(utu)* is inadequate for the *hau* in question; moreover, the issues posed by Ranapiri transcend reciprocity as such. In any event, Johansen, upon taking up again the three-party transaction, dissipated the advance he had made. Unaccountably, he credited the received understanding that the original donor performs magic on the second party through the goods the latter received from the third, goods that

---

is involved in Tikopian gift exchange (1967). Too, he now has certain critical reservations on Mauss's discussion of the obligations to give, receive, and reciprocate. Yet at one level he would agree with Mauss. Not in the sense of an actual spiritual entity, but in the more generalized social and psychological sense of an extension of the self, the gift does partake of its donor *(ibid.,* pp. 10–11, 15–16).

7  In the original Maori as published by Best, the passage on gifts was actually intercalculated as an explanatory aside between two descriptions of the ceremony. The continuous English translation, however, deletes the main part of the first description, this Best having cited a page earlier (1909, p. 438). Besides, both English and Maori

become *hau* in this context. But since the explication is "not obvious," Johansen found himself compelled to invoke a special unknown tradition, "to the effect that when three persons exchanged gifts and the intermediary party failed, the counter-gift which had stopped with him might be *hau,* i.e., might be used to bewitch him." He then finished gloomily: "However a certain uncertainty is involved in all these considerations and it seems doubtful whether we shall ever attain to actual certainty as regards the meaning of the *hau*" (*ibid.,* p. 118).

## THE TRUE MEANING OF THE HAU OF VALUABLES

I am not a linguist, a student of primitive religions, an expert on the Maori, or even a Talmudic scholar. The "certainty" I see in the disputed text of Tamati Ranapiri is therefore suggested with due reservations. Still, to adopt the current structuralist incantation, "everything happens as if" the Maori was trying to explain a religious concept by an economic principle, which Mauss promptly understood the other way around and thereupon proceeded to develop the economic principle by the religious concept. The *hau* in question really means something on the order of "return on" or "product of," and the principle expressed in the text on *taonga* is that any such yield on a gift ought to be handed over to the original donor.

The disputed text absolutely should be restored to its position as an explanatory gloss to the description of a sacrifical rite.[8] Tamata Ranapiri was trying to make Best understand by this example of gift exchange—example so ordinary that anybody (or any Maori) ought to be able to grasp it immediately—why certain game birds are ceremoniously returned to the *hau* of the forest, to the source of their

---

texts begin with a discussion of witchcraft spells, not apparently related to the ceremonial or the gift exchange, but about which more later.

8. There is a very curious difference between the several versions of Best, Mauss, and Tamati Ranapiri. Mauss appears to deliberately delete Best's reference to the ceremony in the opening phrase. Best had cited "'I will now speak of the *hau,* and the ceremony of *whangai hau'*"; whereas Mauss has it merely, "'Je vais vous [*sic*] parler du *hau.* . .'" (ellipsis is Mauss's). The interesting point is raised by Biggs's undoubtedly authentic translation, much closer to that of Mauss, as it likewise does not mention *whangai hau* at this point: "'Now, concerning the *hau* of the forest.'" However, even in this form the original text linked the message on *taonga* with the ceremony of *whangai hau,* "fostering" or "nourishing *hau,*" since the *hau* of the forest was not the subject of the immediately succeeding passage on gifts but of the consequent and ultimate description of the ceremony.

abundance. In other words, he adduced a transaction among men parallel to the ritual transaction he was about to relate, such that the former would serve as paradigm for the latter. As a matter of fact, the secular transaction does not prove directly comprehensible to us, and the best way to understand it is to work backwards from the exchange logic of the ceremony.

This logic, as presented by Tamati Ranapiri, is perfectly straightforward. It is necessary only to observe the sage's use of *"mauri"* as the physical embodiment of the forest *hau,* the power of increase—a mode of conceiving the *mauri* that is not at all idiosyncratic, to judge from other writings of Best. The *mauri,* housing the *hau,* is placed in the forest by the priests *(tohunga)* to make game birds abound. Here then is the passage that followed that on the gift exchange—in the intention of the informant, as night follows day:[9]

> I will explain something to you about the forest *hau.* The *mauri* was placed or implanted in the forest by the *tohunga* [priests]. It is the *mauri* that causes birds to be abundant in the forest, that they may be slain and taken by man. These birds are the property of, or belong to, the *mauri,* the *tohunga,* and the forest: that is to say, they are an equivalent for that important item, the *mauri.* Hence it is said that offerings should be made to the *hau* of the forest. The *tohunga* (priests, adepts) eat the offering because the *mauri* is theirs: it was they who located it in the forest, who caused it to be. That is why some of the birds cooked at the sacred fire are set apart to be eaten by the priests only, in order that the *hau* of the forest-products, and the *mauri,* may return again to the forest—that is, to the *mauri.* Enough of these matters (Best, 1909, p. 439).

In other words, and essentially: the *mauri* that holds the increase-power *(hau)* is placed in the forest by the priests *(tohunga);* the *mauri* causes game birds to abound; accordingly, some of the captured birds should be ceremoniously returned to the priests who placed the *mauri;* the consumption of these birds by the priests in effect restores the fertility *(hau)* of the forest (hence the name of the ceremony, *whangai hau,* "nourishing *hau").*[10] Immediately then, the ceremonial transaction presents a familiar appearance: a three-party game, with the

9. I use Best's translation, the one available to Mauss. I also have in hand Biggs's interlinear version; it does not differ significantly from Best's.

10. The earlier discussion of this ritual, preceeding the passage on *taonga* in the full Maori text, in fact comments on two related ceremonies: the one just described and another, performed before, by those sent into the forest in advance of the fowling season to observe the state of the game. I cite the main part of this earlier description in Biggs's

priests in the position of an initiating donor to whom should be rendered the returns on an original gift. The cycle of exchange is shown in Figure 4.1.

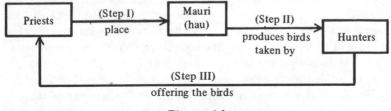

*Figure 4.1*

Now, in the light of this transaction, reconsider the text, just preceding, on gifts among men. Everything becomes transparent. The secular exchange of *taonga* is only slightly different in form from the ceremonial offering of birds, while in principle it is exactly the same—thus the didactic value of its position in Ranapiri's discourse. *A* gives a gift to *B* who transforms it into something else in an exchange with *C,* but since the *taonga* given by *C* to *B* is the product *(hau)* of *A*'s original gift, this benefit ought to be surrendered to *A*. The cycle is shown in Figure 4.2.

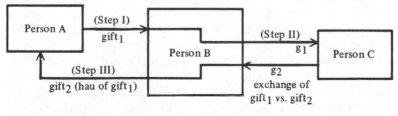

*Figure 4.2*

version: "The *hau* of the forest has two 'likenesses.' 1. When the forest is inspected by the observers, and if birds are observed to be there, and if birds are killed by them that day, the first bird killed by them is offered to the *mauri*. It is simply thrown away into the bush, and is said, 'that's for the *mauri.*' The reason, lest they get nothing in the future. 2. When the hunting is finished (they) go out of the bush and begin to cook the birds for preserving in fat. Some are set aside first to feed the *hau* of the forest; this is the forest *hau*. Those birds which were set aside are cooked on the second fire. Only the priests eat the birds of the second fire, Other birds are set aside for the *tapairu* from which only the women eat. Most of the birds are set aside and cooked on the *puuraakau* fire. The birds of the *puuraakau* fire are for all to eat. . . ." (cf. Best, 1909, pp. 438, 440–41, 449f; and for other details of the ceremonies, 1942, pp. 13, 184f, 316–17).

The meaning of *hau* one disengages from the exchange of *taonga* is as secular as the exchange itself. If the second gift is the *hau* of the first, then the *hau* of a good is its yield, just as the *hau* of a forest is its productiveness. Actually, to suppose Tamati Ranapiri meant to say the gift has a spirit which forces repayment seems to slight the old gentleman's obvious intelligence. To illustrate such a spirit needs only a game of two persons: you give something to me; your spirit *(hau)* in that thing obliges me to reciprocate. Simple enough. The introduction of a third party could only unduly complicate and obscure the point. But if the point is neither spiritual nor reciprocity as such, if it is rather that one man's gift should not be another man's capital, and therefore the fruits of a gift ought to be passed back to the original holder, then the introduction of a third party is necessary. It is necessary precisely to show a *turnover:* the gift has had issue; the recipient has used it to advantage. Ranapiri was careful to prepare this notion of advantage beforehand by stipulating[11] the absence of equivalence in the first instance, as if *A* had given *B* a free gift. He implies the same, moreover, in stressing the delay between the reception of the gift by the third person and the repayment—"a long time passes, and that man thinks that he has the valuable, he should give some repayment to me." As Firth observes, delayed repayments among Maori are customarily larger than the initial gift (1959a, p. 422); indeed, it is a general rule of Maori gift exchange that, "the payment must if possible be somewhat in excess of what the principle of equivalence demanded" (ibid., p. 423). Finally, observe just where the term *hau* enters into the discussion. Not with the initial transfer from the first to the second party, as well it could if it were the spirit in the gift, but upon the exchange between the second and third parties, as logically it would if it were the yield on the gift.[12] The term "profit" is economically and historically inappropriate to the Maori, but it would have

11. And in Best's translation, even reiterating: "'Suppose that you possess a certain article, and you give that article to me, without price. We make no bargain over it.'"
12. Firth cites the following discussion to this point from Gudgeon: "'If a man received a present and passed it on to some third person then there is no impropriety in such an act; but if a return present is made by the third party then it must be passed on to the original grantor or it is a *hau ngaro* (consumed *hau*)'" (Firth, 1959a, p. 418). The lack of consequence in the first of these conditions is again evidence against Mauss's nostalgic *hau,* ever striving to return to its *foyer.*

been a better translation than "spirit" for the *hau* in question.

Best provides one other example of exchange in which *hau* figures. Significantly, the little scene is again a transaction *à trois:*

> I was having a flax shoulder-cape made by a native woman at Rua-tahuna. One of the troopers wished to buy it from the weaver, but she firmly refused, lest the horrors of *hau whitia* descend upon her. The term *hau whitia* means "averted hau" (1900–1901, p. 198).

Only slightly different from the model elaborated by Tamati Rana-piri, this anecdote offers no particular difficulty. Having commissioned the cape, Best had the prior claim on it. Had the weaver accepted the trooper's offer, she would have turned this thing to her own advantage, leaving Best with nothing. She appropriates the product of Best's cape; she becomes subject to the evils of a gain unrightfully turned aside, "the horrors of *hau whitia.*"[13] Otherwise said, she is guilty of eating *hau—kai hau—*for in the introduction to this incident Best had explained,

> Should I dispose of some article belonging to another person and not hand over to him any return or payment I may have received for that article, that is a *hau whitia* and my act is a *kai hau,* and death awaits, for the dread terrors of *makutu* [witchcraft] will be turned upon me (1900–1901, pp. 197–98)![14]

So as Firth observed, the *hau* (even if it were a spirit) does not cause harm on its own initiative; the distinct procedure of witchcraft *(makutu)* has to be set in motion. It is not even implied by this incident that such witchcraft would work through the passive medium of *hau,* since Best, who was potentially the deceived party, had apparently put nothing tangible into circulation. Taken together, the different texts on the *hau* of gifts suggest something else entirely: not

---

13. *Whitia* is the past participle of *whiti. Whiti,* according to H. Williams's dictionary, means: (1) *v.i.,* cross over, reach the opposite side; (2) change, turn, to be inverted, to be contrary; (3) *v.t.,* pass through; (4) turn over, prise (as with a lever); (5) change (Williams, 1921, p. 584).

14. Best's further interpretation lent itself to Mauss's views: "For it seems that that article of yours is impregnated with a certain amount of your *hau,* which presumably passes into the article received in exchange therefore, because if I pass that second article on to other hands it is a *hau whitia"* (1900–1901, p. 198). Thus "it seems." One has a feeling of participating in a game of ethnographic folk-etymology, which we now find, from Best's explanation, is a quite probable game *a quatre.*

that the goods withheld are dangerous, but that withholding goods is *immoral*—and therefore dangerous in the sense the deceiver is open to justifiable attack. " 'It would not be *correct* to keep it for myself,' said Ranapiri, " 'I will become *mate* (ill, or die).' "

We have to deal with a society in which freedom to gain at others' expense is not envisioned by the relations and forms of exchange. Therein lies the moral of the old Maori's economic fable. The issue he posed went beyond reciprocity: not merely that gifts must be suitably returned, but that returns rightfully should be given back. This interpretation it is possible to sustain by a judicious selection among the many meanings of *hau* entered in H. Williams's (1921) Maori dictionary. *Hau* is a verb meaning to "exceed, be in excess," as exemplified in the phrase *kei te hau te wharika nei* ("this mat is longer than necessary"); likewise, *hau* is the substantive, "excess, parts, fraction over any complete measurement." *Hau* is also "property, spoils." Then there is *haumi,* a derivative meaning to "join," to "lengthen by addition," to "receive or lay aside"; it is also, as a noun, "the piece of wood by which the body of a canoe is lengthened."

The following is the true meaning of Tamati Ranapiri's famous and enigmatic discourse on the *hau* of *taonga:*

> I will explain it carefully to you. Now, you have something valuable which you give to me. We have no agreement about payment. Now, I give it to someone else, and, a long time passes, and that man thinks he has the valuable, he should give some repayment to me, and so he does so. Now, that valuable which was given to me, that is the product of [hau] the valuable which was given to me[by you] before. I must give it to you. It would not be right for me to keep it for myself, whether it be something good, or bad, that valuable must be given to you from me. Because that valuable is a return on [hau] the other valuable. If I should hang onto that valuable for myself, I will become ill [or die]."

### ASIDE ON THE MAORI SORCERER'S APPRENTICE

But this understanding of the *hau* of things still risks criticism on its own grounds—of omission, of failure to consider the total context. Both passages, on gifts and on sacrifice, are parts of a yet larger whole, preeceded by still another disquisition on *mauri* as taken by Best from the lips of Ranapiri (1909, pp. 440-441). True, there may be good

reason for leaving this particular prelude aside. Highly obscure, eso-
teric, concerned mainly with the nature and teaching of death-dealing
spells, it seems to have no great bearing on exchange:

> The *mauri* is a spell which is recited over a certain object, of stone, or of
> wood, or something else approved of by the *tohunga* [priest] as a "clinging
> place," a "holding-fast-place," a "dwelling-place" for the *mauri*. Such an
> object is subjected to the "cause-to-be-split" ritual, and left in a hidden part
> of the forest to lie there. The *mauri* is not *tapu*-less. Also it is not the case
> that all of the forest is as *tapu* as the part where the *mauri* lies. Concerning
> the causing-to-be-split, it is a shattering. If a man is taught by a priest
> certain spells, say witchcraft spells, or spells for placing *mauri,* and the
> other Maori spells, and he learns them, then the priest says to that man,
> "Now, there, 'cause-to-be-split' your spells!" That is, be-spell the stone so
> that it is shattered, the man so that he dies, or whatever. If the stone is
> smashed, or the man dies, the spells of that pupil have become very *mana*.
> If the stone does not burst (shatter), or the man die, which has been
> "caused-to-be-split," his spells are not *mana*. They will return and kill him,
> the pupil. If the priest is very old and near to death, that priest will say,
> to his pupil to "cause-to-be-split" his spells against him, that is, the priest.
> The priest dies, so his spells are "split" (shattered) which he taught, and
> are *mana*. Then the pupil lives, and, in due time, he will want to place a
> *mauri*. Now, he is able to place (it) in the forest, or in the water, or on the
> post of the eel-weir which is called *pou-reinga*. It would not be good for
> the spells of that pupil to remain within him, to be not split, that is,
> shattered forth, and, it is the shattering forth, which is the same as shatter
> the stone. If the stone shatters completely, that is good. That is the "caus-
> ing-to-split" (Bigg's translation).

No question that the previous examination of gift and ceremonial
exchange leaves us merely unprepared to understand the *profondeurs*
of this section. Yet the text again speaks of an exchange, which even
superficial study will recognize as formally analogous to the transactions of *taonga* and "nourishing *hau*." The spell passed by priest to
student returns to the former enhanced in value and by way of a third
party. It may very well be that the three sections of the Ranapiri text
are variations on the same theme, unified not only in content but by
a triple replication of the same transactional structure.[15]

15. There is also, of course, a narrative bridge between the section on transmission.

The case is strengthened by a precious datum, again explicated by Firth (1959a, pp. 272-273), apparently from materials supplied by Best (1925a, pp. 1101-1104). Comparing Maori custom with common Melanesian practice in regard to the transmission of magic, Firth was struck by the virtual absence among Maori of any obligation to repay the teacher. In the Maori view, such recompense would degrade the spell, even defile and render it null—with a single exception. The Maori teacher of the most *tapu* black magic *was* repaid—*by a victim!* The apprentice would have to kill a near relative, an act of sacrifice to the gods that empowered the spell even as it restored the gift (Best, 1925a, p. 1063). Or perhaps, as the *tohunga* grew old the death-dealing knowledge would be directed back upon him—proving, incidentally, that scholarly cults are the same all over. Best's description of these customs has exactly the transactional cadence of the passage on gifts, beginning on the same note of nonreturn:

> The old men of Tuhoe and Awa explain it this way: The priest teacher was not paid for his services. If he were, then the arts of magic, etc., acquired by the pupil would not be effectual. He would not be able to slay a person by means of magical spells. But, if you are taught by me, then I will tell you what to do in order to reveal your powers. I will tell you the price that you must pay for your initiation, as—"The equivalent for your knowledge acquired, the disclosing of your powers, must be your own father," or your mother, or some other near relative. Then such powers will be effective. The teacher mentions the price the pupil must pay. He selects a near relative of the pupil as the greatest sacrifice he can pay for his acquirements. A near relative, possibly his own mother, is brought before him, that he may slay her by means of his magical powers. In some cases the teacher would direct his pupil to so slay him, the teacher. Ere long he would be dead. . . . "The payment made by the pupil was the loss of a near relative. As to a payment in goods—what would be the good of that. *Hai aha!*" (Best, 1925a, p. 1103).

This detail in hand, the morphological resemblance between all three parts of the Ranapiri text becomes unmistakable. In the transmission of *tapu* magic, as in the exchange of valuables or the sacrifice of birds, a direct return on the initial gift is excluded. In each instance,

---

of magic and the ceremony, as the former ends with the placing of the *mauri* which is the key element of the latter.

reciprocation passes by way of a third party. This mediation in every case brings issue to the original gift: by the transfer from the second party to the third, some value or effect is added to the thing given by the first party to the second. And one way or another, the first recipient (middle term) is menaced by destruction *(mate)* if the cycle is not completed. Concretely in the text on magic: the *tohunga* gives the spell to the apprentice; the apprentice turns it upon the victim, so enhancing it if he is successful—"the spells of that pupil have become very *mana*"—or dying himself if he fails; the victim belongs to the *tohunga* as compensation for his teaching; alternatively, the apprentice returns his now powerful spell to the aged *tohunga,* that is, he kills him. The cycle is shown in Figure 4.3.

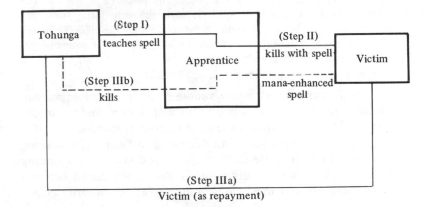

*Figure 4.3*

THE LARGER SIGNIFICANCE OF *HAU*

Returning now to the *hau,* it is clear we cannot leave the term merely with secular connotations. If the *hau* of valuables in circulation means the yeild thereby accrued, a concrete product of a concrete good, still there is a *hau* of the forest, and of man, and these do have spiritual quality. What kind of spiritual quality? Many of Best's remarks on the subject suggest that the *hau*-as-spirit is not unrelated to the *hau*-as-material-returns. Taking the two together, one is able to reach a larger understanding of that mysterious *hau*.

Immediately it is clear that *hau* is not a spirit in the common animistic sense. Best is explicit about this. The *hau* of a man is a quite different thing from his *wairua*, or sentient spirit—the "soul" of ordinary anthropological usage. I cite from one of Best's most comprehensive discussions of *wairua:*

> In the term *wairua* (soul) we have the Maori term for what anthropologists style the soul, that is the spirit that quits the body at death, and proceeds to the spirit world, or hovers about its former home here on earth. The word *wairua* denotes a shadow, any unsubstantial image; occasionally it is applied to a reflection, thus it was adopted as a name for the animating spirit of man. . . . The *wairua* can leave the sheltering body during life; it does so when a person dreams of seeing distant places or people. . . . The *wairua* is held to be a sentient spirit; it leaves the body during sleep, and warns its physical basis of impending dangers, of ominous signs, by means of the visions we term dreams. It was taught by high-grade native priests that all things possess a *wairua,* even what we term inanimate objects, as trees and stones (Best, 1924, vol. 1, pp. 299-301).[16]

*Hau,* on the other hand, belongs more to the realm of animatism than animism. As such it is bound up with *mauri,* in fact, in the writings of the ethnographic experts, it is virtually impossible to distinguish one from the other. Firth despairs of definitively separating the two on the basis of Best's overlapping and often corresponding definitions—"the blurred outline of the distinction drawn between *hau* and *mauri* by our most eminent ethnographic authority allows one to conclude that these concepts in their immaterial sense are almost synonymous" (Firth, 1959a, p. 281). As Firth notices, certain

16. Thus Mauss's simple translation of *hau* as spirit and his view of exchange as a *lien d'âmes* is at least imprecise. Beyond that, Best repeatedly would like to distinguish *hau* (and *mauri*) from *wairua* on the grounds that the former, which ceases to exist with death, cannot leave a person's body on pain of death, unlike *wairua.* But here Best finds himself in difficulty with the material manifestation of a person's *hau* used in witchcraft, so that he is alternatively tempted to say that some part of the *hau* can be detached from the body or that the *hau* as witchcraft is not the "true" *hau.*

contrasts sometimes appear. In reference to man, the *mauri* is the more active principle, "the activity that moves within us." In relation to land or the forest, *"mauri"* is frequently used for the tangible representation of an incorporeal *hau*. Yet is is clear that *"mauri"* too may refer to a purely spiritual quality of land, and, on the other hand, the *hau* of a person may have concrete form—for example, hair, nail clippings, and the like used in witchcraft. It is not for me to unscramble these linguistic and religious mysteries, so characteristic of that Maori "esprit théologique et juridique encore imprécis." Rather, I would emphasize a more apparent and gross contrast between *hau* and *mauri,* on one side, and *wairua* on the other, a contrast that also seems to clarify the learned words of Tamati Ranapiri.

*Hau* and *mauri* as spiritual qualities are uniquely associated with fecundity. Best often spoke of both as the "vital principle." It is evident from many of his observations that fertility and productivity were the essential attributes of this "vitality." For example (the italics in the following statements are mine):

> The *hau* of land is its vitality, *fertility* and so forth, and also a quality which we can only, I think, express by the word prestige (Best, 1900–1901, p. 193).

> The *ahi taitai* is a sacred fire at which rites are performed that have for their purpose the protection of the life principle and *fruitfulness* of man, the land, forests, birds, etc. It is said to be the *mauri* or *hau* of the home (p. 194).

> . . . when Hape went off on his expedition to the south, he took with him the *hau* of the *kumara* [sweet potato], or, as some say, he took the *mauri* of the same. The visible form of this *mauri* was the stalk of a *kumara* plant, it represented the *hau,* that is to say, the vitality and *fertility* of the *kumara* (p. 196; cf. Best, 1925b, pp. 106–107).

> The forest *mauri* has already received our attention. We have shown that its function was to protect the *productiveness* of the forest (p.6).

> Material *mauri* were utilized in connection with agriculture; they were placed in the field where crops were planted, and it was a firm belief that they had a highly beneficial effect on the growing crops (1922, p. 38).

Now, the *hau* and *mauri* pertain not only to man, but also to animals, land, forests and even to a village home. Thus the *hau* or vitality, or *productiveness*, of a forest has to be very carefully protected by means of certain very peculiar rites . . . For *fecundity* cannot exist without the essential *hau* (1909, p. 436).

Everything animate and inanimate possesses this life principle *(mauri)*: without it naught could *flourish* (1924 vol. 1, p. 306).

So, as we had in fact already suspected, the *hau* of the forest is its fecundity, as the *hau* of a gift is its material yield. Just as in the mundane context of exchange *hau* is the return on a good, so as a spiritual quality *hau* is the principle of fertility. In the one equally as in the other, the benefits taken by man ought to be returned to their source, that it may be maintained as a source. Such was the total wisdom of Tamati Ranapiri.

"Everything happens as if" the Maori people knew a broad concept, a general principle of productiveness, *hau*. It was a category that made no distinctions, of itself belonging neither to the domain we call "spiritual" nor that of the "material," yet applicable to either. Speaking of valuables, the Maori could conceive *hau* as the concrete product of exchange. Speaking of the forest, *hau* was what made the game birds abound, a force unseen but clearly appreciated by the Maori. But would the Maori in any case need to so distinguish the "spiritual" and the "material"? Does not the apparent "imprecision" of the term *hau* perfectly accord with a society in which "economic," "social," "political" and "religious" are indiscriminately organized by the same relations and intermixed in the same activities? And if so, are we not obliged once more to reverse ourselves on Mauss's interpretation? Concerning the spiritual specifics of the *hau,* he was very likely mistaken. But in another sense, more profound, he was right. "Everything happens as if" *hau* were a total concept. *Kaati eenaa.*

## Political Philosophy of the Essay on the Gift.

For the war of every man against every man, Mauss substitutes the exchange of everything between everybody. The *hau,* spirit of the donor in the gift, was not the ultimate explanation of reciprocity, only a special proposition set in the context of an historic conception. Here was a new version of the dialogue between chaos and covenant, transposed from the explication of political society to the reconciliation of segmentary society. The *Essai sur le don* is a kind of social contract for the primitives.

Like famous philosophical predecessors, Mauss debates from an original condition of disorder, in some sense given and pristine, but then overcome dialectically. As against war, exchange. The transfer of things that are in some degree persons and of persons in some degree treated as things, such is the consent at the base of organized society. The gift is alliance, solidarity, communion—in brief, peace, the great virtue that earlier philosophers, Hobbes notably, had discovered in the State. But the originality and the verity of Mauss was exactly that he refused the discourse in political terms. The first consent is not to authority, or even to unity. It would be too literal an interpretation of the older contract theory to discover its verification in nascent institutions of chieftainship. The primitive analogue of social contract is not the State, but the gift.

The gift is the primitive way of achieving the peace that in civil society is secured by the State. Where in the traditional view the contract was a form of political exchange, Mauss saw exchange as a form of political contract. The famous "total prestation" is a "total contract," described to just this effect in the *Manuel d'Ethnographie:*

> We shall differentiate contracts into those of total *prestation* and contracts in which the *prestation* is only partial. The former already appear in Australia; they are found in a large part of the Polynesian world . . . and in North America. For two clans, total *prestation* is manifest by the fact that to be in a condition of perpetual contract, everyone owes everything to all the others of his clan and to all those of the opposed clan. The permanent and collective character of such a contract makes it a veritable *traité,* with the necessary display of wealth *vis-a-vis* the other party. The *prestation* is extended to everything, to everyone, at all times . . . (1967, p. 188).

But as gift exchange, the contract would have a completely new political realization, unforeseen and unimagined in the received philosophy and constituting neither society nor State. For Rousseau, Locke, Spinoza, Hobbes, the social contract had been first of all a pact of society. It was an agreement of incorporation: to form a community out of previously separate and antagonistic parts, a superperson of the individual persons, that would exercise the power subtracted from each in the benefit of all. But then, a certain political formation had to be stipulated. The purpose of the unification was to put end to the strife born of private justice. Consequently, even if the covenant was not as such a contract of government, between ruler and ruled, as in medieval and earlier versions, and whatever the differences between the sages over the locus of sovereignty, all had to imply by the contract of society the institution of State. That is to say, all had to insist on the alienation by agreement of one right in particular: private force. This was the essential clause, despite that the philosophers went on to debate its comprehensiveness: the surrender of private force in favor of a Public Power.

The gift, however, would not organize society in a corporate sense, only in a segmentary sense. Reciprocity is a "between" relation. It does not dissolve the separate parties within a higher unity, but on the contrary, in correlating their opposition, perpetuates it. Neither does the gift specify a third party standing over and above the separate interests of those who contract. Most important, it does not withdraw their force, for the gift affects only will and not right. Thus the condition of peace as understood by Mauss—and as in fact it exists in the primitive societies—has to differ politically from that envisioned by the classic contract, which is always a structure of submission, and sometimes of terror. Except for the honor accorded to generosity, the gift is no sacrifice of equality and never of liberty. The groups allied by exchange each retain their strength, if not the inclination to use it.

Although I opened with Hobbes (and it is especially in comparison with *Leviathan*[17] that I would discuss *The Gift*), it is clear that in sentiment Mauss is much closer to Rousseau. By its segmentary morphology, Mauss's primitive society rather returns to the third stage of the *Discourse on Inequality* than to the radical individualism of a

17. I use the Everyman's edition for all citations from *Leviathan* (New York: Dutton, 1950), as it retains the archaic spelling, rather than the more commonly cited *English Works* edited by Molesworth (1839).

Hobbesian state of nature (cf. Cazaneuve, 1968). And as Mauss and Rousseau had similarly seen the oppositions as social, so equally their resolutions would be sociable. That is, for Mauss, an exchange that "extends to everything, to everyone, to all time." What is more, if in giving one gives himself *(hau)*, then everyone spiritually becomes a member of everyone else. In other words, the gift approaches even in its enigmas that celebrated contract in which, "Chacun de nous met en commun sa personne et toute sa puissance sous la suprême direction de la volonté générale; et nous recevons en corps chaque membre comme partie indivisible du tout."

But if Mauss is a spiritual descendant of Rousseau, as a political philosopher he is akin to Hobbes. Not to claim a close historic relation with the Englishman, of course, but only to detect a strong convergence in the analysis: a basic agreement on the natural political state as a generalized distribution of force, on the possibility of escaping from this condition by the aid of reason, and on the advantages realized thereby in cultural progress. The comparison with Hobbes seems to best bring out the almost concealed scheme of *The Gift*. Still, the exercise would have little interest were it not that this "problématique" precisely at the point it makes juncture with Hobbes arrives at a fundamental discovery of the primitive polity, and where it differs from Hobbes it makes a fundamental advance in understanding social evolution.

POLITICAL ASPECTS OF *THE GIFT* AND *LEVIATHAN*

In the perspective of Mauss, as it was for Hobbes, the understructure of society is war. This in a special sense, which is sociological.

The "war of every man against every man," spectacular phrase, conceals an ambiguity; or at least in its insistence on the nature of man it ignores an equally striking structure of society. The state of nature described by Hobbes was also a political order. True that Hobbes was preoccupied with the human thirst for power and disposition to violence, but he wrote too of an allocation of force among men and of their liberty to employ it. The transition in *Leviathan* from the psychology of man to the pristine condition seems therefore at the same time continuous and disjunctive. The state of nature was *sequitur* to human nature, but it also announced a new level of reality that as polity was not even describable in the terms of psychology. This war of each against all is not just the disposition to use force but the *right* to do so, not merely certain inclinations but certain *relations* of power, not simply a passion for supremacy but a sociology of dominance, not only the instinct of competition but the legitimacy of the confrontation. The state of nature is already a kind of society.[18]

What kind? According to Hobbes, it is a society without a sovereign, without "a common Power to keep them all in awe." Said positively, a society in which the right to give battle is retained by the people in severalty. But this must be underlined: it is the right which endures, not the battle. The emphasis is Hobbes's own, in a very important passage that carried the war of nature beyond human violence to the level of structure, where rather than fighting it appears as a *period of time* during which there is no assurance to contrary, and the will to contend is sufficiently known:

> For WARRE , consisteth not in Battell onely, or the act of fighting; but in a tract of time, wherein the Will to contend by Battell is sufficiently known: and therefore the notion of *Time,* is to be considered in the nature of Warre; as it is in the nature of Weather. For as the nature of Foule weather, lyeth not in a shower or two of rain; but in an inclination thereto of many dayes together; So the nature of Warre, consisteth not in actual fighting; but in the known disposition thereto, during all the time there is no assurance to the contrary. All other time is PEACE (Part I, Chapter 13).

Happily, Hobbes frequently used the archaic spelling, "Warre," which gives us the opportunity of taking it to mean something else, a determinate political form. To repeat, the critical characteristic of Warre is free recourse to force: everyone reserves that option in pursuit of his greater gain or glory, and in defense of his person and possessions. Unless and until this partite strength was rendered to a

18. Why this should seem particularly so in *Leviathan* in comparison with the earlier *Elements of Law* and *De Cive* becomes intelligible from McNeilly's recent analysis to the effect that *Leviathan* completes the transformation of Hobbes's argument into a formal rationality of interpersonal relations (in the absence of a sovereign power), which involves abandonment, as concerns the logic of argument, of the prior stress on the content of human passions. Hence if in the early works, "Hobbes attempts to derive political conclusions from certain (very doubtful) propositions about the specific nature of individual human beings . . . in *Leviathan* the argument depends on an analysis of the *formal* structure of the *relations* between individuals" (McNeilly, 1968, p. 5).

collective authority, Hobbes argued, there would never be assurance of peace; and though Mauss discovered that assurance in the gift, both agreed that the primitive order is an absence of law; which is the same as saying that everyone can take the law into his own hands, so that man and society stand in continuous danger of a violent end.

Of course, Hobbes did not seriously consider the state of nature as ever a general empirical fact, an authentic historic stage—although there are some people who "live to this day in that brutish manner," as the savages of many places in America, ignorant of all government beyond the lustful concord of the small family. But if not historical, in what sense was the state of nature intended?

In the sense of Galilean logic, it is sometimes said: a thinking away of the distorting factors in a complex appearance to the ideal course of a body moving without resistance. The analogy is close, but insofar as it slights the tension and the stratification of the complex appearance, it perhaps does not do justice, neither to Hobbes nor to the parallel in Mauss. This "Warre" does exist, if it is only that people "lock their doors behind" and princes are in "constant jealousy." Yet though it exists, it has to be imagined because all appearance is *designed* to repress it, to overlay and deny it as an insupportable menace. So it is imagined in a way that seems more like psychoanalysis than physics: by probing for a hidden substructure that in outward behavior is disguised and transfigured into its opposite. In that event, the deduction of the pristine state is not a direct extension of experimental approximations, still consistent with the empirical even as it is projected beyond the observable. The real is here counterposed to the empirical, and we are forced to understand the appearance of things as the negation rather than the expression of their truer character.

In just this manner, it seems to me, Mauss posited his general theory of the gift on a certain nature of primitive society, nature not always evident—but that exactly because it is contradicted by the gift. It was, moreover, a society of the same nature: Warre. The primitive order is a contrived agreement to deny its inherent fragility, its division at base into groups of distinct interest and matched strength, clanic groups "like the savage people in many places of America," that can join only in conflict or else must withdraw to avoid it. Of course, Mauss did not begin from Hobbesian principles of psychology.

His view of human nature is certainly more nuanced than that "perpetuall and restless desire of Power after power, that ceaseth only in Death."[19] But his view of social nature was an anarchy of group poised against group with a will to contend by battle that is sufficiently known, and a disposition thereto during all that time there is no assurance to the contrary. In the context of this argument, the *hau* is only a dependent proposition. That supposed adoption by the ethnologist of a native rationalization is itself, by the scheme of *The Gift*, the rationalization of a deeper necessity to reciprocate whose reason lies elsewhere: in threat of war. The compulsion to reciprocate built into the *hau* responds to the repulsion of groups built into the society. The force of attraction in things thus dominates the attractions of force among men.

Less spectacular and sustained than the argument from *hau*, that from Warre nevertheless reappears persistently in *The Gift*. For Warre is contained in the premises, constructed by Mauss in the very definition of "total prestation": those exchanges, "undertaken in seemingly voluntary guise . . . but in essence strictly obligatory, *on pain of private or open warfare*" (1966, p. 151; emphasis mine). Similarly: "To refuse to give or to fail to invite is, like refusing to accept, equivalent to a declaration of war; it is to refuse alliance and communion" (pp. 162-163).

Perhaps it strains the point to insist on Mauss's appreciation of the potlatch as a sort of sublimated warfare. Let us pass on to the concluding paragraphs of the essay, where the opposition between Warre and exchange is developed with progressive amplitude and clarity, first in the metaphor of the Pine Mountain Corroboree, finally in a general statement that begins . . .

All the societies we have described above, except our own European, are segmentary societies. Even the Indo-Europeans, the Romans before the *Twelve Tables*, the Germanic societies until very late—up to the Edda—Irish society until the time of its principal literature, all were still based on clans, or at the least great families, more or less undivided internally and isolated from one another externally. All these societies are or were far

___

19. Mauss did note in certain transactions of the present day some "fundamental motives of human activity: emulation between individuals of the same sex, that 'deep-seated imperialism' of men, at base part social, part animal and psychological. . . ." (1966, pp. 258-259). On the other hand, if as Macpherson (1965) argues, Hobbe's conception of human nature is just the bourgeois eternalized, then Mauss is squarely opposed to it (1966, pp. 271-272).

removed from our own degree of unification, as well as from that unity with which they are endowed by inadequate historical study (1966, p. 277).

From this organization, a time of exaggerated fear and hostility, appears an equally exaggerated generosity:

> When, during tribal feasts and ceremonies of rival clans and of families that intermarry or initiate reciprocally, groups visit each other; even when, among more advanced societies—with a developed law of "hospitality"—the law of friendship and contracts with the gods have come to assure the "peace" of the "market" and the towns; for a very long period of time and in a considerable number of societies, men confront each other in a curious frame of mind, of exaggerated fear and hostility and of generosity equally exaggerated, which is however mad in no one's eyes but our own (p. 277).

So the people "come to terms" *(traiter),* happy phrase whose double meaning of peace and exchange perfectly epitomizes the primitive contract:

> In all the societies that have immediately preceded ours and that still surround us, and even in numerous usages of our own popular morality, there is no middle way: either complete trust or complete mistrust. One lays down one's arms, renounces magics and gives everything away from casual hospitality to one's daughters and goods. It is in conditions of this kind that men put aside their self-concern and learnt to engage in giving and returning. But then they had no choice. Two groups of men that meet can only withdraw—or in case of mistrust or defiance, battle—or else come to terms (p. 277).

By the end of the essay, Mauss had left far behind the mystic forests of Polynesia. The obscure forces of *hau* were forgotten for a different explanation of reciprocity, consequent on the more general theory, and the opposite of all mystery and particularity: *Reason.* The gift is Reason. It is the triumph of human rationality over the folly of war—

> It is by opposing reason to emotion, by setting up the will for peace against rash follies of this kind, that peoples succeed in substituting alliance, gift and commerce for war, isolation and stagnation (p. 278).

I stress not only this "reason," but the "isolation" and "stagnation." Composing society, the gift was the liberation of culture. Oscillating permanently between confrontation and dispersion, the segmentary society is otherwise brutish and static. But the gift is progress. That is its supreme advantage—and Mauss's final appeal:

> Societies have progressed in the measure that they themselves, their sub-groups and finally their individuals have been able to stabilize their relations, to give, receive, and to repay. In order to trade it was necessary first to lay down the spear. It is then that one succeeded in exchanging goods and persons, not only between clan and clan, but between tribe and tribe, nation and nation, and, above all, between individuals. It is only consequently that people became capable of mutually creating and satisfying their interests, and finally of defending them without recourse to arms. It is thus that clans, tribes, peoples have learned—and it is thus that tomorrow in our world called civilized the classes, nations, and also individuals must learn—how to oppose without massacring one another, and how to give without sacrificing one to another (pp. 278-279).

The "incommodities" of the Hobbesian state of nature had been likewise a lack of progress. And society was similarly condemned to stagnation. Here Hobbes brilliantly anticipated a later ethnology. Without the State (commonwealth) he is saying, lacking special institutions of integration and control, culture must remain primitive and uncomplicated—just as, in the biological realm, the organism had to remain relatively undifferentiated until the appearance of a central nervous system. In some degree, Hobbes even went beyond modern ethnology, which still only in an unconscious way, and without serious attempt to justify its decision, is content to see in the formation of the state the great evolutionary divide between "primitive" and "civilized," while in the meantime subjecting that famous passage of Hobbes's where it is explained just why the criterion is good, to nasty, brutish and short burlesques. Hobbes at least gave a functional justification of the evolutionary distinction, and an indication that qualitative change would alter the quantity:

> *The incommodities of such a Warre.* Whatsoever therefore is consequent to a time of Warre, where every man is Enemy to every man; the same is consequent to the time, wherein men live without other security, than what their own strength, and their own invention shall furnish them withall. In such condition, there is no place for industry; because the fruit thereof is uncertain: and consequently no Culture of the Earth, no Navigation, nor use of the commodities that may be imported by Sea; no commodious Building; no Instruments of moving, and removing such things as require

much force; no Knowledge of the face of the Earth; no account of Time, no Arts; no Letters; no Society; and which is worst of all, continuall feare, and danger of violent death; And the life of man, solitary, poore, nasty, brutish and short (Part 1, Chapter 13).

But to pursue the resemblance to Mauss, from this insecurity and poverty man seeks to escape: for reasons largely of emotion, according to Hobbes, but by means strictly of *reason*. Menaced by material deprivation and haunted by fear of violent death, men would incline to reason, which "suggesteth certain convenient Articles of Peace, upon which men may be drawn to agreement." Thus Hobbes's well-known Laws of Nature, which are counsels of reason in the interest of preservation, and of which the first and fundamental is *"to seek Peace, and follow it."*

And because the condition of Man, (as hath been declared in the precedent Chapter) is a condition of Warre of every one against everyone; in which case every one is governed by his own Reason; and there is nothing he can make use of, that may not be a help unto him, in preserving his life against his enemyes; It followeth, that in such a condition, every man has a Right to every thing; even to one another's body. And therefore, as long as this naturall Right of every man to every thing endureth, there can be no security to any man, (how strong or wise soever he be,) of living out the time, which Nature ordinarily alloweth men to live. And consequently it is a precept, or generall rule of Reason, *That every man, ought to endeavour Peace, as farre as he has hope of obtaining it; and when he cannot obtain it, that he may seek, and use, all helps, and advantages of Warre.* The first branch of which Rule, containeth the first, and Fundamentall Law of Nature; which is, to seek Peace, and follow it (Part 1, Chapter 14).

That Hobbes had even foreseen the peace of the gift is too strong a claim. But this first law of nature was followed by eighteen others, all in effect designed to realize the injunction that men seek peace, and the second through fifth in particular founded on the same principle of reconciliation of which the gift is merely the most tangible expression—founded also, that is to say, on reciprocity. So in structure the argument unites with Mauss's. To this point, at least, Hobbes understands the suppression of Warre neither through the victory of one nor by the submission of all, but in a *mutual surrender.* (The ethical importance is obvious, and Mauss would duly emphasize it, but theoretically too the point is in opposition to the cult of power and organization that was to mark a later evolutionism—and to which Hobbes went on to contribute.)

On the deeper analogy of reciprocity, one may thus juxtapose to gift exchange Hobbes's second law of nature, *"That a man be willing, when others are so too, as farre-forth, as for Peace, and defence of himselfe he shall think it necessary, to lay down this right to all things; and be contented with as much liberty against other men, as he would allow other men against himselfe";* and the third law, *"That men performe their Covenants made";* and again, the fifth, *"That every man strive to accomodate himselfe to the rest."* But of all these apposite precepts, the fourth law of nature touches nearest the gift:

> *The fourth law of nature, gratitude.* As Justice dependeth on Antecedent Covenant; so does GRATITUDE depend on Antecedent Grace, that is to say, Antecedent Free-gift: and is the fourth Law of Nature; which may be conceived in this Forme, *That a man which receiveth Benefit from another of meer Grace, Endeavour that he which giveth it, have no reasonable cause to repent him of his good will.* For no man giveth, but with intention of Good to himselfe; because Gift is Voluntary; and of all Voluntary Acts, the Object is to every man his own Good; of which if men see they shall be frustrated, there will be no beginning of benevolence, or trust; nor consequently of mutuall help; nor of reconciliation of one man to another; and therefore they are to remain still in the condition of *War;* which is contrary to the first and Fundamentall Law of Nature, which commandeth men to *Seek Peace* (Part I, Chapter 15).

Thus the close correspondance between the two philosophers: including, if not exactly the gift, at least a similar appreciation of reciprocity as the primitive mode of peace; and also, if this more marked in Hobbes than in Mauss, a common respect for the rationality of the undertaking. Furthermore, the convergence continues with a negative parallel. Neither Mauss nor Hobbes could trust in the efficacy of reason alone. Both concede, Hobbes the more explicitly, that reason against the force of an imprinted rivalry is insufficient to guarantee the contract.    Because, says Hobbes, the laws of nature, even if they be reason itself, are contrary to our natural passions, and men cannot be expected unfailingly to obey unless they are generally coerced to do so. On the other hand, to honor the laws of nature without the assurance that others do likewise is unreasonable; for then the good become prey, and the strong arrogant. Men, says Hobbes, are not bees. Men are driven constantly to compete for honor and dignity, out of which arises hate, envy and finally, war. And "covenants without the sword, are but words, and of no strength to secure a man at all." Hobbes consequently is led to this paradox: that the laws of nature cannot succeed outside the frame of a contrived organization, outside the commonwealth. Natural law is established only by artificial Power, and Reason enfranchised only by Authority.

I stress again the political character of Hobbes's argument. The commonwealth put an end to the state of nature but not to the nature of man. Men agreed to surrender their right to force (except in self-defense), and to put all their strength at the disposal of a sovereign, who would bear their person and save their lives. In this conception of state formation, Hobbes once more rings very modern. What more fundamental sense has since been made of the state than that it is a differentiation of the generalized primitive order: structurally, the separation of a public authority out of the society at large; functionally; the special reservation to that authority of coercive force (monopoly control of force)?

> The only way to erect such a Common Power, as may be able to defend them from the invasion of Forraigners, and the injuries of one another, and thereby to secure them in such sort, as that by their owne industry, and by the fruites of the Earth, they may nourish themselves and live content-edly; is, to conferre all their power and strength upon one Man, or upon one Assembly of men, that may reduce all their Wills, by plurality of voices, unto one Will: which is as much as to say, to appoint one Man, or Assembly of men, to beare their Person; and every one to owne, and acknowledge himselfe to be the Author of whatsoever that he that so beareth their Person, shall Act, or cause to be Acted, in those things which conern the Common Peace and safetie; and therein to submit their Wills, every one to his Will, and their Judgements, to his Judgement (Part 2, Chapter 17).

But Mauss's resolution of Warre also had historic merit: it corrected just this simplified progression from chaos to commonwealth, savagery to civilization, that had been the work of classical contract theory.[20] Here in the primitive world Mauss displayed a whole array of intermediate forms, not only of a certain stability, but that did not

20. Hobbes's particular inability to conceive primitive society as such is manifest by

make coercion the price of order. Still, Mauss too was not confident
that reason alone had been responsible. Or perhaps it was just an
afterthought, upon looking back over the peace of the gift, that he saw
in it the signs of an original wisdom. For the rationality of the gift
contradicted everthing he had said before on the subject of *hau*.
Hobbes's paradox was to realize the natural (reason) in the artifical;
for Mauss, reason took the form of the irrational. Exchange is the
triumph of reason, but lacking the embodied spirit of the donor *(hau)*,
the gift is not requited.

A few last words about the fate of *The Gift*. Since Mauss, and
in part by way of rapprochment with modern economics, anthropology has become more consistently rational in its treatment of
exchange. Reciprocity is contract pure and mainly secular, sanctioned perhaps by a mixture of considerations of which a carefully
calculated self-interest is not the least (cf. Firth, 1967). Mauss seems
in this regard much more like Marx in the first chapter of *Capital:*
if it can be said without disrespect, more animistic. One quarter
of corn is exchangeable for *X* hundredweight iron. What is it in
these things, so obviously different, that yet is equal? Precisely,
the question was, for Marx, what *in these things* brings them into
agreement?—and not what is it about these parties to the exchange?
Similarly, for Mauss; "What force is there in the thing given that
makes the beneficiary reciprocate?" And the same kind of answer,
from "intrinsic" properties: here the *hau*, if there the socially necessary labor time. Yet "animistic" is manifestly an improper charac-
terization of the thought involved. If Mauss, like Marx, concentrated
singularly on the anthropomorphic qualities of the things
exchanged, rather than the (thinglike?) qualities of the people, it

---

his assimilation of it, that is of the patriarchal chiefdom, to the commonwealth. This
is clear enough in the passages of *Leviathan* on commonwealths by acquisition, but even
more definitive in the parallel sections of *Elements of Law* and *De Cive.* Thus, in the
latter: "A *father* with his *sons* and *servants,* grown into a civil person by virtue of his
paternal jurisdiction, is called a *family.* This *family,* if through multiplying of *children*
and acquisition of *servants* it becomes numerous, insomuch as without casting the
uncertain die of war it cannot be subdued, will be termed an *hereditary kingdom.* Which
though it differ from an *institutive monarchy,* being acquired by force, in the original
and manner of its constitution; yet being constituted, it hath all the same properties,
and the right of authority is everywhere the same; insomuch as it is not needful to speak
anything of them apart" *(English Works* [Molesworth, ed.], 1839, vol. 2, pp. 121-122).

was because each saw in the transactions respectively at issue a determinate form and epoch of alienation: mystic alienation of the donor in primitive reciprocity, alienation of human social labor in commodity production (cf. Godelier, 1966, p. 143). They thus share the supreme merit, unknown to most "Economic Anthropology," of taking exchange as it is historically presented, not as a natural category explicable by a certain eternal disposition of humanity.

In the total prestations between clan and clan, said Mauss, things are related in some degree as persons and persons in some degree as things. More than irrational, it exaggerates only slightly to say that the process approaches clinical definitions of neurosis: persons are treated as objects; people confuse themselves with the external world. But even beyond the desire to affirm the rationality of exchange, a large section of Anglo-American anthropology has seemed instinctively repelled by the commercialization of persons apparently implied in the Maussian formula.

Nothing could be farther apart than the initial Anglo-Saxon and French responses to this generalized idea of prestation. Here was Mauss decrying the *inhumanity* of modern abstract distinctions between real and personal law, calling for a return to the archaic relation between men and things, while the Anglo-Saxons could only congratulate the ancestors for having finally liberated men from a debasing confusion with material objects. And especially for thus liberating women. For when Lévi-Strauss parleyed the "total prestation" into a grand system of marital exchanges, an interesting number of British and American ethnologists recoiled at once from the idea, refusing for their part to "treat women as commodities."

Without wanting to decide the issue, not at least in these terms, I do wonder whether the Anglo-American reaction of distrust was ethnocentric. It seems to presume an eternal separation of the economic, having to do with getting and spending, and besides always a little off-color, from the social sphere of moral relationships. For if it is decided in advance that the world in general is differentiated as is ours in particular, economic relations being one thing and social (kinship) another, than to speak of groups exchanging women does appear an immoral extension of business to marriage and a slander of all those engaged in the traffic. Still, the conclusion forgets the great lesson of "total prestation," both for the study of primitive economics and of marriage.

The primitive order is generalized. A clear differentiation of spheres into social and economic does not there appear. As for marriage, it is not that commercial operations are applied to social relations, but the two were never completely separated in the first place. We must think here in the same way we do now about classificatory kinship: not that the term for "father" is "extended" to father's brother, phrasing that smuggles in the priority of the nuclear family, but rather that we are in the presence of a broad kinship category that knows no such genealogical distinctions. And as for economics, we are similarly in the presence of a generalized organization for which the supposition that kinship is "exogenous" betrays any hope of understanding.

I mention a final positive contribution of *The Gift*, related to this point but more specific. At the end of the essay, Mauss in effect recapitulated his thesis by two Melanesian examples of tenuous relations between villages and peoples: of how, menaced always by deterioration into war, primitive groups are nevertheless reconciled by festival and exchange. This theme too was later amplified by Lévi-Strauss. "There is a link," he wrote, "a continuity, between hostile relations and the provision of reciprocal prestations. Exchanges are peacefully resolved wars and wars are the result of unsuccessful transactions" (1969, p. 67; cf. 1943, p. 136). But this implication of *The Gift* is, I think, even broader than external relations and transactions. In posing the internal fragility of the segmentary societies, their constituted decomposition, *The Gift* transposes the classic alternatives of war and trade from the periphery to the very center of social life, and from the occasional episode to the continuous presence. This is the supreme importance of Mauss's return to nature, from which it follows that primitive society is at war with Warre, and that all their dealings are treaties of peace. All the exchanges, that is to say, must bear in their material design some political burden of reconciliation. Or, as the Bushman said, "'The worse thing is not giving presents. If people do not like each other but one gives a gift and the other must accept, this brings a peace between them. We give what we have. That is the way we live together'" (Marshall, 1961, p. 245).

And from this comes in turn all the basic principles of an economics properly anthropological, including the one in particular at the heart of succeeding chapters: that every exchange, as it embodies some coefficient of sociability, cannot be understood in its material terms apart from its social terms.

# 5

# On the Sociology
# of Primitive Exchange

In a discussion that has anthropological pretensions, "provisional
generalization" is no doubt a redundant phrase. Yet the present venture needs a doubly cautious introduction. Its generalizations have
developed out of a dialogue with ethnographic materials—many of
these are appended Tylorian fashion as "illustrative materials"—but
no rigorous tests have been applied. Perhaps the conclusions may be
offered as a plea to enthnography rather than a contribution to theory, if these are not again the same thing. At any rate, there follow
some suggestions about the interplay in primitive communities between forms, material conditions, and social relations of exchange.

## Material Flow and Social Relations

What are in the received wisdom "noneconomic" or "exogenous"
conditions are in the primitive reality the very organization of economy.[1] A material transaction is usually a momentary episode in a

1. For the present purpose, "economy" is viewed as the process of provisioning
society (or the "socio-cultural system"). No social relation, institution, or set of institutions is of itself "economic." Any institution, say a family or a lineage order, if it has
material consequence for provisioning society can be placed in an economic context and
considered part of the economic process. The same institution may be equally or more
involved in the political process, thus profitably considered as well in a political context.
This way of looking at economics or politics—or for that matter, religion, education,
and any number of other cultural processes—is dictated by the nature of primitive
culture. Here we find no socially distinct "economy" or "government," merely social
(continued on p. 186)

continuous social relation. The social relation exerts governance: the flow of goods is constrained by, is part of, a status etiquette. "One cannot treat Nuer economic relations by themselves, for they always form part of direct social relations of a general kind," Evans-Pritchard writes: ". . . there is always between them a general social relationship of one kind or another, and their economic relations, if such they may be called, must conform to this general pattern of behavior" (1940, pp. 90–91). The dictum is broadly applicable (cf. White, 1959, pp. 242–245).

Yet the connection between material flow and social relations is reciprocal. A specific social relation may constrain a given movement of goods, but a specific transaction—"by the same token"—suggests a particular social relation. If friends make gifts, gifts make friends. A great proportion of primitive exchange, much more than our own traffic, has as its decisive function this latter, instrumental one: the material flow underwrites or initiates social relations. Thus do primitive peoples transcend the Hobbesian chaos. For the indicative condition of primitive society is the absence of a public and sovereign power: persons and (especially) groups confront each other not merely as distinct interests but with the possible inclination and certain right to physically prosecute these interests. Force is decentralized,

---

groups and relations with multiple functions, which we distinguish as economic, political, and so forth.

That economy thus presents itself as an aspect of things is probably generally acceptable. That the emphasis be the provisioning of *society* may not prove so acceptable. For the concern is not how individuals go about their business: "economy" has not been defined as the application of scarce available means against alternative ends (material ends or otherwise). From means to end "economy" is conceived as *a component of culture* rather than *a kind of human action,* the material life process of society rather than a need-satisfying process of individual behavior. Our purpose is not to analyze entrepreneurs but to compare cultures. We reject the historically specific Business Outlook. In terms of controversial positions recently developed in the *American Anthropologist,* the stand adopted is much more with Dalton (1961; cf. Sahlins, 1962) than with Burling (1962) or LeClair (1962). Also, solidarity is here affirmed with housewives the world over and Professor Malinowski. Professor Firth upbraids Malinowski's imprecision on a point of economic anthropology with the observation that "This is not the terminology of economics, it is almost the language of the housewife" (Firth, 1957, p. 220). The terminology of the present effort similarly departs from economic orthodoxy. This may be justly considered a necessity born of ignorance, but something is to be said as well for the appropriateness, in a study of kinship economies, of the housewife's perspective.

legitimately held in severalty, the social compact has yet to be drawn, the state nonexistent. So peacemaking is not a sporadic intersocietal event, it is a continuous process going on within society itself. Groups must "come to terms"—the phrase notably connotes a material exchange satisfactory on both sides.[2]

Even on its strictly practical side, exchange in primitive communities has not the same role as the economic flow in modern industrial communities. The place of transaction in the total economy is different: under primitive conditions it is more detached from production, less firmly hinged to production in an organic way. Typically, it is less involved than modern exchange in the acquisition of means of production, more involved with the redistribution of finished goods through the community. The bias is that of an economy in which food holds a commanding position, and in which day-to-day output does not depend on a massive technological complex nor a complex division of labor. It is the bias also of a domestic mode of production: of household producing units, division of labor by sex and age dominant, production that looks to familial requirements, and direct access by domestic groups to strategic resources. It is the bias of a social order in which rights to control returns go along with rights to use resources of production, and in which there is very limited traffic in titles or income privileges in resources. It is the bias, finally, of societies ordered in the main by kinship. Such characteristics of primitive economies as these, so broadly stated, are of course subject to qualification in specific instances. They are offered only as a guide to the detailed

2. Economy has been defined as the process of (materially) provisioning society and the definition opposed to the human act of satisfying wants. The great play of instrumental exchange in primitive societies underscores the usefulness of the former definition. Sometimes the peace-making aspect is so fundamental that precisely the same sorts and amounts of stuff change hands: the renunciation of opposed interest is in this way symbolized. On a strictly formal view the transaction is a waste of time and effort. One might say that people are maximizing value, social value, but such is to misplace the determinant of the transaction, to fail to specify the circumstances which produce different material outcomes in different historical instances, to hold fast to the economizing premise of the market by a false assignment of pecuniary-like qualities to social qualities, to take the high road to tautology. The interest of such transactions is precisely that they do not materially provision people and are not predicated on the satisfaction of human material needs. They do, however, decidedly provision society: they maintain social relations, the structure of society, even if they do not to the least advantage the stock of consumables. Without any further assumptions, they are "economic" in the suggested meaning of the term (cf. Sahlins, 1969).

analysis of distribution that follows. It is also advisable to repeat that "primitive" shall refer to cultures lacking a political state, and it applies only insofar as economy and social relations have not been modified by the historic penetration of states.

On a very general view, the array of economic transactions in the ethnographic record may be resolved into two types.[3] First, those "vice-versa" movements between two parties known familiarly as 'reciprocity' $(A \rightleftarrows B)$. The second, centralized movements: collection from members of a group, often under one hand, and redivision within this group:

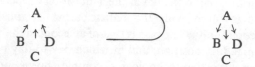

This is "pooling" or "redistribution." On an even more general view, the two types merge. *For pooling is an organization of reciprocities, a system of reciprocities*—a fact of central bearing upon the genesis of large-scale redistribution under chiefly aegis. But this most general understanding merely suggests concentration in the first place on reciprocity; it remains the course of analytic wisdom to separate the two.

Their social organizations are very different. True, pooling and reciprocity may occur in the same social contexts—the same close kinsmen that pool their resources in household commensality, for instance, also as individuals share things with one another—but the precise social relations of pooling and reciprocity are not the same. Pooling is socially a *within* relation, the collective action of a group. Reciprocity is a *between* relation, the action and reaction of two parties. Thus pooling is the complement of social unity and, in Polanyi's term, "centricity"; whereas, reciprocity is social duality and

3. The reader familiar with recent discussions of primitive distribution will recognize my indebtedness to Polanyi (1944, 1957, 1959) on this score, and likewise the departures from Polanyi's terminology and threefold scheme of principles of integration. It is also a pleasure to affirm with Firth that "Every student of primitive economics, in fact, gratefully builds upon the foundations which Malinowski has laid" (Firth, 1959, p. 174).

"symmetry." Pooling stipulates a social center where goods meet and thence flow outwards, and a social boundary too, within which persons (or subgroups) are cooperatively related. But reciprocity stipulates two sides, two distinct social-economic interests. Reciprocity can establish solidary relations, insofar as the material flow suggests assistance or mutual benefit, yet the social fact of sides is inescapable.

Considering the established contributions of Malinowski and Firth, Gluckman, Richards, and Polanyi, it does not seem too sanguine to say that we know fairly well the material and social concomitants of pooling. Also, what is known fits the argument that pooling is the material side of "collectivity" and "centricity." Cooperative food production, rank and chieftainship, collective political and ceremonial action, these are some of the ordinary contexts of pooling in primitive communities. To review very briefly:

The everyday, workaday variety of redistribution is familial pooling of food. The principle suggested by it is that products of collective effort in provisioning are pooled, especially should the cooperation entail division of labor. Stated so, the rule applies not only to householding but to higher-level cooperation as well, to groups larger than households that develop about some task of procurement—say, buffalo impounding in the Northern Plains or netting fish in a Polynesian lagoon. With qualifications—such as the special shares locally accorded special contributions to the group endeavor—the principle remains at the higher, as at the lower, household level: "goods collectively procured are distributed through the collectivity."

Rights of call on the produce of the underlying population, as well as obligations of generosity, are everywhere associated with chieftainship. The organized exercise of these rights and obligations is redistribution:

> I think that throughout the world we would find that the relations between economics and politics are of the same type. The chief, everywhere, acts as a tribal banker, collecting food, storing it, and protecting it, and then using it for the benefit of the whole community. His functions are the prototype of the public finance system and the organization of State treasuries of to-day. Deprive the chief of his privileges and financial benefits and who suffers most but the whole tribe? (Malinowski, 1937, pp. 232–233).

This use "for the benefit of the whole community" takes various forms: subsidizing religious ceremony, social pageantry, or war; underwriting craft production, trade, the construction of technical apparatus and of public and religious edifices; redistributing diverse local products; hospitality and succor of the community (in severalty or in general) during shortage. Speaking more broadly, redistribution by powers-that-be serves two purposes, either of which may be dominant in a given instance. The practical, logistic function—redistribution—sustains the community, or community effort, in a material sense. At the same time, or alternatively, it has an instrumental function: as a ritual of communion and of subordination to central authority, redistribution sustains the corporate structure itself, that is in a social sense. The practical benefits may be critical, but, whatever the practical benefits, chiefly pooling generates the spirit of unity and centricity, codifies the structure, stipulates the centralized organization of social order and social action—

> . . . every person who takes part in the *aŋa* [feast organized by a Tikopia chief] is impelled to participate in forms of cooperation which for the time being go far beyond his personal interests and those of his family and reach the bounds of the whole community. Such a feast gathers together chiefs and their clansfolk who at other times are rivals ready to criticize and slander each other, but who assemble here with an outward show of amity. . . . In addition, such purposive activity subserves certain wider social ends, which are common in the sense that every person or nearly every person knowingly or unknowingly promotes them. For instance, attendance at the *aŋa* and participation in the economic contributions does in fact help to support the Tikopia system of authority (Firth, 1950, pp. 230-231).

So we have at least the outline of a functional theory of redistribution. The central issues are now likely to be developmental ones, the specification by comparison or phylogenetic study of selective circumstances. The economic anthropology of reciprocity, however, is not at the same stage. One reason, perhaps, is a popular tendency to view reciprocity as balance, as unconditional one-for-one exchange. Considered as a material transfer, reciprocity is often not that at all. Indeed, it is precisely through scrutiny of departures from balanced exchange that one glimpses the interplay between reciprocity, social relations and material circumstances.

Reciprocity is a whole class of exchanges, a continuum of forms. This is specially true in the narrow context of material transactions— as opposed to a broadly conceived social principle or moral norm of give-and-take. At one end of the spectrum stands the assistance freely given, the small currency of everyday kinship, friendship, and neighborly relations, the "pure gift" Malinowski called it, regarding which an open stipulation of return would be unthinkable and unsociable. At the other pole, self-interested seizure, appropriation by chicanery or force requited only by an equal and opposite effort on the principle of *lex talionis,* "negative reciprocity" as Gouldner phrases it. The extremes are notably positive and negative in a moral sense. The intervals between them are not merely so many gradations of material balance in exchange, they are intervals of sociability. The distance between poles of reciprocity is, among other things, social distance:

> Unto a stranger thou mayest lend upon usury; but unto thy brother thou shalt not lend usury (Deuteronomy xxiii, 21).

> Native [Siuai] moralists assert that neighbors should be friendly and mutually trustful, whereas people from far-off are dangerous and unworthy of morally just consideration. For example, natives lay great stress on honesty involving neighbors while holding that trade with strangers may be guided by *caveat emptor* (Oliver, 1955, p. 82).

> Gain at the cost of other communities, particularly communities at a distance, and more especially such as are felt to be aliens, is not obnoxious to the standards of homebred use and wont (Veblen, 1915, p. 46).

> A trader always cheats people. For this reason intra-regional trade is rather frowned upon while inter-tribal trade gives to the (Kapauku) businessman prestige as well as profit (Pospisil, 1958, p. 127).

### A Scheme of Reciprocities

A purely formal typology of reciprocities is possible, one based exclusively on immediacy of returns, equivalence of returns, and like material and mechanical dimensions of exchange. The classification thus in hand, one might proceed to correlate subtypes of reciprocity with diverse "variables" such as kinship distance of parties to the transaction. The virtue of this manner of exposition is that it is "scientific," or so it would seem. Among the defects is that it is a conventional metaphor of exposition, not a true history of experiment. It ought to be recognized from the beginning that the distinction of one type of reciprocity from another is more than formal. A feature such as the expectation of returns says something about the spirit of exchange, about its disinterestedness or its interestedness, the impersonality, the compassion. Any seeming formal classification conveys these meanings: it is as much a moral as a mechanical scheme. (That the recognition of the moral quality prejudges the relation of exchange to social "variables," in the sense that the latter are then logically connected to variations in exchange, is not contested. This is a sign that the classification is good.)

The actual kinds of reciprocity are many in any primitive society, let alone in the primitive world taken as a whole. "Vice-versa movements" may include sharing and counter-sharing of unprocessed food, informal hospitality, ceremonious affinal exchanges, loaning and repaying, compensation of specialized or ceremonial services, the transfer that seals a peace agreement, impersonal haggle, and so on and on. We have several ethnographic attempts to cope typologically with the empirical diversity, notably Douglas Oliver's scheme of Siuai transactions (1955, pp. 229–231; cf. Price, 1962, p. 37 f; Spencer, 1959, p. 194 f; Marshall, 1961, and others). In *Crime and Custom*, Malinowski wrote rather broadly and unconditionally about reciprocity; in the *Argonauts*, however, he developed a classification of Trobriand exchanges out of manifold variations in balance and equivalence (Malinowski, 1922, pp. 176–194). It was from this vantage point, looking to the directness of returns, that the *continuum* which is reciprocity was revealed:

> I have on purpose spoken of forms of exchange, of gifts and counter-gifts, rather than of barter or trade, because, although there exist forms of barter pure and simple, there are so many transitions and gradations between that and simple gift, that it is impossible to draw any fixed line between trade on the one hand, and the exchange of gifts on the other. . . . In order to deal with these facts correctly it is necessary to give a complete survey of all forms of payment or present. In this survey there will be at one end the

extreme cases of pure gift, that is an offering for which nothing is given in return [but see Firth 1957, pp. 221, 222]. Then, through many customary forms of gift or payment, partially or conditionally returned, which shade into each other, there come forms of exchange, where more or less strict equivalence is observed, arriving finally at real barter (Malinowski, 1922, p. 176).

Malinowski's perspective may be taken beyond the Trobriands and applied broadly to reciprocal exchange in primitive societies. It seems possible to lay out in abstract fashion a continuum of reciprocities, based on the "vice-versa" nature of exchanges, along which empirical instances encountered in the particular ethnographic case can be placed. The stipulation of material returns, less elegantly, the "sidedness" of exchange, would be the critical thing. For this there are obvious objective criteria, such as the toleration of material unbalance and the leeway of delay: the initial movement of goods from hand to hand is more or less requited materially and there are variations too in the time allowed for reciprocation (again see Firth, 1957, pp. 220–221). Put another way, the spirit of exchange swings from disinterested concern for the other party through mutuality to self-interest. So expressed, the assessment of "sidedness" can be supplemented by empirical criteria in addition to those of immediacy and material equivalence: the initial transfer may be voluntary, involuntary, prescribed, contracted; the return freely bestowed, exacted, or dunned; the exchange haggled or not, the subject of accounting or not; and so forth.

The spectrum of reciprocities proposed for general use is defined by its extremes and mid-point:

Generalized reciprocity, the solidary extreme $(A \xleftarrow{\phantom{---}} B)$[4]

"Generalized reciprocity" refers to transactions that are putatively altruistic, transactions on the line of assistance given and, if possible

---

4. Since the original publication of this essay, Lévi-Strauss's "échange généralisé" has become much more current than our "generalized reciprocity." This is only unfortunate because the two do not refer to the same type (let alone the same universe) of reciprocity. Besides, friends and critics have suggested various alternatives to "generalized reciprocity," such as "indefinite reciprocity," etc. The time for beating a terminological retreat may be near; but for the moment, I am holding on.

and necessary, assistance returned. The ideal type is Malinowski's "pure gift." Other indicative ethnographic formulas are "sharing," "hospitality," "free gift," "help," and "generosity." Less sociable, but tending toward the same pole are "kinship dues," "chiefly dues," and *"noblesse oblige."* Price (1962) refers to the genre as "weak reciprocity" by reason of the vagueness of the obligation to reciprocate.

At the extreme, say voluntary food-sharing among near kinsmen—or for its logical value, one might think of the suckling of children in this context—the expectation of a direct material return is unseemly. At best it is implicit. The material side of the transaction is repressed by the social: reckoning of debts outstanding cannot be overt and is typically left out of account. This is not to say that handing over things in such form, even to "loved ones," generates no counter-obligation. But the counter is not stipulated by time, quantity, or quality: the expectation of reciprocity is indefinite. It usually works out that the time and worth of reciprocation are not alone conditional on what was given by the donor, but also upon what he will need and when, and likewise what the recipient can afford and when. Receiving goods lays on a diffuse obligation to reciprocate when necessary to the donor and/or possible for the recipient. The requital thus may be very soon, but then again it may be never. There are people who even in the fullness of time are incapable of helping themselves or others. A good pragmatic indication of generalized reciprocity is a sustained one-way flow. Failure to reciprocate does not cause the giver of stuff to stop giving: the goods move one way, in favor of the have-not, for a very long period.

### Balanced reciprocity, the midpoint $(A \rightleftharpoons B)$

"Balanced reciprocity" refers to direct exchange. In precise balance, the reciprocation is the customary equivalent of the thing received and is without delay. Perfectly balanced reciprocity, the simultaneous exchange of the same types of goods to the same amounts, is not only conceivable but ethnographically attested in certain marital transactions (e.g., Reay, 1959, pp. 95 f), friendship compacts (Seligman, 1910, p. 70), and peace agreements (Hogbin, 1939, p. 79; Loeb, 1926, p. 204; Williamson, 1912, p. 183). "Balanced reciprocity" may be more loosely applied to transactions which stipulate returns of commensurate worth or utility within a finite and narrow period. Much "gift-exchange," many "payments," much that goes under the ethnographic head of "trade" and plenty that is called "buying-selling" and involves "primitive money" belong in the genre of balanced reciprocity.

Balanced reciprocity is less "personal" than generalized reciprocity. From our own vantage-point it is "more economic." The parties confront each other as distinct economic and social interests. The material side of the transaction is at least as critical as the social: there is more or less precise reckoning, as the things given must be covered within some short term. So the pragmatic test of balanced reciprocity becomes an inability to tolerate one-way flows; the relations between people are disrupted by a failure to reciprocate within limited time and equivalence leeways. It is notable of the main run of generalized reciprocities that the material flow is sustained by prevailing social relations; whereas, for the main run of balanced exchange, social relations hinge on the material flow.

### Negative reciprocity, the unsociable extreme $(A \rightleftarrows B)$

"Negative reciprocity" is the attempt to get something for nothing with impunity, the several forms of appropriation, transactions opened and conducted toward net utilitarian advantage. Indicative ethnographic terms include "haggling" or "barter," "gambling," "chicanery," "theft," and other varieties of seizure.

Negative reciprocity is the most impersonal sort of exchange. In guises such as "barter" it is from our own point of view the "most economic." The participants confront each other as opposed interests, each looking to maximize utility at the other's expense. Approaching the transaction with an eye singular to the main chance, the aim of the opening party, or of both parties, is the unearned increment. One of the most sociable forms, leaning toward balance, is haggling conducted in the spirit of "what the traffic will bear." From this, negative reciprocity ranges through various degrees of cunning, guile, stealth, and violence to the finesse of a well-conducted horse raid. The "reciprocity" is, of course, conditional again, a matter of defense of self-interest. So the flow may be one-way once more, reciprocation contingent upon mustering countervailing pressure or guile.

It is a long way from a suckling child to a Plains Indians' horse-raid. Too long, it could be argued, the classification too widely set. Yet "vice-versa movements" in the ethnographic record do grade into each other along the whole span. It is well to recall, nevertheless, that empirical exchanges often fall somewhere along the line, not directly on the extreme and middle points here outlined. The question is, can one specify social or economic circumstances that impel reciprocity toward one or another of the stipulated positions, toward generalized, balanced, or negative reciprocity? I think so.

## *Reciprocity and Kinship Distance*

The span of social distance between those who exchange conditions the mode of exchange. Kinship distance, as has already been suggested, is especially relevant to the form of reciprocity. Reciprocity is inclined toward the generalized pole by close kinship, toward the negative extreme in proportion to kinship distance.

The reasoning is nearly syllogistic. The several reciprocities from freely bestowed gift to chicanery amount to a spectrum of sociability, from sacrifice in favor of another to self-interested gain at the expense of another. Take as the minor premise Tylor's dictum that kindred goes with kindness, "two words whose common derivation expresses in the happiest way one of the main principles of social life." It follows that close kin tend to share, to enter into generalized exchanges, and distant and nonkin to deal in equivalents or in guile. Equivalence becomes compulsory in proportion to kinship distance lest relations break off entirely, for with distance there can be little tolerance of gain and loss even as there is little inclination to extend oneself. To non-kin—"other people", perhaps not even "people"—no quarter must needs be given: the manifest inclination may well be "devil take the hindmost."

All this seems perfectly applicable to our own society, but it is more significant in primitive society. Because kinship is more significant in primitive society. It is, for one thing, the organizing principle or idiom of most groups and most social relations. Even the category "nonkin" is ordinarily defined by it, that is, as the negative aspect of it, the logical extreme of the class—nonbeing as a state of being. There is something real to this view; it is not logical sophistry. Among ourselves, "nonkin" denotes specialized status relations of positive quality: doctor-patient, policeman-citizen, employer-employee, classmates, neighbors, professional colleagues. But for them, "nonkin" connotes the negation of community (or tribalism); often it is the synonym for "enemy" or "stranger." Likewise the economic relation tends to be a simple negation of kinship reciprocities: other institutional norms need not come into play.

Kinship distance, however, has different aspects. It may be organized in several ways, and what is "close" in one of these ways need not be so in another. Exchange may be contingent on genealogical distance (as locally imputed), that is, on interpersonal kinship status. Or it may hinge on segmentary distance, on descent group status. (One suspects that where these two do not correspond the closer relation governs the reciprocity appropriate in dealings between individual parties, but this ought to be worked out empirically.) For the purpose of creating a general model, attention should also be given to the power of community in stipulating distance. It is not only that kinship organizes communities, but communities kinship, so that a spatial, coresidential term affects the measure of kinship distance and thus the mode of exchange.

> Brothers living together, or a paternal uncle and his nephews living in the same house were, as far as my observation goes, on much closer terms with each other than relatives of similar degrees living apart. This was evident whenever there was a question of borrowing things, of getting help, of accepting an obligation, or of assuming responsibilities for each other (Malinowski, 1915, p. 532; the reference is to the Mailu).

Mankind [to Siuai] consists of relatives and strangers. Relatives are usually interlinked by both blood and marital ties; most of them live nearby, and persons who live nearby are all relatives . . . Transactions among them should be carried out in a spirit devoid of commerciality—preferably consisting of sharing [i.e., "pooling" in terms of the present discussion], nonreciprocable giving, and bequeathing, among closest relatives, or of lending among more distantly related ones. . . . Except for a few very distantly related sib-mates, persons who live far away are not relatives and can only be enemies. Most of their customs are unsuitable for the Siuai, but a few of their goods and techniques are desirable. One interacts with them only to buy and sell—utilizing hard bargaining and deceit to make as much profit from such transactions as possible (Oliver, 1955, pp. 454-455).

Here is one possible model for analyzing reciprocity: the tribal plan can be viewed as a series of more and more inclusive kinship-residential sectors, and reciprocity seen then to vary in character by sectoral position. The close kinsmen who render assistance are particularly near kinsmen in a spatial sense: it is in regard to people of the household, the camp, hamlet, or village that compassion is required, inasmuch as interaction is intense and peaceable solidarity essential. But the quality of mercy is strained in peripheral sectors, strained by kinship distance, so is less likely in exchanges with fellow tribesmen of another village than among covillagers, still less likely in the intertribal sector.

Kinship-residential groupings from this perspective comprise ever-widening comembership spheres: the household, the local lineage, perhaps the village, the subtribe, tribe, other tribes—the particular plan of course varies. The structure is a hierarchy of levels of integration, but from the inside and on the ground it is a series of concentric circles. Social relations of each circle have a specific quality—household relations, lineage relations, and so on—and except as the sectoral divisions be cut through by other organizations of kinship solidarity—say, nonlocalized clans or personal kindreds—relations within each sphere are more solidary than relations of the next, more inclusive sector. Reciprocity accordingly inclines toward balance and chicane in proportion to sectoral distance. In each sector, certain modes of reciprocity are characteristic or dominant: generalized modes are dominant in the narrowest spheres and play out in wider spheres, balanced reciprocity is characteristic of intermediate sectors, chicane of the most peripheral spheres. In brief, a general model of the play of reciprocity may be developed by superimposing the society's sectoral plan upon the reciprocity continuum. Such a model is shown in Figure 5.1.

The plan does not rest alone upon the two terms of sectoral division and reciprocity variation. Something is to be said for the embedded third term, morality. "Far more than we ordinarily suppose," Firth has written, "economic relations rest on moral foundations" (1951, p. 144). Certainly that must be the way the people see it—"Although the Siuai have separate terms for 'generosity,' 'cooperativeness,' 'morality' (that is, rule abiding), and 'geniality,' I believe that they consider

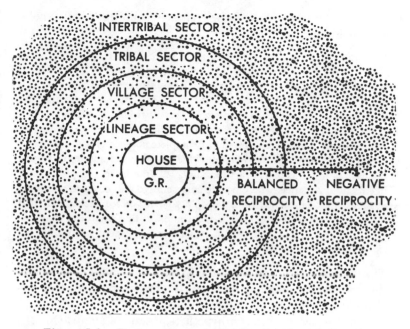

*Figure 5.1.   Reciprocity and Kinship Residential Sectors*

all these to be closely interrelated aspects of the same attribute of goodness . . ." (Oliver, 1955, p. 78). Another contrast with ourselves is suggested, a tendency for morality, like reciprocity, to be sectorally organized in primitive societies. The norms are characteristically relative and situational rather than absolute and universal. A given act, that is to say, is not so much in itself good or bad, it depends on who the "Alter" is. The appropriation of another man's goods or his woman, which is a sin ("theft," "adultery") in the bosom of one's community, may be not merely condoned but positively rewarded with the admiration of one's fellows—if it is perpetrated on an outsider. The contrast with the absolute standards of the Judeo-Christian tradition is probably overdrawn: no moral system is exclusively absolute (especially in wartime) and none perhaps is entirely relative and contextual. But situational standards, defined often in sectoral terms, do seem to prevail in primitive communities and this contrasts sufficiently with our own to have drawn repeated comment from ethnologists. For instance:

> Navaho morality is . . . contextual rather than absolute. . . . Lying is not always and everywhere wrong. The rules vary with the situation. To deceive when trading with foreign tribes is a morally accepted practice. Acts are not in themselves bad or good. Incest [by its nature, a contextual sin] is perhaps the only conduct that is condemned without qualification. It is quite correct to use witchcraft techniques in trading with members of foreign tribes. . . . There is an almost complete absence of abstract ideals. Under the circumstances of aboriginal life Navahos did not need to orient themselves in terms of abstract morality. . . . In a large, complex society like modern America, where people come and go and business and other dealings must be carried on by people who never see each other, it is functionally necessary to have abstract standards that transcend an immediate concrete situation in which two or more persons are interacting (Kluckhohn, 1959, p. 434).

The scheme with which we deal is at least tripartite: social, moral, and economic. Reciprocity and morality are sectorally structured—the structure is that of kinship-tribal groupings.

But the scheme is entirely a hypothetical state of affairs. One can conceive circumstances that would alter the social-moral-reciprocal relations postulated by it. Propositions about the external sectors are particularly vulnerable. (For "external sector" one can generally read "intertribal sector," the ethnic peripherae of primitive communities; in practice it can be set where positive morality fades out or where intergroup hostility is the normal in-group expectation.) Transactions in this sphere may be consummated by force and guile, it is true, by *wabuwabu,* to use the near-onomatopoeic Dobuan term for sharp practice. Yet it seems that violent appropriation is a resort born of urgent requirements that can only, or most easily, be supplied by militant tactics. Peaceful symbiosis is at least a common alternative.

In these nonviolent confrontations the propensity to *wabuwabu* no doubt persists; it is built in to the sectoral plan. So if it can be socially tolerated—if, that is, countervailing peace-enforcing conditions are sufficiently strong—hard bargaining is the institutionalized external relation. We find then *gimwali,* the mentality of the market place, the impersonal (no-partnership) exchange of Trobriand commoners of different villages or of Trobrianders and other peoples. But still *gim-wali* does suppose special conditions, some sort of social insulation that prevents the economic friction from kindling a dangerous confla-gration. In the ordinary case, haggling is actually repressed, partic-ularly, it appears, if the exchange of the border is critical to both sides, as where different strategic specialties move against each other. De-spite the sectoral distance, the exchange is equitable, *utu,* balanced: the free play of *wabuwabu* and *gimwali* is checked in the interest of the symbiosis.

The check is delivered by special and delicate institutional means of border exchange. The means sometimes look so preposterous as to be considered by ethnologists some sort of "game" the natives play, but their design manifestly immunizes an important economic inter-dependence against a fundamental social cleavage. (Compare the dis-cussion of the *kula* in White,1959, and Fortune,1932.) Silent trade is a famous case in point—good relations are maintained by preventing any relations. Most common are "trade-partnerships" and "trade-friendships." The important thing in all varieties is a social suppres-sion of negative reciprocity. Peace is built in, haggling outlawed, and, conducted as a transfer of equivalent utilities, the exchange in turn underwrites the peace. (Trade-partnerships, often developed along lines of classificatory or affinal kinship, particularly incapsulate exter-nal economic transactions in solidary social relations. Status relations essentially internal are projected across community and tribal bound-aries. The reciprocity then may lean over backward, in the direction not of *wabuwabu* but something to the generalized side. Phrased as gift-giving, the presentation admits of delay in reciprocation: a direct return may indeed be unseemly. Hospitality, on another occasion returned in kind, accompanies the formal exchange of trade goods. For a host to give stuff over and above the worth of things brought by his partner is not unusual: it both befits the relation so to treat one's partner while he is traveling and stores up credits. On a wider view, this measure of unbalance sustains the trade partnership, compelling as it does another meeting.)

Intertribal symbiosis, in short, alters the terms of the hypothetical model. The peripheral sector is breached by more sociable relations than are normal in this zone. The context of exchange is now a narrower co-membership sphere, the exchange is peaceful and equitable. Reciprocity falls near the balance point.

Now the assertions of this essay, as I have said, developed out of a dialogue with ethnographic materials. It seems worthwhile to append some of these data to appropriate sections of the argument. Accordingly, Appendix A sets out materials relevant to the present section, "Reciprocity and Kinship Distance." This is not by way of proof, of course—there are indeed certain exceptions, or seeming exceptions, in the materials—but by way of exposition or illustration. Moreover, since the ideas only gradually came over me and the monographs and articles had been in many instances consulted for other purposes, it is certain that data pertinent to reciprocity in the works cited have escaped me. (I hope this is sufficiently apologetic and that the ethnographic notes of Appendix A are of interest to someone besides myself.)

Whatever the value of these notes as exposition of the asserted relation between reciprocity and kinship distance, they must also suggest to the reader certain limitations of the present perspective. Simply to demonstrate that the character of reciprocity is contingent upon social distance—even if it could be demonstrated in an incontestable way—is not to traffic in ultimate explanation, nor yet to specify when exchanges will in fact take place. A systematic relation between reciprocity and sociability in itself does not say when, or even to what extent, the relation will come into play. The supposition here is that the forces of constraint lie outside the relation itself. The terms of final analysis are the larger cultural structure and its adaptive response to its milieu. From this wider view one may be able to stipulate the significant sectoral lines and kinship categories of the given case, and to stipulate too the incidence of reciprocity in different sectors. Supposing it true that close kinsmen would share food, for example, it need not follow that the transactions occur. The total (cultural-adaptive) context may render intensive sharing dysfunctional and predicate in subtle ways the demise of a society that allows itself the luxury. Permit me to quote *in extenso* a passage from Fredrik Barth's brilliant ecological study of South Persian nomads. It shows so well the larger considerations that must be brought to the bar of explanation; in detail it exemplifies a situation that discounts intensive sharing:

The stability of a pastoral population depends on the maintenance of a balance between pastures, animal population, and human population. The pastures available by their techniques of herding set a maximal limit to the total animal population that an area will support; while the patterns of nomadic production and consumption define a minimal limit to the size of the herd that will support a human household. In this double set of balances is summarized the special difficulty in establishing a population balance in a pastoral economy: the human population must be sensitive to imbalances between flocks and pastures. Among agricultural, or hunting and collecting people, a crude Malthusian type of population control is sufficient. With a growing population, starvation and death-rate rise, until a balance is reached around which the population stabilizes. Where pastoral nomadism is the predominant or exclusive pattern, the nomad population, if subjected to such a form of population control, would *not* establish a population balance, but would find its whole basis for subsistence removed. Quite simply, this is because the productive capital on which their subsistence is based is not simply land, it is animals—in other words *food.* A pastoral economy can only be maintained so long as there are no pressures on its practitioners to invade this large store of food. A pastoral population can therefore only reach a stable level if other effective population controls intervene *before* those of starvation and death-rate. A first requirement in such an adaptation is the presence of the patterns of private ownership of herds, and individual economic responsibility for each household. By these patterns, the population becomes fragmented with respect to economic activities, and economic factors can strike differentially, eliminating some members of the population [i.e., through sedentarization] without affecting other members of the same population. This would be impossible if the corporate organization with respect to political life, and pasture rights, were also made relevant to economic responsibility and survival (Barth, 1961, p. 124).

Now, about the incidence of reciprocity in the specific case, here is something else to consider—the people may be stingy. Nothing has been said about sanctions of exchange relations nor, more importantly, about forces that countervail. There are contradictions in primitive economies: inclinations of self-interest are unleashed that are incompatible with the high levels of sociability customarily demanded. Malinowski long ago noticed this and Firth (1926) in an early paper on Maori proverbs skillfully brought to light the clash, the subtle interplay, between the moral dictates of sharing and narrow economic interests. The widespread mode of family production for use, it might be remarked, acts to brake outputs at comparatively low levels even as it orients economic concern inward, within the household. The mode of production thus does not readily lend itself to general economic solidarity. Suppose sharing is morally called for, say by the destitution of a near kinsman, all the things that make sharing good and proper may not evoke in an affluent man the inclination to do it. And even as there may be little to gain by assisting others, there are no iron-clad guarantees of such social compacts as kinship. The received social-moral obligations prescribe an economic course, and the publicity of primitive life, increasing the risk of evoking jealousy, hostility, and future economic penalty, tends to keep people on course. But, as is well known, to observe that a society has a system of morality and constraints is not to say that everyone acquiesces in it. There may be *biša-baša* times, "particularly in the late winter, when the household would hide its food, even from relatives" (Price,1962, p. 47).

That *biša-baša* is the pervasive condition of some peoples is not embarassing to the present thesis. The Siriono, everyone knows, parley hostility and crypto-stinginess into a way of life. Interestingly enough, the Siriono articulate ordinary norms of primitive economic intercourse. By the norm, for instance, the hunter should not eat the animal he has killed. But the *de facto* sector of sharing is not merely very narrow, "sharing rarely occurs without a certain amount of mutual mistrust and misunderstanding; a person always feels that it is he who is being taken advantage of," so that "The bigger the catch the more sullen the hunter" (Holmberg,1950, pp. 60, 62; cf. pp. 36, 38–39). The Siriono are not thereby different in kind from the run of primitive communities. They simply realize to an extreme the potentiality elsewhere less often consummated, the possibility that structural compulsions of generosity are unequal to a test of hardship. But then, the Siriono are a band of displaced and deculturated persons. The whole cultural shell, from rules of sharing through institutions of chieftainship and Crow kinship terminology, is a mockery of their present miserable state.

### Reciprocity and Kinship Rank

It is by now apparent—it is made apparent by the illustrative materials of Appendix A—that in any actual exchange several circumstances may simultaneously bear upon the material flow. Kinship distance, while perhaps significant, is not necessarily decisive. Something may be said for rank, relative wealth and need, the type of goods whether food or durables, and still other "factors." As a tactic of presentation and interpretation, it is useful to isolate and separately consider these factors. Accordingly, we move on to the relation between reciprocity and kinship rank. But with this proviso: propositions about the covariation of kinship distance or of kinship rank and reciprocity can be argued separately, even validated separately to the extent to which it is possible to select instances in which only the factor at issue is in play—holding "other things constant"—but the propositions do not present themselves separately in fact. The obvious course of further research is to work out the power of the several "variables" during combined plays. At best only the beginnings of this course are suggested here.

Rank difference as much as kinship distance supposes an economic relation. The vertical, rank axis of exchange—or the implication of rank—may affect the form of the transaction, just as the horizontal kinship-distance axis affects it. Rank is to some extent privilege, *droit du seigneur,* and it has its responsibilities, *noblesse oblige.* The dues and duties fall to both sides, both high and low have their claims, and feudal terms indeed do not convey the economic equity of kinship ranking. In its true historic setting *noblesse oblige* hardly cancelled out the *droits du seigneur.* In primitive society social inequality is more the organization of economic equality. Often, in fact, high rank is only secured or sustained by o'ercrowing generosity: the material advantage is on the subordinate's side. Perhaps it is too much to see the relation of parent and child as the elemental form of kinship ranking and its economic ethic. It is true, nevertheless, that paternalism is a common metaphor of primitive chieftainship. Chieftainship is ordinarily a relation of higher descent. So it is singularly appropriate that the chief is their "father," they his "children," and economic dealings between them cannot help but be affected.

The economic claims of rank and subordination are interdependent. The exercise of chiefly demand opens the way to solicitation from below, and vice versa—not uncommonly a moderate exposure to the "larger world" is enough to evoke native reference to customary chiefly dues as local banking procedure (cf. Ivens, 1927, p. 32). The word then for the economic relation between kinship ranks is "reciprocity." The reciprocity, moreover, is fairly classed as "generalized." While not as sociable as the run of assistance among close kinsmen, it does lean toward that side of the reciprocity continuum. Goods are in truth *yielded* to powers-that-be, perhaps on call and demand, and likewise goods may have to be *humbly solicited* from them. Still the rationale is often assistance and need, and the supposition of returns correspondingly indefinite. Reciprocation· may be left until a need precipitates it, it bears no necessary equivalence to the initial gift, and the material flow can be unbalanced in favor of one side or the other for a long time.

Reciprocity is harnessed to various principles of kinship rank. Generation-ranking, with the elders the privileged parties, may be of significance among hunters and gatherers not merely in the life of the family but in the life of the camp as a whole, and generalized reciprocity between juniors and seniors a correspondingly broad rule of social exchange (cf. Radcliffe-Brown,1948, pp. 42–43). The Trobrianders have a name for the economic ethic appropriate between parties of different rank within common descent groups—*pokala.* It is the rule that "Junior members of a sub-clan are expected to render gifts and services to their seniors, who in return are expected to confer assistance and material benefits on the juniors" (Powell,1960, p. 126). Even where rank is tied to genealogical seniority and consummated in office power — chieftainship properly so called—the ethic is the same. Take Polynesian chiefs, office holders in large, segmented polities: supported on the one hand by various chiefly dues, they are freighted, as many have observed, with perhaps even greater obligations to the underlying population. Probably always the "economic basis" of primitive politics is chiefly generosity—at one stroke an act of positive morality and a laying of indebtedness upon the commonalty. Or, to take a larger view, the entire political order is sustained by a pivotal flow of goods, up and down the social hierarchy, with each gift not merely connoting a status relation but, as a generalized gift not directly requited, compelling a loyalty.

In communities with established rank orders, generalized reciprocity is enforced by the received structure, and once in operation the exchange has redundant effects on the rank system. There is a large range of societies, however, in which rank and leadership are in the main achieved; here reciprocity is more or less engaged in the *formation* of rank itself, as a "starting mechanism." The connection between reciprocity and rank is brought to bear in the first case in the form, "to be noble is to be generous," in the second case, "to be generous is to be noble." The prevailing rank structure influences economic relations in the former instance; the reciprocity influences hierarchical relations in the latter. (An analogous feedback occurs in the context of kinship distance. Hospitality is frequently employed to suggest sociability—this is discussed later. John Tanner, one of those "feral Whites" who grew to manhood among the Indians, relates an anecdote even more to the point: recalling that his Ojibway family was once saved from starvation by a Muskogean family, he noted that if any of his own people ever afterwards met any of the latter,"he would call him 'brother,' and treat him as such" (Tanner,1956, p. 24).)

The term "starting mechanism" is Gouldner's. He explains in this way how reciprocity may be considered a starting mechanism:

> . . . it helps to initiate social interaction and is functional in the early phases of certain groups before they have developed a differentiated and customary set of status duties. . . . Granted that the question of origins can readily bog down in a metaphysical morass, the fact is that many concrete social systems [perhaps "relations and groups" is more apt] do have determinate beginnings. Marriages are not made in heaven. . . . Similarly, corporations, political parties, and all manner of groups have their beginnings. . . . People are continually brought together in new juxtapositions and combinations, bringing with them the possibilities of new social systems. How are these possibilities realized? . . . Although this perspective may at first seem somewhat alien to the functionalist, once it is put to him, he may suspect that certain kinds of mechanisms, conducive to the crystallization of social systems out of ephemeral contacts, will in some measure be institutionalized or otherwise patterned in any society. At this point he would be considering "starting mechanisms." In this way, I suggest, the norm of reciprocity provides one among many starting mechanisms (Gouldner, 1960, pp. 176–177).

Economic imbalance is the key to deployment of generosity, of generalized reciprocity, as a starting mechanism of rank and leadership. A gift that is not yet requited in the first place "creates a something between people": it engenders continuity in the relation, solidarity—at least until the obligation to reciprocate is discharged. Secondly, falling under "the shadow of indebtedness," the recipient is constrained in his relations to the giver of things. The one who has benefited is held in a peaceful, circumspect, and responsive position in relation to his benefactor. The "norm of reciprocity," Gouldner remarks, "makes two interrelated minimal demands: (1) people should help those who have helped them, and (2) people should not injure those who have helped them" (1960, p. 171). These demands are as compelling in the highlands of New Guinea as in the prairies of Peoria—"Gifts [among Gahuka-Gama] have to be repaid. They constitute a debt, and until discharged the relationship of the individuals involved is in a state of imbalance. The debtor has to act circumspectly towards those who have this advantage over him or otherwise risk ridicule" (Read, 1959, p. 429). The esteem that accrues to the generous man all to one side, generosity is usefully enlisted as a starting mechanism of leadership *because it creates followership.* "Wealth in this finds him friends," Denig writes of the aspiring Assiniboin, "as it does on other occasions everywhere" (Denig, 1928–29, p. 525).

Apart from highly organized chiefdoms and simple hunters and gatherers, there are many intermediate tribal peoples among whom pivotal local leaders come to prominence without yet becoming holders of office and title, of ascribed privilege and of sway over corporate political groups. They are men who "build a name" as it is said, "big-men" they may be reckoned, or "men of importance," "bulls," who rise above the common herd, who gather followers and thus achieve authority. The Melanesian "big-man" is a case in point. So too the Plains Indian "chief." The process of gathering a personal following and that of ascent to the summits of renown is marked by calculated generosity—if not true compassion. Generalized reciprocity is more or less enlisted as a starting mechanism.

In diverse ways, then, generalized reciprocity is engaged with the rank order of the community. Yet we have already characterized the economics of chieftainship in other transactional terms, as redistribution (or large-scale pooling). At this juncture the evolutionist question is posed: "When does one give way then to the other, reciprocity to redistribution?" This question, however, may mislead. Chiefly redistribution is not different in principle from kinship-rank reciprocity. It is, rather, based upon the reciprocity principle, a highly organized form of that principle. Chiefly redistribution is a centralized, formal organization of kinship-rank reciprocities, an extensive social integration of the dues and obligations of leadership. The real ethnographic world does not present us with the abrupt "appearance" of redistribution. It presents approximations and kinds of centricity. The apparent course of wisdom is to hinge our characterizations—of rank-reciprocities versus a system of redistribution—on formal differences in the centralization process, and in this way to resolve the evolutionist issue.

A big-man system of reciprocities may be quite centralized and a chiefly system quite decentralized. A thin line separates them, but it is perhaps significant. Between centricity in a Melanesian big-man economy such as Siuai (Oliver, 1955) and centricity in a Northwest Coast chiefdom such as the Nootka (Drucker, 1951), there is little to choose. A leader in each case integrates the economic activity of a (more or less) localized following: he acts as a shunting station for goods flowing reciprocally between his own and other like groups of society. The economic relation to followers is also the same: the leader is the central recipient and bestower of favors. The thin line of difference is this: the Nootka leader is an officeholder in a lineage (house group), his following is this corporate group, and his central economic position is ascribed by right of chiefly due and chiefly obligation. So centricity is built into the structure. In Siuai, it is a personal achievement. The following is an achievement—a result of generosity bestowed—the leadership an achievement, and the whole structure will as such dissolve with the demise of the pivotal big-man. Now I think that most of us concerned with "redistributive economies"have come to include Northwest Coast peoples under this head; whereas assigning Siuai that status would at least provoke disagreement. This suggests that the political organization of reciprocities is implicitly recognized as a decisive step. Where kinship-rank reciprocity is laid down by office and political grouping, and becomes *sui generis* by virtue of customary duty, it takes on a distinctive character. The distinctive character may be usefully named—chiefly redistribution.

A further difference in economies of chiefly redistribution is worth remarking. It is another difference in centricity. The flow of goods both into and out of the hands of powers-that-be is for the most part unintegrated in certain ethnographic instances. Subordinates in severalty and on various occasions render stuff to the chief, and often in severalty receive benefits from him. While there is always some massive accumulation and large-scale handout—say during rites of chieftainship—the prevailing flow between chief and people is fragmented into independent and small transactions: a gift to the chief from here, some help given out there. So aside from the special occasion, the chief is continuously turning over petty stocks. This is the ordinary situation in the smaller Pacific island chiefdoms—e.g. Moala (Sahlins, 1962), apparently Tikopia—and it may be generally true of pastoralist chiefdoms. On the other hand, chiefs may glory in massive accumulations and more or less massive dispensations, and at times too in large stores on hand congealed by pressure on the commonalty. Here the independent act of homage or *noblesse oblige* is of less significance. And if, in addition, the social scale of chiefly redistribution is extensive—the polity large, dispersed, and segmented—one confronts a measure of centricity approximating the classical magazine economies of antiquity.

Appendix B presents illustrative ethnographic materials on the relation between rank and reciprocity. (See the citation from Malo under B.4.2 and from Bartram under B.5.2 on magazine economies of various scale.)

### Reciprocity and Wealth

According to their [the Yukaghir] way of thinking, "a man who possesses provisions must share them with those who do not possess them" (Jochelson, 1926, p. 43).

This habit of share and share alike is easily understandable in a community where everyone is likely to find himself in difficulties from time to time, for it is scarcity and not sufficiency that makes people generous, since everybody is thereby ensured against hunger. He who is in need to-day receives help from him who may be in like need tomorrow (Evans-Pritchard, 1940, p. 85).

One of the senses of previous remarks on rank and reciprocity is that rank distinctions, or attempts to promote them, tend to extend generalized exchange beyond the customary range of sharing. The same upshot may come of wealth differences between parties, often anyhow associated with rank differences.

If one is poor and one's comrade is rich, well, there are certain constraints on acquisitiveness in our dealings—at least if we are to remain comrades, or even acquaintances, for very long. There are particularly restraints on the wealthier, if not a certain *richesse oblige*.

That is to say, given some social bond between those who exchange, differences in fortune between them compel a more altruistic (generalized) transaction than is otherwise appropriate. A difference in affluence—or in capacity to replenish wealth—would lower the sociability content of balanced dealing. As far as the exchange balances, the side that cannot afford it has sacrificed in favor of the side that did not need it. The greater the wealth gap, therefore, the greater the demonstrable assistance from rich to poor that is necessary just to maintain a given degree of sociability. Reasoning further on the same line, the inclination toward generalized exchange deepens where the economic gap amounts to oversupply and undersupply of customary requirements and, especially, of urgent stuff. The thing to look for is food-sharing between haves and have-nots. It is one thing to demand returns on woodpecker scalps, yet one spares a dime—brother!—for even a hungry stranger.

The "brother" is important. That scarcity and not sufficiency makes people generous is understandable, functional, "where everyone is likely to find himself in difficulties from time to time." It is most understandable, however, and most likely, where kinship community and kinship morality prevail. That whole economies are organized by the combined play of scarcity and differential accumulation is no secret to Economic Science. But then the societies involved do not wrest a livelihood as limited and uncertain as the Nuer's, nor do they meet hardship as kinship communities. It is such circumstances precisely that make invidious accumulation of fortune intolerable and dysfunctional. And if the affluent do not play the game, they ordinarily can be forced to disgorge, in one way or another:

A Bushman will go to any lengths to avoid making other Bushmen jealous of him, and for this reason the few possessions the Bushmen have are constantly circling among members of their groups. No one cares to keep a particularly good knife too long, even though he may want it desperately, because he will become the object of envy; as he sits by himself polishing a fine edge on the blade he will hear the soft voices of the other men in his band saying: "Look at him there, admiring his knife while we have nothing." Soon somebody will ask him for his knife, for everybody would like to have it, and he will give it away. Their culture insists that they share with each other, and it has never happened that a Bushman failed to share objects, food, or water with other members·of his band, for without very rigid co-operation Bushmen could not survive the famines and droughts that the Kalahari offers them (Thomas, 1959, p. 22).

Should the potential for poverty be extreme, as for food collectors such as these Bushmen, best that the inclination to share out one's abundance be made lawful. Here it is a technical condition that some households day in and day out will fail to meet their requirements. The vulnerability to food shortage can be met by instituting continuous sharing within the local community. I think this the best way to interpret tabus that prohibit hunters from eating game they bring down, or the less drastic and more common injunction that certain large animals be shared through the camp—"the hunter kills, other people have, say the Yukaghir" (Jochelson, 1926, p. 124). Another way to make food-sharing the rule, if not a rule, is to freight it heavily with moral value. If this is the case, incidentally, sharing will break out not merely in bad times but especially in good. The level of generalized reciprocity "peaks" on the occasion of a windfall: now everyone can cash in on the virtues of generosity:

> They gathered almost three hundred pounds [of tsi nuts]. . . . When the people had picked all they could find, when every possible bag was full, they said they were ready to go to Nama, but when we brought the jeep and began to load it they were already busy with their endless preoccupation, that of giving and receiving, and had already begun to give each other presents of tsi. Bushmen feel a great need to give and receive food, perhaps to cement relationships with each other, perhaps to prove and strengthen their dependence upon each other; because the opportunity to do this does not occur unless huge quantities of food are at hand. Bushmen always exchange presents of foods that come in huge quantities, these being the meat of game antelope, tsi nuts, and the nuts of the mangetti trees, which at certain seasons are scattered abundantly all through the mangetti forests. As we waited by the jeep Dikai gave a huge sack of tsi to her mother.

Her mother gave another sack to Gao Feet's first wife, and Gao Feet gave a sack to Dikai. Later, during the days that followed, the tsi was distributed again, this time in smaller quantities, small piles or small bagfuls, after that in handfuls, and, last, in very small quantities of cooked tsi which people would share as they were eating . . . (Thomas, 1959, pp. 214–215).

The bearing of wealth differences upon reciprocity, of course, is not independent of the play of rank and kinship distance. Real situations are complicated. For instance, wealth distinctions probably constrain assistance in some inverse proportion to the kinship distance of the sides to exchange. It is poverty in the in-group particularly that engenders compassion. (Conversely, helping people in distress creates very intense solidarity—on the principle of "a friend in need. . . .") On the other hand, material distinctions between distant relatives or aliens may not commensurately, or even at all, incline the affluent party to be charitable. If the interests had been opposed to begin with, well now the desperate traffic will bear more.

The observation is frequently made that any accumulation of wealth—among such and such people—is followed hard upon by its disbursement. The *objective* of gathering wealth, indeed, is often that of giving it away. So, for example, Barnett writes of Northwest Coast Indians that "Accumulation in any quantity by borrowing or otherwise is, in fact, unthinkable unless it be for the purpose of immediate redistribution" (1938, p. 353). The general proposition may be allowed that the material drift in primitive societies tends on the whole away from accumulation towards insufficiency. Thus: "In general it may be said that no one in a Nuer village starves unless all are starving" (Evans-Pritchard, 1951, p. 132). But in view of foregoing remarks there must be qualification. The incline toward have-nots is steeper for more urgently than for less urgently required goods, and it is steeper within local communities than between them.

Supposing some tendency to share in favor of need, even if qualified by community, it is possible to draw further inferences about economic behavior in general scarcity. During lean food seasons the incidence of generalized exchange should rise above average, particularly in the narrower social sectors. Survival depends now on a double-barreled quickening of social solidarity and economic cooperation (see Appendix C, e.g. C.1.3). This social and economic consolidation conceivably could progress to the maximum: normal reciprocal relations between households are suspended in favor of pooling of resources for the duration of emergency. The rank structure is perhaps mobilized and engaged, either in governance of pooling or in the sense that chiefly food reserves are now put into circulation.

Yet the reaction to depression "all depends": it depends on the social structure put to test and on the duration and intensity of the shortage. For the forces that countervail are strengthened in these *biša-baša* times, the tendency to look to household interests especially, and also the tendency for compassion to be more-than-proportionately expended on close kin in need than on distant kin in the same straits. Probably every primitive organization has its breaking-point, or at least its turning-point. Every one might see the time when cooperation is overwhelmed by the scale of disaster and chicanery becomes the order of the day. The range of assistance contracts progressively to the family level; perhaps even these bonds dissolve and, washed away, reveal an inhuman, yet most human, self-interest. Moreover, by the same measure that the circle of charity is compressed that of "negative reciprocity" is potentially expanded. People who helped each other in normal times and through the first stages of disaster display now indifference to each others' plight, if they do not exacerbate a mutual downfall by guile, haggle, and theft. Put another way, the whole sectoral scheme of reciprocities is altered, compressed: sharing is confined to the innermost sphere of solidarity and all else is devil take the hindmost.

Implicit in these remarks is a plan of analysis of the normal sectoral system of reciprocities in the given case. The prevailing reciprocity scheme is some vector of the quality of kin-community relations and the ordinary stresses developing out of imbalances in production. But it is the emergency condition that concerns us now. Here and there in the illustrative materials to this section we see the two predicted reactions to depressed food supplies, both more sharing and less. Presumably the governing conditions are the community structure on one side and the seriousness of shortage on the other.

A final remark under the head of reciprocity and wealth. A community will, if suitably organized, tighten not only under economic threat but in the face of other present danger, of external political-military pressure, for example. In this connection, two notes on the economics of native war parties are included in the illustrative materials appended to the present section (Appendix C: C.1.10 and C.2.5). They illustrate an extraordinary intensity of sharing (generalized reciprocity) between haves and have-nots during preparations for attack. (Likewise, the experience of recent wars would show that transactions move a long way from yesterday's dice game in the barracks to today's sharing of rations or cigarettes on the front line.) The sudden outbreak of compassion is consistent with what has been said of sociability, sharing, and wealth differences. Generalized reciprocity is not merely the sole exchange congruent with the now serious interdependence, it strengthens interdependence and so the chances of each and all to survive the noneconomic danger.

Ethnographic data relevant to the propositions of this section may be found in Appendix C).

### Reciprocity and Food

The character of the goods exchanged seems to have an independent effect on the character of exchange. Staple foodstuffs cannot always be handled just like anything else. Socially they are not quite like anything else. Food is life-giving, urgent, ordinarily symbolic of hearth and home, if not of mother. By comparison with other stuff, food is more readily, or more necessarily, shared; barkcloth and beads more readily lend themselves to balanced gift-giving. Direct and equivalent returns for food are unseemly in most social settings: they impugn the motives both of the giver and of the recipient. From this several characteristic qualities of food transfers appear to follow.

Food dealings are a delicate barometer, a ritual statement as it were, of social relations, and food is thus employed instrumentally as a starting, a sustaining, or a destroying mechanism of sociability:

Food is something over which relatives have rights, and conversely relatives are people who provide or take toll on one's food (Richards, 1939, p. 200).

The sharing of food [among the Kuma] symbolizes an identity of interests. . . . Food is never shared with an enemy. . . . Food is not shared with strangers, for they are potential enemies. A man may eat with his cognatic and affinal relatives and also, people say, with the members of his own clan. Normally, however, only members of the same subclan have an unequivocal right to share each other's food. . . . If two men or the members of two sub-subclans have a serious and lasting quarrel, neither they nor their descendants may use one another's fires. . . . When affinal relatives come together at marriage, the formal presentation of the bride and the pork and the valuables emphasizes the separate identity of the two clans, but the people actually participating in the ceremony share vegetable food informally, unobtrusively, as they might share it with intimate companions within the subclan. This is a way of expressing their common interest in linking the two groups. Symbolically, they belong now to a single group and so are "brothers," as affinal relatives should be (Reay, 1959, pp. 90-92).

Food offered in a generalized way, notably as hospitality, is good relations. As Jochelson says, putting it for the Yukaghir with near-Confucian pith: "hospitality often turns enemies into friends, and strengthens the amicable relations between groups foreign to one another" (1926, p. 125). But then, a complementary negative principle is implied, that food not offered on the suitable occasion or not taken is bad relations. Thus the Dobuan syndrome of suspicion of everyone save the nearest kinfolk finds its clearest expression in the social range of food-sharing and commensality—"Food or tobacco is not accepted except within a small circle" (Fortune,1932, p. 170; on rules proscribing commensality, cf. pp. 74–75; Malinowski,1915, 545). Finally there is the principle that one does not exchange things for food, not directly that is, among friends and relatives. Traffic in food is traffic between foreign interests. (Look how a novelist quite simply suggests that one of his characters is a real bastard: "He brought his blankets to the bare house, took silent supper with the Boss family, insisted on paying them—he could not understand why they pretended reluctance when he offered to pay them; food cost money; they were not in the restaurant business, but food cost money, you could not deny that"—MacKinlay Kantor.)

In these principles of instrumental food exchange there seems little variation between peoples. Of course, the extent to which they are employed, and which of them are employed, vary with the case. Dobuans proscribe intervillage visiting and hospitality, no doubt for good and sufficient reasons. Elsewhere, circumstances ranging from economic interdependence through political strategy enjoin both visiting and the hospitable entertainment of visitors. A detailed look at the circumstances would be beyond the present purview: the point is that where some coming to sociable terms with visitors is desirable, hospitality is an ordinary way of doing it. And the Dobuan syndrome is by no means typical. Ordinarily, "Savages pride themselves in being hospitable to strangers" (Harmon, 1957, p. 43).

Consequently the sphere of generalized exchange in food is sometimes wider than the sphere of generalized exchange in other things. This tendency to transcend the sectoral plan is most dramatized in the hospitality afforded trade partners, or any kinsmen from afar, who make visits the occasion for exchanging presents (see examples in Appendix A). Here are people whose dealings in durables are consciously balanced out—or even potentially run on *caveat emptor*—by some miracle charitably supplying one another with food and shelter. But then hospitality counters the *wabuwabu* lurking in the background, and provides an atmosphere in which direct exchange of presents and trade goods can be equitably consummated.

There is logic in an undue tendency to move food by generalized reciprocity. Like exchange between rich and poor, or between high and low, where food is concerned a greater inclination to sacrifice seems required just to sustain the given degree of sociability. Sharing needs to be extended to more distant relatives, generalized reciprocity broadened beyond ordinary sectoral limits. (It might be recalled from the Appendixes to previous sections that generosity is distinctively associated with food dealing.)

About the only sociable thing to do with food is to give it away, and the commensurably sociable return, after an interval of suitable decency, is the return of hospitality or assistance. The implication is not only a rather loose or imperfect balance in food dealing, but specifically a restraint on exchanges of food for other goods. One notes with interest normative injunctions against the sale of food among peoples possessed of primitive currencies, among certain Melanesian and California tribes for instance. Here balanced exchange is run of the mill. Money tokens serve as more or less general equivalents and are exchanged against a variety of stuff. But not *food*stuff. Within a broad social sector where money talks for other things, staples are insulated against pecuniary transactions and food shared perhaps but rarely sold. Food has too much social value—ultimately because it has too much use value—to have exchange value.

> Food was not sold. It might be given away, but being "wild stuff" should not be sold, according to Pomo etiquette. Manufactured articles only were bought and sold, such as baskets, bows and arrows (Gifford, 1926, p. 329; cf. Kroeber, 1925, p. 40, on the Yurok—same sort of thing).

> [To the Tolowa-Tututni] food was only edible, not saleable (Drucker 1937, p. 241; cf. DuBois, 1936, pp. 50-51).

> The staple articles of food, taro, bananas, coconuts, are never sold [by Lesu], and are given to kindred, friends, and strangers passing through the village as an act of courtesy (Powdermaker, 1933, p. 195).

In a similar way, staple foodstuffs were excluded from balanced trading among Alaskan Eskimo—"The feeling was present that to trade for food was reprehensible—and even luxury foods that were exchanged between trade partners were transferred as presents and apart from the main trading" (Spencer, 1959, pp. 204-205). It would seem that common foodstuffs are likely to have an insulated "circuit of exchange," separate from durables, particulary wealth." (See Firth, 1950; Bohannan, 1955; Bohannan and Dalton, 1962, on "spheres of exchange"). Morally and socially this should be so. For a wide range of social relations, balanced and direct food-for-goods transactions (conversions) would rend the solidary bonds. Distinctve categorizations of food versus other goods, i.e. "wealth," express the sociological disparity and protect food from dysfunctional comparisons of its worth—as among the Salish:

> Food was not classed as "wealth" [i.e. blankets, shell ornaments, canoes, etc.]. Nor was it treated as wealth . . . "holy food," a Semiahmoo informant called it. It should be given freely, he felt, and could not be refused. Food was evidently not freely exchanged with wealth. A person in need of food might ask to buy some from another household in his community, offering wealth for it, but food was not generally offered for sale (Suttles, 1960, p. 301; Vayda, 1961).

But an important qualification must in haste be entered. These food and nonfood spheres are sociologically based and bounded. The immorality of food-wealth conversions has a sectoral dimension: at a certain socially peripheral point the circuits merge and thus dissolve. (At this point, food-for-goods exchange is a "conveyance" in Bohannan and Dalton's usage.) Food does not move against money or other stuff within the community or tribe, yet it may be so exchanged outside these social contexts, and not merely under duress but as use and wont. The Salish *did* customarily take food, "holy food," to affinal relatives in other Salish villages and received wealth in return (Suttles, 1960). Likewise, Pomo *did* "buy"— at any rate gave beads for—acorns, fish, and like necessities from other communities (Kroeber, 1925, p. 260; Loeb, 1926, pp. 192–193). The separation of food and wealth cycles is contextual. Within communities these are insulated circuits, insulated by community relations; they are kept apart where a demand of return on necessities would contradict prevailing kinship relations. Beyond this, in the intercommunity or intertribal sector, the insulation of the food circuit may be worn through by frictions of social distance.

(Foodstuffs, incidentally, are not ordinarily divorced from the circuit of labor assistance. On the contrary, a meal is in the host of primitive societies the customary return for labor solicited for gardening, housebuilding, and other domestic tasks. "Wages" in the usual sense is not at issue. The feeding amounts to an extraordinary extension to other relatives and to friends of the household economy. Rather than a tentative move toward capitalism, it is perhaps better understood by a principle something to the opposite: that those who participate in a productive effort have some claim on its outcome.)

### On Balanced Reciprocity

We have seen generalized reciprocity in play in instrumental ways, notably as a starting mechanism of rank distinction and also, in the form of hospitality, as mediator of relations between persons of different communities. Balanced reciprocity likewise finds instrumental employments, but especially as formal social compact. Balanced reciprocity is the classic vehicle of peace and alliance contracts, substance-as-symbol of the transformation from separate to harmonious interests. Group prestations are the dramatic and perhaps the typical form, but there are instances too of interpersonal compact sealed by exchange.

Here it is useful to recall Mauss's dictum: "In these primitive and archaic societies there is no middle path. . . . When two groups of men meet they may move away or in case of mistrust or defiance they may resort to arms; or else they can come to terms." And the terms ought to balance, insofar as the groups are "different men." The relations are too tenuous to long sustain a failure to reciprocate—"Indians notice such things" (Goldschmidt, 1951, p. 338). They notice a lot of things. Goldschmidt's Nomlaki Indians in fact articulate a whole set of glosses and paraphrases of Maussian principle, among them:

> When enemies meet they call to one another. If the settlement is friendly they approach closer and spread out their goods. One man would throw something in the middle, one man from the other side would throw in something for it and take the traded material back. They trade till one side has traded everything. The ones that have some left make fun of those who have run out, bragging about themselves. . . . This trade takes place on the border line (Goldschmidt, 1951, p. 338).

Balanced reciprocity is willingness to give for that which is received. Therein seems to be its efficacy as social compact. The striking of equivalence, or at least some approach to balance, is a demonstrable foregoing of self-interest on each side, some renunciation of hostile intent or of indifference in favor of mutuality. Against the preexisting context of separateness, the material balance signifies a new state of affairs. This is not to deny that the transaction is consequential in a utilitarian sense, as it may well be—and the social effect perhaps compounded by an equitable exchange of different necessities. But whatever the utilitarian value, and there need be none, there is always a "moral" purpose, as Radcliffe-Brown remarked of certain Andaman transactions: "to provide a friendly feeling . . . and unless it did this it failed of its purpose."

Among the many kinds of contract struck as it were by balanced exchange, the following seem most common:

## FORMAL FRIENDSHIP OR KINSHIP

These are interpersonal compacts of solidarity, pledges of brotherhood in some cases, friendship in others. The alliance may be sealed by exchange of identical goods, the material counterpart of some exchange of identities, but at any rate the transaction is likely to balance and the exchange is of distant for close relationship (e.g., Pospisil, 1958, pp. 86-87; Seligman, 1910, pp. 69-70). An association once so formed may well become more sociable over time, and future transactions both parallel and compound this trend by becoming more generalized.

### AFFIRMATION OF CORPORATE ALLIANCES

One may place in this category the various feasts and entertainments reciprocally tendered between friendly local groups and communities, such as certain of the interclan vegetable-heap presentations in the New Guinea Highlands or inter-village social feasts in Samoa or New Zealand.

### PEACE-MAKING

These are the exchanges of settlement, of cessation of dispute, feud, and warfare. Both interpersonal and collective hostilities may be thus quieted by exchange. " 'When an equivalence is struck', parties to an Abelam argument are satisfied: 'talk is thrown away' " (Kaberry, 1941–42, p. 341). That is the general principle.

One may wish to include wergeld payments, compensations for adultery, and other forms of compounding injury in this category, as well as the exchanges that terminate warfare. They all work on the same general principle of fair trade. (Spencer provides an interesting Eskimo example: when a man received compensation from the abductor of his wife, the two men "inevitably" became friendly, he writes, "because they had conceptually effected a trade" [1959, p. 81]. See also Denig, 1928–29, p. 404; Powdermaker, 1933, p. 197; Williamson, 1912, p. 183; Deacon, 1934, p. 226; Kroeber, 1925, p. 252; Loeb, 1926, pp. 204-205; Hogbin, 1939, pp. 79, 91-92; etc.).

MARITAL ALLIANCE

Marriage prestations are of course the classic form of exchange as social compact. I have little to add to the received anthropological discussion, except a slight qualification about the character of reciprocity in these transactions, and even this may be superfluous.

It does sometimes miss the point, however, to view marital exchange as perfectly balanced prestation. The transactions of marriage, and perhaps contingent future affinal exchange as well, are often not exactly equal. For one thing, an asymmetry of quality is commonplace: women move against hoes or cattle, *toga* against *oloa*, fish against pigs. In the absence of some secular convertability, or of a mutual standard of value, the transfer seems to an extent one of incomparables; neither equivalent nor total, the transaction may be of incommensurables. In any event, and even where the same sorts of things are exchanged, one side or the other may be conceived to benefit unduly, at least for the time being. This lack of precise balance is socially of the essence.

For unequal benefit sustains the alliance as perfect balance could not. Truly, the people concerned—and/or the ethnographer—might muse that in the fullness of time accounts between affines even out. Or losses and gains may be cancelled by circular or statistical patterns of alliance. Or some balance in goods, at least, may obtain in the total political economy, where the flow of payments upwards (against a flow of women downwards) through a series of ranked lineages is reversed by redistribution from the top (cf. Leach, 1951). Yet it is socially critical that over a certain term, and perhaps forever, the exchange between two groups united by a marriage has not been balanced. Insofar as the things transferred are of different quality, it may be difficult ever to calculate that the sides are "even-steven." This is a social good. The exchange that is symmetrical or unequivocally equal carries some disadvantage from the point of view of alliance: it cancels debts and thus opens the possibility of contracting out. If neither side is "owing" then the bond between them is comparatively fragile. But if accounts are not squared, then the relationship is maintained by virtue of "the shadow of indebtedness," and there will have to be further occasions of association, perhaps as occasions of further payment.

Moreover, and quite obviously, an asymmetrical exchange of different things lends itself to alliance that is complementary. The marital bond between groups is not always, maybe not even usually, some sort of fifty-fifty partnership between homologous parties. One group surrenders a woman, another gets her; in a patrilineal context the wife-receivers have secured continuity, something at the expense of the wife-givers, at least on this occasion. There has been a differential transfer: the groups are socially related in a complementary and asymmetrical way. Likewise, in a ranked lineage system the giving of women may be a specification of the set of subordinate-superordinate relations. Now in these cases, the several rights and duties of alliance are symbolized by the differential character of transfers, are attached to complementary symbols. Asymmetrical prestations secure the complementary alliance once again as perfectly balanced, symmetrical, or all-out total prestations would not.

The casual received view of reciprocity supposes some fairly direct one for-one exchange, balanced reciprocity, or a near approximation of balance. It may not be inappropriate, then, to footnote this discussion with a respectful demur: that in the main run of primitive societies, taking into account directly utilitarian as well as instrumental transactions, balanced reciprocity is not the prevalent form of exchange. A question might even be raised about the stability of balanced reciprocity. Balanced exchange may tend toward self-liquidation. On one hand, a series of honorably balanced dealings between comparatively distant parties builds trust and confidence, in effect reduces social distance, and so increases the chances for more generalized future dealings—as the initial blood-brotherhood transaction creates a "credit rating," as it were. On the other hand, a renege acts to sever relations—as failure to make returns breaks a trade-partnership—if it does not actually invite chicanery in return. May we conclude that balanced reciprocity is inherently unstable? Or perhaps that it requires special conditions for continuity?

The societal profile of reciprocity, at any rate, most often inclines toward generalized modes. In the simpler hunting groups the generalized assistance of close kinship seems usually dominant; in neolithic chiefdoms this is supplemented by kinship-rank obligations. There are nonetheless societies of certain type in which balanced exchange, if not exactly dominant, acquires unusual prominence. Interest attaches to these societies, not alone for the emphasis on balanced reciprocity, but for what goes with it.

The well known "labor exchange" in Southeast Asian hinterland communities brings these immediately to mind. Here is a set of peoples who, placed against the main run of primitive societies, offer departures in economy, and social structure as well, that cannot fail to kindle a comparative interest. The well-described Iban (Freeman 1955, 1960), Land Dayak (Geddes,1954, 1957; cf. Provinse,1937) and Lamet (Izikowitz,1951) belong in the class—some Philippine peoples may as well, but I am uncertain how far the analysis about to be suggested will work for the Philippines.

Now these societies are distinctive not only for uncommon internal characteristics of economy but for unusual external relations—unusual, that is, in a strictly primitive milieu. They are hinterlands engaged by petty market trade—and perhaps also by political dominance (e.g. Lamet)—to more sophisticated cultural centers. From the perspective of the advanced centers, they are backwaters serving as secondary sources of rice and other goods (cf. VanLeur, 1955, especially pp. 101f, for some hints about the economic significance of hinterland provisioning in Southeast Asia). From the hinterlands view, the critical aspect of the intercultural relation is that the subsistence staple, rice, is exported for cash, iron tools, and prestige goods, many of the last quite expensive. It is suggested—with all the deference that must be supplied by one who has no research experience in the area—that the peculiar social-economic character of Southeast Asian hinterland tribes is congruent with this unusual deployment of household subsistence surpluses. The implication of an external trade in rice is not merely an internal ban on sharing it, or a corresponding requirement of quid-pro-quo in intracommunity dealings, but departure from ordinary characteristics of primitive distribution in virtually all respects.

The engagement with the market makes a key minimal demand: that internal community relations permit household accumulation of rice, else the amounts required for external exchange will never be forthcoming. This stipulation must prevail in the face of limited and uncertain modes of rice production. The fortunate households cannot be responsible for the unfortunate; if internal leveling is encouraged then the external trade relations are simply not sustained.

The set of consequences for the economy and polity of the hinterland tribal communities appear to include: (1) Different households, by virtue of variations in ratio and number of effective producers, amass different amounts of the subsistence-export staple. The productive differences range between surfeit above and deficit below family consumption requirements. These differences, however, are not liquidated by sharing in favor of need. Instead (2) the intensity of sharing within the village or tribe is low, and (3) the principal reciprocal relation between households is a closely calculated balanced exchange of labor service. As Geddes remarks of the Land Dayak: " . . co-operation beyond the household, except on business lines where every service must have an equal return, is at a low level" (1954, p. 34). Balanced labor-exchange, of course, maintains the productive advantage (accumulation capacity) of the family with more adult workers. The only goods that customarily move in generalized reciprocity are game and perhaps large domestic animals sacrificed in family ceremonies. Such items are widely distributed through the community (cf. Izikowitz, 1951), much as hunters would share them, but the sharing of meat is not as decisive in structuring interfamilial relations as the lack of sharing decreed by export of staples. (4) Even household commensality may be rather rigidly supervised, subjected to accounting of each person's rice dole in the interest of developing an exchange reserve, hence less sociable than ordinary primitive commensality (compare, for example, Izikowitz, 1951, pp. 301–302 with Firth, 1936, pp. 112–116). (5) Restricted sharing of staples, demanded by articulation with the siphoning market, finds its social complement in an atomization and fragmentation of community structure. Lineages, or like systems of extensive and corporate solidary relations, are incompatible with the external drain on household staples and the corresponding posture of self-interest required *vis-à-vis* other households. Large local descent groups are absent or inconsequential. Instead, the solidary relations are of the small family itself, with various and changing interpersonal kin ties the only such nexus of connection between households. Economically, these extended kin ties are weak ones:

> A household is not only a distinct unit, but one which minds its own business. Perforce, it has to do so, because it ˙ ıs with other households no formal relations, sanctioned by custom, on which it can rely for certain support. Indeed, the absence of such structured relationships is a condition

of the society as at present organized. In the main economic affairs, cooperation with others is based upon contract and not primarily upon kinship.
... As a result of this situation, ties which persons have with others in the
community tend to be widespread, but limited to sentiment and sociability, often sadly so (Geddes, 1954, p. 42).

(6) Prestige apparently hinges upon obtaining exotic items—Chinese
pottery, brass gongs, etc.—from the outside in exchange for rice or
work. Prestige does not, obviously cannot, rest on generous assistance to one's fellows in the manner of a tribal big-man. The exotic
goods figure internally as ceremonial display items and in marriage
prestations—thus insofar as status is linked to them it is principally
as possession and ability to make payments, again not through giving
them away. ("Wealth does not help a man to become chief because
it gives him power to distribute largesse. Riches rarely incline a Dayak
to charity, although they may to usury "[Geddes,1954,p.50] No one
then obligates others very much. No one creates followers. As a result
there are no strong leaders, a fact which probably contributes to the
atomization of the community and may have repercussions on the
intensity of land use (cf. Izikowitz,1951).

In these Southeast Asian communities, the prevalence of balanced
reciprocity does seem connected with special circumstances. But then
the circumstances suggest that it is not legitimate to involve these
peoples in the present context of tribal economics. By the same token,
their use in debating issues of primitive economics, as Geddes uses the
Land Dayak to argue against "primitive communism," seems not very
pertinent. Perhaps they are best classed with peasants—so long as one
does not thereupon suggest, as is unfortunately often done under the
label "economic anthropology," that "peasant" and "primitive" belong together in some undifferentiated type of economy distinguished
negatively as whatever-it-is that is outside the province of orthodox
economic analysis.

There are, however, incontestable examples of societal emphasis on
balanced reciprocity in primitive settings. Primitive monies serving as
media of exchange at more or less fixed rates argue this. The monies
amount to the suggested special mechanisms for maintaining balance.
It is worthwhile to inquire into their incidence and their economic and
social concomitants.

Yet this is not to be hazarded without some formal definition of "primitive money," a problem approaching the status of a classic dilemma in comparative economics. On one side, any thing that has a "money use"—as we know money uses: payments, exchange, standard, etc.—may be taken for "money." If so, probably every society enjoys the dubious benefits, inasmuch as some category of goods is usually earmarked for certain payments. The alternative is less relativistic and therefore seems more useful for comparative generalizations: to agree on some minimal use and quality of the stuff. The strategy, as Firth suggests, is not to question "What is primitive money?" but "What is it useful to include in the category of primitive money?" (1959, p. 39). His specific suggestion, which as I understand it centrally involves the medium-of-exchange function, does indeed appear useful. ("My own view is that to entitle an object to be classified as money, it should be of a generally acceptable type, serving to facilitate the conversion of one object or service into terms of another and used as a standard of value thereby" [Firth, 1959, pp. 38-39].)

Let "money" refer to those objects in primitive societies that have token value rather than use value and that serve as means of exchange. The exchange use is limited to certain categories of things—land and labor are ordinarily excluded—and is brought to bear only between parties of certain social relation. In the main it serves as an indirect bridge between goods (C-M-C') rather than commercial purposes (M-C-M'). These limitations would justify the phrase "primitive money." If all this is agreeable, it further appears that pristine developments of primitive money are not broadly spread through the ethnographic scene, but are restricted to certain areas: especially western and central Melanesia, aboriginal California, and certain parts of the South American tropical forest. (Monies may also have developed in pristine contexts in Africa, but I am not expert enough to disentangle their distribution from archaic civilizations and ancient "international" trade.)

This is also to say that primitive money is associated with an historically specific type of primitive economy, an economy with a marked incidence of balanced exchange in peripheral social sectors. It is not a phenomenon of simple hunting cultures—if I may be permitted, cultures of a band level. Neither is primitive money characteristic of the more advanced chiefdoms, where wealth tokens though certainly encountered tend to bear little exchange load. The regions noted—Melanesia, California, South American tropical forest—are (or were) occupied by societies of an intermediate sort, such as have been called "tribal" (Sahlins,1961; Service,1962) or "homogeneous" and "segmented tribes" (Oberg,1955). They are distinguished from band systems not merely for more settled conditions of life—often associated with neolithic versus paleolithic production—but principally for a larger and more complex tribal organization of constituent local groupings. The several local settlements of tribal societies are bound together both by a nexus of kin relations and by cross-cutting social institutions, such as a set of clans. Yet the relatively small settlements are autonomous and self-governing, a feature which in turn distinguishes tribal from chiefdom plans. The local segments of the latter are integrated into larger polities, as divisions and subdivisions, by virtue of principles of rank and a structure of chieftainships and subchieftainships. The tribal plan is purely segmental, the chiefdom pyramidal.

This evolutionary classification of social-cultural types is admittedly loose. I hope not to raise an issue over it, for it has been offered merely to direct attention to contrasting structural features of primitive-money areas. They are precisely the kinds of features that, given previous argumentation, suggest an unusual incidence of balanced reciprocity. A greater play of balanced exchange in tribal over band societies is argued in part by a greater proportion of craft goods and services in the societal economic output. Foodstuffs, while still the decisive share of a tribal economic product, decline relatively. Transactions in durables, more likely to be balanced than food transactions, increase. But more important, the proportion of peripheral-sector exchange, the incidence of exchange among more distantly related people, is likely to be considerably greater in tribal than in band societies. This is understandable by reference to the more definite segmental plan of tribes, which is also to say the more definite sectoral breaks in the social structure.

The several residential segments of tribes are comparatively stable and formally constituted. And a corporate political solidarity is as characteristic of the tribal segment as it is lacking in flexible camp-and-band arrangements of hunters. Tribal segmental structure is also more extensive, including perhaps internal lineage groupings in the political segments, the set (and sometimes segmentary subsets) of political segments, and the tribal-foreigner division. Now the accretion over band organization is particularly in peripheral structure, in the development of the intratribal and intertribal sectors. Here is where exchange encounters increase, whether these be instrumental, peacemaking exchanges, or frankly materialistic dealings. The accretion in exchange then is in the social areas of balanced reciprocity.

A chiefdom, in further contrast, liquidates and pushes out peripheral sectors by transforming external into internal relations, by including adjacent local groups within enclaving political unions. At the same time, the incidence of balanced reciprocity is depressed, in virtue of both the "internalization" of exchange relations and their centralization. Balanced exchanges should thus decline in favor of more generalized with the attainment of a chiefdom level. The implication for primitive money is perhaps illustrated by its absence in the Trobriands, despite the fact that this island of chiefdoms is set in a sea of money-using tribes, or by the progressive attentuation in exchange-uses of shell beads moving northward from tribal California to proto-chiefdom British Columbia.

The hypothesis about primitive money—offered with due caution and deference—is this: it occurs in conjunction with unusual incidence of balanced reciprocity in peripheral social sectors. Presumably it facilitates the heavy balanced traffic. The conditions that encourage primitive money are most likely to occur in the range of primitive societies called "tribal" and are unlikely to be served by band or chiefdom development. But a qualification must in haste be entered. Not all tribes provide circumstances for monetary development and certainly not all enjoy primitive money, as the term is here understood. For the potentiality of peripheral exchange is maximized only by some tribes. Others remain relatively inner-directed.

First, peripheral sectors become scenes of intensive exchange in conjunction with regional and intertribal symbiosis. An areal ecological regime of specialized tribes, the respective families and communities of which are in trade relation, is probably a necessary condition for primitive money. Such regimes are characteristic of California and Melanesia—about South America I am not prepared to say—but in other tribal settings symbiosis is not characteristic and the intertribal (or interregional) exchange sector comparatively underdeveloped. Perhaps just as important are circumstances that put premiums on delayed exchange and so on tokens that store value in the interim. The outputs of interdependent communities, for example, may be una-voidably unbalanced in time—as between coastal and inland peoples, where an exchangeable catch of fish cannot always be met by comple-mentary inland products. Here a currency acceptable on all sides very much facilitates interdependence—so that shell beads, say, taken for fish at one time can be converted for acorns at another (cf. Vayda, 1954; Loeb, 1926). Big-man leadership systems, it would seem from Melanesia, may likewise render delayed balanced exchange function-al. The tribal big-man operates on a fund of power consisting of food, pigs, or the like, stuffs with the common quality that they are not easy to keep around in large amounts over long periods. But, at the same time, the extractive devices for accumulating these political funds are underdeveloped, and collection of goods for a climactic giveaway would have to be gradual and thus technically difficult. The dilemma is resolvable by monetary manipulations: by converting wealth into tokens and by calculated deployment of money in loans and exchange, so that a time will come when a massive call on goods can be made and the whole fund of wealth, given away, converted into status.

### An Afterthought

It is difficult to conclude with a dramatic flourish. The essay has not a dramatic structure—its main drift seems downhill. And a sum-mary would be needlessly repetitive.

But there is a curiosity worth remarking. Here has been given a discourse on economics in which "economizing" appears mainly as an exogenous factor! The organizing principles of economy have been sought elsewhere. To the extent they have been found outside man's presumed hedonist propensity, a strategy for the study of primitive economics is suggested that is something the reverse of economic orthodoxy. It may be worth while to see how far this heresy will get us.

# Appendix A

*Notes on Reciprocity and Kinship Distance*

A.1.0     *Hunters and Gatherers* — Generally, sectoral breaks in reciprocity not always as definite as for neolithic peoples, but variation in reciprocity by interpersonal kinship distance apparent. Generalized reciprocity often consists of specific obligations to render goods to certain kinsmen (kinship dues) rather than altruistic assistance. Notable differences between the handling of foods and durables.

A.1.1     *Bushmen* — The !Kung term lack of generosity or failure to reciprocate "far-hearted"—a felicitious choice of words, from our perspective.

    Three social-material breaking points in reciprocity are apparent in Marshall's (1961) paper on !Kung exchange: (1) a range of close kin in the camp with whom meat is shared, often as customary obligation; (2) more distant kin within the camp and other Bushmen, with whom economic relations are characterized by "gift-giving" of durables in a more balanced fashion and transactions in meat that approximate "gift-giving"; (3) "trade" with Bantu. Marshall's materials are rich and indicate the play of various social considerations and sanctions determining specific transactions. Large game moves through a camp in several waves. Initially it is pooled in the hunting party by the taker, with shares going also to the arrow. "In the second distribution [here we move into reciprocity proper] close kinship is the factor which sets the pattern of the giving. Certain obligations are compulsory. A man's first obligation at this point, we were told, is to give to his wife's parents. He must give to them the best he has in as generous portions as he can, while still fulfilling other primary obligations, which are to his own parents, his spouse, and offspring [note, these cook and eat meat separately]. He keeps a portion for himself at this time and from it would give to his siblings, to his wife's siblings, if they are present, and to other kin, affines, and friends who are there, possibly only in small quantities by then. Everyone who receives meat gives again, in another wave of sharing, to his or her parents, parents-in-law, spouses, offspring, siblings, and others. The meat may be cooked and the quantities small. Visitors, even though they are not close kin or affines, are given meat by the people whom they are visiting" (Marshall, 1961, p. 238). Beyond the range of close kin, giving meat is a matter of individual inclination in which friendship, obligation to return past favors, and other considerations come into account. But this giving is definitely more balanced: "In the later waves of sharing when the primary distribution and the primary kinship obligations have been fulfilled, the giving of meat from one's own portion has the quality of gift-giving. /Kung society requires at this point only that a person should give with reasonable generosity in proportion to what he has received and not keep more than an equitable amount for himself in the end, and that the person who receives a gift of meat must give a reciprocal gift some time in the future" (p. 239). Marshall reserves "gift-giving" to the exchange of durables; this occurs also, and importantly, between /Kung of different bands. One should neither refuse such gifts nor fail to make a return. Much of the gift-giving is instrumental, having principally social effects. Even asking for a thing, claimed one man, "formed a love" between people. It means "he still loves me, that is why he is asking." And Marshall adds laconically, "At least it forms a something between people, I thought" (p. 245). "Gift-giving" is distinguishable from "trade" both in form of reciprocity and social sector. "In reciprocating [a gift] one does not give the same object back again but something of comparable value. The interval of time between receiving and reciprocating varied from a few weeks to a few years. Propriety requires that there be no unseemly haste. The giving must not look like trading" (p. 244). The mechanics of trading are not specified. "Negotiation" however is mentioned; the implication is of haggle. The social sphere is in any case clear: "The /Kung do not trade among themselves. They consider the procedure undignified and avoid it because it is too likely to stir up bad feelings. They trade with

Bantu, however, in the settlements along the B.P. border. . . . The odds are with the Bantu in the trading. Big, aggressive, and determined to have what they want, they easily intimidate the Bushmen. Several !Kung informants said that they tried not to trade with Herero if it was possible to avoid it because, although the Tswana were hard bargainers, the Herero were worse" (p. 242).

Intense generalized reciprocity within Bushmen camps and bands—especially food-sharing—is also indicated by Thomas (1959, pp. 22, 50, 214–215) and Schapera (1930, pp. 98–101, 148). Interband exchange, however, is characterized as "barter" by Schapera (1930, p. 146; cf. Thomas's amusing anecdote of the trouble that developed between a man and woman of different groups over an unrequited gift presented to the father of the former by the woman's father [1959, pp. 240–242].)

Theft reported unknown to them (Marshall, 1961, pp. 245–246; Thomas, 1959, pp. 206). However, Schapera implies it exists (1930, p. 148).

A.1.2    *Congo Pygmies* — In general, the scheme of reciprocity looks very much like the Bushmen's, including a rather impersonal exchange with "Negroes" (Putnam, 1953, p. 322; Schebesta 1933, p. 42; Turnbull, 1962). Hunting spoils, large game especially, are shared out in the camp, on a kinship-distance basis it appears—Putnam implies that first the family shares, then the "family group" gets shares (1953, p. 332; cf. Schebesta, 1933, pp. 68, 124, 244).

A.1.3    *Washo* — "Sharing obtained at every level of Washo social organization. Sharing also decreased as kinship and residence distances increased" (Price, 1962, 37). It is difficult to say where "trade" leaves off and "gift-giving" begins, but "In trade there tended to be immediate reciprocation while gift exchange often involved a time lapse. Trade also tended to be competitive and to increase with less intense social ties. Trade involved explicit negotiation and social status was secondary as a factor in the transaction" (p. 49).

A.1.4    *Semang* — Sharp sectoral break in reciprocity at the "family group" (band) border: "Each family contributes from its own food, already cooked and prepared, to every other family. If one family on any particular day is unusually well supplied, they give generously to all kindred families, even if it leaves them with too little. If other families not belonging to the group are in the camp, they do not share, or only to a very small extent, in the distribution" (Schebesta, n.d., p. 84).

A.1.5    *Andamans* — Radcliffe-Brown's (1948) account suggests a higher level of generalized reciprocity within the local group, particularly in food dealings and in transactions between junior and senior generations (cf. pp. 42–43), and more balanced forms of reciprocity between people of different bands, particularly in durables. The exchange of presents is characteristic of interband meetings, an exchange that could amount to swapping local specialties. In this sector, "It requires a good deal of tact to avoid the unpleasantness that may arise if a man thinks he has not received things as valuable as he has given" (p. 43; cf. pp. 83–84; Man, n.d., p. 120).

A.1.6    *Australian Aboriginals* — A number of formal, compulsory kin dues and also formal precedence orders for sharing food and other goods with relatives of the camp (see Elkin, 1954, 110–111; Meggitt, 1962, pp. 118, 120, 131, 139, etc.; Warner, 1937, pp. 63, 70, 92–95; Spencer and Gillen, 1927, p. 490).

A strong obligation to share out food in the horde (Radcliffe-Brown, 1930–31, p. 438; Spencer and Gillen, 1927, pp. 37–39).

Yir-Yiront exchange seems to parallel the Bushman scheme (above). Sharp notes that reciprocity varies on both sides of the set of customary kin dues, toward balance beyond and toward generalized reciprocity in the narrowest sphere of closest kin. Giving to persons outside the range of those entitled dues "amounts to compulsory exchange. . . . But there is also irregular giving, though within a relatively narrow social range, for which the incentives seem to be chiefly sentimental, and which may be considered altruistic;

this may lead to a desire to acquire property in order to give it away" (Sharp, 1934–35, pp. 37–38).

On the connection between assistance and close kinship: Meggitt observes of the Walbiri that ". . . a man who has several spears parts with them willingly; but, should he have only one, his son or father should not ask for it. If he is asked, the man usually gives the single article to an actual or close father or son, but he refuses distant 'fathers' and 'sons' " (Meggitt, 1962, p. 120).

Balanced reciprocity, in various specific guises, is characteristic of the well-known interband and intertribal trade exchange, which is often effected by trade partners who are classificatory kin (see, for example, Sharp, 1952, pp. 76–77; Warner, 1937, pp. 95, 145).

A.1.7 *Eskimo* — High level of generalized reciprocity in the camp, associated by Birket-Smith with "the fellowship of the settlement." This concerns food in the main, particularly large animals, and especially during the winter season (Birket-Smith, 1959, p. 146; Spencer, 1959, pp. 150, 153, 170; Boas, 1884–85, p. 562; Rink, 1875, p. 27).

Taken all in all, Spencer's study of the North Alaskan Eskimo suggests significant differences between the reciprocity appropriate among kinsmen, among trade partners, and among nonkin who are also not trade partners. These variations concern durables, especially trade goods. Nonkin within the camp would presumably be given some food if they are short, but trade goods are exchanged with them, as well as with outsiders (who are not trade partners), in an impersonal "bidding" transaction (reminiscent of Brazilian Indians' "trade game"). Trade partnerships are formed—on quasi-kin or institutional-friendship lines—between coastal and inland men; the exchange is of local specialties. Partners deal without haggle, indeed try to extend themselves, yet without balance (or near balance) in exchange the partnership would dissolve. Trade relations are specifically distinguished by Spencer from kinship-generalized reciprocity. Thus kinsmen do not need to enter into partnership, he says,

for "A relative would always be of assistance, an arrangement which pointed primarily to the sharing of food and
granting of shelter" (Spencer, 1959, pp. 65–66). Again: "One
would not form a partnership with a brother, the theory
being that one secured assistance and aid from one's close
relatives in any case" (p. 170).

A.1.8    *Shoshoni* — When a family did not have a great deal to share
out, as when only seeds or small animals had been taken, that
given out was to close relatives and neighbors (Steward,
1938, pp. 74, 231, 240, 253). There seems to have been a
fairly high level of generalized reciprocity in the village,
which Steward links to the "high degree of [kin] relationship
between village members" (p. 239).

A.1.9    *Northern Tungus* (mounted hunters)— Much sharing within the clan, but food sharing most intense within the few
families of a clan that nomadized together (Shirokogoroff,
1929, pp. 195, 200, 307). According to Shirokogoroff, gift-
giving among Tungus was not reciprocal, and Tungus re-
sented Manchu expectations on his head (p. 99); however, he
also wrote that gifts were given to guests (over and above
ordinary hospitality) and these items should be reciprocated
(p. 333). Reindeer sold only outside the clan; inside, pass as
gifts and assistance (pp. 35–36).

A.2.0    *Oceania* — The sectoral system of reciprocities is often more
clear and more definite, especially in Melanesia. In Polynesia
it is overriden by centralization of reciprocities in chiefly
hands or by redistribution.

A.2.1    *'Gawa (Busama)* — Hogbin contrasts maritime intertribal
trade through partnerships and inland trade with unrelated
peoples, saying of the latter exchange: "The parties seem
slightly ashamed, however, and conclude their arrangements
outside the village. [Note the literal exclusion of impersonal
exchange from the 'Gawa village:] Commerce it is considered, should be carried on away from where people live,
preferably alongside the road or the beach (the native-owned
store at Busama is located fifty yards from the nearest dwell-

ing). The Busama sum up the situation by saying that the maritime people give one another presents but insist on a proper return from the bushmen. The basis of the distinction is that on the coast activities are confined to relatives, but so few of the beach folk have kinsmen in the hill country that most transactions take place of necessity between comparative strangers. [Hogbin mentions elsewhere that the bush trade is often recent.] A certain amount of migration and intermarriage has taken place around the seaboard, and every coastal native has kinsmen in some of the other shore villages, especially those close at hand. When trading by sea it is with these, and these only, that he makes exchanges. Kinship ties and bargaining are considered to be incompatible, and all goods are handed over as free gifts offered from motives of sentiment. Discussion of values is avoided, and the donor does the best he can to convey the impression that no thought of a counter gift has entered his head. Yet at a later stage, when a convenient opportunity arises, hints are dropped of what is expected, whether pots, mats, baskets, or food. . . . Most of the visitors go home with items at least as valuable as those with which they came. Indeed, the closer the kinship bond the greater the host's generosity is, and some of them return a good deal richer. A careful count is kept, however, and the score is afterwards made even. . . . [The account goes on to give examples and to note that failure to balance will cause termination of the partnership. Now, contrast the foregoing with reciprocity in the intravillage sector:] It is significant that when a Busama acquired a string bag from a fellow villager, as has recently become possible, he always gives twice what he would pay to a more distant relative [i.e., trading partner] on the north coast. 'One is ashamed,' the people explain, 'to treat those with whom one is familiar like a tradesman'" (Hogbin, 1951, pp. 83–86). The variation in reciprocity by linear-kinship distance is also worth noting: "A presentation [of a pig] from a close relative imposes the usual obligation to return an animal of equivalent size on some future occasion, but no money changes hands either when the original gift is made or later. A similar obligation exists between distant kinsmen, but in this case each pig has also to be paid for at its full market price. The transaction is in line with earlier practice, except that dog's teeth then served as payment. The members of the purchasers' group help him nowadays with a few shillings, just as formerly they would have given him a string or two of teeth" (p. 124).

A.2.2    *Kuma* — Generalized reciprocity is prevalent within such small-scale descent groups as the "sub-subclan"—"a bank and a labour force for its members" (Reay, 1959, p. 29)—and the subclan (p. 70). The interclan sector is characterized by balanced exchange, by "the general emphasis on exact reciprocity between groups" (p. 47; see also pp. 55, 86–89, 126). In the external sector, balance is appropriate between trade-partners, but without a partnership the transaction inclines toward negative reciprocity. "In Kuma trading, there are two distinct forms: institutionalized transactions through trading partners, and casual encounters along the trade routes. In the former, a man is content to conform to the ruling scale of values . . . but in the latter he haggles for a bargain, trying to gain a material advantage. The term for 'trading partner' is, most significantly, a verb form, 'I together I-eat.' . . . He is, as it were, drawn into the 'in-group' of clansmen and affines, the people who should not be exploited for private ends" (pp. 106–107, 110). Hospitality runs alongside the balanced exchange of trade goods between partners, and "to exploit a partner for material gain is to lose him" (p. 109). Nonpartnership exchange is mostly a recent development.

A.2.3    *Buin Plain, Bougainville* — Sectoral distinctions in reciprocity among the Siuai have been indicated in previous textual citations. A few further aspects can be mentioned here. First, on the extremely generalized reciprocity appropriate among very close kinship: "Gift-giving among close relatives over and beyond the normal expectations of sharing ["sharing" as Oliver defines it is the "pooling" of the present essay] cannot entirely be reduced to conscious expectation of reciprocity.

A father might rationalize the giving of tidbits to his son by explaining that he expected to be cared for by the latter in his old age, but I am convinced that some giving between, say, father and son does not involve any desire or expectation for reciprocation" (Oliver, 1955, p. 230). Loans of productive goods normally brought over-and-above returns ("interest"), but not from close relatives (p. 229). Exchange between distant relatives and trade partners is *ootu:* it is characterized by approximate equivalence but is distinguished from "sales" involving shell money (as the sale of craft goods) by the possibility of deferring payments in *ootu* (pp. 230–231). In trade-partner transactions, also, giving above going rates is creditable, so that balance is achieved perhaps only over the long term (see pp. 297, 299, 307, 350–351, 367–368).

Sectoral variations in the economy of the Buin neighbors of the Siuai (the Terei, apparently) so impressed Thurnwald that he suggested the existence of three "kinds of economics: (1) the husbandry [pooling] within the family . . . ; (2) the inter-individual and inter-familial help among near relatives and members of a settlement united under a chief; (3) the inter-communal relations manifested by barter between individuals belonging to different communities or strata of society" (Thurnwald, 1934–35, p. 124).

A.2.4  *Kapauku* —The difference in reciprocity between interregional and intraregional sectors of the Kapauku economy has been noted in textual citation (above). Also notable is the fact that kinship and friendship ties lower customary rates of exchange in Kapauku shell-money dealings (Pospisil, 1958, p. 122). The Kapauku data are rendered obscure by an inappropriate economic terminology. So-called "loans," for example, are generalized transactions—" 'take it without repayment in the immediate future' " (p. 78; see also p. 130)—but the social context and extent of these "loans" is not clear.

A.2.5  *Mafulu* — Excepting pig-exchange, which the ethnographer discounts as a ceremonial affair, "Exchange and barter is generally only engaged in between members of different communities and not between those of the same community" (Williamson, 1912, p. 232).

A.2.6   *Manus* — Affinal exchanges, ordinarily between Manus of the same or different villages, are distinguished by long-term credit, compared with the short-term credit of trade friendship or market exchange (Mead, 1937, p. 218). Trade-friendship exchange, while more or less balanced, is in turn to be differentiated from the more impersonal "market" exchange with Usiai bushfellows. The trade friendships are developed with people of distant tribes, sometimes on long-standing kinship ties. Some credit is extended trade friends, as well as hospitality, but market exchange is direct: the Usiai are viewed as furtive and hostile, "whose eye is ever on driving a sharp bargain, whose trade manners are atrocious" (Mead, 1930, p. 118; see also Mead, 1934, pp. 307–308).

A.2.7   *Chimbu* — "Mutual help and sharing characterize relations among subclan members. A man may call upon a fellow subclansman for help whenever he needs it; he may ask any wife or daughter of a member of his subclan to give him food when she has some. . . . However, it is only the most prominent men who can count on such services from persons outside their own subclan" (Brown and Brookfield, 1959–60, p. 59; on the exception of "prominent men," compare Appendix B, "Reciprocity and Kinship Rank"). The pig-exchanges and other exchanges between clans argue balance in the external sector here, as elsewhere in the New Guinea Highlands (compare, for example, Bulmer, 1960, pp. 9–10).

A.2.8   *Buka Passage* — The total of internal reciprocity seems limited by comparison with external trade, but there are some indications of generalized exchange in internal sectors as contrasted with balanced, though not haggled, external exchange. In Kurtatchi village, requests from own sibmates of the same sex for areca or coconuts are honored without repayment though the recipients are open to counter request; otherwise, no giving of something for nothing—save that near relatives may take a man's coconuts (Blackwood, 1935, pp. 452, 454; compare p. 439 f on trade).

A.2.9    *Lesu* — "Free gifts" (generalized reciprocity) are especially rendered relatives and friends, most especially certain types of kinsmen. These gifts are food and betel. Between villages and moieties there are various balanced transactions (Powdermaker, 1933, pp. 195–203).

A.2.10    *Dobu* — As is well known, a very narrow sector of economic trust and generosity, including only *susu* and household. Outside of this, theft a possibility. Intervillage affinal exchanges more or less balanced, with village mates helping the sponsoring *susu* meet its obligations (Fortune, 1932).

A.2.11    *Trobriands* — The sociology of the reciprocity continuum described by Malinowski is only partly sectoral; rank considerations (compare below) and affinal obligations notably intrude. "Pure gift," however, is characteristic of family relations (Malinowski, 1922, pp. 177–178); "customary payments, re-paid irregularly, and without strict equivalence" include *urigubu* and contributions to a kinsman's mortuary-ceremony fund (p. 180); "gifts returned in economically equivalent form" (or almost equivalent form) include intervillage presentations at visits, exchanges between "friends" (apparently these are especially or exclusively outside the village), and, it seems, the "secondary" trade in strategic goods between kula partners (pp. 184–185); "ceremonial barter with deferred payment" (not haggled) is characteristic between kula partners and between partners in the inland-coastal, vegetables versus fish exchange *(wasi)* (pp. 187–189; cf. p. 42); "trade, pure and simple," involving haggling, mainly in nonpartner exchange between members of "industrial" and other villages within Kiriwina (pp. 189–190). The last type is *gimwali,* it is characteristic also of vegetable-fish exchange in the absence of partnership and overseas exchange accompanying *kula,* again in the absence of partnership (cf. pp. 361 f).

A.2.12    *Tikopia* — Near kinsmen and neighbors are privileged economically (e.g. Firth, 1936, p. 399; 1950, p. 203) and are expected to render economic assistance in various ways (e.g.

Firth, 1936, p. 116; 1950, p. 292). The necessity of a *quid pro quo* seems to increase with kinship distance—thus "forced exchange" (also known ethnographically as "coercive gift") is a transaction of the more distant sector: "The importance of the social category comes out . . . in cases such as when a man wants a coconut-grating stool. If he knows of a close kinsman who has an extra one, he goes and asks for it and should get it without ceremony. 'You give me a stool for myself; your stools are two.' It is said that the kinsman 'rejoices' to give it because of the tie between them. Sooner or later he in turn comes and asks for something he fancies and this too will be handed over freely. Such freedom of approach obtains only between members of a small kinship group and depends upon the recognition of a principle of reciprocity. If a man is going to apply to someone not of his own kin, a 'different man' as the Tikopia say, then he cooks food, fills a large basket, and tops it off with an ordinary piece of bark-cloth or even a blanket. Armed with this he goes to the owner and asks for the article. He is usually not refused" (Firth, 1950, p. 316).

A.2.13     *Maori* — A large part of the internal circulation, here of the village especially, was centralized in chiefly hands—it was generalized enough but run on the principles of chiefly due and *noblesse oblige* (cf. Firth, 1959). The external exchanges (intervillage, intertribal) involved more direct and equivalent reciprocation, although prestige of course accrued to liberality (cf. Firth, 1959, pp. 335–337, 403–409, 422–423). Maori proverb: "In winter a relation, in autumn a son; "signifying 'he is only a distant relative at the time of cultivation when there is heavy work to be tackled, but in the time after harvest when all is finished, and there is plenty of food to be eaten, he calls himself my son' " (Firth, 1926, p. 251).

A.3.0      *Notes from here and there.*

A.3.1      *Pilaga* — Henry's well-known study (1951) of food-sharing in a Pilaga village is here cited with caution. We have to deal with a disrupted and resettled population. Also, during the period of Henry's observations a great portion of the men were away working on sugar plantations. It was, moreover, the "hungry time" of the Pilaga year. "Thus we are dealing with an economic system from which a considerable number of productive persons had been withdrawn, and during a period of scarcity, with the society functioning at low ebb" (Henry, 1951, p. 193). (The intense food-sharing under these miserable conditions is consistent with propositions developed below on the relation between reciprocity and need.) I assume that most if not all the instances of sharing were of the generalized reciprocal sort, the giving out of larger stocks that had come to hand, rendering assistance and the like. The assumption is consistent with examples offered by Henry and with the lack of balance he records in individuals' outgo and income. Trade with other groups, reported by Henry to have occurred, is not considered in the study in question. The principal value of this study for the present discussion is its specification of the incidence of food-sharing by social distance. The obligation to share food is highest among those closest in kinship-residential terms. "Membership in the same household [a multifamily and multidwelling group making up a section of the village] constitutes a very close tie; but membership in the same household plus a close kinship tie is the closest of bonds. This is objectified in food-sharing, those having the closest bond sharing food most often" (p. 188). The conclusion is supported by analysis of particular cases. (In one of these, the association between sharing and close relations was working the other way around—a woman was sharing food heavily with a man whom she wanted to, and eventually did, marry.) "The cases reviewed so far concerning distribution within the household [section of the village] may be summarized as follows: the answer to the question, *to which individual or family did each individual or family give most often?* can be answered only through quantitative analysis of the behavior of individuals and families. When this is done four points emerge: (1) The Pilaga distributes most of his product to members of his own household. (2) He does not distribute equally to all. (3) A variety of factors enter to prevent his distributing equally to all; *(a)* differences in genealogical ties, *(b)* differences of obligations among the people of the household with respect to their obligations outside it, *(c)* stability of residence, *(d)* dependency needs, *(e)* marital expectations, *(f)* fear of shamans, and *(g)* special food taboos. (4) When common residence and close genealogical ties combine, the highest rate of interchange of products between families so related is present" (p. 207). The sectoral incidence of food-sharing is shown in the following chart (adapted from Henry's *Table IV*, p. 210).The other section of the village, for which Henry did not have as numerous records—because they were wandering about the forest a good deal—does not show the same trend (also *Table IV*). The second column is in three of four instances larger than the first—more sharing across the village than within the "household" section. But this section of the village is not comparable to the other (tabulated above) because in the former people were "more closely integrated [i.e. closely related] than those at the other end, thus much of what takes the form of *distribution,* the transfer of produce from the producer to another person, in No. 28's part of the village [tabulated below], takes the form of *commensality* at No. 14's end of the village. Hence the percentage of product distributed by No. 14's people to persons within the section . . . appears low, while that distributed to other classes [sectors] seems high" (p. 211; Henry's emphases). Since Henry does not consider commensality among different families of the same "household" as food-sharing, the seeming exception may be in fairness disregarded.

| Family | Per cent of Times Sharing Food with Families in | | |
|:---:|:---:|:---:|:---:|
| | Own household section of village | The other household section of the village | Outsiders, of other villages |
| I | 72 | 18 | 10 |
| II | 43 | 0 | 7 |
| III | 81 | 16 | 3 |
| IV | 55 | 34 | 11 |

A.3.2   *Nuer* — Intensive food-sharing, hospitality, and other generalized reciprocities in Nuer smaller local groups (hamlet
sections of the village) and cattle camps (Evans-Pritchard,
1940, pp. 21, 84–85, 91, 183; 1951, pp. 2, 131–132; Howell,
1954, p. 201). Not much exchange in the intratribal (extra-
village) sector except the instrumental transactions of bridewealth and feud settlement (as compensations, of their
nature balanced). Nuer specifically distinguish internal
reciprocity from trade with Arabs by the directness (tem-
porally) of the latter exchange (Evans-Pritchard, 1956, p.
223 f). Relations with neighboring tribes, especially Dinka,
notoriously appropriative, amounting in the main to seizure
of loot and territory through violence.

A.3.3   *Bantu of North Kavirondo* — Intensive informal hospitality
among neighbors. Exchanges of balanced sort are principally
in durables, with craftsmen, but the rates most favor neigh-
bor-clansmen, are higher for the clansman who is not a
neighbor, most dear for strangers (Wagner, 1956, pp. 161–
162).

A.3.4   *Chukchee* — Certain amount of generosity and assistance
within Chukchee camps (see citations in Sahlins, 1960).
Theft from the herds of other camps common (Bogoras,
1904–09, p. 49). Aboriginal trade between maritime and
reindeer Chukchee, and some trade across the Bering Straits:
apparently the trade more or less balanced; some of it was
silent and all of it conducted with considerable mistrust
(Bogoras, 1904–09, pp. 53, 95–96).

A.3.5   *Tiv* — Clear differentiation at least between external ("market") and internal spheres. A "market" distinguishable from
the several varieties of gift: the last imply "a relationship
between the two parties concerned which is of a permanence
and warmth not known in a 'market,' and hence—though
gifts should be reciprocal over a long period of time—it is
bad form overtly to count and compete and haggle over
gifts" (Bohannan, 1955, p. 60). A "market" is competitive

and exploitative: "In fact, the presence of a previous relationship makes a 'good market' impossible: people do not like to sell to kinsmen since it is bad form to demand as high a price from kinsmen as one might from a stranger" (p. 60).

A.3.6    *Bemba* — A centralized system of reciprocities (chiefly redistribution) is, analogously to Polynesia, the main part of the larger economy; a very limited inter-tribal exchange sector (Richards, 1939, p. 221 f). Various dues to close relatives by kin type (pp. 188 f). Apart from hospitality to visiting kinsmen, chiefs and, nowadays, strangers, food-sharing is ordinarily characteristic in a narrow circle of close kin—but apparently in a wider circle during scarcities (pp. 108–109, 136 f, 178–182, 186, 202–203). The money that has been introduced is not much used in internal exchange, but when it is, "People buying from relatives pay less than the normal rate, and usually add some service to the transaction" (p. 220). ". . . I have often seen women take a pot of beer and conceal it in a friend's granary on the reported arrival of some elderly relative. To refuse hospitality with a pot of beer sitting on the hearth would be an impossible insult, but a bland assertion that 'Alas, Sir, we poor wretches. . . . We have nothing to eat here' is sometimes necessary. This would not be done in the case of a near relative, but only with a more distant kinsman of a classificatory type, or one of the well-known 'cadgers' of a family" (p. 202).

# Appendix B

*Notes on Reciprocity and Kinship Rank*

B.0.0    These materials deal with kinship-rank reciprocities both in simple form and in the context of chiefly redistribution.

B.1.0    *Hunting-Gathering Peoples*

B.1.1    *Bushmen* — "No Bushman wants prominence, but Toma [a band headman] went further than most in avoiding prominence; he had almost no possessions and gave away everything that came into his hands. He was diplomatic, for in exchange for his self-imposed poverty he won the respect and following of all the people there" (Thomas, 1959, p. 183). "We did hear people say . . . that a headman may feel that he should lean well to the generous side in his giving, for his position as headman sets him out from the others a little and he wants whatever attention this attracts not to be envious. Someone remarked that this could keep a headman poor" (Marshall, 1961, p. 244).

B.1.2   *Andamans* — "Generosity is esteemed by the Andaman Islanders as one of the highest of virtues and is unremittingly practiced by the majority of them," Radcliffe-Brown writes (1948, p. 43). He notes that the person who does not work and must needs be given food sinks in esteem, while Man remarked that the generous person rises in esteem (Man, n.d, p. 41). There is a definite generation-status influence on reciprocity. Although at least sometimes appearing as givers of food—on occasions of collective sharing of game—elders are privileged in regard to juniors: "It is considered a breach of good manners ever to refuse the request of another. Thus if a man be asked by another to give him anything that he may possess, he will immediately do so. If the two men are equals a return of about the same value will have to be made. As between an older married man and a bachelor or a young married man, however, the younger would not make any request of such a nature, and if the older asked the younger for anything, the latter would give it without always expecting a return" (Radcliffe-Brown, 1948, pp. 42–43).

B.1.3   *Eskimo* — Influence and prestige accrued to the North Alaskan Eskimo whale boat leader or caribou hunting leader at least in part by virtue of the stuff he doled out in ostensibly generous fashion (Spencer, 1959, pp. 144, 152 f, 210 f; 335–336, 351). Great men noted for their great generosity (pp. 154–155, 157). Stinginess as usual deplorable (p. 164).

B.1.4   *Carrier* — A big-man, slighted by a fur trader, boasts that he is just as good a chief as the trader: "'When it is the proper season to hunt the beaver, I kill them; and of their flesh I make feasts for my relations. I, often, feast all the Indians of my village; and, sometimes, invite people from afar off, to come and partake of the fruits of my hunts . . . ' " (Harmon, 1957, pp. 143–144; cf. 253–254).

B.2.0    *Melanesia* — I have elsewhere presented a general study of the economics of big-man leadership in western Melanesian societies (Sahlins, 1963). Generalized reciprocity is here the decisive "starting mechanism" of ranking. A following is developed through private assistance to individuals, a tribal name (renown) through large-scale giveaways, often of pigs and vegetable foods. The wherewithal for his generosity comes initially from the aspiring big-man's own household from his nearest relatives: he capitalizes in the beginning on kinship dues and by finessing the generalized reciprocity appropriate among close kin. He often enlarges his household at an early phase, perhaps by taking additional wives. A leader's career is well under way when he is able to link other men and their families to his faction, to harness their production to his ambition by helping them in some big way. He cannot, however, extend these people too far: some material benefits must accrue to followers on pain of encouraging their discontent and his downfall.

Most examples that follow are of big-man systems. The concluding cases are different: chiefdoms or protochiefdoms in which generalized reciprocity between ranks is apparent in a redistributive context.

B.2.1    *Siuai* — The most thorough exposition of Melanesian big-man economics is Oliver's (1955) study. The development of influence and prestige through generalized transactions is richly described. There are several peripheral features likewise of interest in the present context. Notable is the influence of rank on customary rates of balance in shell money dealings: "One great advantage of being a leader lies in one's ability to buy things more cheaply ('When a mumi [big-man] sends out thirty spans of *mauai* to purchase a pig for a feast, the pig owner would be ashamed to send along a pig worth less than forty'). On the other hand, this commercial advantage of the leader is usually counterbalanced by the traditional exercise of *noblesse oblige"* (p. 342). So, "the most praiseworthy thing a man can do is to exceed the transactional requirements of ordinary trade and kin relationships by paying generously (in goods) for all goods and services he receives, by giving goods to persons to whom he is not directly obligated, and by doing these things after the manner of great leaders of the past" (p. 456; cf. pp. 378, 407, 429–430).

Thurnwald writes of another Buin Plain people that *mamoko,* the reward given by a big-man to his followers, "is considered an act of liberality, for which there is no obligation. Any gift of friendship is described by the same name. A surplus payment over the price agreed is also called *mamoko. Totokai* is the excess payment of a kitere [follower] to his *mumira* [leader] for ensuring his good will and his willingness to credit him with *abuta* [shell money] on another occasion. *Dakai* designates a payment for reconciliation or reparation between men of equal position" (Thurnwald, 1934–35, p. 135). The variation of reciprocity by rank difference is clear.

B.2.2    *'Gawa (Busama)* — Clubhouse leaders and, especially, outstanding village leaders are typical western Melanesian bigmen. Hogbin writes: "The man who is generous over a long period thus has many persons in his debt. No problem arises when these are of the same status as himself—the poor give one another insignificant presents, and the rich exchange sumptuous offerings. But if his resources are greater than theirs they may find repayment impossible and have to default. Acutely conscious of their position, they express their humility in terms of deference and respect. . . . The relation of debtors and creditors forms the basis of the system of leadership" (Hogbin, 1951, p. 122). The leaders were "men who ate bones and chewed lime—they presented the best meat to others, leaving only scraps for themselves, and were so free with areca nuts and pepper that they had no betel mixture left. Folk-tales about legendary headmen of the past relate that, although these men had 'more pigs than anyone could count and bigger gardens than are made now,' they gave everything away" (p. 123; cf. pp. 118 f). The main run of clubhouse leaders were reluctantly placed in that position. The work was hard— "His hands are never free from earth, and his forehead continually drips with sweat" (p. 131)—and the material rewards nil. The principal big-man of the village, however, was ambitious. "It is frequently insisted that the headmen were so jealous of their reputation that they went to the trouble of inventing excuses for giving food away" (p. 139). Low rank was the reward of stinginess, and he who is prepared to take advantage of others, "He sinks to the bottom of the social ladder. . . ." (p. 126).

B.2.3   *Kaoka (Guadalcanal)* — A main-run big-man economy (Hogbin, 1933–34; 1937–38). "Reputation . . . is enhanced not by accumulating wealth in order to use it for one's self but by giving it away. Every event of importance in a person's life—marriage, birth, death and even the construction of a new house or canoe—is celebrated by a feast, and the more feasts a man gives, and the more lavish he is in providing food, the greater is his prestige. The social leaders are those who give away most" (Hogbin, 1937–38, p. 290).

B.2.4   *Kapauku* — Described by the ethnographer as sort of upland New Guinea capitalists. The big-man pattern, however, is an ordinary (sweet potato) garden variety. "Loans" and "credit" put out by Kapauku big men (*tonowi,* generous richman) are not interest bearing in the standard sense (see above, A.2.4); they are means of developing status through generosity (Pospisil, 1958, p. 129). "The society views its ideal man as a most generous individual, who through the distribution of his fortune satisfies the needs of many people. Generosity is the highest cultural value and an attribute necessary for acquiring followers in political and legal life" (p. 57). The big-man's status sinks if he loses the wherewithal for generosity (p. 59); if he is excessively demanding he is likely to face an egalitarian rebellion— " '. . . you should not be the only rich man, we should all be the same, therefore you only stay equal with us'. . . . was the reason given by the Paniai people for killing Mote Juwopija of Madi, a *tonowi* who was not generous enough" (p. 80; cf. pp. 108–110). Wealth is not enough: ". . . a selfish individual who hoards his money and does not lend [*sic*] it, never sees the time when his word will be taken seriously and his advice and decisions followed, no matter how rich he may become. The people believe that the only justification for becoming rich is to be able to redistribute the accumulated property among one's less fortunate fellows, a procedure which also gains their support" (pp. 79–80). Big-men buy more cheaply than prevailing rates (p. 122). One big-man summed up well, if cynically, the rank-generating impetus delivered by generalized reciprocity. " 'I am a headman,' he said, 'not because the people like me but because they owe me money and are afraid' " (p. 95).

B.2.5    *New Guinea Highlands* — The big-man pattern, here worked out in a segmented lineage context, is general in the Highlands. "The Kuma 'big men' or 'men of strength' . . . who can command much wealth, are entrepreneurs in the sense that they control the flow of valuables between clans by making fresh presentations on their own account and choosing whether or not to contribute to others. Their profit in these transactions is incremental reputation. . . . The aim is not simply to be wealthy, nor even to act as only the wealthy can act: it is to be *known* to be wealthy. Further, a man does not really achieve his ambition until he can be seen to act as if wealth itself were of no account" (Reay, 1959, p. 96; see pp. 110–111, 130). There is also the usual Melanesian corollary of the big-man, the "rubbish man." "A man is a 'rubbish man' of no consequence if he has not enough food to offer many friends and relatives as well as meet his personal requirements" (p. 23).

The use of generalized reciprocity as a mechanism of status differentiation in another Highland instance (Kyaka) is succinctly put by Bulmer: "These supporters of a leader are normally in a state of mutual obligation with him, having been helped by him with bridewealth payment and the like, or expecting help of this kind. Such assistance obligates them to channel through him such pigs of their own as they are putting into the Moka [interclan pig-exchange]" (Bulmer, 1960, p. 9).

B.2.6    *Lesu* — "A rich man might pay five *tsera* for a pig for which another man would pay four. The more he pays the more prestige the buyer has. Everyone then knows he is a rich man. On the other hand, the owner of a pig would gain prestige if he sold it for four *tsera* when he might have received five'" (Powdermaker, 1933, p. 201).

B.2.7    *To'ambaita (N. Malaita)* — Another good description of a typical big-man order, conforming in all essential respects to those already discussed (Hogbin, 1939, pp. 61 f; 1943–44, pp. 258 f).

B.2.8    *Manus* — The Manus have—or had, in their "old lives"—a big-man pattern (Mead, 1934; 1937a). Their clans, however, were also ascriptively divided into two ranks, *lapan* (high) and *lau* (low). This ranking was, according to Mead, not of great political significance, but its economic side is of interest nonetheless. "Between *lapan* and *lau* there is a type of mutual helpfulness expected, not unlike a slight version of the feudal relationship—the *lapan* takes care of the economic needs of the *lau* and the *lau* works for the *lapan*" (Mead, 1934, pp. 335–336).

For discussion of other big-men systems see Sahlins, 1963. Among the well-described ones are the Arapesh (Mead, 1937a; 1938; 1947), the Abelam (Kaberry, 1940–41; 1941–42), and Tangu (Burridge, 1960). Deacon struck the general note: "Yet for all that the Malekulan is, as has been said, grasping and bourgeois in his attitude toward wealth, generosity and consideration for one's debtors are held up as virtues. . . . To be stingy is to sink in public esteem; to be openhanded is to acquire fame, honour, and influence" (Deacon, 1934, p. 200).

B.2.9    *Sa'a* — The generalized reciprocity principle in the context of a small scale redistributive system. "The good chief and the commoners regarded one another as mutually dependent on each other, and the people loved a chief who by his feasts brought glory on the place, and one of the reasons why [the chief] Wate'ou'ou was called. . . 'he who keeps the canoe on a straight course,' was because he was good at feasts" (Ivens, 1927, p. 255). "Stowed away safely in the lodge in bags is the chief's possession in money, which in a measure is what Doraadi called the 'panga,' the 'bank' of the village because it is drawn on for communal purposes such as feasts or the payments of blood money. The Sa'a chiefs were wealthy men owing to the contributions made to them on public occasions by the commoners" (p. 32). "Chief and priest were exempted from the obligation to make a return for gifts received which held always in the case of commoners" (p. 8). "Chiefs were said to *kuluhie hänue,* succour the land, to draw the people up who came to them for protection, and the word *kulu,* draw or lift up, appears in the compound *mänikulu'e,* glorious, a word associated with feasts and chiefs" (p. 129, cf. pp. 145, 147–148, 160 f, 221 f).

B.2.10    *Trobriands* — Generalized rank reciprocity organized as redistribution. The underlying ethic was reciprocal assistance between chiefs and people. Malinowski's many statements of the economic obligations of chieftainship include several which highlight the status implications of generosity. For example: ". . . to possess is to be great, and . . . wealth is the indispensable appanage of social rank and attribute of personal virtue. But the important point is that with them to possess is to give. . . . A man who owns a thing is naturally expected to share it, to distribute it, to be its trustee and dispenser. And the higher the rank the greater the obligation. . . . Thus the main symptom of being powerful is to be wealthy, and of wealth is to be generous. Meanness, indeed, is the most despised vice, and the only thing about which the natives have strong moral views, while generosity is the essence of goodness" (1922, p. 97). Again: "Not in all cases, but in many of them, the handing over of wealth is the expression of the superiority of the giver over the recipient. In others, it represents subordination to a chief, or a kinship relation or relationship-in-law" (p. 175). *"Relationship between Chiefs and Commoners.*—The tributes and services given to a chief by his vassals on the one hand, and the small but frequent gifts which he gives them, and the big and important contribution which he makes to all tribal enterprises are characteristic of this relationship" (p. 193). The Trobriand chief's difficulties in holding on to his betel, and the little strategems he employed to save some for himself, are famous anecdotes of the introductory anthropology course (Malinowski, 1922, p. 97).

B.3.0    *American Plains* — Plains Indian chiefs were local equivalents of Melanesian big-men. The pattern is much the same; the cultural idiom varies. Generalized reciprocity here again a decisive starting mechanism of leadership. Military honors were an important attribute of leaders, but influence rested as much or more on generous dispositions of horses, of loot, of meat, of help to the poor and widowed, and the like. The chief's faction was a roving band, a cluster of lesser and often dependent people, for whose well-being the chief felt responsible and upon whom he might draw economically. Wealth in horses was an ultimate necessity for a band chief: the loss of this fund of generosity was the loss of influence.

B.3.1    *Assiniboin* — "The chief of a band is little more than the nominal father of all and addresses them as his children in a body" (Denig, 1928–29, p. 431). "A chief must give away all to preserve his popularity and is always the poorest in the band, yet he takes good care to distribute his gifts among his own relatives or the rich, upon whom he can draw at any time he be in need" (p. 449; cf. pp. 432, 525, 547–548, 563; on the element of calculation in Assiniboin generosity, see pp. 475, 514–515).

B.3.2    *Kansa-Osage* —"The chiefs and candidates for public preferment render themselves popular by their disinterestedness and poverty. Whenever any extraordinary success attends them in the acquisition of property, it is only for the benefit of their meritorious adherents, for they distribute it with a profuse liberality, and pride themselves in being esteemed the poorest man in the community" (Hunter, 1823, p. 317).

B.3.3   *Plains Cree* —"It is not an easy thing to be a chief. Look at this chief now. He has to have pity on the poor. When he sees a man in difficulty he must try to help him in whatever way he can. If a person asks for something in his tipi, he must give it to him willingly and without bad feeling" (Mandelbaum, 1940, p. 222; cf. pp. 195, 205, 221 f, 270–271).

B.3.4.   *Blackfoot* — The same pattern, in essence (Ewers, 1955, pp. 140–141, 161 f, 188–189, 192–193, 240 f ).

B.3.5   *Comanche* — The same (Wallace and Hoebel, 1952, pp. 36, 131, 209 f, 240).

B.4.0   *Polynesia* — I have elsewhere offered studies of the economies of Polynesian chieftainship (Sahlins, 1958; 1963). Redistribution is the transactional form, generalized reciprocity the principle. The few notes here highlight particularly the principle.

B.4.1   *Maori* — Firth's excellent analysis of Maori economics provides the *mise en scène* for considerations of rank-reciprocity in Polynesia. I cite two long passages: "The prestige of a chief was bound up with his free use of wealth, particularly food. This in turn tended to secure for him a larger revenue from which to display his hospitality, since his followers and relatives brought him choice gifts. . . . Apart from lavish entertainment of strangers and visitors, the chief also disbursed wealth freely as presents among his followers. By this means their allegiance was secured and he repaid them for the gifts and personal services rendered to him. All payment among the Maori was made in the form of gifts. There was thus a continual reciprocity between chief and people. The chief also acted as a kind of capitalist, assuming the initiative in the construction of certain 'public works' if the term may be so used. It was by his accumulation and possession of wealth, and his subsequent lavish distribution of it, that such a man was able to give the spur to these important tribal enterprises. He was a kind of channel through which wealth flowed, concentrating it only to pour it out freely again" (Firth, 1959a, p. 133). "The quantity and quality of . . . gifts received tended to increase with the rank and hereditary position of the chief in the tribe, his prestige, and the following which he was able to gather around him. But the relationship was by no means one-sided. If the income of a chief was largely dependent on his prestige and influence and the regard of his people, this in its turn was contingent upon his liberal treatment of them. There were constant calls upon his resources. His slaves and immediate dependents had to be fed, he was expected to assist those of his tribesmen who came to him in need, a crowd of relatives—and the Maori bonds of kinship stretched far—looked to him for a generous repayment of all the small social services they rendered him, and for an occasional *douceur* as a mark of appreciation of their loyalty. When presents of foodstuffs were made to him by people of other tribes his regard for his reputation required that he should distribute a considerable portion of them among his tribespeople. For all gifts made to him a return was expected, of equivalent or even greater value. . . . Again, the calls of hospitality were never ending. Entertainment had to be provided on a lavish scale for visiting chiefs and their adherents. . . . Moreover, on occasions of the birth, marriage or death of any people of rank in the village his personal resources were drawn upon to a serious extent, while the occasional provision of a large feast also drained him of food supplies. In this connection he seems to have exercised control of the communal stores of food which he commanded to be disbursed as required. If the chief's use of wealth be reviewed, then, it is seen that to the varied sources which provided him with his stores of goods corresponded a number of serious liabilities. The result was that a sort of equilibrium was maintained between income and expenditure. In general, at no time was the chief the possessor of enormous quantities of valuables, though the system of receipt and redistribution of goods allowed a great quantity of them to flow through his hands" (pp. 297–298; cf. pp. 130 f, 164, 294 f, 345–346).

B.4.2    *Hawaii* — Chiefs had extensive call on the labor, the resources and products of the underlying (*makaainana*) population, as well as control over certain specialists and enjoyment of certain sumptuary perquisites. The chiefdom, often embracing the whole of a large island, was an elaborate collection-redistribution apparatus. "It was the practice for kings [i.e. paramount chiefs of individual islands] to build storehouses in which to collect food, fish, tapas [bark cloth], malos [men's loin cloths], pa-us [women's loin skirts], and all sorts of goods. These store-houses were designed by the Kalaimoku [chief's executive] as a means of keeping the people contented, so they would not desert the king. They were like the baskets that were used to entrap the *hinalea* fish. The *hinalea* thought there was something good within the basket, and he hung round the outside of it. In the same way the people thought there was food in the storehouses, and they kept their eyes on the king. As the rat will not desert the pantry . . . where he thinks food is, so the people will not desert the king while they think there is food in his storehouse" (Malo, 1951, p. 195). The tendency at the highest levels of chieftainship, however—and despite well meaning advice of counselors—was to press too heavily on the lesser chiefs and people, with the result that, as Malo puts it, "Many kings were put to death by the people because of their oppression of the *makaainana* [commonality]" (p. 195; cf. pp. 58, 61; Fornander, 1880: pp. 76, 88, 100–101, 200–202, 227–228, 270–271).

B.4.3    *Tonga* — A fine native statement of the chiefly economic ethic, attributed by Mariner to the chief Finau. Upon Mariner's explanation of the value of money: "Finow replied that the explanation did not satisfy him; he still thought it a foolish thing that people should place a value on money, when they either could not or would not apply it to any useful (physical) purpose. 'If,' said he, 'it were made of iron, and could be converted into knives, axes and chisels, there would be some sense in placing a value on it; but as it is, I see none.

If a man,' he added, 'has more yams than he wants, let him exchange some of them away for pork or *gnatoo* [bark cloth]. Certainly money is much handier, and more convenient, but then, as it will not spoil by being kept, people will store it up, instead of sharing it out, as a chief ought to do, and thus become selfish; whereas, if provisions were the principal property of man, and it ought to be, as being both the most useful and the most necessary, he could not store it up, for it would spoil, and so he would be obliged either to exchange it away for something else useful, or share it to his neighbors, and inferior chiefs and dependents, for nothing.' He concluded by saying 'I understand now very well what it is that makes the Papalangis ["Europeans"] so selfish—it is this money!' " (Mariner, 1827 i, pp. 213–214).

Conversely, the upward flow: ". . . the practice of making presents to superior chiefs is very general and frequent. The higher class of chiefs generally make a present to the king, of hogs or yams about once a fortnight. These chiefs, about the same time, receive presents from those below them, and these last from others, and so on, down to the common people" (p. 210; cf. Gifford, 1929).

B.4.4    *Tahiti* — From indications of the Duff missionaries, it looks as if Ha'amanimani, the Tahitian priest-chief, acted faithfully to the ideal expressed by Finau: "Manne Manne was very urgent for sails, rope, anchor, etc. for his vessel, none of which articles we had to spare: on which account, though the captain gave him his own cocked hat and a variety of articles, he was still discontented; saying, 'Several people told me that you wanted Manne Manne, and now I am come, you give me nothing.' An observation similar to this he once made to the missionaries: 'You give me,' says he, 'much parow (talk) and much prayers to the Eatora, but very few axes, knives, scissars, or cloth.' The case is, that whatever he receives he immediately distributes among his friends and dependents; so that for all the numerous presents he had received, he had nothing now to shew, except a glazed hat, a pair of breeches, and an old black coat, which he had fringed with red feathers. And this prodigal behavior he excuses, by saying that, were he not to do so, he should never be a king, nor even remain a chief of any consequence" (Duff missionaries, 1799, pp. 224–225). For all this it is apparent from the Duff journal as well as other early reports (e.g. Rodriguez, 1919) that Tahitian high chiefs might accumulate considerable stocks of goods and especially that they had very considerable power to demand foodstuffs from the underlying population. The traditional counsel was the same as in Hawaii—"Your household must not be accused of food hiding. Let not your name be associated with hidden foods or hidden goods. The hands of the Arii must be always open; on these two things rest your prestige" (Handy, 1930, p. 41)—but apparently Tahitian chiefs were inclined, as it is said, to "eat the powers of the government too much." (Yet see also Davies, 1961, p. 87 note 1.)

B.4.5    *Tikopia* — A stream of gifts flow from below to the Tikopia chief, but then his obligation to be generous is at least as great as his ability to accumulate things. Generosity indeed was a jealousy guarded chiefly prerogative: "Chiefs are recognized as being proper persons to control large quantities of food, to have a number of valued objects stored away in their houses. . . . But the stocks which they accumulate are expected to be dispersed in a manner which will yield benefit to their people. Great accumulation by a commoner must also be followed by a corresponding dispersal. But such a man would incur the charge from the chiefly families of *fia pasak* 'desiring to boast,' and would be watched by them lest he attempt to usurp some of their privileges. According to precedent in Tikopia history they would probably take an opportunity either to seize his goods or to kill him" (Firth, 1950, p. 243). The Tikopia chiefs, in short, would not tolerate starting mechanisms. This is not true throughout Polynesia. In the Marquesas, for example, upward mobility through "accumulating and dispensing wealth" was possible (Linton, 1939, pp. 150, 153, 156–157; Handy, 1923, pp. 36–37, 48, 53). (On other aspects of the reciprocity between Tikopia chiefs and people see Firth, 1936, pp. 382–383, 401–403; 1950, pp. 34, 58, 109 f, 172, 188, 190, 191, 196, 212 f, 321).

B.5.0   *Miscellaneous*

B.5.1   *Northwestern North America* — Generalized reciprocity per-
meated the political economy of the Northwest Coast Indians, both in the potlatch giveaways between chiefs and in the
internal relation of chiefs and their respective followers. The
Nootka are a clearly described case in point. Chiefs acquired
a variety of dues: from the first catch of salmon traps, early
pickings of berry patches, from large catches of fish taken by
their people, and the like (e.g., Drucker, 1951, pp. 56–57,
172, 255, 272, *et passim).* Conversely, " 'Every time a chief
got a lot of food of any kind, he gave a feast to give it away
to his people' " (p. 370; see also Suttles, 1960, pp. 299–300;
Barnett, 1938; Codere, n.d.).

  The Tolowa-Tututni political economy is the same in principle as that prevailing to the north, albeit a slighter version.
Drucker characterizes the chief-follower relation as "symbiotic"—"The relationship uniting the rich-man and his kinfolk was essentially a symbiotic one. It is said that some of
the richest men never worked; their henchmen hunted and
fished for them. In return the rich-man gave feasts, and in
lean times would share his stores with his people. He bought
wives for the young men, or at least contributed most of the
payment; but it was also he who accepted and held the bride
prices paid for their sisters and daughters. Perhaps most
important of all; it was the rich-man who was obliged to pay
compensation for wrongs his henchmen committed, to save
them, and himself, from retaliation . . . he received a lion's
share of any indemnities paid for injuries to one of them"
(Drucker, 1937, p. 245; for indications of similar rank-reciprocity in California see Kroeber, 1925, pp. 3, 40, 42, 55;
Goldschmidt, 1951, pp. 324–325, 365, 413; Loeb, 1926, pp.
238–239).

B.5.2   *Creek* — One of the finest descriptions of chiefly redistribution, again run on the underlying principle of generalized
reciprocity, appears in W. Bartram's late eighteenth-century
account of the Creek: "After the feast of the busk is over, and

all the grain is ripe, the whole town again assemble, and every man carries of the fruits of his labour, from the part [of the town field] first allotted to him, which he deposits in his own granary; which is individually his own. But previous to their carrying off their crops from the field, there is a large crib or granary, erected in the plantation, which is called the king's crib; and to this each family carries and deposits a certain quantity, according to his [apparently meaning "their"] ability or inclination, or none at all if he so chooses, this in appearance seems a tribute or revenue to the mico [chief], but in fact is designed for another purpose, i.e. that of a public treasury, supplied by a few and voluntary contributions, and to which every citizen has the right of free and equal access, when his own private stores are consumed, to serve as a surplus to fly to for succour, to assist neighboring towns whose crops have failed, accommodate strangers, or travellers, afford provisions or supplies, when they go forth on hostile expeditions, and for all other exigencies of the state; and this treasure is at the disposal of the king or mico; which is surely a royal attribute to have an exclusive right and ability in a community to distribute comfort and blessings to the necessitous" (Bartram, 1958, p. 326; cf. Swanton, 1928, pp. 277–278).

B.5.3  *Kachin* — "In theory then people of superior class receive gifts from their inferiors. But no permanent economic advantage accrues from this. Anyone who receives a gift is thereby placed in debt *(hka)* to the giver. . . . Paradoxically therefore although an individual of high-class status is defined as one who receives gifts . . . he is all the time under a social compulsion to give away more than he receives. Otherwise he would be reckoned mean and a mean man runs the danger of losing status" (Leach, 1954, p. 163).

B.5.4  *Bemba* — Exhibits classic redistributive economy, a classic generalized reciprocity between chief and people. ". . . the distribution of cooked food is an attribute of authority, and therefore prestige, and . . . its reception puts a man under an obligation to return to the giver respect, service, or reciprocal

hospitality" (Richards, 1939, p. 135). The paramount is most
engaged in the distributive process, and this "is of course
necessary to the chief if he is to make gardens and conduct
tribal business through his councillors. But it is more than
this. The giving of food, as in most African tribes, is an
absolutely essential attribute of chieftainship, just as it is of
authority in the village or household, and the successful organization of supplies at the capital seems to be associated in
the Bemba mind with the security and well-being of the
whole tribe itself. . . . The whole institution of the *kamitembo*
[the sacred kitchen and storehouse of the tribe] illustrates to
my mind that close association between authority and the
power to distribute provisions on which the tribal organization depends. The chief owns the food and receives tribute,
and the chief provides for his subjects and distributes cooked
food to them. Both of these attributes are symbolized in the
*kamitembo* house" (pp. 148, 150). "I never heard a chief
boast to another about the size of his granaries, but often
about the amount of food brought to him and distributed by
him. In fact chiefs particularly valued the fact that some of
their food was brought to them and not grown in their gardens, for it gave them some kind of resource to fall back
upon. The Bemba say: 'We will shake the tree until it gives
up its fruit,' that is to say, we will nag the big man until he
divides his supplies. If a chief attempted to dry meat and keep
it for subsequent division his followers would sit and stare at
it and talk about it until he was forced to give them some,
but supplies brought irregularly from other villages provided
constant fresh resources" (p. 214). "The people still definitely
prefer their ruler to have a big granary. It gives them, I think,
a sense of security—a feeling of certainty that there will be
food at the capital and a knowledge that they are working for
a powerful and successful man. . . . Besides this, a hungry
man has technically the right to call upon his chief for help.
I did not hear of this claim being made very often, but still,
in a sense, the *umulasa* [tribute-labour] garden and *umulasa*
granary are recognized as belonging to the people. A man can
steal from the tribute garden of a chief, but not from those

of his wives, and I have sometimes heard old natives speak with pride of 'our' granary, adding, 'It was we who filled it to overflowing.' Thus the commoner got by his labour the sense of supernatural support, a personal approach to his chief, food in return for his work, support in time of starvation, and . . . leadership in economic pursuits. The chief in return got extra supplies of food to distribute, the means of supporting his tribal council, the necessary labour for tribal undertakings such as road-building, and last, but not least, prestige" (p. 261; cf. pp. 138, 169, 178–180, 194, 215, 221, 244 f, 275, 361–362).

B.5.5　*Pilagá* — Generosity is no starting mechanism, but it is a sustaining mechanism of rank. In Henry's tables (1951, pp. 194, 197, 214) it is the chief who gives more goods (and to more people) than anyone else. Henry comments regarding this: "It will . . . be observed that in no case is the contribution of his [i.e. the chief's] family to any family equaled or exceeded by any other family. As a matter of fact, No. 28 [the chief] himself alone contributes on an average of 35% of the income, i.e. food received of each family. Thus the role of the chief and his family in Pilaga society is to support others. The chief and his family thus become *the unifying factor in the village*. It is this that gives meaning to the use of the father term for the chief and the child term for the members of the village. . . . The position of the chief, despite the 'prestige' it carries also entails burdens. All the people are his children *(kokotepi)* for whom he is responsible. Hence the word for chief, *salyaranik,* signifies one who is heavy" (pp. 214–215).

# Appendix C

*Notes on Reciprocity and Wealth*

C.0.0　*Reciprocity and Wealth* — The following notes mostly concern societies already considered in other contexts. The citations illustrate particularly the association between wealth

differences and generosity (generalized reciprocity). That
food is the item so often shared is significant. Examples that
indicate sharing in favor of need between socially distant
parties—those who would ordinarily enter balanced exchange—especially underscore the assertions of this section.

C.1.0    *Hunters and gatherers*

C.1.1    *Andamans* — "It has been stated above that all food is private property and belongs to the man or woman who has
obtained it. Everyone who has food is expected, however, to
give to those who have none. . . . The result of these customs
is that practically all the food obtained is evenly distributed
through the whole camp . . ." (Radcliffe-Brown, 1948, p. 43).

C.1.2    *Bushmen* — "Food, whether vegetable or animal, and water
are also private property, and belong to the person who has
obtained them. Everyone who has food is, however, expected
to give to those who have none. . . . The result is that
practically all food obtained is evenly distributed through the
whole camp" (Schapera, 1930, p. 148). Compare these last
two quotations! It is an extremely rare fortune in anthropology, and fills one with humble awe, to enter the presence of
a great natural law. Actually, the elided parts of these citations indicate some difference in manner of distribution. An
older married man among the Andamanese will share out
food after he has reserved sufficient for his family; a younger
man hands over the pigs to elders for distribution (see also
Radcliffe-Brown, 1948, pp. 37–38, 41; Man, n.d., pp. 129,
143 note 6). The one who takes game or veldkos among the
Bushman does the sharing out, according to Schapera.
    The Andamanese who is lazy or helpless is still given food,
despite the probability or certainty of no reciprocation (Radcliffe-Brown, 1948, p. 50; Man, n.d., 25). A lazy hunter fares
badly among the Bushmen; a crippled one is abandoned by
all save his nearest relations (Thomas, 1959, pp. 157, 246; see
also Marshall, 1961, on Bushman sharing).

C.1.3    *Eskimo* — The Alaskan seal-hunter is often solicited for
meat, especially in lean winter months, and these requests are

very rarely refused (Spencer, 1959, pp. 59, 148–149). "In times of food shortage, it was the successful hunter and his family who might go hungry, since in his generosity he gave away whatever he had at hand" (p. 164). Notable are the obligations of the fortunate toward non-kin in the camp: "Generosity was a primary virtue and no man could risk a miserly reputation. Thus anyone in the community, whether inland or coastal, could ask aid of a man of wealth and it was never refused. This might mean that the men of wealth would be obliged to support an entire group in times of stress. Here, too, aid was extended to non-kin" (p. 153; presumably these non-kin might at other times enter balanced exchanges, as in the "bidding game"—see A.1.7). Lazy people take advantage of a hunter's bounty, and do not necessarily reciprocate even if they have their own stores (pp. 164–165; see also pp. 345–351, 156–157 for giveaways in which poor stand to gain materially).

Generally among Eskimo large game is "common property," though smaller animals are not; yet the hunter might in any case invite people of the camp to a meal (Rink, 1875, p. 28 f; Birket-Smith, 1959, p. 146; see also Boas, 1884–85, pp. 562, 574, 582; Weyer, 1932, pp. 184–186).

Spencer's note of the reaction of Alaskan Eskimo to the Great Depression of the 1930s is of interest in the context of economic behavior during general shortage. "More so than in a time of prosperity, the community sense of in-group consciousness appears to have developed. Those who did engage in hunting were obliged by custom to share their catch—seal, walrus, caribou, or any other game—with the less fortunate members of the community. But while this factor of sharing operated between non-kin, the economic circumstances of the period furthered the aboriginal family system as a cooperative institution. Families worked together and extended their joint efforts to the benefit of the community at large. The return to the aboriginal social patterns at a time of economic stress appears to have lent the family system a force which it still possesses. As may be seen, however, the cooperative arrangement between non-kin in the community tends to break down with the addition of new wealth" (Spencer, 1959, pp. 361–362).

C.1.4    *Australian Aboriginals* — Local communities of Walbiri or of friendly tribes could drop in on neighboring Walbiri when in need. They were welcomed, even if the hosts' supplies were limited, but there was some degree of balance in the economic relationship. The requests of hungry communities "often took the form of appeals to actual kinship ties and, couched in these terms, could hardly be refused. The suppliants, then or later, made gifts of weapons, hair-string, red ochre and the like to express their gratitude and, equally important, to rid themselves of feelings of shame or embarrassment" (Meggitt, 1962, p. 52). In lean seasons among the Arunta, everyone shared in available supplies, ordinary generation, sex, and kinship-status considerations notwithstanding (Spencer and Gillen, 1927 i, pp. 38–39, 490).

C.1.5    *Luzon Negritos* — Large quantities of food are shared; whenever a good find is made neighbors are invited to partake until it is eaten up (Vanoverbergh, 1925, p. 409).

C.1.6    *Naskapi* — The same (e.g. Leacock, 1954, p. 33).

C.1.7    *Congo Pygmies* — A hunter cannot very well refuse—in view of public opinion—to share out game in the camp (Putnam, 1953, p. 333). Larger animals, at least, were generally shared through extended family groups; vegetables were not so distributed unless some family had none and then others "come to their assistance" (Schebesta, 1933, pp. 68, 125, 244).

C.1.8    *Western Shoshoni* — Essentially the same customary sharing of large game, and of lesser family supplies in favor of need, in the camp (Steward, 1938, pp. 60, 74, 231, 253; cf. also pp. 27–28 on helping families whose traditional pinion haunts were not bearing).

C.1.9    *Northern Tungus (mounted hunters)* — The hunting spoil, by the custom of *nimadif,* went to the clan—"in other words, the fruit of the hunting does not belong to the hunter, but to the clan" (Shirokogoroff, 1929, p. 195). There was great readiness to assist clansmen in need (p. 200). Reindeer were allocated to the poor of the clan following epizootics, with the results that families holding over sixty deer were not to be seen (p. 296).

C.1.10 *Northern Chipewayan and Copper Indians* — Samuel Hearne notices an outbreak of "disinterested friendship" among members of his crew as they prepare to attack some Eskimos: "Never was reciprocity of interest more generally regarded among a number of people, than it was on the present occasion by my crew, for not one was a moment in want of anything that another could spare; and if ever the spirit of disinterested friendship expanded the heart of a Northern Indian, it was here exhibited in the most extensive meaning of the word. Property of every kind that could be of general use now ceased to be private, and every one who had any thing that came under that description seemed proud of an opportunity of giving it, or lending it to those who had none, or were most in want of it" (Hearne, 1958, p. 98).

C.2.0 *Plains Indians* — In many northern tribes there was insufficiency of good buffalo horses and unequal possession of them. Those without horses, however, did not suffer for food in consequence; the meat circulated to have-nots, in various ways. For example:

C.2.1 *Assiniboin* — Denig notes that in a large camp men who lacked horses, and the old and infirm as well, would follow the hunt, taking meat as they would but leaving the hide and choice parts for the hunter, and they got as much meat as they wanted (Denig, 1928–29, p. 456; cf. p. 532). When food was scarce people would spy out lodges that were better supplied and drop in at mealtimes, as "No Indian eats before guests without offering them a share, even if it is the last portion they possess" (p. 509; cf. p. 515). The successful horse raider might be flattered so by old men upon his return from the raid that by the time he reached his lodge he ("frequently") had given all the loot away (pp. 547–548).

C.2.2 *Blackfoot* — The poor in horses might borrow from the wealthy—the latter thus adding to the number of followers—

and people whose herds had been depleted by misfortune were particularly so helped by those more fortunate (Ewers, 1955, pp. 140–141). A person who borrowed a horse for a chase might return to the owner the best of the meat taken, but this evidently was conditional upon the horse-owner's own supply (pp. 161–162). If borrowing was not possible, the man would have to rely on the "rich" for meat and usually had to take the lean (pp. 162–163; but see pp. 240–241). A case cited of an amputee warrior thereafter supplied with a lodge, horses and food by his band (p. 213). Those who captured horses on raids were supposed afterward to share their loot with less fortunate comrades, but arguments were frequent here (p. 188; compare with Plains Ojibway generosity before the raid, C.2.5). Note how wealth differences generalize exchange: in intratribal trading, rich men paid more dearly for things than did others; the average man, for example, gave two horses for a shirt and leggings, the rich man three to nine horses for the same thing (p. 218). A man, in addition, frequently gave horses to the needy "to get his name up," and the poor might take advantage of the rich by giving small presents to the latter or simply praising them loudly in the hopes of a horse return (p. 255). Ewers thus summarizes the economic relation between rich and poor: "Generosity was felt to be a responsibility of the wealthy. They were expected to loan horses to the poor for hunting and moving camp, to give food to the poor, and to give away horses occasionally. They were expected to pay more in intratribal barter than were Indians who were not well to do. If the man of wealth had political ambitions it was particularly important that he be lavish with his gifts in order to gain a large number of followers to support his candidacy" (p. 242).

The reaction to general shortage was heightened sharing. Lean winter periods were common: "Then the wealthy, who had put up extensive winter supplies the previous fall, had to share their food with the poor" (Ewers, 1955, p. 167). The rank structure of the band was also engaged to organize relief: hunters had to turn over their bag to the band chief, who had it cut up and divided equally to each family. When game became more plentiful, this "primitive form of food rationing" was discontinued and the chief stepped out of the central distributive role (pp. 167–168).

C.2.3   *Plains Cree*— The same inclination of those better off to share meat to people without horses, to give horses away on occasion—for which from the poor one received in return not meat but fealty (Mandelbaum, 1940, p. 195)—and other generosities found in the Plains in connection with wealth differences (pp. 204, 221, 222, 270–271; see also Wallace and Hoebel, 1952, p. 75 *et passim* on the Comanche; Coues on the Mandan (village Indians), 1897, p. 337).

C.2.4   *Kansa*— Hunter writes that if one party to an agreed exchange could not meet his obligations due to ill health or bad hunting luck, he was not dunned, nor did friendly relations with his creditors cease. But one who failed of his obligations for reason of laziness was a bad Indian and would be abandoned by his friends—such types, however, were rare (Hunter, 1823, p. 295). Moreover, ". . . no one of respectable standing will be allowed to experience want or sufferings of any kind, while it is in the power of others of the same community to prevent it. In this respect they are extravagantly generous; always supplying the wants of their friends from their own superabundance" (p. 296).

Generalized reciprocity apparently intensified during shortage. "Whenever a scarcity prevails, they reciprocally lend, or rather share with each other, their respective stores, till they are all exhausted. I speak now of those who are provident, and sustain good characters. When the case is otherwise, the wants of such individuals are regarded with comparative indifference; though their families share in the stock, become otherwise common from public exigency" (p. 258).

C.2.5   *Plains Ojibway*— Tanner and his Ojibway family, destitute, reach a camp of Ojibway and Ottawa; the chiefs of the camp meet to consider their plight and one man after another volunteers to hunt for Tanner's people; Tanner's FaBrWi is stingy to them, but her husband beats her for it (Tanner, 1956, pp. 30–34). In similar circumstances, an Ojibway lodge insisted on silver ornaments and other objects of value in return for giving Tanner's family some meat one winter. This insistence on exchange struck Tanner as despicable, for his people were hungry—"I had not before met with such an instance among the Indians. They are commonly ready to divide what provisions they have with any who come to them in need" (p. 47; see also pp. 49, 60, 72–73, 75, 118, 119).

During a period of epidemic and general food shortage in an Ojibway camp, Tanner and another hunter managed to kill a bear. "Of the flesh of this animal," he wrote, "we could not eat a mouthful, but we took it home and distributed to every lodge an equal portion" (p. 95). On another similar occasion, an Indian who had shot two moose tried to get Tanner to secretly share them, keeping the meat from the rest of the camp. Tanner, a better Indian than this, refused, went out hunting, killed four bears and distributed the meat to the hungry (p. 163).

On special economic behavior of the warpath: if a man of the war party was short of moccasins or ammunition he took out one of that object and walked about the camp before a person well supplied; the latter ordinarily gave over the thing desired without the necessity of anyone speaking, or else, the leader of the party went from man to man taking what was needed by the person who was short (p. 129).

C.3.0   *Miscellaneous*

C.3.1   *Nuer* — See the citations in the text of this section: "Kinsmen must assist one another, and if one has a surplus of a good thing he must share it with his neighbors. Consequently no Nuer ever has a surplus" (Evans-Pritchard, 1940, p. 183). Generalized reciprocity characteristic between haves and have nots, especially if close kin and neighbors, in the compact dry season camps, and during seasons of generally low supplies (pp. 21, 25, 84–85, 90–92; 1951, p. 132; Howell, 1954, pp. 16, 185–186).

C.3.2   *Kuikuru (upper Xingú)* — The contrast between the handling of the major crop, manioc, and the disposition of maize is an instructive illustration of the relation of sharing to supplies on hand. Kuikuru households are in general self-sufficient; there is little sharing between them, especially of manioc which is produced with ease and in quantity. But during Carneiro's stay, maize was planted by only five men of the village, and their harvest was divided through the community (Carneiro, 1957, p. 162).

C.3.3    *Chukchee* — Despite an anthropological reputation something to the contrary, the Chukchee are remarkably generous "toward everyone who is in need" (Bogoras, 1904–09, p. 47). This includes aliens, such as poor Lamut families who got sustenance from neighboring rich Chukchee without payment, and also starving Russian settlements in whose favor Chukchee have slaughtered their herds for little or no return (p. 47). At the annual fall slaughter, about one-third of the deer were given to guests, who need not make returns, especially if poor; neighboring camps, however, might exchange slaughtered beasts at this time (p. 375). At serious setbacks to herds, neighboring camps—these need not be related—might render assistance (p. 628). Tobacco is highly valued by Chukchee but is not hoarded when scarce; ". . . the last pipeful be divided or smoked by turns" (pp. 549, 615 f, 624, 636–638).

C.3.4    *California-Oregon* — The Tolowa-Tututni "rich-man" was, as we have noted, a source of aid to his people (Drucker, 1937). Poorer people depended on the bounty of richer. "Food was shared by the provident with the improvident within the village group" (DuBois, 1936, p. 51). Of the Yurok, Kroeber writes that food was sometimes sold, "but no well-to-do man was guilty of the practice" (1925, p. 40), implying that the exchange would be generalized rather than balanced (selling) in this case. Similarly Kroeber remarks that small gifts among the Yurok were ordinarily reciprocated, as "Presents were clearly a rich man's luxury" (p. 42; cf. p. 34 on the liberal disposition of fish by successful fishermen). Meat, fish and the like taken in large quantities by

Patwin families went to the village chief for distribution to
families most in need; a family, moreover, might demand
food of fortunate neighbors (McKern, 1922, p. 245).

C.3.5    *Oceania* —The Melanesian big-man complex, wherever it
exists, argues the prevalence of generalized reciprocity in
exchange between people of different fortune.

The Duff missionaries' description of Tahitian generosity,
especially of *richesse oblige,* is probably too good to be true,
anyhow too good to be analytically adequate: "All are friendly and generous, even to a fault; they hardly refuse anything
to each other if importuned. Their presents are liberal, even
to profusion. Poverty never makes a man contemptible; but
to be affluent and covetous is the greatest shame and reproach. Should any man betray symptoms of incorrigible
avariciousness and refuse to part with what he has in time
of necessity, his neighbors would soon destroy all his property, and put him on a footing with the poorest, hardly leaving
a house to cover his head. They will give the clothes from
their back, rather than be called peere, peere, or stingy"
(1799, p. 334).

Firth's discussion of Maori sharing in favor of need is
more measured: "At a time of shortage of provisions . . .
persons did not as a rule keep to themselves the product of
their labour, but shared it out among the other people of the
village" (Firth, 1959, p. 162). It is as true in the forests of
New Zealand as the savannahs of the Sudan that "Starvation
or real want in one family was impossible while others in the
village were abundantly supplied with food" (p. 290).

Of interest in connection with responses to general scarcity
is the development in food-poor Polynesian atolls of reserve
lands administered in group interests, the products of which
were periodically pooled by communities (e.g. Beaglehole, E.
and P., 1938; Hogbin, 1934; MacGregor, 1937). The restudy of
Tikopia by Firth and Spillius, however, provides probably
the most comprehensive report of the reaction of a primitive
society to prolonged and intense food shortage. The reaction
proceeded far: while traffic in food did not develop, theft

certainly did and contraction of foodsharing to the household sphere did too. These latter responses, increases in negative reciprocity and diminution of the sector of generalized exchange, were apparently progressive, augmenting as the crisis deepened. It is impossible to do justice here to Firth's and Spillius' analyses, but it is at least useful to excerpt some remarks from Firth's summary of exchange behavior during the famine: "In general it can be said . . . that while morals degenerated under the strain of famine, manners remained. At the times of greatest food shortage the ordinary modes of serving food were kept up. . . . But while in matters of hospitality all the *forms* of etiquette continued to be maintained throughout the period of famine, its *substance* radically altered. No longer was food actually shared with visitors. Moreover, after food had been cooked it was . . . concealed—sometimes even locked up in a box. . . . In this development kinship ties were affected, though not quite in the same way as the more general rules of hospitality. Kin who called in were treated as ordinary visitors; food was not shared with them. . . . In many cases if food was left in a house a member of the household remained behind to guard it. Here, it was stated to Spillius, the inmates were often not so much afraid of theft by strangers but of the inroads of kin who normally would have been welcome to come and take what they pleased. In the definition of kin interests that took place under the stress of famine there was some atomization of the larger kin groups on the consumption side and a closer integration of the individual household group. (This normally meant elementary family but often included other kin.) Even at the height of the famine it appeared that within an elementary family full sharing of food continued to be the norm. The atomization tended to be most strong where food was most desparately short—and it must be remembered that supplies varied considerably in different groups, depending on their size and their wealth in land. But in one respect the strength of kin ties was manifested, in the common practice of pooling supplies, especially where food—though scarce—was not desperately short. Closely related households 'linked

ovens' *(tau umu)* by each drawing upon its own stock of food
and then sharing in the work of the oven and in a common
meal . . . the Tikopia avoided where possible their general
responsibility or undefined responsibility for kin during the
famine but showed no disposition to reject responsibility
which had been specifically defined by the undertaking.
What the famine did was to reveal the solidarity of the
elementary family. But it also brought out the strength of
other kin ties personally assumed . . ." (Firth, 1959, pp.
83–84).

C.3.6    *Bemba* —High incidence of generalized reciprocity associated with differential food stocks, and also during general
hunger seasons. Thus, "If a man's crops are destroyed by
some sudden calamity, or if he has planted insufficient for his
needs, relatives in his own village may be able to help him
by giving him baskets of grain or offering him a share in their
meals. But if the whole community has been visited by the
same affliction, such as a locust swarm or a raider elephant,
the householder will move himself and his family to live with
other kinsmen in an area where food is less scarce. . . .
Hospitality of this sort is commonly practised in the hunger
season, when families go all over the country 'looking for
porridge' . . . or 'running from hunger' . . . . Hence the legal
obligations of kinship result in a particular type of food
distribution, both within the village and the surrounding
neighbourhood, which is not found in those modern communities in which a more individual domestic economy is practised" (Richards, 1939, pp. 108–109). "The economic
conditions under which [a Bemba woman] lives necessitate
reciprocal sharing of foodstuffs, rather than their accumulation, and extend the individual's responsibility outside her
own household. Plainly, therefore, it does not pay a Bemba
woman to have very much more grain than her fellows. She
would merely have to distribute it, and during the recent
locust scourge the villagers whose gardens escaped destruction complained that they were not really better off than their
fellows for 'our people come and live with us or beg us for
baskets of millet' " (pp. 201–202).

C.3.7     *Pilagá*— Henry's *Table I* (1951, p. 194) indicates that all unproductive persons in the village studied—it was, recall, a period of very low supplies—received food from more people than they gave food to. The "negative" balance of these cases—old and blind, old women, etc.—varies from -3 to -15 and the eight persons listed as unproductive make up more than half of those showing such negative balance. This is contrary to the general Pilaga trend: "It will be at once clear from the tables that the Pilaga *on the whole* gives to more people than he receives from, but that, with the unproductive Pilaga the situation is reversed" (pp. 195–197). The negative balance of unproductive people shows as well in the number of transactions as in the number of people given to minus received-from (p. 196). In *Table III,* presenting the approximate ratios of food quantity received to food quantity given away, ten persons are listed as unproductive and for eight of these income exceeded out-go; six persons are listed as very or exceptionally productive and four had out-go over income, one had income over out-go and one had income equal to out-go (p. 201). I take these figures to mean that those who had food shared it out to those who had none, in the main.

# 6

# Exchange Value and the Diplomacy of Primitive Trade

Anthropological economics can respectably claim one theory of value on its own, fashioned from empirical encounters in its own province of primitive and peasant economies. Here, in many of the societies, have been discovered "spheres of exchange" which stipulate for different categories of goods differential standing in a moral hierarchy of *virtu*. This is anything but a theory of exchange value. The diverse values put on things depend specifically on barriers to their interchange, on the inconvertibility of goods from different spheres; and as for the transactions ("conveyances") within any one sphere, no determinants of the rates have yet been specified (cf. Firth, 1965; Bohannan and Dalton,1962; Salisbury,1962). So ours is a theory of value in nonexchange, or of nonexchange value, which may be as appropriate to an economy not run on sound business principles as it is paradoxical from a market standpoint. Still it is plain that anthropological economics will have to complete its theory of value with a theory of exchange value, or else abandon the field at this juncture to the forces of business as usual: supply, demand,and equilibrium price.

This essay constitutes a reconnaissance with a view toward defending the terrain as anthropological territory. But it will be in every sense a venture in "Stone Age Economics"—and rather of the earlier phase than the later. Its intellectual weapons are the crudest choppers, capable only of indelicate blows at the objective, and likely soon to crumble against refactory empirical materials.[1]

1. I do not attempt here a general theory of value. The principal concern is exchange
(continued on p. 278)

For the facts are difficult. True they are often disconcerting from the orthodox vantage of supply and demand and generally remain so even if, in the absence of price-fixing markets, one agrees to meanings of "supply" and "demand" more relevant than the current technical definitions (that is, the quantities that would be made available and taken up over a series of prices). The same facts, however, are just as perturbing to anthropological convictions, such as those that begin from the prevalence in the primitive economies of "reciprocity," whatever that means. Indeed, the facts are perturbing precisely because we rarely bother to say what it does mean, as a rate of exchange.

But then, a "reciprocity" that comprehends precise material rates is rarely encountered. The characteristic fact of primitive exchange is indeterminancy of the rates. In different transactions, similar goods move against each other in different proportions—especially so in the ensemble of ordinary transactions, the everyday gift giving and mutual aid, and in the internal economy of kinship groups and communities. The goods may be deemed comparable to all intents by the people involved, and the variation in rates occur within the same general time period, place, and set of economic conditions. In other words, the usual stipulations of market imperfection seem not to blame.

Nor is the variability of reciprocity attributable to that supreme imperfection, higgle-haggle, where an interconnection between different deals is lacking and competition reduced to its ultimate term of an oriental confrontation between buyer and seller. Although it would account theoretically for the indeterminancy, bargaining is too marginal a strategy in the primitive world to bear the burden of a general explanation. To most primitive peoples it is completely unknown; among the rest, it is mostly an episodic relation with strangers.

(If I may be allowed here an impertinent aside, in no way justified

---

value. By the "exchange value" of a good *(A),* I mean the quantity of other goods *(B, C,* etc.) received in return for it—as in the famous couplet "The value of a thing/Is just as much as it will bring." For the historical economies in question, it remains to be seen whether this "exchange value" approximates the Ricardian-Marxist "value," the average social labor embodied in the product. Were it not for the ambiguity introduced by spheres of exchange in assigning goods different relative standing, the term "relative value" might be more acceptable all around than "exchange value"; where the context allows, I substitute the former term. "Price" is reserved for exchange value expressed in money terms.

by an impressive personal ignorance of Economics, the ready supposition of extreme circumstances, amounting to the theoretical null or limiting case, seems nevertheless characteristic of attempts to apply the formal business apparatus to primitive economies: demand with the substitution potential and elasticity of a market for food in a beleaguered city, the supply sensitivity of a fish market in the late afternoon—not to mention the appreciation of mother's milk as "enterprise capital" [Goodfellow, 1939] or the tautological dispensation of failures to take the main chance by invocation of a local preference for social over material values. It is as if primitive peoples somehow manage to construct a systematic economy under those theoretically marginal conditions where, in the formal model, system fails.)

In truth, the primitive economies seem to defy systematization. It is practically impossible to deduce standard going rates from any corpus of transactions as ethnographically recorded (cf. Driberg, 1962, p. 94; Harding, 1967; Pospisil, 1963; Price, 1962, p. 25; Sahlins, 1962). The ethnographer may conclude that the people put no fixed values on their goods. And even if a table of equivalences is elicited—by whatever dubious means—actual exchanges often depart radically from these standards, tending however to approximate them most in socially peripheral dealings, as between members of different communities or tribes, while swinging wildly up and down in a broad internal sector where considerations of kinship distance, rank, and relative affluence are effectively in play. This last qualification is important: the material balance of reciprocity is subject to the social sector. Our analysis of exchange value thus begins where the last chapter, on "the sociology of primitive exchange," left off.

The discussion in Chapter 5 argued at length the social organization of material terms. To recapitulate very briefly: from one vantage, the tribal plan presents itself as a series of concentric spheres, beginning in the close-knit inner circles of homestead and hamlet, extending thence to wider and more diffuse zones of regional and tribal solidarity, to fade into the outer darkness of an intertribal arena. This is at once a social and moral design of the tribal universe, specifying norms of conduct for each sphere as are appropriate to the degree of common interest. Exchange too is moral conduct and is so regulated. Hence, reciprocity is generalized in the innermost sectors: the return of a gift only indefinitely prescribed, the time and amount of reciprocation left contingent on the future needs of the original donor and abilities of the recipient; so the flow of goods may be unbalanced, or even one-way, for a very long period. But on leaving these internal spheres and uncertain repayments, one discovers a sector of social relations so tenuous they can only be sustained by an exchange at once more immediate and balanced. In the interest of a long-term trade, and under the social protection of such devices as "trade partnership," this zone may even extend to intertribal relations. Beyond the internal economy of variable reciprocity is a sphere, of greater or less expanse, marked by some correlation between the customary and *de facto* rates of equivalence. Here, then, is the area of greatest promise to research on exchange rates.

In the same way as the origin of money has traditionally been sought in external markets, and for many of the same reasons, the quest for a primitive theory of value turns to exterior spheres of transaction. Not only is balanced dealing there enjoined, but the exchange circuits of the internal economy tend to disintegrate and combine, as the immorality of "conversion" is rendered irrelevant by social distance. Goods that were separated from each other inside the community are here brought into equivalence. Attention especially should be directed to transactions between trade friends and trade kinsmen, for these relationships stipulate economic equity and going rates. Accordingly, the inquiry that follows shall concentrate upon partnership trade, and, out of practical considerations, upon a few empirical cases only, chosen however from areas of the Pacific famous for an indigenous commerce.

### Three Systems of Trade

We shall examine three areal exchange networks, constituting besides three different structural and ecological forms: the Vitiaz Straits and Huon Gulf systems of New Guinea, and the intertribal trade chain of northern Queensland, Australia. In each case a certain play of supply/demand is detectable in the rates of exchange. Yet the existence of this supply/demand influence renders the trade even less comprehensible than would its absence. For the kind of market competition that alone in economic theory gives supply and demand such power over exchange value is completely absent from the trade in question.

The essentials of the Queensland network are exhibited in Figure 6.1 (constructed after the brief description provided by Sharp, 1952). In structure it is a simple chain of trade, band linked to band along a line running approximately 400 miles south from the Cape York coast. Each group is limited to contacts with its immediate neighbors, thus only indirectly related to bands further along the line. The trade itself proceeds in the form of gift exchange between elders standing as classificatory brothers. Working out of Yir-Yoront, Sharp could give few details of the axe-spear exchange running the length of the

A. Trading Groups

A    (sources of sting ray spears)


B   YIR-YIRONT
(some spears)
                                    150 miles

C


                            "Further South"
D


E    (Quarry source of stone axes)

B. Rates of exchange at various points

at B    YIR-YIRONT,    12 Spears  =  1 Axe

C                       1 spear  =  1 Axe

D                       1 Spear  =  "Several Axes" (presumably)

*Figure 6.1.  Queensland Trade Chain (after Sharp, 1952)*

chain, but the information is sufficient to document the effect of supply/demand on the terms of transaction. This by the simple principle that if, in an areal network, the exchange rate of a good *(A)* in terms of another *(B)* rises in proportion to distance from the source of *A*, it is reasonable to suppose that the relative value of *A* is increasing *pari passu* with "real" costs and scarcities, that is, with declining supply, and probably also with increasing demand. The differences in spear-axe exchange ratios along the Queensland chain would reflect the double play of this principle. At Yir-Yiront, near the northern source of spears, 12 of them must be given for a single axe; about 150 miles south, that much closer to the source of axes, the rate falls to one to one; in the extreme south the terms (apparently) become one spear for "several" axes. A point then for supply and demand, and apparently for orthodox Economic Theory.

The trade system of the Vitiaz Straits arrives at the same effect but by different organizational means (Figure 6.2). Articulated from the center by the voyages of Siassi Islanders, the Vitiaz network is but one of several similar circles established in Melanesia under the aegis of Phoeneican-like middlemen. In their own areas, the Langalanga of Malaita, the Tami Islanders, the Arawe of New Britain, the Manus of the Admiralties and the Bilibili of New Guinea ply a similar trade. This mercantile adaptation merits a short comment.

The trading groups are themselves marginally if centrally situated, often perched precariously on stilt-house platforms in the middle of some lagoon, without a *mow* of arable land to call their own or any other resources save what the sea affords them—lacking even wood for their canoes or fibers for their fishnets. Their technical means of production and exchange are imported, let alone their main stocks in trade. Yet the traders are typically the richest people of their area. The Siassi occupy about one three-hundredths of the land in the Umboi subdistrict (which includes the large island of that name), but they make up approximately one quarter of the population (Harding, 1967, p. 119).[2] This prosperity is the dividend of trade, amassed from a number of surrounding villages and islands, themselves better endowed by nature but tempted to commerce with the Siassi for

---

2. "The Manus . . . most disadvantageously placed of all the tribes in that part of the archipelago, are nevertheless the richest and have the highest standard of living" (Mead, 1937, p. 212).

A. Section of the Siassi Trade Sphere.

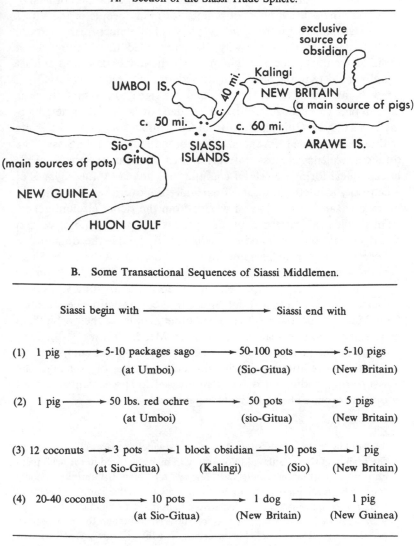

B. Some Transactional Sequences of Siassi Middlemen.

Siassi begin with ⟶ Siassi end with

(1)  1 pig ⟶ 5-10 packages sago ⟶ 50-100 pots ⟶ 5-10 pigs
                (at Umboi)              (Sio-Gitua)          (New Britain)

(2)  1 pig ⟶ 50 lbs. red ochre ⟶ 50 pots ⟶ 5 pigs
                (at Umboi)              (sio-Gitua)          (New Britain)

(3) 12 coconuts ⟶ 3 pots ⟶ 1 block obsidian ⟶ 10 pots ⟶ 1 pig
                (at Sio-Gitua)      (Kalingi)              (Sio)       (New Britain)

(4)  20-40 coconuts ⟶ 10 pots ⟶ 1 dog ⟶ 1 pig
                (at Sio-Gitua)      (New Britain)       (New Guinea)

*Figure 6.2. Middleman Gains of Siassi Traders (from Harding, 1967)*

reasons ranging from material to marital utility. The Siassi regularly exchanged fish for root crops with adjacent villages of Umboi Island; they were the sole suppliers of pottery for many people of the Vitiaz region, transhipping it from the few places of manufacture in northern New Guinea. In the same way they controlled the distribution of obsidian from its place of origin in northern New Britain. But at least equally important, the Siassi constituted for their trade partners a rare or exclusive source of bridewealth and prestige goods—such items as curved pigs' tusks, dogs' teeth, and wooden bowls. A man in neighboring areas of New Guinea, New Britain, or Umboi could not take a wife without some trade beforehand, direct or indirect, with the Siassi. The total consequence of Siassi enterprise, then, is a trade system of specific ecological form: a circle of communities linked by the voyages of a centrally located group, itself naturally impoverished but enjoying on balance an inward flow of wealth from the richer circumference.

This ecological pattern depends upon, is the precipitate of certain arrangements on the plane of exchange. Although the domains of different trading peoples sometimes overlap, a group such as Siassi fairly monopolizes carrying within its own sphere. There the "competition" is dramatically imperfect: the several and far-flung villages of the circumference are without direct intercourse with one another. (The Manus went so far as to prevent other peoples of their orbit from owning or operating seagoing canoes [cf. Mead, 1961, p. 210]). Capitalizing on the lack of communication between distant communities, and with an eye always toward enhancing the rates of exchange, the Siassi during traditional times were pleased to spread fantastic tales about the origins of goods they transmitted:

> . . . cooking pots are distributed from three widely-separated locations on the mainland [New Guinea]. No pottery in manufactured in the archipelago [that is, Umboi, nearby islands, and western New Britain], and people there who receive pots via the Siassis (and earlier the Tamis) previously were not even aware that clay-pots were man-made products. Rather, they were regarded as exotic products of the sea. Whether the non-pottery peoples originated this belief is uncertain. The Siassis, however, elaborated and helped to sustain such beliefs, as everyone since has learned. Their story was that the pots are the shells of deep-water mussels. The Sios [of New Guinea] make a specialty of diving for these mussels and, after eating

the flesh, sell the empty "shells" to the Siassi. The deception, if it added to their value, was justified by the vital part that pots have in overseas trade (Harding, 1967, pp. 139-140).

By my understanding (based on a brief visit) the Siassi in these tales were exaggerating more directly the effort of production than the scarcity of the pots, on the local principle that "big-fella work" is worth "big-fella pay." The most advanced mercantile guile was imbricated in a most innocent labor theory of value. It is only consistent that the customary partnership of the Vitiaz network, a kind of trade-friendship (*pren*, N-M), is several degrees removed in sociability from the trade-kinship of the Queensland system. True, the exchanges between Siassi and their partners followed standard rates. But, secure in their middlemen position and indispensable to their "friends," towards whom they were not profoundly compelled to be considerate, the Siassi in the context of these rates were charging what the traffic would bear. Exchange values not only varied locally with supply/demand—judging again by the difference in terms according to distance from origin (Harding, 1967, p. 42 passim)—but monopolistic sharp practice may have afforded discriminatory gains. As the transactional sequences show (Figure 6.2), the Siassi, by voyaging here and there, could in principle turn a dozen coconuts into a pig, or that one pig again into five. An extraordinary tour of primitive *passe-passe*—and another apparent victory for the businesslike interpretation of indigenous trade.[3]

The same confidence in the received economic wisdom is not as readily afforded by the Huon Gulf system, for here goods of special-

3. Local demand in the Manus trade system is indicated by an unusual device. In Manus transactions with Balowan, where sago is scarce, one package of sago offered by Manus will bring ten mud hen's eggs from Balowan; but the equivalent of a package of sago offered by Manus to Balowan in shell money commands only three mud hen's eggs. (Clearly if the Manus anywhere can convert these several items they make a killing.) Similarly, in Manus daily trade with Usiai land people, demand is indicated by unequal ratios of the following sort: one fish from Manus=ten taro or forty betel nut from Usiai; whereas one cup of lime from Manus=four taro or eighty betel nut from Usiai. Mead comments: "Betel-chewing need is matched against betel chewing need, to coerce the sea people [Manus] into providing lime for the land peoples" (Mead, 1930, p. 130). That is to say, when the Usiai want lime, they offer betel nut, as the Manus can realize more betel in exchange for lime than for fish; if Usiai wanted fish, they would have brought taro. On the labor advantage to Manus in this trade, and the gains appreciated through supply/demand variations in different parts of the Manus network, see Schwartz, 1963, pp. 75, 78.

ized local manufacture are transacted at uniform rates throughout the network (Hogbin, 1951). Nevertheless, a simple analysis will show that supply and demand are once more at work.

The semicircular coastal network of the Gulf again unites ethnically heterogeneous communities (Figure 6.3). Trade, however, is effected through reciprocal voyaging: people of a given village visit and in turn are visited by partners from several other places, both up and down the coast, although usually from the nearer rather than the more distant vicinity. The trade partners are kinsmen, their families linked by previous intermarriage; their commerce accordingly is a sociable gift exchange, balanced at traditional rates. Certain of these rates are indicated in Table 6.1.

Local specialization in craft and food production within the system is attributed by Hogbin to natural variations in resource distribution. A single village or small group of adjacent villages has its characteristic specialty. Since voyaging ranges are limited, centrally situated

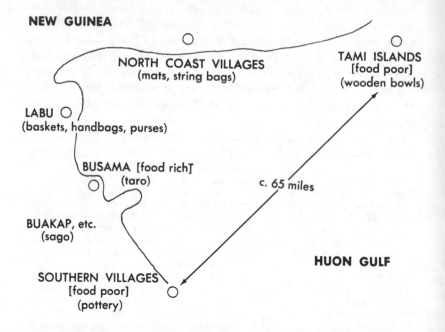

*Figure 6.3.  Huon Gulf Trade Network (from Hogbin, 1951)*

Table 6.1.   *Customary equivalents in trade, Huon  Gulf*
*trade network (data from Hogbin, 1951, pp. 81-95)*

### I.  Busama

| For | | Busama gives |
|---|---|---|
| 1 large pot | = | c. 150 pounds taro or 60 pounds sago |
| 24-30 large pots | = | 1 small canoe |
| 1 small pot | = | c. 50 pounds taro or 20 pounds sago |
| 1 mat | = | 1 small pot |
| 3 mats | = | 1 large pot (or 2 shillings)* |
| 4 purses | = | 1 small pot (or 1 shilling for 2) |
| 1 basket | = | 2 large bowls (or one pound) |
| 1 bowl (usual size) | = | 10-12 shillings (more for larger bowls) |

### II.  North Coast Villages

| For | | North Coast villages give |
|---|---|---|
| 1 large pot | = | 4 string bags or 3 mats (or 6-8 shillings) |
| 1 small pot | = | 1 mat (or 2 shillings) |
| 4 purses | = | 1 mat (or 1 shilling for 2) |
| 1 basket | = | 10 mats (or one pound) |
| 1 carved bowl | = | food, unknown quantity |

### III.  Labu

| For | | Labu gives |
|---|---|---|
| 2 large pots | = | 1 woven basket (or 6-8 shillings) |
| 1 small pot | = | 4 purses (or 2 shillings) |
| 1 string bag | = | 3 purses (or 2 shillings) |
| 1 carved bowl | = | 10-12 shillings |

### IV  Pottery villages

| For | | Pottery villages give |
|---|---|---|
| 150 pounds taro or 60 pounds sago= | | 1 large pot |
| 50 pounds taro or 20 pounds sago= | | 1 small pot |
| 4 string bags | = | 1 large pot |
| 1 mat | = | 1 small pot |
| 3 mats | = | 1 large pot |
| 4 purses | = | 1 small pot |
| 1 basket | = | 2 large pots |
| 1 carved bowl | = | 8 shillings |
| 1 small canoe | = | 24-30 pots |

*Except in exchange for bowls, money was rarely used in the trade at the time of study.

communities act as middlemen in the transmission of specialized goods produced towards the extremities of the Gulf. The Busama, for instance, from whose vantage the trade was studied, send southward the mats, bowls, and other goods manufactured on the north coast, and send northward the pots made in the southern villages.

Like other New Guinea trade networks, the Huon system was not entirely closed. Each coastal village had truck with peoples of its own immediate hinterland. Moreover the Tami Islanders, themselves long-distance voyagers, connected the Huon on the north with the Siassi sphere; in traditional times the Tami disseminated within the Gulf obsidian that had originated in New Britain. (Potters in the southern villages likewise exported their craft further south, although little is known about this trade.) A question is thus presented: Why isolate the Huon Gulf as a distinct "system"? There is a double justification. First, on the material plane the several villages apparently comprise an organic community, retaining within their own sphere the great majority of locally produced goods. Secondly, on the organizational level, this kinship trade of a determinate form, and evidently also the uniform series of exchange rates, seem to be restricted to the Gulf.[4]

For those inclined to belittle the practical (or "economic") significance of primitive trade, the Huon Gulf network affords a salutory antidote. Certain villages would not have been able to exist as constituted in the absence of trade. In the meridional reaches of the Gulf, cultivation encounters natural difficulties, and sago and taro have to be obtained from the Buakap and Busama districts (see Figure 6.3 and Table 6.1). "Without trade, indeed, the southern peoples [the pottery makers] could not long survive in their present environment" (Hogbin, 1951, p. 94). Likewise, the soil available to the Tami Islanders of the northeast is inadequate: "Much of [their] food has to be imported" (p. 82). In the event, food exports from fertile areas such as Busama comprise an important fraction of local production: taro "upwards of five tons monthly" is sent out of the community, principally to four southern villages; whereas Busama themselves consume 28 tons monthly (direct human subsistence). By the ample dietary standards prevailing at Busama (p. 69) the taro exported could feed another

4. I cannot however verify these assertions; in the event they prove invalid certain suggestions of the following paragraphs will require modification.

community of 84 people. (The average village population along the Gulf is 200-300; Busama, with more than 600 people, is exceptionally large.) Globally, then, the Huon Gulf presents an ecological pattern precisely the opposite of the Vitiaz Straits: the peripheral communities are here naturally poor, the center rich, and there is on balance a strategic flow of wealth from the latter to the former.

Allowing certain surmises, the dimensions of this flow can be read from the exchange ratios of central to peripheral goods. Busama taro, for example, is traded against southern pottery at a rate of 50 pounds of taro to one small pot or 150 pounds to one large pot. Based on a modest personal acquaintance with the general area, I judge this rate very favorable to pots in terms of necessary labor time. Hogbin seems to hold the same opinion (p. 85). In this connection, Douglas Oliver observed of southern Bougainville, where one "medium-sized" pot is valued at the same shell money rate as 51 pounds of taro, that the latter "represents an incomparably larger amount of labor" (1949, p. 94). In terms of effort, the equations of the Busama-pottery village trade appear to be unbalanced. By the rates prevailing, the poorer communities are appropriating to their own existence the intensified labor of the richer.

Nevertheless, this exploitation is veiled by a disingenuous equation of labor values. Although it appears to fool no one, the deception does give a semblance of equity to the exchange. The potters exaggerate the (labor) value of their product, while the Busama complain merely of its use value:

> Although etiquette prevents argument, I was interested to observe when accompanying some Busama on a trading journey southwards how the Buso [pottery] villagers kept exaggerating the labour involved in pot making. "We toil all day long at it from sunrise to sunset," one man told us over and over again. "Extracting the clay is worse than gold mining. How my back aches! There's always the chance, too, that in the end the pot will develop a crack." The members of our [Busama] party murmured polite agreement but subsequently brought the conversation round to the inferior quality of present-day pots. They confined themselves to generalitites, accusing no one in particular, but it was apparent that here was an attempt at retaliation (Hogbin, 1951, p. 85).

Rates of exchange are, as noted, fairly uniform throughout the

Gulf. In any of the villages, for instance, where mats, "purses" and/or pots are customarily exchanged, one mat-four purses-one small pot. These rates hold regardless of distance from the point of production: a small pot is valued at one mat either in the southern villages where pottery is made or on the north coast where mats are made. The direct implication, that centrally situated middlemen take no gains in the turnover of peripheral goods, is affirmed by Hogbin. There are no "profits" to Busama in transferring southern pots to the north or northern mats to the south (Hogbin, 1951, p. 83).

The simple principle posed to detect supply-demand influences in the Vitiaz and Queensland systems, where exchange values varied directly by distance from the site of production, is therefore not applicable to the Huon Gulf. But then the shape of the Huon "market" is different. Technically it is less imperfect. Potentially at least, a given community has more than one supplier of a given good, so that those tempted to exact special gains run the risk of being by-passed. Hence the Busama rationalization of their failure to take middlemen tolls: "Each community needs the products of all the rest, and the natives freely admit their willingness to sacrifice economic gain to keep within the exchange ring." (p. 83). All this does preclude the possibility of supply/demand effects on exchange rates. The possibility is transposed rather to the higher level of the network as a whole. It becomes a question of whether the relative value of one good in terms of another reflects the respective aggregate supply/demand throughout the Gulf.

A remarkable exception to uniform rates, amounting it would seem to a violation of the most elementary principles of good business and common sense, suggests this is exactly the case. The Busama pay 10-12 shillings for Tami Islander bowls and exchange them in the southern villages for pots worth eight shillings.[5] In explanation the Busama say of the southern potters: " 'They live in such hungry country. Besides we want pots for use for ourselves and to exchange for mats and things' " (Hogbin, 1951, p. 92). Now, the explanation in terms of pots contains an interesting implication in terms of the taro which the Busama themselves produce. The Busama clearly suffer penalties in their southern trade because of the limited demand for

5. Cash has particularly replaced the pigs' tusks traditionally traded for Tami bowls, corresponding to a replacement of the latter by European currency in the brideprices of the Finschhafen area.

taro throughout the Gulf, especially on the part of the northern villages, where a variety of craft goods are produced. The "market" for taro is effectively restricted to the southern potters. (In Hogbin's exchange table [Table 6.1] taro is noted only in the southern trade; reference to taro disappears from the description of northern trade.) But if Busama taro has little exchangeability, the pots manufactured exclusively in the south are everywhere in demand. More than an item of consumption, these pots become for Busama a capital item of trade, without which they would be cut off to the north, so for which they are willing to pay dearly in labor costs. Thus the classic business forces *are* in play in this sense: the relative value of Busama taro in terms of southern pots represents the respective demands for these goods in the Huon Gulf as a whole.[6]

The point may be made in a more abstract way. Suppose three villages, $A$ and $B$ and $C$, each the producer of a special good, $x$, $y$, and $z$ respectively, and linked in a chain of trade such that $A$ exchanges with $B$ and $B$ again with $C$. Consider then the exchange of $x$ against $y$ between villages $A$ and $B$:

| Villages: | $A$ | $B$ | $C$ |
|-----------|-----|-----|-----|
| goods: | $x$ | $y$ | $z$ |

Assuming none of these products superabundant, the quantity of $y$ surrendered by $B$ to obtain $x$ will depend in part on the demand for $y$ as compared to $x$ in village $C$. If in village $C$ the demand for $x$ is much greater than demand for $y$, then $B$, with a view toward the eventual acquisition of $z$, is willing to pay more dearly in $y$ to obtain

6. Belshaw reports a trade system in the southern Massim apparently similar in exchange value conditions to the Huon Gulf (1955, pp. 28–29, 81–82). He notes, however, that rates of certain items—areca nuts, pots, and stick tobacco—do vary locally with demand. I may not fully understand his argument, which is phrased in shilling equivalents, but what it seems to show, when taken in conjunction with the published table of exchange ratios (pp. 82–83), is that values of these goods in terms of each other reflect respective supply and demand in the southern Massim as a whole, not that their exchange values vary locally from place to place (except perhaps in modern shilling deals). A particular good would command more or less of another, depending on the global supply/demand, but whatever the ratio in one place it is the same in another. The published tables seem to indicate fairly uniform customary exchange rates: for example, one pot is traded for one "bunch" or one "bundle" of areca nuts at several locations (Tubetube, Bwasilake, Milne Bay), whereas two sticks of tobacco are given for one "bunch" of areca at Sudest and one pot for two sticks of tobacco at Sumarai (pp. 81-82).

*x* from *A*. Conversely, if in C the demand for *y* greatly outweighs *x*, then *B* will tend to hold back *y* in the exchange with village *A*. Thus the rate on the exchange of local products between any two villages would summarize the demands of all villages in the system.

I open a long parenthesis. Although the analysis is justifiably broken off at this point, with the understanding that Huon Gulf exchange values respond to ordinary market forces, one is tempted nevertheless to press the issue further, into a domain at once more speculative and more real, wherein is discovered not only a certain confirmation of the thesis but insights into the ecology, the structural limits and the history of such a system.

In the key example that unlocked the above analysis, the Busama were content to absorb a net loss on Tami bowls, hoping that way to encourage the flow of pottery from the south. As it was but one exchange in an interdependent sequence, the transaction proved unintelligible in itself. The three-village model facilitated understanding, but still it could not adequately represent all the constraints finally materialized in the sale of the bowl. For behind this transaction lay a whole series of preliminary exchanges by which Tami bowls were carried from place to place around the Gulf, effecting in the process a large preliminary redistribution of local specialities. It is in the hope of specifying this redistribution, and the material pressures developing therefrom, that further speculation is hazarded.

A four-village model is now required. To ease the re-entry into reality, we can retain the original three *(A, B,* and *C),* while identifying *B* as Busama and *A* then as the potters, and adding a fourth village, *T,* to represent Tami with its specialized product, *t* (bowls). Suppose, too, although it is not exactly the case, that the export goods of each community are liberally demanded by all the others; and that, more nearly true, each community exchanges only with the village or villages directly contiguous. The objective of the exercise will be to pass Tami bowls *(t)* from one end of the sequence to the other, determining thus the total distribution of specialized products that would result.

In the hope of explaining better that notable sale of Tami bowls by Busama to the potters *(A),* the exchanges first will be played out *à trois* between villages *B* (Busama), *C,* and *T* (Tami). By the initial moves then, *T* and *C* exchange their respective items, *t* and *z,* and villages

*B* and *C* theirs, *y* and *z*. Leaving aside the question of quantities traded, the types of goods would, after this first round, assume the following distribution:

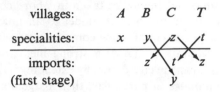

The second round, designed to carry an amount of *t*, bowls, to community *B* (and of *y* to *T*) already presents certain difficulties—not insurmountable yet symptomatic of the pressures accumulating within the system, and of its destiny. Under the given conditions, however, there is little choice. Village *C* is unlikely to accept *z* from *B* in exchange for *t*, since *C* already produces *z*; hence, *B* can only again offer *y* to *C* to acquire *t*, at that probably but part of the *t* in *C*'s possession. In the same way *T* passes more *t* to *C* to obtain *y*. This done, the three-village chain is completed: goods from one terminus (*A* still excluded) appear at the other.

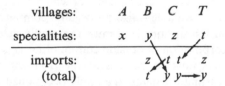

Completed—but perhaps also finished. At this juncture, *B* (usama) finds herself in an embarrassing relation to the global distribution of specialities and imports, her possibilities of further trade drastically reduced. *B* (usama) has nothing to put into circulation that villages down the line, *C* and *T*, do not already have, and have probably in quantities proportional to their proximity to *B*. Hence the strategic importance of village *A*, the potters, to Busama. Busama's continued participation in the exchange network hinges now on escaping from it, on opening a trade with *A*, which is also to say that the continuity of the trade system as a whole depends on its expansion. And in this strategic overture, the pottery of *A* must present itself to *B* not only as a use value but as the only good enjoying exchangeability for the goods of *C . . . T.* The transaction between *B* and *A* masses and brings to bear against the pottery of *A* the weight of all the other goods already in the system. Hence the exchange rates unfavorable to the goods of *B* (usama) and the losses taken in labor "costs."

May one read from an abstract model to an unknown history? Composed in the beginning of a few communities, a trade system of the Huon type would soon know a strong inclination to expand, diversifying its products in circulation by extending its range in space. Peripheral communities in particular, their bargaining position undermined during the initial stages of trade, are impelled to search further afield for novel items-in-trade. The network propogates itself at its extremities by a simple extension of reciprocity, coupling in new and, it is reasonably argued, by preference exotic communities, those that can supply exotic goods.

(The hypothesis may for other reasons be attractive to students of Melanesian society. Confronted by extensive trade chains such as the *kula,* anthropologists have been inclined at once to laud the complexity of the "areal integration" and wonder how it could possibly have come about. The merit of the dynamic outlined is that it makes a simple segmentary accretion of trade—of which Melanesian communities are perfectly capable—also an organic complication.)

But an expansion so organized must eventually determine its own limits. The incorporation of outside communities is achieved only at a considerable expense to villages at the frontiers of the original system. Transmitting the demand already occasioned by the internal redistribution of local specialities, these peripheral villages develop outside contacts on terms greatly disadvantageous to themselves in labor costs. The process of expansion thereby defines an ecological perimeter. It can continue passably enough through regions of high productivity, but once having breached a marginal ecological zone its further advance becomes unfeasible. Communities of the marginal zone may be only too happy to enter the system on the favorable terms offered them, but they are themselves in no position to support the costs of further expansion. Not that they, become now the peripheral outposts of the network, cannot entertain any trade beyond. Only that the trade system as organized, as an interrelated flow of goods governed by uniform procedures and rates, here discovers a natural boundary. Goods that pass beyond this limit must do so under other forms and rates of exchange; they pass into another system.[7]

Deduction thus rejoins reality. The ecological structure of the Huon system is exactly as stipulated theoretically: relatively rich villages in the central positions, relatively poor villages at the extremes, and by the terms of trade a current of value and strategic goods moving from central to marginal locations. End of parenthesis.

Summarizing to this juncture, in the three Oceanic trade systems under review, exchange-values are responsive to supply and demand—at least insofar as supply and demand are inferable from the real distribution of the goods in circulation. Business as usual.

### Rate Variations over Time

Furthermore, the evidence so far reviewed, in the main spatially derived, can be supplemented by observations taken over time at specific Melanesian trade sites. Temporal variations of exchange value follow the same iron laws—with one reservation: the rates tend to remain stable in the short run, unaffected by even important changes in supply and demand, although they do adjust in the long run.

Seasonal fluctuations of supply, for example, generally leave the terms of trade untouched. Salisbury suggests of the Tolai (New Britain) inland-coastal exchange that it could not otherwise be managed:

> The net movement of *tabu* [shell money] from inland to coast, and vice-versa, is small. This conflicts with the impression one gets at different seasons, that all coastals are buying taro and not earning any *tabu*, or that inlanders are buying up all the fish for ceremonials and not selling much taro. If prices were fixed by current supply-demand ratios, they could vary widely and unpredictably. It is in just such a context that a trade in fixed equivalences is highly desirable, with the "traditional" prices being those that provide an equal balance over the long term. (Salisbury, 1966, p. 117 n.)

Over a quite long term, however, "traditional" *Tolai* equivalencies do vary. Exchange rates for food in 1880 were only 50–70 percent of

---

7. Thus Huon Gulf goods may well pass through Tami into the Siassi–New Britain area, but probably under different trade terms, for the Tami islanders act as middlemen in a part of this area, very like the Siassi and probably also to some net advantage.

the 1961 rates. Apart from some overall growth in shell-money stocks, the dynamics of this change are not altogether clear. But elsewhere in Melanesia, long-term revisions in exchange value have clearly ensued from the increased supplies of goods (and even shell monies) pumped into local trade systems by Europeans. An observation from Kapauku illustrates both tendencies here at issue, the short-run sluggishness[8] of customary rates—although Kapauku are not famous for their fair trading—and a long-run sensitivity:

> In general, however, the fluctuation of price because of temporary imbalance of the supply-demand level is rather infrequent . . . [But] a steady increase of supply may bring about a steady decline of the actual price. The permanence of this state has an effect upon the customary price which tends to be identified with the actual payments. Thus, before 1945, when iron axes had to be brought from the coastal people, the customary price was 10Km for an axe. The coming of the white man and the resulting increase and direct supply of axes, reduced the old price to half the former amount. The process is still going on and the actual price in 1956 tended to fall below the customary price of 5Km per axe (Pospisil, 1958, pp. 122-123; cf. Dubbeldam, 1964).

By 1959 an axe could be had for only two units of native currency (2Km) (Pospisil, 1963, p. 310). Still, the Kapauku example is extraordinary, since the economy includes a large sector of bargained exchange where going rates may vary radically from transaction to transaction, as well as develop long-term trends capable of communication to the balanced reciprocity sector (cf. Pospisil,1963, pp. 310-311).

8. In speaking of short-term sluggishness in the face of supply and demand unbalance, it is necessary to bear in mind that the reference is to customary rates, especially if the economy includes a sector of haggling. Bargaining proceeds from various degrees of desperation and advantage, personal positions that do not individually represent the aggregate supply and demand and result in marked differences from transaction to transaction in rates of exchange. In Marshall's terms, bargainers can come to an equilibrium, but only fortituitously to *the* equilibirum (1961, pp. 791-793). Unless and until other people get into the bargaining, both on the demand side and the supply side, such paired haggling does not constitute a "market principle" nor influence price in the way envisioned by the competitive model. Certain ethnographic suggestions that prices in one or another primitive society are even more responsive to supply/demand than in our markets, insofar as they derive from the haggling sector, ought to be treated with suspicion. In any event, these kinds of fluctuations are not involved in the present discussion of short-term stability.

The case is simpler in the Australian New Guinea Highlands, where the bulk of trade is carried at standardized rates and between special partners. Here currency values have dropped substantially since Europeans put large quantities of shell money into circulation (Gitlow, 1947, p. 72; Meggitt, 1957–58, p. 189; Salisbury, 1962, pp. 116-117). The same process has been observed outside Melanesia: the variations in exchange value of horses in the intertribal trade of the American Plains, due to changes in supply conditions. (Ewers, 1955, pp. 217f).

No doubt examples of such sensitivity to supply and demand could be multiplied. Yet more examples would only make matters more unintelligible—by *any* prevailing theory of exchange value. This theoretical embarrassment is noteworthy and critical, and although I may not resolve it I would count the essay a success to have raised it. Nothing really is explained by remarking that exchange value in primitive trade corresponds to supply/demand. For the competitive mechanisms by which supply and demand are understood to determine price in the market place do not exist in primitive trade. It becomes far more mysterious that exchange ratios should respond to supply and demand than that they remain unaffected.

## The Social Organization of Primitive and Market Trade

Supply and demand are operative in the self-regulating market, pushing prices toward equilibrium, by virtue of a two-sided competition between sellers over buyers, and between buyers over sellers. This double competition, symmetrical and inverse, is *the* social organization of formal market theory. Without it, supply and demand cannot be realized in price—so it is always present also, if only implicitly, in textbooks on microeconomics. In the theoretically perfect case, all deals are interconnected. All parties in question have access to each other as well as full knowledge of the market, such that buyers are in a position to compete among themselves by paying more (if necessary and possible), sellers by asking less. In the event of an oversupply relative to the quantity in demand at a given price, sellers contest for the limited patronage by reducing prices; then, certain sellers withdraw because they are unable to support the reduction, even as more buyers find the terms attractive, until a price is reached that clears the market. In the opposite circumstance, buyers bid up prices until the quantity available meets the quantity demanded. The "demand crowd" clearly has no solidarity *inter se* and as against the supply crowd, or vice versa. It is the exact opposite of trade between communities of different tribes, where internal relations of kinship and amity would stand against the competition required by the business model—particularly in the context of an economic confrontation with outsiders. *Caveat emptor,* perhaps; but tribal sociability and homebred morality constitute an unlikely arena for economic infighting—for no man can have honor and profit in his own camp.

The alienated intersections of supply curves and demand curves in the economists' diagrams presuppose a certain structure of competition. Very different are the procedures of primitive trade. Anyone cannot just get into the act, enter the lists against people of his own side in quest of the exotic goods offered by visiting strangers. Once under way, usually in fact beforehand, trade is an exclusive relation with a specific outside party. The traffic is canalized in parallel and insulated transactions between particular pairs.[9] Where trade is handled through parnerships, exactly who exchanges with whom is prescribed in advance: social relations, not prices, connect up "buyers" and "sellers." Lacking a trade contact, a man may not be able to get what he wants at any price.[10] There is no evidence anywhere, so far as I know, of competitive bidding among members of a trading party for the custom of each other's partners; there is only the occasional observation that it is expressly forbidden.[11] Haggling likewise, where

9. Or else the trade of their respective communities is arranged between representative chiefs, who redistribute the proceeds within their groups, for example, certain Pomo trade (Loeb, 1926, pp. 192-193), or in the Marquesas (Linton, 1939, p. 147). On corporate partnerships between groups, see below.

10. Oliver provides an example from Siuai of the difficulty of trade—even between people of the same ethnic group—in the absence of partnership: "It is not a simple matter to purchase a pig. Owners become fond of their beasts and are often loath to give them up. A would-be purchaser cannot merely let it be known that he is interested in buying, and then sit at home and await orders. . . . One situation was observed in which a hopeful purchaser visited a potential seller every day for nine days before finally concluding the transaction: all for a [small] pig worth 20 spans of mauai! It is no wonder, then, that institutionalized arrangements have developed whereby acquiring a pig becomes simplified. One of these is the taovu [trade partner] relationship already described" (Oliver, 1955, p. 350).

it is practiced, is a discrete relation between individuals, not a free-for-all. The nearest documented approach to open-market trading appears to be, on one hand, a kind of auctioning, involving competition within the demand party only, as testified in certain Eskimo and Australian materials (Spencer, 1959, p. 206; Aiston, 1936–37, pp. 376-377);[12] on the other hand, Pospisil adduces a single example of a Kapauku competing with other sellers by lowering his price on a pig for a prospective buyer—but, interestingly enough, the man tried to come to this agreement in secret (1958, p. 123). The double and interrelated competition intrinsic to the business model, competition by which the forces of supply and demand are understood to regulate price, is generally not apparent in the conduct of primitive exchange, and only exceptionally is it half-approximated.

There is always the possibility of *implicit* rate competition among buyers and among sellers. I can only say I have not succeeded in construing it from existing descriptions.[13] Nor would it seem wise to be cynical about the moral force of customary exchange rates, one of the few guarantees of equity and continuity in a context pregnant with

11. " . . . it is a serious offense [among the Sio of northeast New Guinea] to steal or to attempt to lure away another person's trade-friend. In the old days, a man would attempt to kill an errant trade-friend as well as his new partner" (Harding, 1967, pp. 166-167). The following also suggests competitive impotence in trade: "One Komba man [an inland tribe] who is esteemed for his generosity complained that some Sio [trade-] friends were being intentionally impolite to him. He was very offended: 'They want me to visit [that is, exchange with] them, but I am only one man. What do they want me to do, cut off my arms and legs and distribute them around?' " (p. 168)

12. Again, as bargained rates, auctioned rates are indeterminate and are unlikely to indicate *the* equilibrium. Aiston writes of the Australian *pitcheri* narcotic auction: "Intrinsic value had nothing to do with the sales; it was quite likely that a big bag of pitcheri would be exchanged for a single boomerang, but it was just as likely to be exchanged for half a dozen boomerangs and perhaps a shield and a *pirra;* it always depended on what the buyer and seller wanted; sometimes when the seller had as much as he could carry he would give a bag in exchange for food for his party (1936–37, pp. 376-377).

13. Or at least I have not construed any definite or general covert price competition. There is one form of trade that possibly admits it—certain of the so-called "markets" or "market meetings" in Melanesia. This arrangement, of which Blackwood (1935) provides several examples, might reasonably be considered a corporate trade partnership between communities, the members of which meet at traditional places and prearranged times, and are free to trade with any opposite number who shows up. The trade is in customary products, is regulated by customary rates of equivalence, and customarily proceeds without haggle—and little enough of any talk. Blackwood did see one

hostility. More important, where customary rates prevail, and especially where trade is by partnership, there are alternative strategies to
competitive undercutting which avoid the material disadvantage of
lowering selling rates or raising offers: one alternative is to acquire
more partners for trade on the usual terms; another, to be examined
later in more detail, is to overpay one's partner for the time being,
obliging him thus to reciprocate within a reasonable period on pain
of losing dignity or partnership, so completing the transaction at
normal rates. No question that there may be competition for volume
of external trade. Internal prestige systems often hinge on it. But it
does not develop as price manipulation, product differentiation, or the
like. The standard manoeuvre is to increase the number of outside
partners, or else to step up trade with existing partners.

There are no markets properly so-called in these Melanesian soci-
eties.Very likely there are none in any of the archaic societies. Bohannan and Dalton (1962) were wrong to speak of a "market principle,"
even peripheral, in this context. They were misled on two counts by
transactions such as the *gimwali,* the bargaining of Trobriand nonpartnership trade. For one, they read the market from a type of

---

woman try to get more than the customary rate for a load of her produce—i. e., try
to haggle—but she was foiled (1935, p. 440). There remains, however, the choice of
particular partners and inspection of the goods offered; although hawking is not indicated, it is conceivable that women of a side compete with each other by varying the
quantity or quality of their "standard" loads (cf. Blackwood, 1935, p. 443, on variations
of certain loads).

One other possibility of implicit competition, more general than this, is discussed
further along in the text.

Furthermore, there are two rather exceptional conditions of trade on which we have
already put a construction of business-like competition. One was the mixed economy
(Kapauku), combining bargaining and balanced reciprocity sectors whose differences
in rates presumably would incline people, insofar as social relations permit, to withhold
goods from one sector for the better returns available in the other. Or again, as in the
Huon Gulf, two or more villages may handle the same good, and other communities
have access to more than one of these suppliers. The marketlike effect in both cases
would be equalization of rates over the different sectors or communities. But this
interpretation does not solve the critical problems. How is the trend of indeterminate
rates in the bargaining sector transposed to the customary rates of balanced partnership
exchange, such that the latter too realize the influence of supply/demand? Likewise,
in trade networks competitively patterned at the community level, it remains difficult
to understand just how relative value is adjusted to supply and demand. For exchange
still is conducted at customary rates between pairs of customary partners.

competition not essential to it, an overt conflict between buyer and seller.[14] Secondly, they read the market from a type of transaction taken alone, impersonal and competitive, without reference to the global organization of these exchanges. The mistake should serve to underline Polyani's sometimes insistence (1959) that transactions be understood as types of *integration,* not simply as types *(tout court).* "Reciprocity," "redistribution," and market exchange were in the master's treatment not mere forms of economic transaction but modes of economic organization. The determinate forms of transaction found in markets, such as sale and (occasionally) bargaining, are encountered also in a number of primitive instances. But lacking a symmetrical and inverse competition among buyers and among sellers, these exchanges are not integrated as market systems. Unless and until Trobriand haggling was so integrated (not traditionally the case) it would afford no indication of a market principle or of a peripheral market. Markets properly so-called, competitive and price fixing, are universally absent from primitive society.

But then, if the trade is not classically constituted to absorb supply-demand pressure by price changes, the sensitivity we have observed in Melanesian exchange values remains an intriguing mystery.

### A Primitive Theory of Exchange Value

I propose no definitive solution to the mystery. Once the inadequacy of formal economic theory is realized, and the complete unsophistication of anthropological economics thereby discovered, it is absurd to hope for more than partial and underdeveloped explanations. But I do have one such primitive theory of value. As in the good Economics tradition, it has an air of the "never-never"; yet it is consistent

14. Interesting that Marx reproached Proudhon for the same mistake: "Il ne suffit pas, à M. Proudhon, d'avoir éliminé du rapport de l'offre et de la demande les éléments dont nous venons de parler. Il pousse l'abstraction aux dernières limites, en fondant tous les producteurs en *un seul* producteur, tous les consommateurs en *un seul* consommateur, et en etablissant la lutte entre ces deux personnages chimériques. Mais dans le monde réel les choses se passent autrement. La concurrence entre *ceux* qui offrent et la concurrence entre ceux qui demandent, forment un élément nécessaire de la lutte entre les acheteurs et les vendeurs, d'où résulte la valeur venale" (Marx, 1968 [1847], pp. 53–54).

with the observed conduct of certain trade, and it does suggest reasons for the responsiveness of customary values to supply/demand. The idea is addressed exclusively to partnership trade. The essence of it is that rates are set by social tact, notably by the diplomacy of economic good measure appropriate to a confrontation between comparative strangers. In a series of reciprocal exchanges the alternating appearance of this overbalance, first on the part of one partner then the other, would with hardly less certainty than open price competition establish an equilibrium rate. At the same time, the guiding principle of "generosity" should give the agreed rate some semblance of *the* equilibrium i.e., of supply/demand.

It has to be understood that trade between primitive communities or tribes is a most delicate, potentially a most explosive, undertaking. Anthropological accounts document the risks of trading ventures in foreign territory, the uneasiness and suspiciousness, the facility of a translation from trading goods to trading blows. "There is a link," as Lévi-Strauss writes, "a continuity, between hostile relations and the provision of reciprocal prestations. Exchanges are peacefully resolved wars, and wars are the result of unsuccessful transactions" (1969, p. 67).[15] If primitive society succeeds by the gift and by the clan in reducing the state of Warre to an internal truce (see Chapter 4), it is only to displace outward, onto the relations between clans and tribes, the full burden of such a state. In the external sector the circumstances are radically Hobbesian, not only lacking that "common Power to keep them all in awe" but without even that common kinship that might incline them all to peace. In trade, moreover, the context of the confrontation is the acquisition of utilities; and the goods, as we have seen, may very well be urgent. When people meet who owe each other nothing yet presume to gain from each other something, peace of trade is the great uncertainty. In the absence of external guarantees, as of a Sovereign Power, peace must be otherwise secured: by extension of sociable relations to foreigners—thus, the trade-friendship or trade-kinship—and, most significantly, *by the terms of exchange itself*. The economic ratio is a diplomatic manoeuvre. "It requires a good deal of tact on the part of everyone concerned," as

15. " 'While trading, Indians won't hand a foreigner both the bow and the arrows at the same time' " (Goldschmidt, 1951, p. 336).

Radcliffe-Brown wrote of Andamanese interband exchange, "to avoid the unpleasantness that may arise if a man thinks that he has not received things as valuable as he has given. . . . " (1948, p. 42). The people must come to terms. The rate of exchange takes on functions of a peace treaty.

Intergroup exchange does not simply answer to the "moral purpose" of making friends. But whatever the intent and however utilitarian, it will not do to make enemies. Every transaction, as we already know, is necessarily a social strategy: it has a coefficient of sociability demonstrated in its manner, and in its rates by the implied willingness to live and let live, the disposition to give full measure in return. As it happens, the safe and sane procedure is not just measure-for-measure, a reciprocity precisely balanced. The most tactful strategy is economic *good measure,* a generous return relative to what has been received, of which there can be no complaints. One remarks in these intergroup encounters a tendency to *overreciprocate:*

> The object of the exchange [between people of different Andamanese bands] was to produce a friendly feeling between the two persons concerned, and unless it did this it failed of its purpose. *It gave great scope for the exercise of tact and courtesy.* No one was free to refuse a present that was offered to him. *Each man and woman tried to out-do the others in generosity.* There was a sort of amiable rivalry as to who could give away the greatest number of valuable presents [Radcliffe-Brown, 1948, p. 84; emphasis mine.]

The economic diplomacy of trade is "something extra" in return. Often it is "something for the road": the host outdoes his visiting friend, who made the initial presentation, a "solicitory gift" in token of friendship and the hope of safe conduct, and of course in the expectation of reciprocity. Over the long run accounts may balance, or rather one good turn begets another, but for the time being it is critical that some unrequited good measure has been thrown in. Literally a margin of safety, the exceeding generosity avoids at no great cost "the unpleasantness that may arise if a man thinks he has not received things as valuable as he has given," which is to say the unpleasantness that could be occasioned by cutting too fine. At the same time, the beneficiary of this generosity has been put under obligation: he is "one down"; so the donor has every right to expect equal good treatment the next time around, when *he* becomes the stranger and guest of his trade partner. On the widest view, as Alvin Gouldner has divined, these slight unbalances sustain the relation (Gouldner, 1960, p. 175).

The procedure of transitory unbalance, bringing generous returns from the home party to solicitory gifts, is not unique to the Andamans but in Melanesia rather common. It is the appropriate form between trade kinsmen of the Huon Gulf:

> Kinship ties and bargaining are considered to be incompatible, and all goods are handed over as free gifts offered from motives of sentiment. Discussion of value is avoided, and the donor does the best he can to convey the impression that no thought of a counter gift has entered his head. . . . Most of the visitors . . . go home with items at least as valuable as those with which they came. Indeed, the closer the kinship bond, the greater the host's generosity is, and some of them return a good deal richer. A careful count is kept, however, and the score is afterwards made even. (Hogbin, 1951, p. 84)

Or again, the Massim *Kula:*

> The offering of the *pari,* of landing gifts by the visitors, returned by the *talo'i,* or farewell gifts from the hosts fall into the class . . . of presents more or less equivalent. . . . The local man will as a rule [Malinowski seems to mean by this phrase "invariably"] contribute a bigger present, for the *talo'i* always exceeds the *pari* in quantity and value, and small presents are also given to the visitors during their stay. Of course, if in the *pari* there were included gifts of high value, like a stone blade or a good lime spoon, such solicitary gifts would always be returned in strictly equivalent form. The rest would be liberally exceeded in value (Malinowski 1922, p. 362)[16]

Suppose, then, this procedure of reciprocal good measure, as is actually characteristic of the Huon Gulf trade. A series of transactions in which the partners alternately manifest a certain generosity must stipulate by inference a ratio of equivalence between the goods exchanged. One arrives in due course at a fairly precise agreement on exchange values.

Table 6.2 presents a simple demonstration: two goods, axes and spheres, exchanged between two partners, $X$ and $Y$, over a series of

16. Cf. Malinowski, 1922, p. 188 on the unbalances in fish–yam exchange between partners of different Trobriand villages. For other examples of trade partner good measure in reciprocation see also Oliver, 1955, pp. 229, 546; Spencer, 1959, p. 169; cf. Goldschmidt, 1951, p. 335.

Table 6.2. *Determination of exchange value
through reciprocal good measure*

| | Partner X gives | Partner Y gives |
|---|---|---|
| Round I (X is visitor) | 3 spears ⟶ <br> ⟵ <br> [∴ 3 spears < 2 axes] | 2 axes |
| Round II (Y is visitor) | ⟵ <br> 6 spears ⟶ <br> [∴ 9 spears > 4 axes] <br> but if 3 spears < 2 axes, 6 spears < 4 axes <br> ∴ 7-8 spears = 4 axes; or c. 2:1] | 2 axes |
| Round III (X is visitor) | 1-3 spears ⟶ <br> ⟵ | 1-3 axes |

reciprocal visits beginning with $X$'s visit and initial gift to $Y$. After the first round, the two axes given by $Y$ are understood generous in return for the three spears brought by $X$. At the end of the second round, in which $Y$ first compounded $X$'s indebtedness by two axes and was then himself indebted by $X$'s gift of six spears, the implication is that nine spears exceed four axes in value. It follows at this juncture that seven to eight spears equals four axes, or taking into account the indivisibilities, a rate of 2 : 1 prevails. There is of course no necessity to continually escalate gifts. At the end of the second series, $Y$ is down the equivalent of about one spear. Should $X$ bring one to three spears the next time and $Y$ reciprocate one to three (or better, two or three) axes, a fair average balance is maintained. Note also that the rate is something each party mechanically agrees upon, insofar as each understands the current balance of credit and indebtedness, and if any serious misunderstanding does arise the partnership breaks down— which likewise stipulates the rate at which trade must proceed.

Considering the comparisons (perhaps invidious) of trade returns likely to be made with fellows of one's own side, these understandings of equivalence stand a chance of becoming common understandings. Comparison of trade returns are the nearest thing to implicit internal competition I am able to construe. Presumably, information thus gained might be applied next time against one's trade partner of the other community. There seems to be very little evidence on this point, however, or on just how precise is the available information of compatriots' dealings—in some instances transactions with outside partners are conducted privately and rather furtively (Harding, 1967).

The example before us is specifically a simple model case, supposing reciprocal visiting and a standard presentation procedure. It is conceivable that different trade arrangements have some other calculus of exchange value. If, for instance, $X$ of the simple model was a trader-voyager, always on the visiting side, and if the same etiquette of generosity held, the actual ratio would probably favor $X$'s spears more, insofar as $Y$ would be repeatedly obliged to be magnaminous. Indeed, if $X$ consistently presented three spears, and $Y$ consistently returned two axes, the same ratio could be maintained for four rounds without $X$ being down after his initial gift, even though a rate of approximately 2 : 1 is calculable midway through the second round (Table 6.3). A 3 : 2 customary rate could in that event develop. Either

*Table 6.3. Rate determination: one-way visiting*

|  | X gives | Y gives | X's Calculable Debt |
|---|---|---|---|
| Round I | 3 spears ⟶ <br> ⟵ 2 axes <br><br> [∴ 3 spears < 2 axes] |  | [– ? spears] |
| Round II | 3 spears ⟶ <br> [∴ 6 spears > 2 axes <br> ∴ 4-5 spears ≡ 2 axes] <br> ⟵ 2 axes <br> [∴ 6 spears < 4 axes <br> ∴ 2 spears ≡ 1 axe] |  | [–2 spears] |
| Round III | 3 spears ⟶ <br> ⟵ 2 axes |  | [+1 spear] <br> [–3 spears] |
| Round IV | 3 spears ⟶ <br> ⟵ 2 axes <br><br> [∴ 3 spears = 2 axes?] |  | [0 spears] <br> [–4 spears] |

way there are obvious advantages to the voyaging group—though they must bear all the transport, so that the gains over the rate for reciprocal visiting will parallel "supply-cost" differences.

This second example is only one of many possible permutations of exchange rate determination. Even in one-way voyaging, the etiquette of presentation and counterpresentation may be more complicated than that supposed (for example, Barton, 1910). I bring the example forward merely to suggest the possibility that different formalities of exchange generate different exchange rates.

No matter how complex the strategy of reciprocity by which an equilibrium is finally determined, and however subtle our analysis, it remains to be known exactly what has been determined economically. How can it be that a rate fixed by reciprocal generosity expresses the current average supply and demand? Everything depends on the meaning and practice of that capital principle, "generosity." But the meaning is ethnographically uncertain, and therein lies the major weakness of our theory. Only these few facts, not celebrated either for their repetition in the documents, are known: that those who bring a certain good to the exchange are related to it primarily in terms of labor value, the real effort required to produce it, while those to whom the good is tendered appreciate it primarily as a use value. That much we know from incidents to the Huon Gulf and Siassi trade, wherein the labor of manufacture was exaggerated by the suppliers but the product thereof depreciated by the takers—both sides in hopes of influencing terms of trade in their own favor (see above). From this steadfast devotion to the main chance, one has to work back by a kind of inverted logic to the possible meaning of "generosity." Supposing the necessity of reciprocal good measure, it would follow that each party has to consider, in addition to the virtues of the goods he receives, the relative utility to the other party of the goods he gives, and in addition to the labor he has expended himself, the work also of the other. "Generosity" has to bring use value into relation with use value, and labor with labor.

If so, "generosity" will bring to bear on the rate of exchange some of the same forces, operating in the same direction, as affect price in the marketplace. In principle, goods of higher real cost will evoke higher returns. In principle too, if goods of greater utility oblige the recipient to greater generosity, it is as much as saying that price is disposed to increase with demand.[17] Thus compensating efforts to the producer and utilities to the receiver, the rates set by tactful diplomacy will express many of the elemental conditions that are resumed otherwise in the economist's supply curves and demand curves. Into both would enter, and to the same general effects, the real difficulties of production, natural scarcities, the social uses of goods, and the possibilities of substitution. In many respects the opposite of market competition, the etiquette of primitive trade may conduct by a different route to a similar result. But then, there is from the beginning a basic similarity: the two systems share the premise that the trader should be satisfied materially, the difference being that in the one this is left solely to his own inclination while in the other it becomes the responsibility of his partner. To be a diplomatically satisfactory "price" however, the price of peace, the customary exchange ratio of primitive trade should approximate the normal market price. As the mechanisms differ, this correspondence can only be approximate, but the tendency is one.

### Stability and Fluctuation of Exchange Rates

Provisionally at least, we come to the following conclusion: the material conditions expressed familiarly by the terms "supply" and "demand" are likewise subsumed in the understandings of good treatment built into the procedure of Melanesian trade. But then, how do exchange ratios remain immune to short-lived changes in supply/demand?

Certain reasons for this short-term stability have already been mentioned. First, the customary rates have moral force, understandable from their function as standards of fair conduct in an area where tenuous intergroup relations constantly menace the peace of trade.

17. Further, it appears the empirical case that a discrepancy in labor values can be sustained by an equivalence in utilities (cf. Godelier, 1969). "Need" is matched to "need," perhaps at the real expense of one party—although, as we have seen, the norm of equal work may still be maintained by ideological ruse and pretense. This kind of discrepancy would be most likely where the goods traded belong to different spheres of exchange within one or both trading communities, for example, manufactured goods for food, especially where the craft goods are used also in such as bridewealth payments. Then the high social utility of a small amount of one good (the manufactured good) is compensated by a large quantity of the item of lesser status. This may be an important secret in the "exploitation" of richer areas by poorer (e.g., Siassi).

And although moral practice everywhere may be vulnerable to expediency, it is usually not so easy to change the rules. Secondly, in the event of an unbalance of quantities on hand relative to demand (at the prevailing rate of exchange), partnership trade opens more attractive alternatives to cutting the "asking price" or raising the offer: better to find new partners for trade at old rates; or else to embarrass an existing partner by a large overpayment, obliging him to extend himself and later on reciprocate, again thus defending the usual rate. The last is not an hypothetical tactic of my own devising. Consider this Busama technique for encouraging a supply of pigs:

> The difference between the native method of doing business and our own was made plain by an exchange which took place early in 1947. The Salamaua area had suffered more damage than the northern settlements, most of which still had their pigs. On the resumption of voyages after the Japanese defeat, a man from Bukawa' had the notion of bringing a young sow to a Busama kinsman named Boya. The animal was worth about £ 2, but hints indicated that pots would be more acceptable than money. A collection of ten was required for a reasonable equivalent, and as Boya had only five to spare he informed his relatives that anyone prepared to assist would in due course receive a piglet. This invitation was accepted, and twenty-two pots were contributed, making a total of twenty-seven. All were handed over to the visitor, rather to his surprise, as he confessed to me in private. Yet such generosity was not as absurd as it may appear: by giving so much Boya imposed an obligation on his guest to bring across another sow (Hogbin, 1951, pp. 84–85).

The success of Boya's manoeuvre was made possible only by the social qualitites of the trade relation. Partnership is not merely the privilege but the duty of reciprocity. Specifically it comprehends the obligation to *receive* as well as to *repay*. Some people may end up with more of a certain good than they needed, expected or bargained for, but the point is they did not bargain for it. A trade friend is prevailed upon to accept things for which he has no use; thereupon, he will have to repay—for no good "economic" reason. Father Ross of Mt. Hagen seems not to have appreciated the spiritual ethic involved:

> The missionary told the author that natives who have traded with him, and who are in needy circumstances at the moment, will come to the mission station with items possessing no material value and which have no utility to the missionary. The natives seek to trade these items in exchange for

things they need. Upon his refusal the natives point out to him that his conduct is not proper, for according to their view he is their friend and should accept a thing which he does not need so as to assist them when they need such help. They will say to him, "You buy our food, we sell you our pigs, our boys work for you. Therefore you should buy this thing which you claim you do not want, and it is not right for you to refuse to purchase it" (Gitlow, 1947, p. 68).[18]

Working the same principle, the people of the hinterland above Sio (northeast New Guinea) may overcome their coastal partners' reluctance to trade:

> The Sios also, of course, frequently accept goods which they do not need at the time. When I asked one Sio man why he had four bows (most men have more than one), he replied: "If a bush [trade–] friend comes with a bow, you have to help him" (Harding, 1967, pp. 109-110).

Finally, a striking example of the same, appended by Malinowski to his description of fish-yam exchange *(wasi)* between different Trobriand communities. To this day, Malinowski noted, inland yam growers continued to insist on their coastal partners' obligation to receive, thus periodically teasing from the latter a supply of fish, and at the usual terms, though the fishing people could occupy themselves much more profitably diving for pearls. Money thus remained the servant of custom, and partnership the master of indigenous exchange rates:

> Nowadays, when the fishermen can earn about ten or twenty times more by diving for pearls than by performing their share of the *wasi,* the exchange is as a rule a great burden on them. It is one of the most conspicuous examples of the tenacity of native custom that in spite of all the temptation

18. The misunderstanding is cultural and economic, obviously independent of race and religion: " . . . Nuer do not regard purchase from an Arab merchant in the way in which we regard purchase from a shop. It is not to them an impersonal transaction, and they have no idea of price and currency in our sense. Their idea of purchase is that you give something to a merchant who is thereby put under an obligation to help you. At the same time you ask him for something you need from his shop and he ought to give it to you because, by taking your gift, he has entered into a reciprocal relationship with you. Hence *kok* has the sense of 'to buy' or 'to sell.' The two acts are an expression of a single relationship of reciprocity. As an Arab merchant regards the transaction rather differently misunderstandings arise. In the Nuer way of looking at the matter what is involved in an exchange of this kind is a relation between persons rather than between things. It is the merchant who is 'bought' rather than the goods. . . . " (Evans-Pritchard, 1956, pp. 223-224).

which pearling offers them, and in spite of the great pressure exerted upon them by white traders, the fishermen never try to evade a *wasi,* and when they have received the inaugurating gift, the first calm day is always given to fishing, and not to pearling (Malinowski, 1922, p. 188 n).

So acting to maintain the stability of exchange values, the trade partnership merits a more general and respectful interpretation of its economic significance. The primitive trade partnership is a functional counterpart of the market's price mechanism. A current supply-demand imbalance is resolved by pressure on trade partners rather than exchange rates. Where in the market this equilibrium is effected by a change in price, here the social side of the transaction, the partnership, absorbs the economic pressure. The rate of exchange remains undisturbed—although the temporal rate of certain transactions may be retarded. The primitive analogue of the business price mechanism is not the customary exchange rate; it is the customary exchange relation.

Short-term consistency of exchange values is thus accomplished. Yet the same deflection of the pressure from the rate of exchange to the relation of partnership makes the latter all the more vulnerable to a sustained discrepancy of supply-demand. Suppose a continuing and/or widening disparity between the traditional exchange rate and the amount of goods actually disposable—due, it may be, to some new facility in the acquisition of one of the goods at issue. Then partnership trade increases the material pressure in the course of repeatedly resolving it. Holding steady the terms of exchange, the tactic of overpayment proves equitable and endurable only if the supply-demand unbalance is reversible. Otherwise, an inherent tendency to accumulate volume makes it unsupportable. For by an attack on a partner's obligation to receive, granted his possible delay in response, exchange proceeds always at the quantity sought by the most importunate party. In this respect, the inducement to production and exchange exceeds even the dynamic of the competitive market.

That is to say, at any permutation of supply moving above or below demand at a certain price, the volume of exchange implied by partnership trade is greater than the analogous market equilibrium. Perhaps the available quantity of pigs is momentarily less than the quantity demanded at a rate of one pig = five pots; *tant pis* for the pig raisers: they will have to deliver more at the same rate, to the point that all the pots are exhausted. In the open market, the total quantity transacted would be lower, and on terms more favorable to the trade in pigs.

Plain to view that, if the disparity persists between the going rates and the goods on hand, partnership trade must discover its limits as an equilibrating mechanism, always making a supply available to the demand and always on the usual terms. Taken at the social level, the trade becomes irrational: one group enters into economic development by pre-emption of another group's labor. Nor could the harassed set of partners be expected to indefinitely countenance the imbalance, any more than a society that tolerated the procedure could be expected to continue indefinitely. On the individual level the irrationality most likely presents itself as a disutility to accumulation, more concrete than the unrequited cost of production. There must come a moment, after a man is in possession of five bows, or perhaps it is ten, or maybe twenty, when he begins to wonder about the advisability of collecting all the stuff his partner seems intent on unloading. What happens then, when people become unwilling or unable to meet their trade obligations? If we knew, it would unlock the last of the mysteries empirically posed by Melanesian trade: the observed tendency of exchange values to adjust over the long run, if not over the short, to changes in supply/demand. For the apparent solution is to evaluate the rates. But how?

By a relocation of trade, a revision of partnerships. We know, on one hand, what happens when a trade partner is disinclined to reciprocate. The sanction everywhere is dissolution of the partnership. For a time a man can stall, but if he delays too long, or fails in the end to make the adequate return, the trade relation is broken off. In such an event, moreover, the volume of exchange declines, and the pressure to trade thus mounts. On the other hand, we also know (or we suppose) that the process by which exchange value is determined in the first place, i.e. through reciprocal good measure, incorporates current average supply-demand conditions. The solution, thus, to a persistent disconfirmity between exchange values and supply/demand would be a social process by which old partnerships are terminated and new ones negotiated. Perhaps even the network of trade will have to be modified, geographically and ethnically. But in any case, a fresh start, going through with new partners the traditional tactful manoeuvres of reciprocal overpayment, restores the correspondance between exchange value and supply/demand.

This model, if hypothetical, corresponds to certain facts, such as the social organization of the deflation experienced in Melanesian trade networks during the postcontact period. The indigenous trade continued for some time without the benefit of businesslike competition. But the same Europeans who brought excessive quantities of axes, shells or pigs also happened to impose peace. In the colonial era the sphere of Melanesian safe-conduct expanded, the social horizons of tribal communities widened. A significant reshuffling and extension of trade contacts became possible. And a revaluation of trade rates as well: as, for example, in the coast-hinterland trade of Huon Gulf, on the whole more recently opened up, and apparently much more sensitive to supply/demand than the traditional maritime trade (Hogbin, 1951, p. 86; cf. Harding, 1967).

Which leads to a final suggestion: depending on the social qualities of the trade relation, the rates of exchange in differently organized trade systems are probably differentially sensitive to changes in supply/demand. The precise nature of the partnership becomes significant: it may be more or less sociable, so admitting of longer or shorter delays in reciprocation—trade-kinship, for example, probably longer than trade-friendship. The prevailing relation has a coefficient of economic fragility, and the entire system accordingly a certain responsiveness to variations of supply/demand. The simple matter of customary privacy or publicity may be similarly consequential; perhaps it is feasible (for all one knows) to secretly come to new terms with old partners. And what freedom is given within the system to recruit new partners? Aside from the difficulties of breaking paths into villages or ethnic groups previously outside the system, partnerships may be by custom inherited and the set of contacts thus closed, or perhaps more readily contracted and the exchange values thereby more susceptible to revision. In brief, the economic flexibility of the system depends on the social structure of the trade relation.

If the process as outlined does truly describe long-term variations in exchange value, then at a high level of generalization and with a great deal of imperfection it is like business competition. Of course the differences are profound. In primitive trade, the path to economic equilibrium lay not across the play of autonomous individuals or firms fixing a price through the parallel contentions of buyers and sellers. It began rather from the interdiction of competition within the community of either, traversed a structure of institutional arrangements that with varying facility brought together partners mutually obliged to be generous, upon separating those not so inclined, to negotiate in the end an analogous "price." The similarity to market trade appears when abstraction is made of all this—and of the protracted space-time scale, perhaps in reality a changeover of decades from trade with one ethnic group to partnerships in another. Then the primitive system, globally considered, does bring those particular persons into relations of trade, and at those rates, as reasonably reflect the availability and utility of goods.

But what is the theoretical status of this residual resemblance? First appreciated in its bourgeois form, does this make it the analytical private property of conventional Economics? One might fairly judge not, for in its bourgeois form the process is not general, while in its general form it is not bourgeois. The conclusion to this aspect of Melanesian trade will serve as well for the whole: a primitive theory of exchange value is also necessary, and perhaps possible—without saying it yet exists.

# Bibliography

Aiston, G.
  1936–37. "The Aboriginal Narcotic Pitcheri," *Oceania* 7: 372–77.
Allan, William
  1949. *Studies in African Land Usage in Northern Rhodesia.* Rhodes-Livingstone Papers, No. 15.
  1965. *The African Husbandman.* Edinburgh: Oliver and Boyd.
Althusser, Louis
  1966. *Pour Marx.* Paris: Maspero.
Althusser, Louis, Jacques Ranciere, et al.
  1966. *Lire le Capital.* 2 vols. Paris: Maspero.
Anonymous
  n.d. *Apercu d'histoire et d'économie: Vol. 1, Formations précapitalistes.* Moscow: Editions du Progrès.
Awad, Mohamed
  1962. "Nomadism in the Arab Lands of the Middle East," in *The Problems of the Arid Zone,* Proceedings of the Paris Symposium, UNESCO.
Barnett, H. G.
  1938. "The Nature of the Potlatch," *American Anthropologist* 40: 349–58.
Barth, Fredrik
  1961. *Nomads of South Persia.* London: Allen and Unwin, for Oslo University Press.

Barton, F. R.
   1910. "Motu-Koita Papuan Gulf Expedition (Hiri)," in C. G. Seligman (ed.), *The Melanesians of British New Guinea.* Cambridge: At the University Press.
Bartram, William
   1958. *The Travels of William Bartram.* Edited by Francis Harper. New Haven, Conn.: Yale University Press (first published 1791).
Basedow, Herbert
   1925. *The Australian Aboriginal.* Adelaide, Australia: Preece.
Beaglehole, Ernest, and P. Beaglehole
   1938. *Ethnology of Pukapuka.* Bernice P. Bishop Museum Bulletin No. 150.
Belshaw, Cyril
   1955. *In Search of Wealth.* American Anthropological Association Memoir No. 80.
Bennett, Wendell C.
   1931. *Archeology of Kauai.* Bernice P. Bishop Museum Bulletin No. 80.
Best, Elsdon
   1900–01. "Spiritual Concepts of the Maori," *Journal of the Polynesian Society* 9:173-99; 10:1-20.
   1909. "Maori Forest Lore . . . Part III," *Transactions of the New Zealand Institute* 42:433-81.
   1922. *Spiritual and Mental Concepts of the Maori.* Dominion Museum Monographs No. 2.
   1924. *The Maori.* 2 vols. Memoirs of the Polynesian Society No. 5.
   1925a. *Tuhoe: The Children of the Mist.* Memoirs of the Polynesian Society No. 6.
   1925b. *Maori Agriculture.* Dominion Museum Bulletin No. 9.
   1942. *Forest Lore of the Maori.* Dominion Museum Bulletin No. 14.
Biard, le Père Pierre
   1897. "Relation of New France, of its Lands, Nature of the Country, and of its Inhabitants . . . ," in R. G. Thwaites (ed.), *The Jesuit Relations and Allied Documents,* Vol. 3. Cleveland: Burrows. (First French edition, 1616.)
Birket-Smith, Kaj
   1959. *The Eskimos.* 2nd Ed. London: Methuen.
Blackwood, Beatrice

1935. *Both Sides of Buka Passage.* Oxford: At the Clarendon Press.
Bleak, D. F.
1928. *The Naron.* Cambridge: At the University Press.
Boas, Franz
1884–85. "The Central Eskimo," *Smithsonian Institution, Bureau of American Ethnology, Anthropological Reports* 6:399–699.
1940. *Race, Language and Culture.* New York: Free Press.
Boeke, J. H.
1953. *Economics and Economic Policy of Dual Societies.* New York: Institute of Pacific Relations.
Bogoras, W.
1904–19. *The Chukchee.* American Museum of Natural History Memoirs No. 11 (2–4).
Bohannan, Paul
1954. *Tiv Farm and Settlement.* Colonial Research Studies No. 15. London: H. M. Stationery Office.
1955. "Some Principles of Exchange and Investment Among the Tiv," *American Anthropologist* 57:60–70.
Bohannan, Paul, and Laura Bohannan
1968. *Tiv Economy.* Evanston: Northwestern University Press.
Bohannan, Paul, and George Dalton (eds.)
1962. *Markets in Africa.* Evanston: Northwestern University Press.
Bonwick, James
1870. *Daily Life and Origin of the Tasmanians.* London: Low and Merston.
Boukharine, N.
1967. *La Théorie du matérialism historique.* Paris: Editions Anthropos (First Russian edition, 1921).
Braidwood, Robert J.
1952. *The Near East and the Foundations for Civilization.* Eugene: Oregon State System of Higher Education
1957. *Prehistoric Men.* 3rd ed. Chicago Natural History Museum Popular Series, Anthropology, Number 37.
Braidwood, Robert J., and Gordon R. Willey (eds.)
1962. *Courses Toward Urban Life.* Chicago: Aldine.
Brown, Paula, and H. C. Brookfield
1959–60. "Chimbu Land and Society," *Oceania* 30:1–75.
1963. *Struggle for Land.* Melbourne: Oxford University Press.

Bücher, Carl
1907. *Industrial Evolution.* New York: Holt
Bulmer, Ralph
1960–61. "Political Aspects of the Moka Ceremonial Exchange System Among the Kyaka People of the Western Highlands of New Guinea," *Oceania* 31:1–13.
Burling, Robbins
1962. "Maximization Theories and the Study of Economic Anthropology," *American Anthropologist* 64:802–21.
Burridge, Kenelm
1960. *Mambu: A Melanesian Millenium.* London: Methuen.
Carneiro, Robert L.
1957. Subsistence and Social Structure: An Ecological Study of the Kuikuru Indians, Ph.D. dissertation, University of Michigan. Ann Arbor, Michigan: University Microfilms.
1960. "Slash-and-Burn Agriculture: A Closer Look at its Implications for Settlement Patterns," in A. F. C. Wallace (ed.), *Men and Cultures.* Philadelphia: University of Pennsylvania Press.
1968. "Slash-and-Burn Cultivation among the Kuikuru and its Implications for Cultural Development in the Amazon Basin," in Y. Cohen (ed.), *Man in Adaptation: The Cultural Present.* Chicago: Aldine (Reprinted from *Anthropologica* Supplement No. 2, 1961).
Cazaneuve, Jean
1968. *Sociologie de Marcel Mauss.* Paris: Presses universitaires de France.
Chayanov, A. V.
1966. *The Theory of Peasant Economy.* Homewood, Ill.: Richard D. Irwin for the American Economic Association.
Chowning, Ann and Ward Goodenough
1965–66. "Lakalai Political Organization," *Anthropological Forum* 1:412–73.
Clark, Colin, and Margaret Haswell
1964. *The Economics of Subsistence Agriculture.* London: MacMillan.
Clark, Graham
1953. *From Savagery to Civilization.* New York: Schuman.
Clark, W. T.

1938. "Manners, Customs, and Beliefs of the Northern Bega," *Sudan Notes and Records* 21:1–29.

Codere, Helen
(n.d.) *Fighting with Property.* American Ethnological Society Monograph 18. New York: Augustine.
1968. "Money-Exchange Systems and a Theory of Money," *Man,* (n.s.) 3:557–77.

Colson, Elizabeth
1960. *Social Organization of the Gwembe Tonga.* Manchester: At the University Press for the Rhodes-Livingstone Institute.

Conklin, Harold C.
1957. *Hanunóo Agriculture.* Rome: Food and Agriculture Organization of the United Nations.
1959. "Population-Land Balance under Systems of Tropical Forest Agriculture," *Proceedings of the Ninth Pacific Science Congress* 7:63.
1961. "The Study of Shifting Cultivation," *Current Anthropology* 2:27-61.

Cook, Scott
1966. "The Obsolete 'Anti-Market' Mentality: A Critique of the Substantive Approach to Economic Anthropology," *American Anthropologist* 63:1–25.

Coues, Elliot (ed.)
1897. *The Manuscript Journals of Alexander Henry and of David Thompson, 1799–1814.* 2 vols. New York: Harper.

Curr, E. M.
1965. *Recollections of Squatting in Victoria, then Called the Port Phillip District, from 1841–1851.* (First edition, 1883) Melbourne: At the University Press.

Dalton, George
1961. "Economic Theory and Primitive Society," *American Anthropologist* 63:1–25.

Davies, John
1961. *The History of the Tahitian Mission 1799–1830.* Edited by C. W. Newbury. Cambridge: At the University Press.

Deacon, A. Bernard
1934. *Malekula: A Vanishing People in the New Hebrides.* London: Routledge.

Denig, Edwin T.
1928-29. "Indian Tribes of the Upper Missouri," *Smithsonian Institution Bureau of American Ethnology, Annual Report* 46:395-628.
deSchlippe, Pierre
1956. *Shifting Cultivation in Africa.* London: Routledge and Kegan Paul.
Douglas, Mary
1962. "Lele Economy as Compared with the Bushong," in G. Dalton and P. Bohannan (eds.), *Markets in Africa.* Evanston: Northwestern University Press.
1963. *The Lele of Kasai.* London: Oxford University Press.
Driberg, J. H.
1923. *The Lango.* London: Fisher, Unwin.
Drucker, Philip
1937. "The Tolowa and their Southwest Oregon Kin," *University of California Publications in American Archaeology and Ethnology* 36:221-300.
1939. "Rank, Wealth, and Kinship in Northwest Coast Society," *American Anthropologist* 41:55-65.
1951. *The Northern and Central Nootkan Tribes.* Smithsonian Institution Bureau of American Ethnology Bulletin 144. Washington, D.C.: U.S. Government Printing Office.
Dubbledam, L. F. B.
1964. "The Devaluation of the Kapauku-Cowrie as a Factor of Social Disintegration," in James Watson (ed.), *New Guinea: The Central Highlands. American Anthropologist 66,* Special Publication.
DuBois, Cora
1936. "The Wealth Concept as an Integrative Factor in Tolowa-Tututni Culture," in *Essays Presented to A. L. Kroeber.* Berkeley: University of California Press.
Duff Missionaries
1799. *A Missionary Voyage to the Southern Pacific Ocean Performed in the Years 1796, 1797, 1798 in the Ship Duff . . . [etc.]* London: T. Chapman.
Elkin, A. P.
1952-53. "Delayed Exchange in Wabag Sub-District, Central

Highlands of New Guinea," *Oceania* 23:161–201.

1954. *The Australian Aborigines.* 3rd Ed. Sydney: Angus and Robertson.

Engels, Frederick

1966. *Anti-Dühring.* New York: International Publishers. (New World Paperbacks; first German edition 1878.)

Evans-Pritchard, E. E.

1940. *The Nuer.* Oxford: At the Clarendon Press.

1951. *Kinship and Marriage Among the Nuer.* Oxford: At the Clarendon Press.

1956. *Nuer Religion.* Oxford: At the Clarendon Press.

Ewers, John C.

1955. *The Horse in Blackfoot Indian Culture.* Smithsonian Institution Bureau of American Ethnology, Bulletin No. 159. Washington, D.C.: U.S. Government Printing Office.

Eyre, Edward John

1845. *Journals of Expeditions of Discovery into Central Australia, and Overland from Adelaide to King George's Sound, in the Years 1840–41.* 2 vols. London: Boone.

Firth, Raymond

1926. "Proverbs in Native Life, with Special Reference to Those of the Maori," *Folklore* 37:134–53; 245–70.

1936. *We, the Tikopia.* London: Allen and Unwin.

1951. *Elements of Social Organization.* London: Watts.

1959a. *Economics of the New Zealand Maori.* 2nd Ed. Wellington: R. E. Owen, Government Printer.

1959b. *Social Change in Tikopia.* New York: Macmillan.

1965. *Primitive Polynesian Economy.* 2nd ed. London: Routledge and Kegan Paul.

1967. "Themes in Economic Anthropology: A General Comment," in R. Firth (ed.), *Themes in Economic Anthropology.* London: Tavistock, ASA Monograph 6.

Firth, Raymond (ed.)

1957. *Man and Culture: An Evaluation of the Work of Bronislaw Malinowski.* London: Routledge and Kegan Paul.

Forde, C. Daryll

1946. "Native Economies of Nigeria," in M. F. Perham (ed.), *The Economics of a Tropical Dependency.* London: Faber and Faber.

1963. *Habitat, Economy and Society.* 8th ed. London: Methuen.

1964. *Yakö Studies.* London: Oxford University Press.

Fornander, Abraham

1878-85. *An Account of the Polynesian Race.* 3 vols. Londong: Trübner.

Fortune, Reo

1932. *Sorcerers of Dobu.* New York: Dutton.

Freeman, J. D.

1955. *Iban Agriculture.* Colonial Research Studies No. 18. London: H. M. Stationery Office.

Geddes, W. R.

1954. *The Land Dayaks of Sarawak.* Colonial Research Studies No. 14. London: H. M. Stationery Office.

1957. *Nine Dayak Nights.* Melbourne: Oxford University Press.

Gifford, E. W.

1926. "Clear Lake Pomo Society," *University of California Publications in American Archaeology and Ethnology* 18:287-390.

1929. *Tongan Society.* Bernice P. Bishop Museum Bulletin No. 61.

Gitlow, Abraham L.

1947. *Economics of the Mount Hagen Tribes.* American Ethnological Society Monographs No. 12.

Gluckman, Max

1943. *Essays on Lozi Land and Royal Property.* Rhodes-Livingstone Papers, No. 10.

Godelier, Maurice

1966. *Rationalité et irrationalité en économie.* Paris: Maspero.

1969. "La 'monnaie de sel' des Baruya de Nouvelle-Guinée," *L'Homme* 9 (2):5-37.

Goldschmidt, Walter

1951. "Nomlaki Ethography," *University of California Publications in American Archaeology and Ethnology* 42:303-443.

Goodfellow, D. M.

1939. *Principles of Economic Sociology.* London: Routledge and Sons

Gorz, Andre

1967. *Le socialisme difficile.* Paris: Seuil.

Gouldner, Alvin

1960. "The Norm of Reciprocity: A Preliminary Statement,"

*American Sociological Review* 25:161–78.

Grey, Sir George

1841. *Journals of Two Expeditions of Discovery in North-West and Western Australia, During the Years 1837, 38, and 39.* . . . 2 vols. London: Boone.

Grinnell, George Bird

1923. *The Cheyenne Indians.* New Haven, Conn.: Yale University Press.

Guillard, J.

1958. "Essai de mesure de l'activité d'un paysan Africain: le Toupouri," *L'Agronomie Tropicale* 13:415–28.

Gusinde, Martin

1961. *The Yamana.* 5 vols. New Haven, Conn.: Human Relations Area Files. (German edition 1931.)

Handy, E. S. Craighill

1923. *The Native Culture in the Marquesas.* Bernice P. Bishop Museum Bulletin No. 9.

1930. *History and Culture in the Society Islands.* Bernice P. Bishop Museum Bulletin No. 79.

1932. *Houses, Boats, and Fishing in the Society Islands.* Bernice P. Bishop Museum Bulletin No. 90.

1940. *The Hawaiin Planter.* Bernice P. Bishop Museum Bulletin No. 161.

Harding, Thomas G.

1967. *Voyagers of the Vitiaz Strait.* The American Ethnological Society Monograph 44. Seattle: University of Washington Press.

Harmon, Daniel Williams

1957. *Sixteen Years in the Indian Country: The Journal of Daniel Williams Harmon, 1800–1816.* Edited by W. K. Lamb. Toronto: Macmillan.

Harris, Marvin

1968. *The Rise of Anthropological Theory.* New York: Thomas Y. Crowell.

Haury, Emil W.

1962. "The Greater American Southwest," in J. Braidwood and G. R. Willey (eds.), *Courses toward Urban Life.* Chicago: Aldine.

Hearne, Samuel

1958. *A Journey from Prince of Wales' Fort in Hudson's Bay to the*

*Northern Ocean, 1769, 1770, 1771, 1772.* Edited by R. Glover. Toronto: Macmillan.

Henry, Jules
1951. "The Economics of Pilagá Food Distribution," *American Anthropologist* 53:187–219.

Herskovits, Melville J.
1952. *Economic Anthropology.* New York: Knopf.

Hiatt, L.
1965. *Kinship and Conflict.* Canberra: Australian National University.

Hodgkinson, Clement
1845. *Australia, from Port Macquarie to Moreton Bay, with Descriptions of the Natives.* London: Boone.

Hoebel, E. Adamson
1958. *Man in the Primitive World.* 2nd Ed. New York: McGraw-Hill.

Hogbin, H. Ian
1933–34. "Culture Change in the Solomon Islands: Report of Field Work in Guadalcanal and Malaita," *Oceania* 4:233–67.
1934. *Law and Order in Polynesia,* New York: Harcourt, Brace.
1934–35a. "Native Culture of Wogeo: Report of Field Work in New Guinea," *Oceania* 5:308–37.
1934–35b. "Trading Expeditions in Northern New Guinea," *Oceania* 5:375–407.
1937–38. "Social Advancement in Guadalcanal, Solomon Islands," *Oceania* 8:289–305.
1938–39. "Tillage and Collection: A New Guinea Economy," *Oceania* 9:127–51.
1939. *Experiments in Civilization.* London: Routledge.
1943–44. "Native Councils and Native Courts in the Solomon Islands." *Oceania* 14:258–83.
1951. *Transformation Scene: The Changing Culture of a New Guinea Village.* London: Routledge and Kegan Paul.

Holmberg, Allan R.
1950. *Nomads of the Long Bow.* Smithsonian Institution, Institute of Social Anthropology, Publication No. 10. Washington, D.C.: U.S. Government Printing Office.

Howell, P. P.
   1954. *A Manual of Nuer Law.* London: Oxford University Press.
Hunter, John D.
   1823. *Memoirs of a Captivity Among the Indians of North America.* London: Longmans.
Ivens, W. G.
   1927. *Melanesians of the Southeast Solomon 'Islands.* London: Kegan, Paul, Trench, Trübner.
Izikowitz, Karl Gustave
   1951. *Lamet: Hill Peasants in French Indochina.* Etnologiska Studier 17. Göteborg: Etnologiska Museet.
Jochelson, Waldermar
   1926. "The Yukaghir and the Yukaghirzed Tungus," *American Museum of Natural History Memoirs* 13:1–469.
Johansen, J. Prytz
   1954. *The Maori and His Religion.* Copenhagen: Musksgaard.
Kaberry, Phyllis M.
   1940–41. "The Abelam Tribe, Sepik District, New Guinea: A Preliminary Report," *Oceania* 11:233–58, 345–67.
   1941–42. "Law and Political Organization in the Abelam Tribe, New Guinea," *Oceania* 12:79–95, 205–25, 331–63.
Kelly, Raymond C.
   1968. "Demographic Pressure and Descent Group Structure in the New Guinea Highlands," *Oceania* 39:36–63.
Kluckhohn, Clyde
   1959. "The Philosophy of the Navaho Indians," in M. H. Fried (ed.), *Readings in Anthropology,* vol. 2. New York: Crowell.
Kroeber, A. L.
   1925. *Handbook of the Indians of California.* Smithsonian Institution Bureau of American Ethnology Bulletin 78. Washington, D.C.: U.S. Government Printing Office.
Lafargue, Paul
   1909. *The Right to be Lazy.* Chicago: Kerr. (First French edition 1883.)
Landtman, Gunnar
   1927. *The Kiwai Papuans of British New Guinea.* London: Macmillan.

Leach, E. R.

1951. "The Structural Implications of Matrilateral Cross Cousin Marriage," *Journal of the Royal Anthropological Institute* 81:23–55.

1954. *The Political Systems of Highland Burma.* London: Bell.

Leacock, Eleanor

1954. *The Montagnais "Hunting Territory" and the Fur Trade.* American Anthropological Association Memoir No. 78.

LeClair, Edward E., Jr.

1962. "Economic Theory and Economic Anthropology," *American Anthropologist* 64:1179–1203.

Lee, Richard

1968. "What Hunters Do for a Living, or, How to Make Out on Scarce Resources," in R. Lee and I. DeVore (eds.), *Man the Hunter.* Chicago: Aldine.

1969. "/Kung Bushman Subsistance: An Input-Output Analysis," in A. Vayda (ed.), *Environment and Cultural Behavior.* Garden City, N.Y.: Natural History Press.

Lee, Richard B., and Irven DeVore (eds.)

1968. *Man the Hunter.* Chicago: Aldine.

LeJeune, le Père Paul

1897. "Relation of What Occurred in New France in the Year 1634," in R. G. Thwaites (ed.), *The Jesuit Relations and Allied Documents,* Vol. 6. Cleveland: Burrows. (First French edition, 1635.)

Lévi-Strauss, Claude

1943. "Guerre et commerce chez les Indiens de l'Amerique du Sud," *Renaissance* 1:122–39.

1961. *Tristes Tropiques.* New York: Atheneum.

1966. "Introduction à l'oeuvre de Marcel Mauss," in M. Mauss, *Sociologie et anthropologie.* Paris: Presses Universitaires de France.

1969. *The Elementary Structures of Kinship.* London: Eyre and Spottiswoode.

Lewthwaite, Gordon R.

1964. "Man and Land in Early Tahiti: Polynesian Agriculture through European Eyes," *Pacific Viewpoint* 5:11–34.

1966. "Man and the Sea in Early Tahiti: Maritime Economy through European Eyes," *Pacific Viewpoint* 7:28–53.

Linton, Ralph
  1939. "Marquesan Culture," in A. Kardiner, *The Individual and His Society*. New York: Columbia University Press.
Loeb, Edwin M.
  1926. "Pomo Folkways," *University of California Publications in American Archaeology and Ethnology* 19:149–409.
Lothrup, Samuel K.
  1928. *The Indians of Tierra del Fuego*. New York: Museum of the American Indian, Heye Foundation.
Lowie, Robert H.
  1938. "Subsistence," in F. Boas (ed.), *General Anthropology*. Boston: Heath.
  1946. *An Introduction to Cultural Anthropology*. (2nd ed.) New York: Rinehart.
McArthur, Margaret
  1960. "Food Consumption and Dietary Levels of Groups of Aborigines Living on Naturally Occurring Foods," in C. P. Mountford (ed.), *Records of the Australian-American Scientific Expedition to Arnhem Land, Vol. 2: Anthropology and Nutrition*. Melbourne: Melbourne University Press.
McCarthy, Frederick D., and Margaret McArthur
  1960. "The Food Quest and the Time Factor in Aboriginal Economic Life," in C. P. Mountford (ed.), *Records of the Australian-American Scientific Expedition to Arnhem Land, Vol. 2: Anthropology and Nutrition*. Melbourne: Melbourne University Press.
MacGregor, Gordon
  1937. *Ethnology of the Tokelau Islands*. Bernice P. Bishop Museum Bulletin No. 146.
McKern, W. C.
  1922. "Functional Families of the Patwin," University of California Publications in American Archaeology and Ethnology 13 (7):236–58.
McNeilly, F. S.
  1968. *The Anatomy of Leviathan*. London: Macmillan.
MacPherson, C. B.
  1965. "Hobbes's Bourgeois Man," in K. C. Brown (ed.), *Hobbes Studies*. Oxford: Blackwell.
Malinowski, Bronislaw
  1915. "The Natives of Mailu," *Transactions of the Royal Society of*

*South Australia* 39:494–706.

1921. "The Primitive Economics of the Trobriand Islanders," *Economic Journal* 31:1–16.

1922. *Argonauts of the Western Pacific.* (3rd imp. 1950.) London: Routledge and Kegan Paul.

1935. *Coral Gardens and Their Magic.* Vol. 1. New York: American Book Co.

1939. "Anthropology as the Basis of Social Science," in Cattel, Cohen, and Travers (eds.), *Human Affairs.* London: Macmillan.

Malo, David

1951. *Hawaiian Antiquities.* Bernice P. Bishop Museum Special Publications No. 2.

Man, Edward Horace

(n.d) *On the Aboriginal Inhabitants of the Andaman Islands.* (Reprinted from the *Journal of the Royal Anthropological Institute.)* London: RAI.

Mandel, Ernest

1962. *Traite d'économie marxiste.* 2 Vols. Paris: Julliard.

Mandelbaum, David G.

1940. "The Plains Cree," *American Museum of Natural History-Anthropological Papers* 37:155–316.

Mariner, William

1827. *An Account of the Tongan Islands in the South Pacific Ocean.* 3 vols., 3rd ed. Edited by J. Martin. Edinburgh: Constable.

Marshall, Alfred

1961. *Principles of Economics.* 8th ed. London: Macmillan.

Marshall, Lorna

1961. "Sharing, Talking, and Giving: Relief of Social Tensions Among /Kung Bushmen," *Africa* 31:231–49.

Marx; Karl

1967a. *Capital.* 3 vols. (First German editions, 1867, 1893, 1894.) New York: International Publishers.

1967b. *Fondaments de la critique de l'économie politique.* 2 vols. (Manuscripts of 1857–1858, "Grundrisse der Kritik der Politischen okonomie," first published in Moscow, 1939.) Paris: Editions Anthropos.

1968. *Misère de la philosophie.* (First edition, in French, 1847.) Paris: Editions Sociales.

Mathew, John
1910. *Two Representative Tribes of Queensland.* London: Unwin.
Mauss, Marcel
1966. "Essai sur le don: Forme et raison de l'échange dans les sociétés archaiques," in *Sociologie et anthropologie.* (First published 1923–24 in *L'Année Sociologique.)* Paris: Presses Universitaires de France.
1967. *Manuel d'ethnographie.* (First published 1947.) Paris: Payot.
Mead, Margaret
1930. "Melanesian Middlemen," *National History* 30:115–30.
1934. "Kinship in the Admiralty Islands," *American Museum of Natural History-Anthropological Papers,* 34:181–358.
1937a. "The Manus of the Admiralty Islands," in M. Mead (ed.), *Cooperation and Competition among Primitive Peoples.* New York: McGraw-Hill.
1937b. "The Arapesh of New Guinea," in M. Mead (ed.), *Cooperation and Competition among Primitive Peoples.* New York: McGraw-Hill.
1938. "The Mountain Arapesh I. An Importing Culture," *American Museum of Natural History-Anthropological Papers* 36:139–349.
1947. "The Mountain Arapesh III. Socio-economic Life," *American Museum of Natural History-Anthropological Papers* 40:159–232.
Meggitt, Mervyn
1956–57. "The Valleys of the Upper Wage and Lai Rivers, Western Highlands, New Guinea," *Oceania* 27:90–135.
1957–58. "The Enga of the New Guinea Highlands: Some Preliminary Observations," *Oceania* 28:253–330.
1962. *Desert People.* Sydney: Angus and Robertson.
1964. "Indigenous Forms of Government Among the Australian Aborigines," *Bijdragen tot de Taal- Land- en Volkenkunde* 120:163–80.
Meillassoux, Claude
1960. "Essai d'interprétation du phénomène économique dans les sociétés traditionelles d'autosubsistence," *Cahiers d'Etudes Africaines* 4:38–67.
1964. *Anthropologie économique des Gouro de Côte d'Ivoire.* Paris: Mouton.

Nadel, S. F.
1942. *A Black Byzantium*. London: Oxford University Press.
Nash, Manning
1967. " 'Reply' to reviews of *Primitive and Peasant Economic Systems,"* *Current Anthropology* 8:249–50.
Needham, Rodney
1954. "Siriono and Penan: A Test of Some Hypotheses," *Southwestern Journal of Anthropology,* 10:228–32.
Nilles, John
1950–51. "The Kuman of the Chimbu Region, Central Highlands, New Guinea," *Oceania* 21:25–26.
Oberg, Kalervo
1955. "Types of Social Structure in Lowland South America," *American Anthropologist* 57:472–87.
Oliver, Douglas
1949. *Studies in the Anthropology of Bougainville, Solomon Islands.* Papers of the Peabody Museum of American Archaeology and Ethnology, Harvard University. Vol. 29, 1–4. Cambridge, Mass.: The Museum.
1955. *A Solomon Island Society.* Cambridge, Mass.: Harvard University Press.
Pirenne, Henri
1955. *A History of Europe.* New York: University Books. (Translated from the 8th French ed., 1938.)
Pirie, N. W.
1962. "Future Sources of Food Supply: Scientific Problems," *Journal of the Royal Statistical Society (Series A)* 125:399–417.
Polanyi, Karl
1944. *The Great Transformation.* New York: Rinehart.
1947. "Our Obsolete Market Mentality," *Commentary* 3:109-17.
1957. "The Economy as Instituted Process," in K. Polanyi, C. Arensberg and H. Pearson (eds.), *Trade and Market in the Early Empires.* Glencoe: The Free Press.
1959. "Anthropology and Economic Theory," in M. Fried (ed.), *Readings in Anthropology.* Vol. 2. New York: Crowell.
Pospisil, Leopold
1958. *Kapauku Papuans and Their Law.* Yale University Publications in Anthropology No. 54.

1959–60. "The Kapauku Papuans and Their Kinship Organization," *Oceania* 30:188–205.

1963. *Kapauku Papuan Economy.* Yale University Publications in Anthropology No. 67.

Powdermaker, Hortense

1933. *Life in Lesu.* New York: Norton.

Powell, H. A.

1960. "Competitive Leadership in Trobriand Political Organization," *Journal of the Royal Anthropological Institute* 90:118–45.

Price, John Andrew

1962. *Washo Economy.* Nevada State Museum Anthropological Papers No. 6.

Provinse, John H.

1937. "Cooperative Ricefield Cultivation Among the Siang Dyaks of Borneo," *American Anthropologist* 39:77–102.

Putnam, Patrik

1953. "The Pygmies of the Ituri Forest," in Carelton S. Coon (ed.), *A Reader in General Anthropology.* New York: Holt.

Quimby, George I.

1962. "A Year with a Chippewa Family, 1763–1764," *Ethnohistory* 9:217–39.

Radcliffe-Brown, A. R.

1930–31. "The Social Organisation of Australian Tribes," *Oceania* 1:34–63, 206–56, 322–41, 426–56.

1948. *The Andaman Islanders.* Glencoe: The Free Press. (First edition 1922).

Read, K. E.

1946–47. "Social Organization in the Markham Valley, New Guinea," *Oceania* 17:93–118.

1949–50. "The Political System of the Ngarawapum," *Oceania* 20:185–223.

1959. "Leadership and Consensus in a New Guinea Society," *American Anthropologist* 61:425–36.

Reay, Marie

1959. *The Kuma.* Carlton: Melbourne University Press.

Redfield, Robert

1953. *The Primitive World and its Transformations.* Ithaca, N.Y.: Cornell University Press.

Richards, Audrey I.
   1961. *Land, Labour and Diet in Northern Rhodesia.* 2nd ed. London: Oxford University Press.
Rink, Henry
   1875. *Tales and Traditions of the Eskimo.* Edinburgh: Blackwood.
Rivers, W. H. R.
   1906. *The Todas.* London: Macmillan.
Robbins, Lionel
   1935. *An Essay on the Nature and Significance of Economic Science.* 2nd ed. London: Macmillan.
Rodriguez, Maximo
   1919. "Daily Narrative Kept by the Interpreter Maximo Rodriguez at the Island of Amat, Otherwise Otahiti, in the Year 1774," in B. G. Corney (ed.), *The Quest and Occupation of Tahiti by Emissaries of Spain . . . 1772–1776.* Vol. 3. London: Hakluyt Society.
Rousseau, Jean-Jacques
   1964. *Oeuvres complètes.* 4 vols. Paris: Bibliothèque de la Pléiade.
Sahlins, Marshall D.
   1958. *Social Stratification in Polynesia.* Monograph of the American Ethnological Society. Seattle: University of Washington Press.
   1960. "Political Power and the Economy in Primitive Society," in Dole and Carneiro (eds.), *Essays in the Science of Culture in Honor of Leslie White.* New York: Crowell.
   1961. "The Segmentary Lineage: An Organization of Predatory Expansion," *American Anthropologist* 63:322–45.
   1962a. "Review of *Sociological Aspects of Economic Growth* " (B. F. Hoselitz), *American Anthropologist* 64:1063–73.
   1962b. *Moala: Culture and Nature on a Fijian Island.* Ann Arbor: University of Michigan Press.
   1963. "Poor Man, Rich Man, Big-Man, Chief: Political Types in Melanesia and Polynesia," *Comparative Studies in Society and History* 5:285–303.
   1969. "Economic Anthropology and Anthropological Economics," *Social Science Information* 8 (5):13–33.
Sahlins, Marshall, and Elman R. Service (eds.)
   1960. *Evolution and Culture.* Ann Arbor: University of Michigan Press.

Salisbury, Richard
   1962. *From Stone to Steel.* Cambridge: At the University Press.
   1966. "Politics and Shell-Money Finance in New Britain," in Marc
      J. Swartz, Victor W. Turner, and Arthur Tuden (eds.), *Political
      Anthropology.* Chicago: Aldine.
Schapera, I.
   1930. *The Khoisan Peoples of South Africa.* London: Routledge.
Schebesta, Paul
   (n.d.) *Among the Forest Dwarfs of Malaya.* London: Hutchinson.
   1933. *Among Congo Pygmies.* London: Hutchinson.
Schwartz, Theodore
   1963. "Systems of Areal Integration: Some Considerations Based
      on the Admiralty Islands of Northern Melanesia," *Anthropologi-
      cal Forum* 1:56–97.
Scudder, Thayer
   1962. *The Ecology of the Gwembe Tonga.* Manchester: Manchester
      University Press.
Seligman, C. G.
   1910. *The Melanesians of British New Guinea.* Cambridge: At the
      University Press.
Service, Elman R.
   1962. *Primitive Social Organization.* New York: Random House.
   1963. *Profiles in Ethnology.* New York: Harper & Row.
Sharp, Lauriston
   1934-35. "Ritual Life and Economics of the Yir-Yiront of Cape
      York Peninsula," *Oceania* 5:19–42.
   1952. "Steel Axes for Stone-Age Australians," *Human Organiza-
      tion* 11:17–22.
   1958. "People without Politics," in V. F. Ray (ed.), *Systems of
      Political Control and Bureaucracy in Human Societies.* American
      Ethnological Society. Seattle: University of Washington Press.
Shirokogoroff, S. M.
   1929. *Social Organization of the Northern Tungus.* Shanghai: Com-
      mercial Press.
Smyth, R. Brough
   1878. *The Aborigines of Victoria.* 2 vols. Melbourne: Government
      Printer.
Spencer, Baldwin, and F. J. Gillen
   1899. *The Native Tribes of Central Australia.* London: Macmillan.

1927. *The Arunta.* 2 vols. London: Macmillan.
Spencer, Joseph E.
    1966. *Shifting Cultivation in Southeastern Asia.* University of California Publications in Geography. Berkeley: University of California Press.
Spencer, Robert F.
    1959. *The North Alaskan Eskimo: A Study in Ecology and Society.* Smithsonian Institution Bureau of American Ethnology Bulletin 171. Washington, D.C.: U.S. Government Printing Office.
Stewart, Julian
    1938. *Basin-Plateau Aboriginal Sociopolitical Groups.* Smithsonian Institution Bureau of American Ethnology Bulletin 120. Washington, D.C.: U.S. Government Printing Office.
Steward, Julian H., and Louis C. Faron
    1959. *Native Peoples of South America.* New York: McGraw-Hill.
Stewart, C. S.
    1828. *Journal of a Residence in the Sandwich Islands, during the Years 1823, 1824, and 1825.* New York: Haven.
Suggs, Robert C.
    1961. *The Archaeology of Nuku Hiva, Marquesas Islands, French Polynesia.* American Museum of Natural History-Anthropological Papers, 49 (1).
Suttles, Wayne
    1960. "Affinal Ties, Subsistence and Prestige Among the Coast Salish," *American Anthropologist* 62: 296–305.
Swanton, John R.
    1928. "Social Organization and Social Usages of the Indians of the Creek Confederacy," *Smithsonian Institution Bureau of Ethnology-Annual Report* 42:23–472.
Tanner, John
    1956. *A Narrative of the Captivity and Adventures of John Tanner.* Edited by E. James. Minneapolis: Ross & Haines.
Terray, Emmanuel
    1969. *Le marxisme devant les sociétés "primitives."* Paris: Maspero.
Thomas, Elizabeth Marshall
    1959. *The Harmless People.* New York: Knopf.
Thomson, Donald F.

1949a. *Economic Structure and the Ceremonial Exchange Cycle in Arnhem Land.* Melbourne: Macmillan.

1949b. "Arnhem Land: Explorations Among an Unknown People," *The Geographical Journal* 113:1–8, 114, 54–67.

Thurnwald, Richard

1932. *Economics in Primitive Communities.* London: Oxford.

1934–35. "Pigs and Currency in Buin," *Oceania* 5:119-41.

Titiev, Mischa

1944. *Old Oraibi.* Papers of the Peabody Museum of American Archaeology and Ethnology, Harvard University, vol. 22 (1).

Turnbull, Colin

1962. *The Forest People.* Garden City, N.Y.: Doubleday and the American Museum of Natural History.

1965. *Wayward Servants.* Garden City, N.Y.: Natural History Press.

Turner, Victor

1957. *Schism and Continuity in an African Society.* Manchester: Manchester University Press.

Van der Post, Laurens

1958. *The Lost World of the Kalahari.* New York: Morrow.

Vanleur, J. C.

1955. *Indonesian Trade and Society.* The Hague and Bandung: vanHoeve.

Vanoverbergh, Morice

1925. "Negritoes of Northern Luzon," *Anthropos* 20:148–99, 399–443.

Vayda, A. P.

1954. "Notes on Trade Among the Pomo Indians of California," mimeographed. Columbia University Interdisciplinary Project: Economic Aspects of Institutional Growth.

1961. "A Re-examination of Northwest Coast Economic Systems," *Transactions of the New York Academy of Sciences* (Series 2) 23:618–24.

Veblen, Thorstein

1914. *The Instinct of Workmanship.* New York: Macmillan

1915. *Imperial Germany and the Industrial Revolution.* New York: Macmillan.

Wagner, Guntar
1956. *The Bantu of North Kavirondo.* 2 vols. London: Oxford University Press for the International African Institute.

Wallace, Ernest, and E. A. Hoebel
1952. *The Comanches, Lords of the South Plains.* Norman: University of Oklahoma Press.

Warner, W. Lloyd
1964. *A Black Civilization* (Harper "Torchback" from the edition of 1958; first edition 1937). New York: Harper & Row.

Weyer, E. M.
1932. *The Eskimos.* New Haven, Conn.: Yale University Press.

White, Leslie A.
1949. *The Science of Culture.* New York: Farrar, Strauss.
1959. *The Evolution of Culture.* New York: McGraw-Hill.

Williams, Herbert
1921. *A dictionary of the Maori Language.* Auckland, N.Z.: Williams and Northgate.

Williams, William
1892. *A Dictionary of the New Zealand Language.* Auckland, N.Z.: Williams and Northgate.

Williamson, Robert W.
1912. *The Mafulu: Mountain People of British New Guinea.* London: Macmillan.

Woodburn, James
1968. "An Introduction to Hadza Ecology," in R. Lee and I. DeVore (eds.), *Man the Hunter.* Chicago: Aldine.

Woodburn, James (director)
1966. "The Hadza" (film available from the anthropological director, Department of Anthropology, London School of Economics).

Worsley, Peter M.
1961. "The Utilization of Food Resources by an Australian Aboriginal Tribe," *Acta Ethnographica* 10:153–90.

Worthington, Edgar B.
1961. *The Wild Resources of East and Central Africa.* Colonial Research Studies London: H. M. Stationery Office.

# Index

for use-value; Reciprocity;
Sharing; Solidarity
Corporate alliances, 221, 225, 228
Costs, labor, 291
Courtesy, 218, 273
Credit, 240
Crisis, 124, 144, 273, 274
revealatory, 128, 141, 143
Crowd, demand, 298
Cultivation, 48, 57, 71, 73, 104,
105, 106, 141, 242
slash-and-burn, 42-43, 48-49
Culture
design, 33
evolution, 35
Cycle, 42, 73, 139, 140, 144, 145,
146, 159, 165, 219

Dancing, 58, 68, 136
Deceit, 198
Decentralization, 146, 186-87
Decisions, main domestic, 77
Deduction, 295
functionalist, 97
Deflation, 313
Delay, 193
Democracy, 10
Demography, 23, 27, 34, 43-48,
50-51
Dependency, 244, 254, 256, 258
ratio, 89, 94
Descent
matrilineal, 54
patrilineal, 54
Destruction, by Europeans, 24-25
Development, economic, 82, 312
Dialectic, 169
Diet, 6-7, 9, 14, 18, 38-39, 72, 103,
125, 126, 141, 212-13
Difficulties, symptomatic, 293
Dignity, 136, 139, 179, 300
Diminishing returns, 33, 34
Diplomacy, 303, 308
Discontinuity, 99
Dislocation, 20, 243
Dispersion, 95-99

Distance
segmentary, 197
social, 191, 196, 202, 211, 219,
223, 243, 264, 280
Distribution, 244, 250, 254, 255,
259, 261-63, 264, 270, 271, 274,
286, 293
analysis of, 188
global, 293
real, 295
Diversion, 65
Diversity, 32, 154
DMP, 74, 79-81, 82, 86-92, 95, 96,
97, 98, 101, 102, 110, 123, 129,
131, 135
as anti-surplus system, 82, 87
defined, 79
Dobuan culture, 200, 216-17, 241
Dogomba, 45
Domestic group, defined, 77
Drought, 49, 212
Dynamics, 294, 296, 311

Eatora, 133, 257
Ecology, 25, 33, 34-35, 36, 42-43,
50-51, 131, 141, 142, 202-3,
229, 280, 283, 288-89, 292, 294
Economic Man, 13
Economics
and economizing, 230
anthropological, 3, 8, 27, 51, 73,
85, 121, 180, 181, 182-83, 190,
226, 277, 301
infighting and confrontation, 298
kinds, 239
orthodox theory of, 282, 301, 314
politics of, 132, 134ff.
Economy, 6, 67, 76, 224, 296
afflicted, 8, 243
business, 3, 4
finite objectives, 86
household, 82, 94, 101-30
hunting-gathering, 1-38, *passim*
market, 2, 224
organization of, 4, 12, 37, 74, 75